Knowledge Acquisition Tools for Expert Systems

Knowledge-Based Systems

One of the most successful and engaging initiatives in Artificial Intelligence has been the development of knowledge-based systems (or, expert systems) encoding human expertise in the computer and making it more widely available. Knowledge-based system developments are at the leading edge of the move from information processing to knowledge processing in Fifth Generation Computing.

The Knowledge-Based Systems Book Series publishes the work of leading international scientists addressing themselves to the spectrum of problems associated with the development of knowledge-based systems. The series will be an important source for researchers and advanced students working on knowledge-based systems as well as introducing those embarking on expert systems development to the state-of-the-art.

Volume 2 has been compiled from the International Journal of Man–Machine Studies:

Volume 26   Number 1   January 1987
Volume 26   Number 2   February 1987
Volume 26   Number 4   April 1987

Volume 27   Number 2   August 1987
Volume 27   Number 3   September 1987

Knowledge Acquisition Tools for Expert Systems

Knowledge-Based Systems
Volume 2

edited by

J. H. Boose
Boeing Computer Services,
P.O. Box 24346,
Seattle, Washington 98124–0346,
U.S.A.

and

B. R. Gaines
Department of Computer Sciences,
University of Calgary,
Calgary, Alberta T2N 1N4
Canada

1988

ACADEMIC PRESS

Harcourt Brace Jovanovich, Publishers
London   San Diego   New York   Berkeley   Boston
Sydney   Tokyo   Toronto

ACADEMIC PRESS LIMITED
24/28 Oval Road
LONDON NW1 7DX

United States Edition published by
ACADEMIC PRESS INC.
San Diego, CA 92101

British Library Cataloguing in Publication Data
Is available

ISBN: 0-12-115920-5

Typeset by The Universities Press (Belfast) Ltd
Printed in Great Britain at the University Press, Cambridge

Contributors

G. ABRETT *BBN Laboratories, 10 Moulton Street, Cambridge, MA 02238, U.S.A.*

A. M. AGOGINO *Department of Mechanical Engineering, University of California, Berkeley 5136, Etcheverry Hall, Berkeley, CA 94720, U.S.A.*

J. H. ALEXANDER *Computer Research Laboratory, Tektronix Laboratories, P.O. Box 500, Beaverton, OR 97077, U.S.A.*

J. BENTOLILA *Department of Computer Science, Carnegie-Mellon University, Pittsburgh, Pennsylvania 15213, U.S.A.*

J. H. BOOSE *Boeing Computer Services, P.O. Box 24346, Seattle Washington 98124–0346, U.S.A.*

J. M. BRADSHAW *Knowledge Systems Laboratory, Boeing Advanced Technology Center 77–64, Boeing Computer Services, P.O. Box 24346, Seattle, WA 98124, U.S.A.*

G. H. BREAUX *Carnegie Group Inc., 650 Commerce Court, Station Square, Pittsburgh, Pa 15219, U.S.A.*

J. A. BREUKER *University of Amsterdam, Herengracht 196, 1016 BS Amsterdam, The Netherlands*

M. H. BURSTEIN *BBN Laboratories, 10 Moulton Street, Cambridge, MA 02238, U.S.A.*

P. R. COHEN *Experimental Knowledge Systems Laboratory, Department of Computer and Information Science, University of Massachusetts, Amherst, Massachusetts 01003, U.S.A.*

D. M. COMBS *Medical Computer Science Group, Knowledge Systems Laboratory, Departments of Medicine and Computer Science, Stanforth University School of Medicine, Stanforth, California 94305–5479, U.S.A.*

N. M. COOKE *Computing Research Laboratory and Department of Psychology, New Mexico State University, Las Cruces, NM 88003, U.S.A.*

P. DE KLERK *Carnegie Group Inc., 650 Commerce Court, Station Square, Pittsburgh, Pa 15219, U.S.A.*

J. DIEDERICH *Research Division "Expert Systems", Institute for Applied Information Technology, German Research Institute for Mathematics and State Processing, Schloß Birlinghoven, Postfach 1240, D-5205, Sankt Angustin 1, West Germany*

D. EHRET *Department of Computer Science, Carnegie-Mellon University, Pittsburgh, Pennsylvania 15213, U.S.A.*

L. ESHELMAN *Department of Computer Science, Carnegie-Mellon University, Pittsburgh, Pennsylvania 15213, U.S.A.*

L. M. FAGAN *Medical Computer Science Group, Knowledge Systems Laboratory, Departments of Medicine and Computer Science, Stanforth University School of Medicine, Stanforth, California 94305–5479, U.S.A.*

M. J. FREILING *Computer Research Laboratory, Tektronix Laboratories, P.O. Box 500, Beaverton, OR 97077, U.S.A.*

B. R. GAINES *Department of Computer Science, University of Calgary, Calgary, Alberta T2N 1N4, Canada*

W. A. GALE *AT & T. Bell Laboratories 2C278, 600 Mountain Avenue, Murray Hill, NJ 07974, U.S.A.*

C. GARG-JANARDIN *School of Industrial Engineering, Purdue University, West Lafayette, Indiana 47907, U.S.A.*

S. GENETET *Department of Computer Science, Carnegie-Mellon University, Pittsburgh, Pennsylvania 15213, U.S.A.*

M. GRIMES *Department of Computer Science, Carnegie-Mellon University, Pittsburgh, Pennsylvania 15213, U.S.A.*

T. R. GRUBER *Experimental Knowledge Systems Laboratory, Department of Computer and Information Science, University of Massachusetts, Amherst, Massachusetts 01003, U.S.A.*

S. A. HAYWARD   *STC Technology Ltd., Six Hills House, London Road, Stevenage, Herts., SG1 1YB, U.K.*
R. L. JOSEPH   *Carnegie Group Inc., 650 Commerce Court, Station Square, Pittsburgh, Pa 15219, U.S.A.*
G. S. KAHN   *Carnegie Group Inc., 650 Commerce Court, Station Square, Pittsburgh, Pa 15219, U.S.A.*
C. M. KITTO   *Knowledge Systems Laboratory, Boeing Advanced Technology Center, Boeing Computer Services, P.O. Box 24346, Seattle, WA 98124, U.S.A.*
G. KLINKER   *Department of Computer Science, Carnegie-Mellon University, Pittsburgh, Pennsylvania 15213, U.S.A.*
S. MARCUS   *Department of Computer Science, Carnegie-Mellon University, Pittsburgh, Pennsylvania 15213, U.S.A.*
M. MAY   *Research Division "Expert Systems", Institute for Applied Information Technology, German Research Institute for Mathematics and Data Processing, Schloß Birlinghoven, Postfach 1240, D-5205, Sankt Angustin 1, West Germany*
J. McDERMOTT   *Department of Computer Science, Carnegie Mellon University, Pittsburgh, Pennsylvania 15213, U.S.A.*
J. E. McDONALD   *Computing Research Laboratory and Department of Psychology, New Mexico State University, Las Cruces, NM 88003, U.S.A.*
S. L. MESSICK   *Computer Research Laboratory, Tektronix Laboratories, P.O. Box 500, Beaverton, OR 97077, U.S.A.*
E. A. MOORE   *Applicon/Schlumberger, 4251 Plymouth Road, Ann Arbor, MI 48105, U.S.A.*
K. MORIK   *Technical University Berlin, Institute for Applied Computer Science, Computer-based Informations Systems, Project KIT-Leaner, Sekr. FR 5–8, Frankslinstr. 28/29, D-1000, Berlin 10, West Germany*
M. A. MUSEN   *Medical Computer Science Group, Knowledge Systems Laboratory, Departments of Medicine and Computer Science, Stanforth University School of Medicine, Stanforth, California 94305–5479, U.S.A.*
E. P. O. PLANTINGA   *Department of Computer Science, Redeemer College, Ancaster, Ontario, L9*
A. RAPPAPORT   *Neuron Data, 444 High Street, Palo Alto, CA 94301, U.S.A.*
S. REGOCZEI   *Computer Studies, Trent University, Peterborough, Ontario, K9J 7B8, Canada*
S. REHFUSS   *Computer Research Laboratory, Tektronix Laboratories, P.O. Box 500, Beaverton, OR 97077, U.S.A.*
I. RUHMANN   *Research Division "Expert Systems", Institute for Applied Information Technology, German Research Institute for Mathematics and Data Processing, Schloß Birlinghoven, Postfach 1240, D-5205, Sankt Angustin 1, West Germany*
G. SALVENDY   *School of Industrial Engineering, Purdue University, West Lafayette, Indiana 47907, U.S.A.*
M. L. G. SHAW   *Department of Computer Science, University of Calgary, Alberta, Canada T2N 1N4*
E. H. SHORTLIFFE   *Medical Computer Science Group, Knowledge Systems Laboratory, Departments of Medicine and Computer Science, Stanforth University School of Medicine, Stanforth, California 94305–5479, U.S.A.*
S. J. SHULMAN   *Computer Research Laboratory, Tektronix Laboratories, P.O. Box 500, Beaverton, OR 97077, U.S.A.*
M. TAN   *Department of Computer Science, Carnegie Mellon University, Pittsburgh, Pennsylvania 15213, U.S.A.*
B. J. WIELINGA   *University of Amsterdam, Herengracht 196, 1016 BS Amsterdam, The Netherlands*

Preface

The initial success of expert system developments and the development of a number of reasonably domain-independent software support systems for the encoding and application of knowledge have opened up the possibility of widespread usage of expert systems. In particular, Fifth Generation Computing System development programs worldwide assume this will happen and are targeted on knowledge processing rather than information processing. However, what Feigenbaum has termed *knowledge engineering,* the reduction of a large body of knowledge to a precise set of facts and rules, has already become a major bottleneck impeding the application of expert systems in new domains. We need to understand more about the nature of expertise in itself and to be able to apply this knowledge to the elicitation of expertise in specific domains.

The problems of knowledge engineering have been stated clearly:

> "Knowledge acquisition is a bottleneck in the construction of expert systems. The knowledge engineer's job is to act as a go-between to help an expert build a system. Since the knowledge engineer has far less knowledge of the domain than the expert, however, communication problems impede the process of transferring expertise into a program. The vocabulary initially used by the expert to talk about the domain with a novice is often inadequate for problem-solving; thus the knowledge engineer and expert must work together to extend and refine it. One of the most difficult aspects of the knowledge engineer's task is helping the expert to structure the domain knowledge, to identify and formalize the domain concepts." (Hayes-Roth, Waterman & Lenat 1983)

The knowledge acquisition bottleneck has become the major impediment to the development and application of effective knowledge-based systems. Many research groups around the world have been working on knowledge acquisition methodologies, techniques and tools to overcome this problem. In 1985, members of a number of these groups realized that there had been rapid progress in knowledge acquisition research and application. However there was subtantial duplication of effort and limited communication between researchers, and therefore it would be valuable for a workshop to be held that would encourage the sharing of results and experience.

The American Association for Artificial Intelligence agreed to sponsor such a workshop. John Boose of Boeing Advanced Technology Centre and Brian Gaines of the Knowledge Science Institute at the University of Calgary agreed to organize it. Other researchers agreed to contribute effort to the organization and refereeing of papers, resulting in a program and local arrangements committee of: Jeffrey Bradshaw, Boeing Advanced Technology Centre, William Clancey, Stanford University, Catherine Kitto, Boeing Advanced Technology Centre, Janusz Kowalik, Boeing Advanced Technology Centre, John McDermott, Carnegie-Mellon University, Ryszard Michalski, University of Illinois, Art Nagai, Boeing Advanced Technology Centre, Gavriel Salvendy, Purdue University, and Mildred Shaw, University of Calgary.

The response to the call for papers for the Workshop on Knowledge Acquisition for Knowledge-Based Systems (KAW) was overwhelming. The intention was to hold a discussion-intensive meeting of some 35 highly involved researchers. In practice over 120 papers were submitted and some 500 applications to attend were received from about 30 countries. Apart from increasing the refereeing and organizational problems beyond all expected bounds, this response indicated the magnitude and impact of the knowledge acquisition bottleneck and the worldwide interest.

These submissions resulted in 60 people attending the first *Knowledge Acquisition for Knowledge-Based Systems Workshop* (*KAW*) from November 3–7, 1986, at the Banff Centre in Banff, Canada. Each of the 120 papers submitted was refereed by five to seven referees and 42 papers were finally selected. Much of the rejected material was of high-quality and it would have been possible to base a major conference on the material and requests to attend. However, it was decided that the priority at that stage should remain that of establishing in-depth communication between research groups.

It was also clear that it was important to disseminate the workshop material as widely as possible, and arrangements were made to publish revised versions of the papers in the *International Journal of Man–Machine Studies* after the Workshop. These papers have now been gathered together as the first two volumes of the *Knowledge-Based Systems* series.

The table below shows the format of the first KAW. It was very effective in establishing a network linking the community of knowledge acquisition researchers

Knowledge Acquisition for Knowledge-Based Systems *AAAI Workshop, Banff, November 1986*	
Structure	Residential workshop Accomodation, meals and sessions together Attendance limited to 60 (originally 35) 120 papers submitted, 43 accepted Several hundred requests to attend
Overview/ Summary Papers	Gaines—Overview of Knowledge Acquisition Clancey—Cognition and Expertise McDermott—Interactive Interviewing Tools I Boose—Interactive Interviewing Tools II Salvendy—Analysis of Knowledge Structures Michalski—Learning
Mini- Conference	Cognition & Expertise 6, Learning 8 Analysis of Knowledge Structures 7 Interactive Interviewing Tools 16
Workshops on Major Issues	Cognition & Expertise Interactive Interviewing Tools Learning Knowledge Representation
Panels on other Issues	Knowledge Acquisition Methodology/Training Reasoning with Uncertainty
Papers and Books	Preprint volume of all papers to attendees Four special issues of IJMMS in 1987 Two books, Academic Press 1988

worldwide. It resulted in two further KAWs in 1987, a second one at Banff again sponsored by the American Association for Artificial Intelligence (AAAI), and the first European KAW (EKAW) in London and Reading, England, sponsored by the Institute of Electrical Engineers. Papers from these workshops have again been published in the *International Journal of Man–Machine Studies* and constitute the third volume of the *Knowledge-Based Systems* series.

In 1988, the third AAAI-KAW was held at Banff in November with a theme of integration of methodologies, and the second EKAW was held at Bonn, Germany, in June with sponsorship from the Gesselschaft für Mathematik and the German Chapter of the ACM. A specialist workshop on the Integration of Knowledge Acquisition and Performance tools was held at the AAAI Annual Conference in St Paul in August. Sessions and tutorials on knowledge acquisition have become prevalent at a wide variety of conferences concerned with knowledge-based systems worldwide.

These two volumes based on the first AAAI-KAW at Banff contain a wide range of material representing foundational work in knowledge acquisition problems, methodologies, techniques and tools from the major research groups worldwide. All those contributing hope that access to this material will enable other researchers and practitioners to expedite their own developments through the shared knowledge and experience documented here.

Knowledge acquisition research is still in its early stages and there are many fundamental problems to be solved, new perspectives to be generated, tools to be developed, refined and disseminated, and so on—the work seems endless. Like many modern technologies, knowledge acquisition requires a large-scale cooperative international effort. It is virtually impossible for one research and dvelopment group to have world-class expertise in all the issues, technologies and experience necessary to develop integrated knowledge acquisition tools for a wide range of knowledge-based systems.

We wish to thank the many people who have been involved in organizing these workshops and the organizations that have given them sponsorship and publicity. We have a fundamental debt to those who put in place the computer communication networks worldwide, such as UseNet, that have made the world a global village and enable networks such as ours to operate effectively. We are particularly grateful to the AAAI for its role in sponsoring the North American Workshops and for providing such effective means of disseminating information to the massive community of those now involved in knowledge-based systems research.

We sometimes wonder how we have become so involved in the bureaucracy of organizing workshops and networks when our personal priorities are hacking new knowledge acquisition tools. However, the stimulation of discussions with colleagues at the workshops and across the networks is vital to the direction of our own research. We hope the books will make this stimulation widely available and bring a new generation of researchers into the knowledge acquisition network.

We have attempted to structure the material by dividing it between two books. However, we must make it very clear that the division between the books and into sections in this volume is our own. It is somewhat arbitrary in places, and was not discussed with the contributors. There are many cross-connections between papers in different sections. There is tool-oriented material in this volume and fundamental material in the other. The reader will find it worthwhile to browse through both volumes to get a feel for the many different perspectives present and interactions possible.

John Boose and Brian Gaines

Contents

Knowledge Acquisition Tools for Expert Systems

B. R. GAINES

Department of Computer Science, University of Calgary, Calgary, Alberta T2N 1N4, Canada

J. H. BOOSE

Boeing Computer Sciences, P.O. Box 24346, Seattle, Washington 98124-0346, U.S.A.

1. Introduction

This volume contains the papers concerned with tools for knowledge acquisition from the AAAI Knowledge Acquisition for Knowledge-Based System Workshop in November 1986, in Banff, Canada. We have not split them into sections because of the diversity of topics and techniques covered by many of the papers. This is inevitable when integrated systems of tools are being developed that draw on many techniques. There were also keynote addresses, panels and group discussions at the workshop that addressed major themes but did not result in published papers. This paper attempts to capture the essential issues raised in these other presentations.

2. Plenary Papers

Plenary talks were given on the first day by members of the program committee. Each speaker was asked to summarize papers in their area and give an overview of their views on the area. Topics covered relevant to this volume were:

2.1 INTERACTIVE KNOWLEDGE ACQUISITION TOOLS I, JOHN McDERMOTT, CARNEGIE–MELLON UNIVERSITY

Why build intelligent interactive knowledge acquisition tools? 'Smart' means being able to get more mileage out of a few pieces of information than anyone would think you could.

Users of interactive knowledge acquisition tools include AI programmers, programmers, and domain experts. The user may see the structure of the representation (e.g., TEIRESIAS), the problem-solving strategy (e.g., Roget, SALT), or the domain model (e.g., OPAL).

Several interactive knowledge acquisition tools were evaluated in terms of systems built, the system's inference engine, the intended user, and sources of strength. The tools included KREME (Abrett and Burstein), TKAW (Kahn, Breaux, Joseph, and De Klerk), KNACK (Klinker, Bentolila, Genetet, Grimes, and McDermott), STUDENT (Gale), SALT (Marcus), OPAL (Musen, Fagan, Combs, and Shortliffe), and MOLE (Eshelman, Ehret, McDermott, and Tan).

2.2 INTERACTIVE KNOWLEDGE ACQUISITION TOOLS II, JOHN BOOSE, BOEING AI CENTER

Another set of interactive knowledge acquisition tools was evaluated in terms of the problem the tool was addressing, the approach, and the tool's feature set. The tools included KITTEN (Shaw and Gaines), NEXPERT (Rappaport), KRITON (Diedrich, Ruhman, and May), INFORM (Moore and Agogino), FIS (De Jong), MUM (Gruber and Cohen), SMEE (Garg), and AQUINAS (Boose, Bradshaw, and Kitto).

To describe the state-of-the-art, tool features and rates of inclusion were listed: domain modelling, eight tools; interviewing methods, seven tools; use of Personal Construct Psychology and repertory grids, five tools; induction methods, five tools; ability to handle multiple experts, two tools; multiple uncertainty representations, two tools; protocol analysis, two tools; text analysis, two tools; learning (simple), two tools; decision analysis, one tool; copy-and-edit, almost all tools.

To show his committment to knowledge acquisition tools, John Boose produced a repertory grid giving his construing 20 tools and an 'ideal tool', Figure 1 shows this

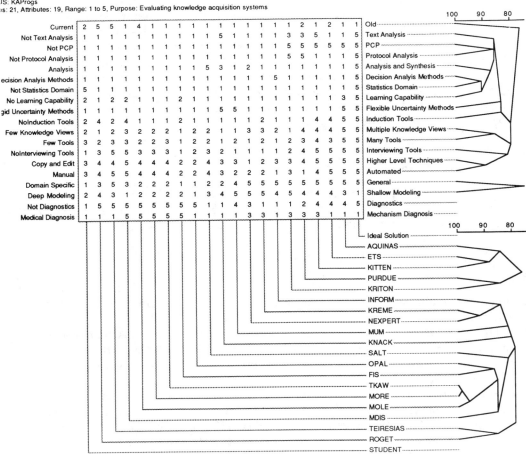

Fig. 1. Repertory grid construing knowledge acquisition tools clustered by FOCUS.

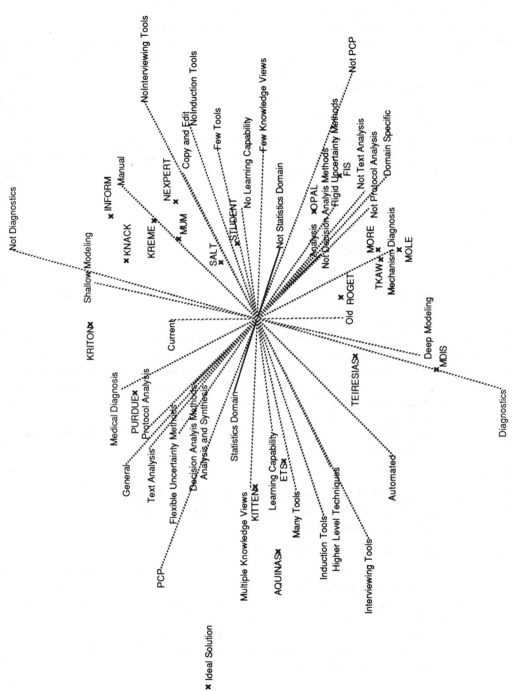

Fig. 2. The tools grid mapped onto its first two principal components.

grid clustered using Shaw's FOCUS algorithm which sorts the original grid and hierarchically clusters it. Note that the 'ideal' tool clusters with no others which is a pretty accurate reflection of the state-of-the-art—we have a long way to go. Figure 2 shows this grid mapped onto its first two principal components. Note also that most of the tool makers were insulated by John's evaluations of their tools which is also a pretty accurate reflection of the state-of-the-art—experts always seem to differ on the most fundamental questions!

3. Working Group Summaries

Attendees participated in several small working groups that attempted to define the aims, objectives, problems, state-of-the-art, and future directions in their areas. The following summaries were presented at the workshop.

3.1 INTERACTIVE KNOWLEDGE ACQUISITION TOOLS, JOHN McDERMOTT, SPOKESPERSON

Aim:
  • Facilitate the production of knowledge-based application programs.

Objectives:
  • Invent or define a way of organizing or classifying tasks and methods at various levels of abstraction.
  • Find a mapping between tasks and methods.
  • Develop a technology that, given some collection of tasks within the idealized task hierarchy, finds the associated method collection within the idealized method hierarchy, integrates and possibly specializes the method collection, and defines what kinds of knowledge are needed to perform the tasks and how that knowledge is to be represented.
  • Build programs (knowledge acquisition tools) that elicit the required knowledge and represent it and the methods that use it as knowledge-based application programs.

Problems:
  • Tasks are ill-defined (i.e. 'configuration, design, interpretation. . . .').
  • Methods are sparse (heuristic classification, Newell's weak methods).
  • Mapping is poorly understood.

State-of-the-art and future directions ('research bets'):
  • Find and clarify a task/method, apply the method to another new task.
  • Pick a task, find a method that allows problem-solving in the task domain, apply the method to another new task. Understand methods in the neighborhood and generalize.
  • Develop languages for defining task and method hierarchies.
  • Look for data to ground ('prove') the task and method hierarchies.
  • Build knowledge-based editors.

Slogan:

'Task + method = knowledge-based application'

The KREME knowledge editing environment

GLENN ABRETT AND MARK H. BURSTEIN

BBN Laboratories, 10 Moulton Street, Cambridge, MA 02238, U.S.A.

One of the major bottlenecks in large-scale expert-system development is the problem of knowledge acquisition: the construction, maintenance, and testing of large knowledge bases. This paper provides an overview of the current state of development of the KREME Knowledge Representation Editing and Modeling Environment. KREME is an extensible experimental environment for developing and editing large knowledge bases in a variety of representation styles. It provides tools for effective viewing and browsing in each kind of representational base, automatic consistency checking, macro-editing facilities to reduce the burdens of large-scale knowledge-base revision and some experimental automatic generalization and acquisition facilities.

1. Introduction

1.1. THE KNOWLEDGE-ACQUISITION PROBLEM

The creation of the large and detailed bodies of knowledge needed to improve the performance of expert systems substantially has proven to be an extremely difficult task. We have identified several factors which make building these very large knowledge bases impractical using current technology:

Knowledge comes in many forms
Human knowledge about the world comes in many forms. Squeezing all the knowledge that an expert system needs into one, or at best two, representational formalisms (e.g. rules and frames) is difficult, time-consuming, and usually an inadequate solution to the task at hand.

Managing large knowledge bases is difficult
As knowledge bases grow in size and complexity they strain the capacities of software tools for knowledge editing, maintenance, and validity checking. Viewpoints at the right level of detail are hard to construct, consistency checking takes up more and more time, and global reorganizations and modifications become virtually impossible to accomplish.

Previously encoded knowledge is not re-used
It is customary to start building a new expert system with an empty knowledge base, even though the completed knowledge base will contain at least some general knowledge about the world. To make matters worse, this general world knowledge is usually entered in a fragmentary and sketchy manner. If general knowledge about the world could be transferred across systems, the gradual accumulation of detail and precision would tremendously enhance the performance of most expert systems.

1

1.2. OVERVIEW OF THE BBN KNOWLEDGE-ACQUISITION PROJECT

Our goal has been to develop an environment in which the problems of knowledge acquisition faced by every knowledge engineer attempting to build a large expert system are minimized. To this end, we have organized the task of developing knowledge-acquisition tools into two stages. During stage one, we have been developing a knowledge representation, editing and modeling environment, dubbed KREME. We believe both knowledge engineers and subject-matter experts with some knowledge of basic knowledge representation techniques will find it easy to use KREME to acquire, edit, and view from multiple perspectives knowledge bases that are several times larger (i.e. 5–10 000 concepts) than those found in most current systems. During phase two of the project, we will be considering more directed kinds of automatic knowledge acquisition; techniques for generating controlled acquisition dialogues, procedures for automatically transforming previously acquired knowledge for use in new tasks, techniques for learning by analogy and learning from examples.

The current version of KREME provides, within a uniform environment, a number of special-purpose editing facilities that permit knowledge to be represented and viewed in a variety of formalisms appropriate to its use, rather than forcing all knowledge to be represented in a single, unitary formalism. In addition to a general editing environment, KREME provides tools to do the kinds of validation and consistency checking so essential during the development or modification of knowledge bases. As the size of knowledge bases grows, and more people become involved in their development, this aspect of knowledge acquisition becomes increasingly important. In the hybrid or multi-formalism representational systems that are becoming prevalent (Rich, 1982; Brachman, Fikes & Levesque, 1983; Vilain, 1985), techniques must be provided for consistency checking not only within a single representational system, but between related systems.

Our approach to consistency maintenance has been to develop a *knowledge integration* subsystem that includes an *automatic frame classifier* and facilities for inter-language consistency maintenance. The frame classifier automatically maintains logical consistency among all of the frames or conceptual class definitions in a KREME frame base. In addition, it can discover implicit class relationships, since it will determine when one definition is logically subsumed by another even when the knowledge engineer has not explicitly stated that relationship. The inter-language consistency maintenance facility checks for inconsistencies in references to frames in knowledge bases specified using other representation languages (e.g. rules, procedures).

A second important area of investigation in developing the KREME editing environment has been the attempt to provide facilities for large-scale revisions of portions of a knowledge base. Our experience indicates that the development of an expert system inevitably requires systematic, large-scale revisions of portions of the developed representation. This is often caused by the addition or redefinition of a task the system is to perform. These kinds of systematic changes to a knowledge base have, to date, only been possible by painstaking piecemeal revision of each affected element, one at a time. Our initial approach has been to provide a *macro-editing* facility, in which the required editing operations can be demonstrated by example and applied to specified sets of knowledge structures atuomatically. We plan to provide a library of such generic macro-editing operations for the most common and conceptually simple (though potentially difficult to describe) operations during phase two of the project.

Finally, we have begun to investigate techniques for *automatic generalization* of concepts defined in a knowledge base. We will describe briefly these experiments as well, in the section on *knowledge extension.*

2. Overview of KREME

KREME attempts to deal with the inextricably related problems of knowledge representation and knowledge acquisition in a unified manner by organizing multiple representation languages and multiple knowledge editors inside a coherent global environment. A key design goal for KREME was to build an environment in which existing knowledge-representation languages, appropriate to diverse types of knowledge, could be integrated and organized as components of a coherent global representation system. The current KREME Knowledge Editor can be thought of as an extensible set of globally coherent operations that apply across a number of related knowledge representation editors, each tailored to a specific type of knowledge. Our approach has been to integrate several existing representation languages in an open ended architecture that allows the extension of each of these languages. In addition, we have provided for the incorporation of additional representation languages to handle additional types of knowledge.

KREME currently contains knowledge editors for four distinct representation languages; one for frames, one for rules, one for procedures, and one for attached behaviors or methods, defined as functions. The rule editor, the procedure editor and the functional method editor are accessible through a global mechanism that treats these types of knowledge as forms of procedural attachment to frames. In the immediate future we plan to add a language for representing causal and other qualitative constraint systems, and several types of instantiation mechanisms, including a truth maintenance system for propositional representations.

Underlying the entire system is a strong notion of meta-level knowledge about knowledge representation and knowledge acquisition. The representation languages were implemented based on a careful decomposition of existing knowledge representation techniques, implemented as combinable objects using FLAVORS (Keene & Moon, 1985). By organizing this meta-level knowledge base modularly, behavioral objects implementing such notions as inheritance and subsumption could be "mixed in" to a variety of representational subsystems making the incorporation of new representations and their editors a reasonably straightforward process. That is, each object in the meta-knowledge base encodes some aspect of a traditional representational technique, and is responsible for its own display, editing and internal forms.

3. The KREME knowledge editing environment

The KREME Knowledge Editor currently consists of three major editor modules; a frame editor, a procedure editor, and a rule editor; and a large tool-box of editing techniques that are shared among the editor modules. This section will describe the global environment and toolbox, later sections will describe the individual editors.

3.1. BASIC EDITING ENVIRONMENT

Each distinct type of representation included in the system (currently concepts, roles, procedures methods and rules) has defined for it one or more editor *views*. A view is a configured collection of windows appearing together on the screen, each of which displays some aspect of the particular piece of knowledge being edited and/or a set of editing operations on it. When the user desires to enter or edit a specific piece of knowledge, the system opens the most appropriate view for the type of knowledge and the editing operation requested. Typically, any aspect of the chunk of knowledge being edited can be changed or viewed in more detail simply by pointing at it. This organization allows knowledge to be viewed by the user from multiple perspectives at the level of detail required.

The editor maintains a level of indirection between the knowledge being edited and the representation of that piece of knowledge in the knowledge base. This is accomplished by a mechanism like that of text editor buffers. Changes are always made to *editor definition objects* which are distinct from the corresponding objects in the actual knowledge base. A stack or list of the active definition objects is always visible to the user. The top item in this list is the definition currently being viewed and edited. The user is free to modify this definition in any way without directly effecting the knowledge base. When the modified definition is to be placed into the knowledge base a defining function appropriate to the type of knowledge (e.g. classification for concepts and roles), is executed and the knowledge base is modified.

Since the editor stack is always visible, it provides one convenient method for browsing. The user may make any definition item currently in the stack the top, visible item by pointing at it. The object will be displayed in the same editor view as when it was last edited.

3.2. WINDOW EDITING TOOLS

There are a number of window subsystems or tools that have been developed and incorporated into the KREME editor to make editing, viewing and browsing in knowledge bases easier and faster. We will now briefly describe some of the most important of them.

The grapher
The KREME grapher is a powerful, generalized facility that rapidly draws lattices of nodes and links. Specific kinds of graphs appear, when appropriate, in a number of editor views. At present, dynamically updated graphs display the parts of the subsumption hierarchy surrounding (i.e. all of the objects subsuming and subsumed by) the concept or role currently being edited in the frame editor. Other concepts may be added to the displayed graph at any time simply by pointing at a node that is already present and requesting all of *its* parents or children be displayed as well. The presence of these graphs greatly facilitates browsing, since any visible node can be pointed at and made the top, current definition being edited. Alternatively, the lisp

form of the object's definition can be temporarily displayed over the graph. In addition to these graphs, a graph can be "popped up" to display networks other than the one normally presented.

One extremely convenient feature of the KREME grapher is that it routinely displays graphs that are much larger than the window through which it is viewed. Simply clicking and dragging the mouse across the graph window causes the grapher to pan smoothly in the direction of mouse motion, making previously obscured portions of the graph instantly visible as though one was moving a window across a larger page. Graphs can also be displayed vertically or horizontally, in a number of different fonts and sizes, and with or without a dynamic overview that provides another convenient method for scrolling. Graphs can also be hardcopied automatically.

Tabular display windows
For editing lists of structured features of objects, we have incorporated into our toolbox a sophisticated kind tabular display window facility. Information displayed in tabular windows can be scrolled both vertically and horizontally, and edited by pointing at a component or a whole row of the table. These windows appear in a number of editor views.

Strucure/text editing windows
Another style of editing commonly found in LISP environments is structure editing. Some KREME Editor views contain windows of this variety, including the *macro editing view* (see section 7). When editing functional methods, the structure editor can also be toggled to act as a ZMACS style editor.

3.3. FILES AND MULTIPLE LANGUAGE SUPPORT

All definitions manipulated by the editor are read and stored in lisp-readable text files of defining forms. Since these files contain formatted lisp forms, they are user-readable, and can be edited offline using an ordinary text editor. In fact, KREME can as easily read files that were developed independently using a text editor or some other frame editor.

Files are read in using the LOAD command. A file can be loaded into a blank KREME knowledge base or can be loaded on top of an already existing knowledge base. This mechanism, which relies heavily on the frame classifier (see section 5) to maintain consistency, enables KREME to organize information from multiple knowledge bases to create a single unified whole.

KREME currently reads and writes definitions in either its own frame language syntax or NIKL syntax, the language upon which it was largely based. This flexibility has made it possible for KREME to be used regularly to examine and update a knowledge base of approximately 1000 roles and concepts for a natural language query system that was built using NIKL. KREME can also read files of MSG [the frame language of the STEAMER (Williams, Hollan & Stevens, 1981) system] defining forms, providing us access to the extensive STEAMER knowledge base of concepts and procedures. We are currently at work in building an interface to files of KEE frame definitions, as well.

We feel that this multiple language handling facility is a crucial feature of KREME and are committed to extending it, where possible, to other representation languages. A rich library of input translation programs will enable a knowledge-base builder, working in KREME, to draw upon many previously existing knowledge bases to create a larger and more detailed whole. It is our opinion that this kind of flexibility will be crucial if knowledge bases developed in different languages are ever to be combined and conveniently modified to create larger ones.

4. The KREME frame editor

Much of the work done in the current implementation of KREME has been focused on building a knowledge editor for a frame representation language. This section will describe the language that the editor works with, its basic structure and operations. Section 5.1 will describe the classifier mechanism that is used within the editor to help maintain correctness and consistency of frame knowledge bases developed with the editor.

4.1. THE KREME FRAME LANGUAGE

A number of frame languages have been developed in recent years to support AI systems (Roberts & Goldstein, 1977; Bobrow, Winograd & KRL Research Group, 1977; Sidner *et al.*, 1981, Moser, 1983, Brachman, *et al.*, 1983; IntelliCorp 1984, Carnegie Group, 1985). These languages have been well researched and extensively tested, and while we had to have some frame language on which to base our initial editor, we did not want to design and implement a new one completely from scratch. Our most important criteria for a suitable frame representation language were that it:

(1) allowed multiple inheritance;
(2) was a logically worked out mature language;
(3) had some mechanism for internal consistency checking;
(4) was built on a modular object-oriented base so that the language could be decomposed in such a way as to make it easily extensible.

NIKL (the definitional or frame language component of KL-TWO) (Moser, 1983; Schmolze & Israel, 1983; Vilain, 1985) seemed an ideal candidate. It is a fully worked-out frame representation language that allows multiple inheritance, is reasonably expressive and, perhaps most importantly, was designed to work effectively with an automatic classification algorithm that could be easily adapted to provide a powerful mechanism for consistency checking and enforcement during knowledge base development. However, no object-implementation of NIKL existed, and the NIKL classifier was not designed to allow *modification* and *reclassification* of previously defined concepts. A second frame language, known as MSG, had been built as part of BBN's STEAMER project and was readily available. MSG is object oriented in both of the above senses but it has no classifier and is not as mature or thoroughly specified a language as NIKL.

To develop KREME, we elected to reimplement NIKL as an object-oriented language using MSG as a guide. the NIKL data structures were decomposed into a modular hierarchy of flavor definitions, and the KREME frame language was then built out of these flavors. This enabled us to incorporate a great deal of the fairly sophisticated instantiation mechanism of MSG with minimal effort. In the process, we were also able to re-implement the NIKL classifier algorithm in a more modular fashion, both to provide the kind of reclassification capability required for a knowledge editing environment, and in anticipation of extending the classifier to deal with the richer semantics of languages like Intellicorp's KEE (IntelliCorp, 1984).

4.1.1. Frame language syntax

The remainder of this section will describe briefly the basic definitional syntax of the KREME frame language. As this syntax closely resembles the formal syntax of NIKL interested readers are referred to Moser (1983) for more detail.

Following NIKL, a KREME frame is called a *concept*. Collections of concepts are organized into a rooted *inheritance* or *subsumption lattice* sometimes referred to as a *taxonomy* of concepts. A single distinguished concept, usually called THING, serves as the root or *most general concept* of the lattice. A concept has a *name*, a textual *description*, a *primitiveness* flag, a list of concepts that it *specializes* or is *subsumed by*, a list of *slots*, a list of *slot equivalences*, and a list of concepts that it is *disjoint from*.

The lists of slots, slot equivalences and disjoint concepts are collectively referred to as the *features* of a concept. If each concept can be thought of as defining a unique category, then features of the concept define the necessary conditions for inclusion in that category. If a concept is not marked as *primitive*, the features also constitute the complete set of sufficient conditions for inclusion in that category.† A concept inherits all features from those concepts above it in the lattice (those concepts that subsume it, and, thus, are more general) and may define additional features that serve to distinguish it from its parent or parents.

Slots (sometimes called role restrictions) consist of a role or slot name, a value restriction, a number restriction and an (optional) default form. The *value restriction* specifies the class of concepts allowed as values for that slot. As in NIKL, value restrictions usually specify a particular concept. We are currently in the process of extending the value restriction language to permit more complex forms containing conjunctions, disjunctions and negations, based on the restriction language for KEE frames (IntelliCorp, 1984). This effort should result in an extended classifier, as well, capable of maintaining consistency among frames in the KEE class of frame languages.

Slot Equivalences describe slots (and slots of slots) that *by definition* must always refer to the same entities.

The role name specified for each KREME slot refers to an object called a *role*. Roles in KREME, as in NIKL and several other frame languages like KRYPTON (Brachman, 1983), and KnowledgeCraft (Carnegie Group, 1985), are actually

---

† Concepts marked as *primitive* (sometimes referred to as *Natural Kinds*) have no complete set of sufficient conditions. For example, and ELEPHANT must, by necessity, be a MAMMAL, but without an exhaustive list of the attributes that distinguish it from other mammals, it must be represented as a primitive concept. The class of WHITE ELEPHANTs, on the other hand, might be completely described as a ELEPHANT, with slot COLOR restricted to WHITE.

distinct, first-class objects that form their own distinct taxonomy, rooted at the most general possible role, usually called RELATION. Roles describe two place relations between concepts. A *role restriction* at a concept is thus a specification of the ways a given role can be used to relate that concept to other concepts.

4.2. FRAME EDITING VIEWS

The frame editor is used to create, edit and browse around in a knowledge base of KREME frames. The current KREME frame editor has four views, each a fixed configuration of windows appearing at once on the screen. Three windows (screen regions) are common to all of these views; the *global command window,* the *editor stack window,* and the *state window.* Figure 1 shows the main concept editing view, which contains most of the windows used for editing portions of a concept's definition. The descriptions of each window below will refer to the numbers superimposed on that figure.

(1)   The *global command window* contains commands that operate on the network as a whole. It is always visible.

(2)   The *editor stack window,* which is also always visible, shows the names of the things being edited and some information about their current edit state (e.g. whether they have been modified). Items in the stack window can be removed from the editor, made the currently visible edit item, or reclassified (if modified) by pointing at them.

(3)   The *state window,* which is visible in all views for concepts and roles, displays the name, textual description, primitive class flag, parents and information on the classification state of the item.

(4)   The *concept graph window* displays a dynamically updated graph of all of the abstractions and specializations of the current concept. This view provides constant visual display of the relative position of the concept being edited in the subsumption hierarchy.

(5)   The *tabular feature window* ordinarily displays a table of (all or just the locally defined) slots for the current concept. Columns in the table show the source of the slot (where it was inherited from), its role name, value and number restrictions, default value, and a description. This window can also be used to display the concept's slot equivalences, disjoint concepts, or a list of all *behaviors* (rules, methods and procedures) defined for the concept (see section 6).

(6)   The *slots command window* contains various commands for editing and displaying the slots of the concept.

(7)   The *Editor Interaction Window* is a Lisp Listener which can be scrolled backward and forward through a history of the current session.

Three other views are currently defined for concepts, and one view is defined for roles. Two of the other concept views are somewhat different configurations of the above windows, the last is the macro and structure editing view described in section 7. A separate view exists for editing role definitions. It contains windows showing a graph of the role taxonomy, highlighting the currently visible role, a window displaying the concepts that restrict the role and third window displaying the role's domain, range and parents.

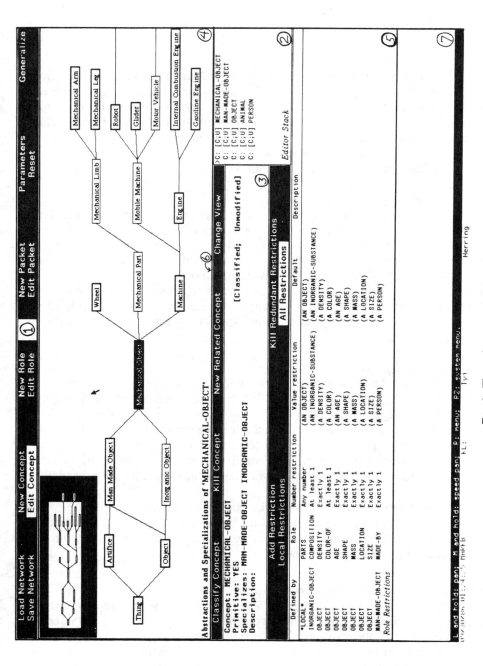

FIG. 1. The main concept editing view.

4.3. FRAME EDITING OPERATIONS

Space does not permit a full description of the functionality of the KREME frame editor so we will very briefly touch upon a few of its more important operations.

Making new concepts

The *New Concept* command in the global command menu initiates the definition of a new concept that is: (1) fully specified by the user; (2) similar to some already defined concept; or (3) a specialization of one or several other defined concepts. When the initial form for the new concept has been specified, the system creates a new concept definition for it and shows this new definition in the main concept view. The user is then free to add details (slots, equivalences, additional parents, etc.) to the new concept definition, classify it, or edit other concepts.

Adding and modifying slots

Whenever the window displaying slots is visible, slots can be added or modified. A new slot is added to the defined slots of the concept with the *Add Slot* command. Any portion of a slot's definition can be entered by typing or by pointing to a visible reference to the desired item. When a role or concept name that is not defined is specified, the system offers to make one with the name given.

Users may modify any locally defined slot or inherited slot. Slots shown in table windows are modified by pointing at the appropriate subform and then either typing in or pointing to a replacement form. Modifying an inherited slot causes the new definition to be locally defined.

Adding and deleting parents

The system displays the classifier determined parents of a concept in two places. The concept graph displays them as part of the abstraction hierarchy of the concept, and the state pane indicates both the defined and direct or computed parents of the concept after the word "*Specializes:*". Since the classifier may have found that the concept being edited specializes some concepts more specific than those given as its defined parents, defined parents that are not direct parents are preceded by a " − ", while classifier determined parents that were not defined parents are preceded by a " + ".

Adding new defined parents to a concept's definition is done by clicking on the word "*Specializes:*" in the state window and typing a concept name or pointing to any visible concept. Parents can be deleted by clicking on their names in the list of parents displayed in the state window.

Changing names and killing concepts and roles

KREME allows the user to change the names of concepts and roles or to delete them completely. Name changing is accomplished simply by pointing at the concept or role's name in the state window and entering a new name. The *Kill* command splices a concept out of the taxonomy by connecting all of its children to all of its parents. There are several complicating issues relating to how concepts are deleted from taxonomies that we do not have time to discuss here.

5. Knowledge integration and consistency maintenance

One of the most time-consuming tasks in building large knowledge bases is maintaining internal consistency. Modification, addition or deletion of knowledge in one part of a knowledge base can have wide-ranging consequences to both the meaning and structure of the knowledge stored in other parts of the knowledge base. A central component of the KREME system design was that it incorporate tools for consistency maintenance both within and across representation languages. These tools are collectively referred to as the *knowledge integrator*. When new knowledge is entered or existing knowledge modified it is the task of the knowledge integrator to propagate, throughout the knowledge base, the changes that this new or modified knowledge entails, and to report any inconsistencies that have been caused by the change.

In essence, the knowledge integrator takes each new or changed chunk of knowledge (e.g. a frame, role, rule or procedure) and determines, first, how the new definition fits into the knowledge base and, second, which other definitions depend on the current one for their meaning within the knowledge base. These dependencies are placed on an agenda and which, in turn, causes them to go through essentially the same process.

The knowledge integration subsystem for frames is basically an extension of the *classification* algorithm developed for the NIKL representation language. The NIKL classifier correctly inserts *new* frames into their proper spot in a taxonomy, by finding the most specific set of concepts whose definitions *subsumed* the definition of the new concept. The KREME classifier was designed additionally to allow existing concepts and roles to be modified and then *reclassified*, so that the effects of redefinitions are automatically propagated throughout the entire frame network. This was accomplished by redesigning the original NIKL classifier to take advantage of the meta-level descriptions of KREME frames and implementing the new classifier using the dependency directed agenda mechanism of the overall knowledge integrator.

5.1. THE FRAME CLASSIFIER

The remainder of this section will give a brief description of the frame classification part of the knowledge integrator, which is the most completely developed portion of the system. For a formal description of the NIKL classifier algorithm see Schmolze & Israel (1983), Schmolze & Lipkis (1983). For a more complete description of a somewhat simpler classifier for an editing environment, see Balzac (1986).

The frame classifier works in essentially two stages, starting from a *concept or role definition*, as supplied by the editor or read from a file. The first stage, called *completion*, refers to the basic inheritance mechanism used by KREME frames to install all inherited features of a concept or role in its internal description. The completion algorithm, when given a set of defined parents and a set of defined features for an object determines the full, logically entailed set of features of that object. The second stage is the actual classification or reclassification of a role or concept. That is, the determination of the complete, most specific set of parents of the object in its respective subsumption hierarchy.

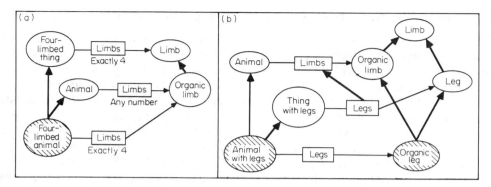

FIG. 2. Two examples of slot completion. (a), inheriting different number and value restrictions; (b), conjoined value restrictions.

5.1.1. Completion

The completion algorithm is broken up into modular chunks that correspond to the decomposition of the frame language. There is a distinct component that deals with slot inheritance, another component that deals with slot equivalence inheritance and so on. This organization makes it quite straightforward to extend the language with new features that handle inheritance in different ways.

Figure 2 shows some of the complexities of slot inheritance. In Fig. 2(a), the most specific *value restriction* for the slot LIMBS at 4-LIMBED-ANIMAL is inherited from one parent (ANIMAL) while the most specific *number restriction*, EXACTLY 4, is inherited from 4-LIMBED-THING. The completion algorithm determines that the restriction for the role LIMBS at the concept 4-LIMBED-ANIMAL must be EXACTLY 4 LIMBS.

Figure 2(b) shows one case for which the effective value restriction must logically be the conjunction of several concepts. Since ANIMAL-WITH-LEGS is both an ANIMAL, and a THING-WITH-LEGS, all of its LIMBS must be both ORGANIC-LIMBs and LEGs. If the concept ORGANIC-LEG, specializing both ORGANIC-LIMB and LEG, exists when ANIMAL-WITH-LEGS is being classified, the integrator will find it and make it the value restriction of the slot LEGS at ANIMAL-WITH-LEGS. If it does not exist, the integrator stops and asks if the user would like to define it (i.e. define a concept that is both an ORGANIC-LIMB and a LEG).

5.1.2. Classification

The second stage of the frame classification algorithm finds all of the *most specific subsumers* of the concept being defined or redefined. This is the actual *classification* stage, and is essentially a special-purpose tree walking algorithm.

The basic classifier algorithm takes a completed definition (i.e. a definition plus all its effective, inherited features) and determines that definition's single appropriate spot in the lattice of previously classified definitions. The result of a classification is a unique set of the most specific objects that subsume the definition and a unique set of the most general objects that are subsumed by the definition. When the classified definition is installed in the lattice all the concepts that subsume its features will be above it in the lattice and all the concepts that are subsumed by its features will be below it.

The classifier is built around a modularly constructed subsumption test that compares the completed sets of features of two objects. The object being classified is repeatedly compared with other, potentially related, objects in the lattice to see whether its completed definition subsumes or is subsumed by those other objects. For one definition to subsume the other, its full set of features must be a subset of the features of the other. As with completion, subsumption testing is partitioned by feature type (i.e. slot, disjoint-class etc). One object subsumes the other when all of its individual feature-type subsumption checks return EQUIVALENT or SUBSUMES, and there is at least one vote for SUBSUMES. The advantage of this kind of modular organization is extensibility. If a new feature type is added to the language one need only define a subsumption predicate for that feature, and objects having that feature will be appropriately classified.

5.2. AN EXAMPLE OF RECLASSIFICATION

The power of frame reclassification in an editing environment can be illustrated with the following relatively simple example. Suppose a knowledge base developer had defined both GASOLINE-POWERED-CAR and INTERNAL-COMBUSTION-POWERED-CAR as specializations of CAR, but had inadvertently defined INTERNAL-COMBUSTION-ENGINE as a kind of GASOLINE-ENGINE. In this situation, the classifier would deduce that INTERNAL-COMBUSTION-POWERED-CAR must be a specialization of GASOLINE-POWERED-CAR, as shown in Fig. 3(a), since the former restricted the role ENGINE to a subclass of the latter's restriction of the same role.

Redefining INTERNAL-COMBUSTION-ENGINE as a kind of ENGINE (rather than a GASOLINE-ENGINE), and then reclassifying, causes all of INTERNAL-COMBUSTION-ENGINE's dependents also to be reclassified, including INTERNAL-COMBUSTION-POWERED-CAR. Since GASOLINE-ENGINE no longer subsumes INTERNAL-COMBUSTION-ENGINE, the restrictions for GASOLINE-POWERED-CAR no longer subsume those of INTERNAL-COMBUSTION-POWERED-CAR, and the classifier therefore finds that

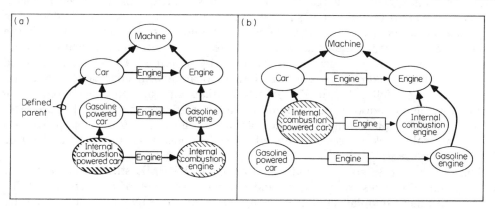

Fig. 3. An example of reclassification. (a), before reclassification; (b), after reclassification.

GASOLINE-POWERED-CAR does not subsume INTERNAL-COMBUSTION-POWERED-CAR. This is shown in Fig. 3(a).

The combination of inconsistency detection during the completion phase and the automatic propagation of classification changes that occurs during reclassification makes KREME a powerful and extremely useful tool for knowledge base development and refinement. Since the effects of reclassification are *immediately* made apparent to users via the dynamically updated graph of the subsumption lattice, they sometimes find that the definitions they have provided have some unanticipated logically entailed effects on their taxonomy. Sometimes these effects are surprising, although correct. Other times, they lead to changes and additions which make the knowledge base more complete and correct.

6. Editing behavioral knowledge

KREME embodies a set of mechanisms for representing and editing behavioral knowledge. One mechanism revolves around the notion of attaching chunks of behavior to frames. Since frames can also be associated with *flavors* (see above) individual behavioral chunks can be (and are) compiled into flavor methods.

A click of a mouse button and the *tabular features window* in the *main concept view* is turned into the toplevel behavior editor. All behaviors currently defined for the concept are shown. Each has a name and a type. There are three types of behaviors currently allowed; Rules, Procedures, and Methods. Existing behaviors can be edited or new ones defined. A modified form of the Symbolics *flavor examiner* can be accessed to show various useful information about method combination and derivation.

Methods are simply flavor methods. Editing a method throws up a text editor window which can be interacted with in normal (Symbolics) editing style or in structure editing style. Editing or inputing a new rule packet accesses the Rule Editor. Editing or inputing a new procedure accesses the Procedure Editor.

6.1. EDITING RULES

The rule language used by KREME is a language called FLEX (Shapiro, 1984), based in large part on the LOOPS rule language. FLEX allows rules to be defined in *rule packets,* which organize sets of rules that are meant to be run together. In the KREME environment, rule packets can be attached to concepts, just as if they were functional methods. In addition, they may be inherited by more specialized concepts. FLEX incorporates a mechanism for dealing with uncertainty, based on EMYCIN (van Melle, 1979). The FLEX runtime environment also provides an elementary history and tracing mechanism, and an explanation system that produces pseudo-English explanations from rule traces. For efficiency, FLEX also provides a means for rule packets to be compiled as LISP code, and run without the rule interpreter present.

The KREME rule editor is built on top of the KREME structure editor. One defines and edits rules by specifying and filling out portions of rule *templates*. The user refines these templates either by using the mouse to copy parts of existing rules or by pointing at slots to be filled and typing in the desired values. Once a rule-set has been developed, the rule editor provides commands to run packets and debug them. It can also generate traces or rule histories paraphrased in pseudo-English. Mechanisms are also provided for deleting and reordering rules, and loading and saving them from files.

The rule editor is also tied to the KREME's knowledge integration subsystem (see section 5 above). At present, all references to slots of frames made in rules are checked for validity by the knowledge integrator. If invalid, the user is alerted, and may switch, if necessary to editing the associated frame. If the problem was simply that he/she named a non-existent slot, a valid one may be selected from a menu. In the near future, the knowledge integrator will also check such cross-references in the opposite direction, as when a slot referred to by some rules is deleted or changed in the frame editor.

6.2. PROCEDURES IN THE KREME ENVIRONMENT

An obvious weakness of many knowledge-representation languages is their inability to handle declaratively expressed knowledge about procedures as partially ordered sequences of actions, particularly if that knowledge is represented at multiple levels of abstraction. Although a number of systems have been developed that do various forms of planning (Ernst & Newell, 1969; Sacerdoti, 1974; Sacerdoti, 1975; Stefik, 1981), most have not encoded their plans in an entirely declarative or inspectable fashion. Certainly the current generation of expert system tools does not provide mechanisms geared to the description of this kind of knowledge. Although it is clear that much of an expert's knowledge about a domain is about procedures and their application, little work has been done on devising ways to capture that information directly.

The STEAMER project (Williams *et al.*, 1981) began to address the issue of declarative representations for procedures in the course of developing a mechanism to teach valid steam-plant operating procedures. The representation system developed for this task had to be directly accessible to the students who were the system's users, and it had to serve as a source of explanations when errors were made. STEAMER was able to describe these procedures, decompose them, show how they were related to similar procedures and, in general, deal with them at the "knowledge level" (Newell, 1981) rather than as pieces of programs or rule sets. Although the syntax of the language was quite primitive, with no previsions for branching or iteration; the mechanisms for procedural abstraction, specialization, and path or reference reformulation that formed the heart of the language seemed to form the kernel of an extremely useful representational facility.

The KREME representation language family includes a descendant of the STEAMER procedure language, built using KREME's library of knowledge representation primitives. Each KREME procedure has a *name,* a *description,* an *action* that the procedure is meant to accomplish, a list of *steps,* and a list of *ordering constraints* that determine the partial ordering of the steps. *Steps* have an *action* and an *object* which names the conceptual class of things that step acts upon. Procedures are attached to specific frames and can be "compiled" into flavor methods.

Each step in a procedure may either be a primitive action or another procedure. If the object of a step defines a procedure for the action of that step then this procedure is said to be a sub-procedure of the enclosing procedure. For example, the ALIGN procedure attached to the concept SUCTION-LINE could have a step ALIGN ⟨PUMP⟩. If the CENTRIFUGAL-PUMP, which is the object of this step for SUCTION-LINEs, defined a procedure for the action ALIGN, then the step ALIGN ⟨PUMP⟩ could be expanded into the steps of the procedure for aligning a centrifugal pump.

6.2.1. *Procedural abstraction and structure mapping*

For knowledge-acquisition purposes, it would be very useful if procedures were represented in an abstraction hierarchy like that for frames. In a strong sense, it seems difficult to define exactly what it means for one abstract procedure to subsume another. However, from an acquisition standpoint, much power can be gained by allowing abstract procedures to form templates upon which more specific procedures can be built, and eventually providing tools for automatic plan refinement like those found in NOAH (Sacerdoti, 1975). For example, if you have some idea about how to grow plants in general, and you want to grow tomatoes, you will use your knowledge about growing plants in general as a starting point for learning about growing tomatoes. The final procedure for growing tomatoes will include some (presumably more detailed) versions of steps in the more general procedure, and may also include steps that are analogous to those used in growing other plants for which more detailed knowledge exists.†

The KREME procedures editor has a mechanism for building templates of new procedures out of more abstract procedures. When a new procedure is being defined at a concept, the procedural abstraction function determines whether any of that concept's parents have a procedure for accomplishing the same action. If so, an initial procedure template is built by combining the steps and constraints of all the inherited, more abstract procedures. The paths (objects) of the steps are adjusted, using the concept's slot equivalences, to use "local" slot names, as much as possible. As yet this facility does not have the ability to do detailed reasoning with constraints on steps, as NOAH does. We expect greatly to expand this capability in the future.

The KREME Procedures language is currently being refined for use in the development of a new training system at BBN. That system will teach diagnostic procedures for the maintenance of a large electronics system. We expect that KREME will greatly ease the knowledge-acquisition problems faced by the developers of that system. It will also provide the first serious test of the effectiveness of the KREME acquisition environment in general.

7. Large-scale revisions of knowledge bases

It seems fairly clear that as knowledge bases grow larger, and the sets of tasks that expert systems are called upon to perform expands, system developers will need better, more automatic methods for revising and reformulating their accumulated knowledge bases of representations. Toward this end, we feel that it is important to

---

† For a detailed discussion of related issues see Carbonell (1986) on derivational analogical planning.

find ways of expressing and packaging conceptually clean *reformulations* of sets of frames and other representations, and begin developing facilities supporting the generation of new representations from old ones.

We are taking two different approaches to this problem. First, we have developed a macro facility for reformulations that can be expressed as sequences of standard, low-level editing operations. This facility allows users to define editing macros that can be applied to sets of frame definitions by giving a single example. Second, we are building a small library of functions providing operations that cannot be defined simply as sequences of low-level editing operations. Our main purpose is to collect and categorize these utilities, and explore their usefulness in a working environment. Our hope is that a large fraction of these operations can be conveniently described using the macro facility, as it is more accessible to an experimental user community than any set of "prepackaged" utilities, and can be more responsive to the, as yet, largely unknown special needs of that community.

7.1. THE MACRO AND STRUCTURE EDITOR

One of the views available when editing concepts in KREME is the *macro and structure editor*. This view (see Fig. 4) provides display and editing facilities for concept definitions, based loosely on the kind of structure editor provided in many LISP environments. The view provides two windows for the display of stylized defining forms for concepts. The *current edit window* displays the definition of the currently edited concept (the top item on the editor stack). The *display window* is available for the display of any number of other concepts. Any concept which is visible in either window can be edited, and features can be copied from one concept to another by pointing. Both windows are scrollable to view additional definitions as required.

There is a menu of commands for displaying and editing definitions that includes the commands *Add Structure, Change Structure, Delete Structure, Display Concept* and *Clear Display*. Arguments (if any) to these commands may be described by pointing or typing. Thus, to delete a slot, one simply clicks on *Delete Structure* and the display of the slot to be deleted. Adding a structure is done by clicking on *Add Structure*, the keyword of the feature class of the concept one wishes to add to (*e.g. Slot*:). The new slot itself may be copied from a displayed concept by pointing, or a new one may be entered from the keyboard. Changing (that is, replacing) a structure can be done by pointing in succession at the *Change Structure* command, the item to be replaced, and the thing to replace it with. In most cases, *Change Structure* can also be invoked simply by pointing at the structure to be replaced, without the menu command.

The last two commands in the structure view's main menu provide the means to change what is displayed in the display window. Pointing at *Display Structure* and then at any visible concept name places the definition of that concept in the display window. *Clear Display* removes all items from the display window. Individual concepts can be deleted from the display window by pointing at them and clicking. The *Edit Concept* command is used to change what is displayed in the current edit window. Editing a new concept moves the old edit concept to the bottom of the display window.

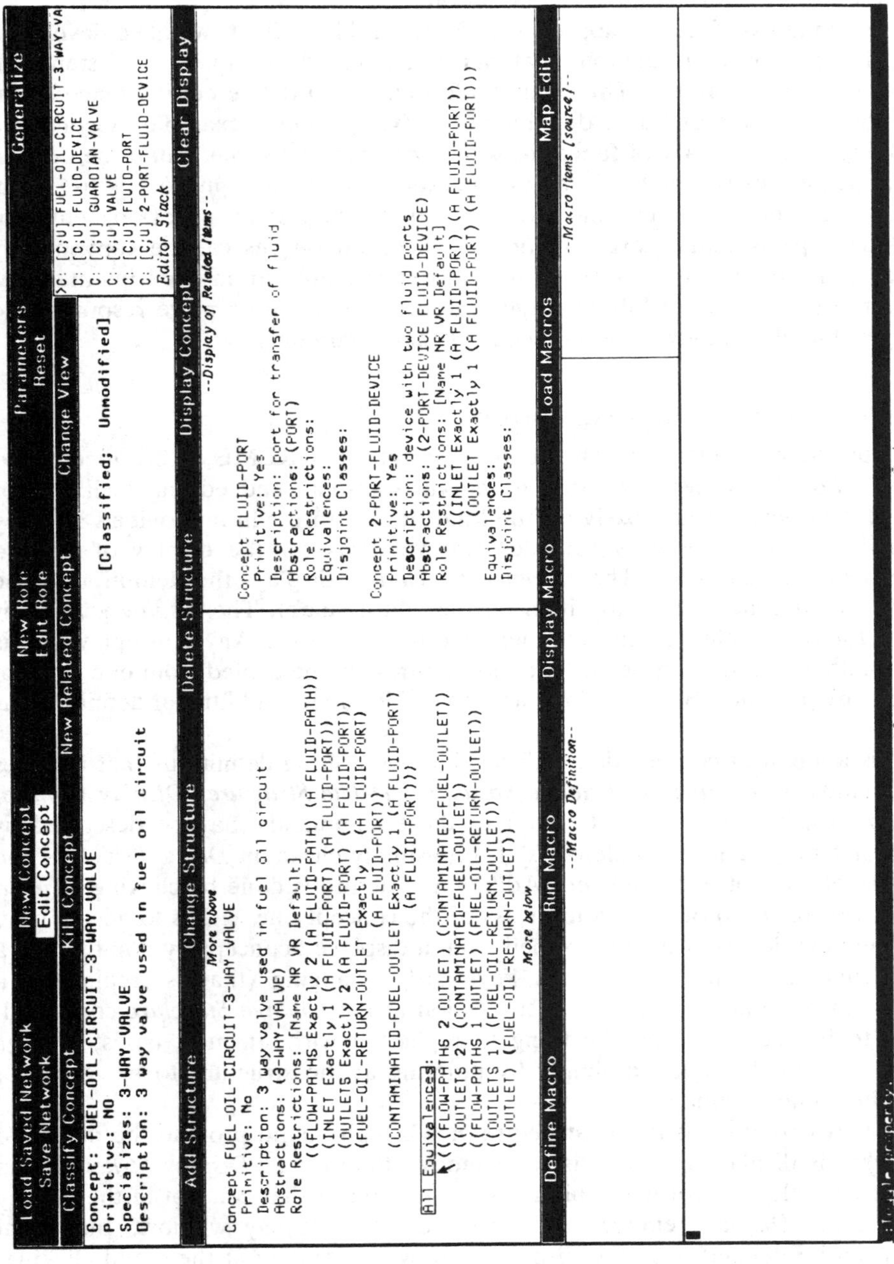

Load Saved Network   New Concept   New Role   Parameters   Generalize
Save Network   Edit Concept   Edit Role   Reset

Classify Concept   Kill Concept   New Related Concept   Change View   >C: [C;U] FUEL-OIL-CIRCUIT-3-WAY-VA
                                                                                     C: [C;U] FLUID-DEVICE
Concept: FUEL-OIL-CIRCUIT-3-WAY-VALVE   [Classified; Unmodified]   C: [C;U] GUARDIAN-VALVE
Primitive: NO   C: [C;U] VALVE
Specializes: 3-WAY-VALVE   C: [C;U] FLUID-PORT
Description: 3 way valve used in fuel oil circuit   C: [C;U] 2-PORT-FLUID-DEVICE

                                                                                     --Editor Stack--

Add Structure   Change Structure   Delete Structure   Display Concept   Clear Display

                                          --More above--   --Display of Related Items--

Concept FUEL-OIL-CIRCUIT-3-WAY-VALVE   Concept FLUID-PORT
Primitive: No   Primitive: Yes
Abstractions: (3-WAY-VALVE)   Description: port for transfer of fluid
Description: 3 way valve used in fuel oil circuit   Abstractions: (PORT)
Role Restrictions: [Name NR VR Default]   Role Restrictions:
  ((FLOW-PATHS Exactly 2 (A FLUID-PATH) (A FLUID-PATH))   Equivalences:
  (INLET Exactly 1 (A FLUID-PORT) (A FLUID-PORT))   Disjoint Classes:
  (OUTLETS Exactly 2 (A FLUID-PORT) (A FLUID-PORT))
  (FUEL-OIL-RETURN-OUTLET Exactly 1 (A FLUID-PORT)   Concept 2-PORT-FLUID-DEVICE
                          (A FLUID-PORT))   Primitive: Yes
  (CONTAMINATED-FUEL-OUTLET Exactly 1 (A FLUID-PORT)   Description: device with two fluid ports
                          (A FLUID-PORT)))   Abstractions: (2-PORT-DEVICE FLUID-DEVICE)
All Equivalences: Role Restrictions: [Name NR VR Default]
  (((FLOW-PATHS 2 OUTLET) (CONTAMINATED-FUEL-OUTLET)   ((INLET Exactly 1 (A FLUID-PORT) (A FLUID-PORT))
  ((OUTLETS 2) (CONTAMINATED-FUEL-OUTLET))   (OUTLET Exactly 1 (A FLUID-PORT) (A FLUID-PORT)))
  ((FLOW-PATHS 1 OUTLET) (FUEL-OIL-RETURN-OUTLET))   Equivalences:
  ((OUTLETS 1) (FUEL-OIL-RETURN-OUTLET))   Disjoint Classes:
  ((OUTLET) (FUEL-OIL-RETURN-OUTLET))
                        --More below--

Define Macro   Run Macro   Display Macro   Load Macros   Map Edit

                  --Macro Definition--   --Macro Items (source)--

FIG. 4. The macro structure editor view.

7.2. DEVELOPING MACRO EDITING PROCEDURES

These operations, together with the globally available commands for defining new concepts and making specializations of old concepts essentially by copying their definitions, provide an extremely flexible environment in which to define and specify modifications of concepts with respect to other defined concepts. Virtually all knowledge editing operations can be done by a sequence of pointing steps using the current edit window and the display window. This style of editing is also used in the rule editor (see section 6.1). The combination of editing features and mouse-based editor interaction style provides an extremely versatile environment for the description, by example, of a large class of editing macros.

In order to have macros, defined essentially by example, work on concepts other than those for which they were defined, the operations recorded cannot refer directly to the concepts or objects which were being edited when the macro was defined. This is handled by a kind of implicit variablization, where the objects named or pointed to are replaced by references to their relationship to the initially edited object. In most cases, these indirect references can be thought of as references to the *location* of the object in the structure editor's display windows. In fact, each new object that is displayed or edited in the course of defining a macro is placed on a stack called the *macro items list,* together with a pointer to the command that caused the item to be displayed. The utility of this form of reference will become clearer with an example.

7.2.1. Macro example: adding pipes between components

When the STEAMER (Williams *et al.,* 1981) system was developed, a structural model of a steam plant was created to represent each component in the steam plant as a frame, with links to all functionally related components e.g. inputs and outputs) represented as slots pointing at those other objects. So, for example, a tank holding water to be fed into a boiler tank through some pipe that was gated by a valve was represented as a frame with an OUTPUT slot whose value was a VALVE. The OUTPUT of that VALVE was a BOILER-TANK. The pipes through which the water was conveyed *were not represented* since they had no functional value in the simulation model. If it had become important to model the pipes, say because they introduced friction or were susceptible to leaks or explosions, then the representational model that STEAMER relied on would have required *massive* revision. Each component object in the system would have needed editing to replace the objects in its INPUT and OUTPUT slots with new frames representing pipes that were in turn connected by their OUTPUT slots to the next component in the system.

One of our goals in developing the KREME macro editor was to be able to make such changes, which are simple to describe but require many tedious editing operations to accomplish, given the number of concepts affected. Figure 5 shows a macro that can be applied to all objects in a system with INPUT and OUTPUT slots, in order to generate and insert PIPEs into those slots. The macro also sets the OUTPUTs of those PIPES to be the concept that was the old value of the OUTPUT slot in the concept edited, and similarly redoes all INPUTs.

Figure 5 shows how the macro is defined, by editing a representation of a tank

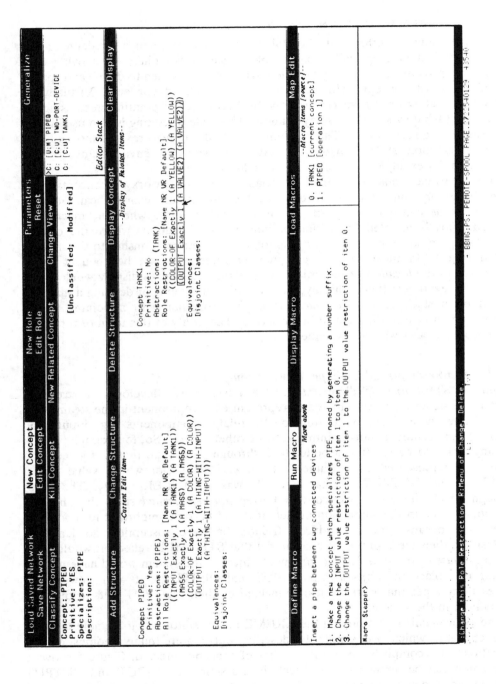

FIG. 5. Steps in PIPE Macro.

(TANK1) connected (by role OUTPUT) to a valve (VALVE2). The sequence of steps required, defined only using the mouse, is also shown in Fig. 5, as it would appear in the *Macro Definition* window of the editor.

Work on macro editing has really just begun. However, it already shows promise as a method for accomplishing a number of large-scale restructurings of knowledge bases which are relatively simple to describe, but tedious to perform. As it stands, the system is already powerful enough to describe a number of transformations between semantically equivalent though functionally and syntactically distinct representations. Macros can also make use of the knowledge integrator to discover relationships in the knowledge base and exploit them. We are building a library of these macro operations so that other users of KREME will not be required to reinvent them.

We see our investigation of macro editing as only the first step in developing a knowledge reformulation facility that will have and make use of more understanding of the logical structure of the represented knowledge as well as providing a basic means of describing procedures to manipulate the syntactic strucure of knowledge representations.

8. Knowledge extension

One of the tasks faced by knowledge engineers in developing robust computerized knowledge bases is getting experts to express their often unconscious *generalizations* about their domains of expertise. While much of the detailed information about particular problems can be accessed and represented by looking at specific examples and problems, the expert's abstract classification of problem types and the abstract features he uses to recognize those problem types are less readily available. Experienced knowledge engineers are often able to discover and define useful generalizations that help organize the knowledge described by a human domain expert. The expert, although not previously aware of such a generalization, will often immediately perceive its relevance to and existence within his own reasoning processes, going so far as to suggest improvements, related generalizations, more abstract generalizations and so forth.

Our initial experiment in knowledge-base extension has been the development of a *frame generalization* algorithm which we will briefly describe. The building of a robust knowledge extension system that can deal with hybrid representation systems in intelligent and useful ways will form the bulk of the work to be done in the next

---

While Editing TANK1:
Click on **Define Macro**. (*Makes Macro Item 0 = TANK1*).

1. Make a new concept which specializes PIPE. (*Creates PIPE0 as item 1*).
2. Change the INPUT value restriction of item 1 (*PIPE0*) to item 0 (*TANK1*).
3. Change the OUTPUT value restriction of item 1 (*PIPE0*) to the OUTPUT value restriction of item 0 (*OUTPUT of TANK1 = VALVE1*).
4. Classify the current edit concept (*Defines PIPE0*).
5. Change the OUTPUT value restriction of item 0 (= *VALVE1*) to item 1 (*PIPE0*).
6. Classify item 0 (*TANK1*).
7. Edit the OUTPUT value restriction of item 1 (*Creates item 2 = VALVE1*).
8. Change the INPUT value restriction of item 2 (*INPUT of VALVE1 = TANK1*) to item 1 (*PIPE0*).
9. Classify all items.

generation KREME system. With our current generalizer, potentially useful generalizations are found by searching for sets of concept features that are shared by several unrelated concepts. Finding concepts with a given set of features is relatively easy since KREME indexes all concepts under each of its features.

When the generalizer finds a set of at least k features shared by at least m concepts, where k and m are user settable parameters, the system forms the most specific concept definition that would enclose all of the features but would still be more general than any concept in the set. Since our simple algorithm has no other external notion of "interestingness" it simply displays this potential new concept definition to the user. For example, given three concepts that are all ANIMALs and independently define the slot WINGS, the generalizer would suggest forming a specialization of ANIMAL with the slot WINGS, that these concepts would all specialize. If the user wanted to introduce this concept, he would respond by naming the new generalization, call it FLYING-ANIMAL, which would then be classified and integrated with the network. The features that are enclosed by this new, more general concept, are automatically removed from each of the more specific concepts being generalized.

9. Conclusion

The goal of the BBN Labs Knowledge Acquisition Project is to build a versatile experimental computer environment for developing the large knowledge bases which future expert systems will require. We are pursuing this goal along two complementary paths. First, we have constructed a flexible, extensible, Knowledge Representation, Editing and Modeling Environment in which different kinds of representations (initially frames, rules, and procedures) can be used. We are now using this environment to investigate acquisition strategies for a variety of types and combinations of knowledge representations. In building and equipping this "sandbox", we have been adapting and experimenting with techniques which we think will make editing, browsing, and consistency checking for each style of representation easier and more efficient, so that knowledge engineers and subject matter experts can work together to build with significantly larger and more detailed knowledge bases than are presently practical.

Now that we are well along in constructing a first, experimental version of the editing environment, we are beginning to address the second aspect of our research plan, the development of more automatic tools for knowledge-base reformulation and extension. An important part of this endeavor is the discovery, categorization and use of explicit knowledge about knowledge representations; methods for viewing different knowledge representations, techniques for describing knowledge-base transformations and extrapolations, techniques for finding and suggesting useful generalizations in developing knowledge bases, semi-automatic procedures of eliciting knowledge from experts, and extensions of consistency checking techniques to provide a mechanism for generating candidate expansions of a knowledge base.

Our ultimate goal is to explore a number of approaches to knowledge acquisition and knowledge editing that could be incorporated into existing and future development environments, not to develop the definitive knowledge editing environment. AI is still a young field, and new knowledge representation techniques will continue to be developed for the foreseeable future. We are attempting to provide a laboratory for experimenting with new representation techniques and new tools for developing knowledge bases. If we are successful, many of the techniques developed in our laboratory will be adopted by the comprehensive knowledge acquisition and knowledge representation systems required to support the development and maintenance of AI systems in the future.

We would like to thank Richard Shapiro for his major contributions to the KREME project. Rich was largely responsible for the rule editor, the macro and structure editor and most of the user interface tools in the current version of the frame editor. We would also like to thank Dr Ed Walker for his comments and contributions to several earlier drafts of this paper.

This research was supported by the Defense Advanced Research Projects Agency of the Department of Defense and was monitored by RADC under contract number F30602-85-c-0005.

References

BALZAC, S. R. (1986). A system for the interactive classification of knowledge. *M.S. Thesis,* M.I.T. Department of Electrical Engineering and Computer Science.

BOBROW, D., WINOGRAD, T. & KRL RESEARCH GROUP. (1977). Experience with KRL-0: one cycle of a knowledge representation language. *Proceedings of the Fifth International Joint Conference on Artificial Intelligence,* Cambridge, Massachussetts, August.

BRACHMAN, R. J., FIKES, R. E. & LEVESQUE, H. J. (1983). Krypton: a functional approach to knowledge representation. *IEEE Computer, Special Issue on Knowledge Representation,* October.

CARBONELL, J. G. (1986). Derivational analogy: a theory of reconstructive problem solving and expertise acquisition. In MICHALSKI, R. S., CARBONELL, J. G. & MITCHELL, T. M. Eds, *Machine Learning, Vol. II.* Los Altos, California: Morgan Kaufmann Publishers, Inc., pp. 371–392.

Carnegie Group, Inc. (1985). *KnowledgeCraft.* Carnegie Group, Inc.

ERNST, G. W. & NEWELL, A. (1969). *GPS: a Case Study in Generality and Problem Solving.* New York: Academic Press.

IntelliCorp. *KEE Software Development System.* IntelliCorp.

KEENE, S. E. & MOON, D. (1985). *Flavors: Object-oriented Programming on Symbolics Computers.* Symbolics, Inc.

VAN MELLE, W. (1979). A domain independent production-rule system for consultation programs. *Proceedings of IJCAI-6,* pp. 923–925.

MOSER, M. (1983). An Overview of NIKL. Section of *BBN Report No. 5421,* Bolt Beranek and Newman Inc.

NEWELL, A. (1981). The knowledge level. *AI Magazine,* **2,** 1–20.

RICH, C. (1982). Knowledge representation languages and predicate calculus: how to have your cake and eat it too. *Proceedings of AAAI,* pp. 192–196.

ROBERTS, B. & GOLDSTEIN, I. P. (1977). The FRL Manual. *A.I. Laboratory Memo 409,* M.I.T.

SACERDOTI, E. E. (1974). Planning in a hierarchy of abstraction spaces. *Artificial Intelligence,* **5,** 115–135.

SACERDOTI, E. D. (1975). A structure for plans and behavior. *109, SRI Artificial Intelligence Center.*

SCHMOLZE, J. & ISRAEL, D. (1983). KL-ONE: semantics and classification. In *Research in Knowledge Representation for Natural Language Understanding, Annual Report: 1 September 1982 to 31 August 1983.* BBN Report No. 5421.

SCHMOLZE, J. G. & LIPKIS, T. A. (1983). Classification in the KL-ONE Knowledge Representation System. *Proceedings of the 8th IJCAI.*

SHAPIRO, R. (1984). FLEX: a tool for rule-based programming. 5643, BBN Laboratories.
SIDNER, C. L., BATES, M., BOBROW, R. J., BRACHMAN, R. J., COHEN, P. R., ISRAEL, D. J., WEBBER, B. L. & WOODS, W. A. (1981). Research in knowledge representation for natural language understanding: annual report. *BBN Report No. 4785*, Bolt Beranek and Newman Inc.
STEFIK, M. (1981). Planning with constraints: MOLGEN. *Artificial Intelligence*, **16**, 111–169.
VILAIN, M. (1985). The restricted language architecture of a hybrid representation system. *Proceedings of IJCAI-85, International Joint Conferences on Artificial Intelligence, Inc.*, pp. 547–551.
WILLIAMS, M., HOLLAN, J. & STEVENS, A. (1981). An overview of STEAMER: an advanced computer-assisted instruction system for propulsion engineering. *Behavior Research Methods and Instrumentation*, **14**, 85–90.

Ontological analysis: an ongoing experiment

James H. Alexander†, Michael J. Freiling, Sheryl J. Shulman, Steven Rehfuss and Steven L. Messick

Computer Research Laboratory, Tektronix Laboratories, PO Box 500, Beaverton, OR 97077, U.S.A.

Knowledge engineering is a complex activity which permeated with problems inherent in the difficulties of choosing the correct abstractions. Knowledge-level analysis has been suggested as a technique to help manage this complexity. We have previously presented a methodology, called ontological analysis, which provides a technique for performing knowledge-level analysis of a problem space. This paper presents the experiences we have gained with knowledge-level analysis. Our experiences are reported and the criteria for a formal knowledge-level analysis language are discussed.

1. Knowledge-level analysis

We have found that neophyte knowledge engineers often "don't know where to start". This roadblock is not usually the result of a lack of understanding about expert systems or representation schemes; but is due to confusion about the appropriate classification of the individual knowledge elements of a domain.

Currently, a knowledge engineer must rely on an intuitive, informal approach to collecting and organizing expert knowledge for a knowledge-based system. Newell (1982) proposed that there should be a *knowledge-level* analysis to guide the development of AI systems, such as expert systems. Recently (Alexander, Freiling, Messick & Rehfuss 1986; Freiling, Rehfuss, Alexander, Messick & Shulman, 1986), we proposed a language and an informal methodology (*ontological analysis*) for use during knowledge-level analysis, to allow us to study knowledge engineering. The goal of ontological analysis is to facilitate the high-level analysis of problem spaces.

We believe most development problems encountered in knowledge-based systems derive from *ad hoc* selection of abstractions. Ontological analysis provides a principled means to analyse and decompose a domain of interest. With the development of our technique, we have identified major conceptual areas which must be represented in a knowledge-level analysis language and have gathered experience on the characteristics of the methodology of knowledge-level analysis. In this paper we present some of the lessons we have learned. These include the advantages and disadvantages of ontological analysis, as well as some features to consider in a language for knowledge-level analysis.

2. An overview of ontological analysis

As a preliminary step, we chose an analysis language loosely based on denotational semantics domain equations. The main goal of this exercise was to gain experience

---

† Current address: US WEST Advanced Technologies, 6200 S. Quebec St. # 170, Englewood, CO 80111, USA.

25

with knowledge-level analysis and to determine how it differs from simply choosing a representation language. This section details ontological analysis as it currently exists and is followed by an evaluation of the method and language.

Ontological analysis, is a technique for the preliminary analysis of a problem-solving domain (Alexander *et al.*, 1986; Freiling *et al.*, 1986). An ontology is a collection of abstract and concrete objects, relationships and transformations that represent the physical and cognitive entities necessary for accomplishing a task. Complex ontologies are constructed in a three step process that concentrates first on the (static) physical objects and relationships, on the (dynamic) operations that can change the task world, and finally on the (epistemic) knowledge structures that guide the selection and use of these operations. To this end, we are developing a family of languages collectively called SPOONS (SPecification Of ONtological Structure).

The most useful and concise of the SPOONS languages is SUPE-SPOONS (SUPErstructure SPOONS; Freiling *et al.*, 1986), which is based on the domain equations of denotational semantics (Gordon, 1979) and algebraic specification (Guttag & Horning, 1980). SUPE-SPOONS consists of two basic statement types:

Domain equations: Site = Building × Campus. These statements define domains, or *types* of knowledge structures.†

Domain function declarations: add_meeting: Meeting → [Meetings → Meetings]. These statements declare the type of specific domain elements.

The right-hand side of statements can be composed of one or more domains or constant elements with operators relating these elements. Four primitive domains, STRING, BOOLEAN, INTEGER and NUMBER, are always assumed to be defined. Other primitive domains can be defined by explicit enumeration of their elements, or by open assignment to some collection of atomic elements.

The operators in the domain equations are of five types:

Discriminated Union: $D + E$. Discriminated union of two domains defines that domain composed of each member of D and E, where original domain identity is preserved. (Generalization).

Cross Product: $D \times E$. Cross product of two domains describes a domain composed of all ordered pairs whose first element is a member of domain D and second element is a member of domain E. (Aggregation).

Domain mapping: $D \rightarrow E$. Mapping of one domain onto another creates a domain consisting of all functions which map domain D onto domain E.

Collection of Sets: $2^{**}D$. The domain consisting of all subsets of D.

Collection of Ordered Sets: D^*. The domain of all ordered sequences of D.

2.1. BUILDING AN ONTOLOGY

In addition to the formal notation, ontological analysis has a taxonomy of knowledge types which clarifies the function of each of the member statements. The

---

† For most purposes, it suffices to think of domains as sets. A more complex semantics is needed if domains are defined recursively (Stoy, 1977) or with multiple equations.

statements fall into three groups:

Static ontology
Defines the physical objects, or primitive objects in a problem space, their properties and relationships. Ontological analysis begins with enumeration of physical objects in the problem space and identification of their inherent properties and relationships. At the level of the static ontology, the analysis performed is quite similar to the entity-relationship model of Chen (1976).

Dynamic ontology
Defines the state space of the problem-solving domain, and the actions that transform the problem from one state to another state. Problem-solving is often characterized as search through a state space (Simon, 1981; Newell & Simon, 1972). Solution of a problem consists of selecting operators whose application transforms the current state into another. The dynamic ontology defines a problem space in terms of configurations of elements from the static ontology, and then defines problem operators as transformations built on the domain of problem states. The dynamic ontology defines which knowledge is unchanged throughout the problem solving process (*i.e.* organizational charts, see the Appendix) and which knowledge changes as the problem is solved (*i.e.* schedules and meeting plans).

Epistemic ontology
Defines the constraints and methods that control the use of knowledge applied to the Static and Dynamic Ontologies. The epistemic ontology defines knowledge structures to guide the selection and use of these operations. The epistemic ontology usually contains two different types of knowledge structures. Some are used to select which operation should be performed. Others control the actual performance of certain operations. In fact, the only knowledge structures that do appear are those needed to guide the operations classified as *heuristic operations* in the dynamic ontology.

3. Evaluation of ontological analysis

We have performed analyses on a wide range of domains including a system troubleshooting Tektronix Oscilloscopes (Alexander *et al.,* 1986; Rehfuss, Alexander, Freiling, Messick & Shulman, 1985; Freiling *et al.,* 1986), MYCIN's medical knowledge domain (Shortliffe, 1984), design rule checking for nMOS circuitry (Lob, 1984), oscilloscope operation and an Intelligent Electronic Calendar (IEC, Staley, in press—an ontology is presented in the Appendix). With each analysis, our understanding of the domain was greatly enhanced; similarly our general understanding of the guiding principles of analysis was more focused.

3.1. EXPERIENCES GAINED USING ONTOLOGICAL ANALYSIS

The following are features of ontological analysis that have proven useful in the analysis of problem spaces.

(1) Technical vocabulary is the primary source of base entities, properties and relationships key to the problem space

We begin our analysis with a paper knowledge base (Freiling, Alexander, Messick, Rehfuss & Shulman, 1985); a description of the task domain in plain English. The paper knowledge base may come from verbal protocols (Ericsson & Simon, 1984), a textbook, a training manual or any convenient source. The technical vocabulary used in the paper knowledge base provides the initial elements of the static ontology. Physical entities are the starting point, their properties and relationships are derived later. This allows for a quick start from a concrete foundation.

(2) Objects are assigned either atomic or derived status in order to clarify intended representations

Two types of object appear in an ontology: atomic and derived objects. Atomic objects (*surrogates* in database terminology; Codd, 1979) cannot be individuated by their properties. Instead they are individuated by identifying tokens ($\langle atomic \rangle$ in SUPE-SPOONS). For a meeting scheduler, for example, meetings can be atomic objects:

$$\text{Meeting} = \langle \text{atomic} \rangle$$
$$\text{Time\_Of\_Meeting} = [\text{Meeting} \rightarrow \text{Time\_Description}]$$

Properties of atomic objects are expressed via functions which map the objects into their property values.

Derived objects refer to those elements of an ontology that represent aggregations of other elements. Derived objects are individuated solely on the basis of common components. For example, consider the following derived object:

$$\text{Gregorian\_Time\_Point} = \text{Year} \times \text{Month} \times \text{Day} \times \text{Hour} \times \{00, 15, 30, 45\}$$

Any two calendar dates are equal if they consist of the same year, the same month, hour and quartile. Only when their composite attributes are identical, are the elements themselves identical.

This distinction ameliorates the problem of representation of identity and partial specification. To be specific, derived objects must be fully specified to allow proper representation in a formal system. Conversely, atomic objects can exist, and be uniquely identified, even when nothing is known about them. Thus, objects which a system only gradually learns facts about should be represented in an atomic manner.

(3) A clear distinction between intensional and extensional entities can be established

There are many cases in knowledge engineering where it is important to distinguish between representatives for the physical objects (the extension), and for descriptions or viewpoints of those objects (the intension). For the Intelligent Electronic Calendar problem (Staley, in press) it was necessary to define units of absolute time, and relate them to descriptions of time units with respect to one of many calendars (for example, to represent the following two descriptions of the same time interval: Gregorian 1986, and Japanese Showa 60).

A common way to achieve the distinction between extensional representatives of real world objects and intensional representatives of descriptions or classes of such objects is to define representatives for the extensional objects with only the bare minimum of structure. In the IEC, for instance,

Real_Time_Point = INTEGER
Real_Time_Interval = (Real_Time_Point × Real_Time_Point)

The primitive points in time are integers; point 0 is associated with 0000 hr on 1 January 1901, by the Gregorian calendar. The points are 15 min apart. Intervals of time can then be represented simply as a pair of points. (There is actually a bit more complexity for dealing with unbounded intervals, see Appendix).

Intensional descriptions with respect to various calendars can be constructed as necessary from different parts of the description.

Intensional_Time_Point =
        Gregorian_Time_Point + Japanese_Imperial_Reign_Time_Point
Gregorian_Time_Point =
        Year × Month × Day × Hour × {00, 15, 30, 45}
Japanese_Imperial_Reign_Time_Point =
        Era × Year × Month × Day × Hour × {00, 15, 30, 45}

Finally, intensional directions can be related to extensional descriptions by the use of various interpretation functions.

interpret : [Intensional_Time_Point → Real_Time_Point]

Extensional identity of descriptions of varying sorts can then be defined as equality of the image under the relevant interpretation functions.

(4) Most relevant abstractions are built through the use of generalization and aggregation.
Generalization and aggregation (Smith & Smith, 1977) are common techniques for building large knowledge structures. These have a direct manifestation in our formalism as discriminated unions and Cartesian Products:

GENERALIZATION: Car = (Compact + Luxury_Car + Truck)
AGGREGATION: Car_Assembly = (Engine × Chassis × Body × Drive_Train)

It is also possible to create implicit aggregations through the use of functions. Thus, the properties of an atomic object are implicitly aggregated through the fact that some particular function defines values for each.

Car = ⟨atomic⟩
Type = [Car → {Compact, Luxury_Car, Truck}]
Has_Engine = [Car → Engine]
Has_Chassis = [Car → Chassis]
Has_Body = [Car → Body]
Has_Drive_Train = [Car → Drive_Train]

Note also that generalizations are implicit in the properties of objects as well. Instances of the domain Car, for example, can be decomposed into Compacts, etc. on the basis of common images under the Type function.

(5) The structures built through ontological analysis highlight consistency or inconsistency of the lower-level structures (Alternatively, compositionality is an important general criteria)

An example of this concept illustrates the usefulness of our methodology. We first encountered the following problem in the process of building a semantic grammar (GLIB; Freiling, Alexander, Feicht & Stubbs, 1984) for use in collecting knowledge about electronic instrument behavior. Table 1 shows a fragment of GLIB that can generate the following atomic signal predicate.

SIGNAL-3 IS HIGH

TABLE 1
Glib fragment

⟨signal value⟩ ::= 'HIGH'	'LOW'
⟨signal⟩ ::= 'SIGNAL-' ⟨integer⟩
⟨atomic signal predicate⟩ ::= ⟨signal⟩ IS ⟨signal value⟩
⟨signal predicate⟩ ::= {atomic signal predicate}
|⟨atomic signal predicate⟩ 'when' ⟨atomic signal predicate⟩

Initially we assumed that this signal predicate would map signals into Boolean values. However, the semantics of two such statements combined with the connective *when* was not at all clear. If *when* was assumed to produce a Boolean itself, then the result would be returned by one of the 16 truth function of two Boolean values, clearly not what we had intended.

SIGNAL-3 IS HIGH when SIGNAL-4 IS LOW

Using domain equations to analyse the problem:

$$Signal = [Time \rightarrow Value]$$
$$Signal\_Predicate = [(Signal \times Signal\_Value) \rightarrow BOOLEAN]$$
$$\equiv [([Time \rightarrow Value] \times Signal\_Value) \rightarrow BOOLEAN],$$

we discovered that our signal predicate as defined was dropping the temporal information to and performing a global comparison with the threshold value. This problem was solved by creating a more appropriate description of the class for *Signal_Predicate,* which follows:

$$Signal\_Predicate =$$
$$[(Signal \times Signal\_Value) \rightarrow [Time \rightarrow BOOLEAN]]$$
$$\equiv [([Time \rightarrow Value] \times Signal\_Value) \rightarrow [Time \rightarrow BOOLEAN]]$$
$$when: [[[Time \rightarrow BOOLEAN] \times [Time \rightarrow BOOLEAN]] \rightarrow [Time \rightarrow BOOLEAN]]$$

Thus, the comparison made by the *Signal_Predicate* is made *at each instant of time,* so that the result is not a single truth value computed from the whole signal, but a truth value for every time unit of the signal. This makes it possible for *when* to preserve its *when* functional character, since the truth function (logical and) is now applied on a point by point basis. The compositional analysis of this type of problem is common to researchers familiar with the techniques of semantics and model theory (Allen, 1981). Techniques like ontological analysis make it available to knowledge engineers.

(6) Use of multiple domain equations points to abstraction difficulties

Often, in the process of creating ontologies, we noticed a tendency to create multiple equations for the same domain, with each equation representing a different emphasis on the meaning of the domain. Invariably, we found that this flagged an improper description of the domain. There were three forms of this problem:

Equations representing successive refinement

$$A: \text{Name} \rightarrow \text{Person}$$
$$A: (\text{First} \times \text{Second}) \rightarrow \text{Person}$$

These equations imply that domain Name can be further refined to (First × Second). The two forms must be reconciled so that they are identical. In this trivial example, the solution would simply be to define Name as (First × Second) and then have A use Name.

Orthogonal definitions of a domain

$$A : B \rightarrow C$$
$$A : D \rightarrow E$$

In this case, A is a function which takes a B into a C, and/or a D into an E. This is not necessarily the same as:

$$A : (B + D) \rightarrow (C + E)$$

since this would also allow two other combinations:

$$A : B \rightarrow E$$
$$A : D \rightarrow C$$

Orthogonal definitions may occur for several reasons:

(1) B is a refinement of D and C a refinement of E. In this case the above example is another instance of refinement:

$$\text{Workstation: Employee} \rightarrow \text{Desk}$$
$$\text{Workstation: Executive} \rightarrow \text{Office.}$$

(2) B and D are not directly comparable, but the function A is intended to apply to both. This implies a unifying abstraction, F, already exists or should be created. B and C are refinements of F. The same argument applies to the relationship of C and E, with a unifying abstraction G. An example could be:

$$\text{pay\_taxes: person} \rightarrow \text{dollars}$$
$$\text{pay\_taxes: corporation} \rightarrow \text{dollars}$$

$$\text{taxable\_entity: person + corporation}$$
$$\text{(a unifying abstraction)}$$

$$\text{pay\_taxes: Taxable\_entity} \rightarrow \text{dollars}$$

(3) *B* and *D* are not comparable at all and no unifying abstraction seems appropriate (their join is Top). In this case the semantics of the function *A* is unknown. It may be intended to be a polymorphic function.

However, if *B* and *D* cannot be rephrased as a common domain (unifying abstraction), and similarly for *C* and *E,* then the function *A* cannot be typed correctly using both domain equations. In that case, *A* has been overgeneralized and should be rephrased as two functions, *A*1 and *A*2.

$$A1:\ B \rightarrow E$$
$$A2:\ D \rightarrow C$$

The appropriateness of polymorphism may be further investigated in the future.

The above cases could be viewed as constraints. Each of the equations must hold true. The ambiguity must be resolved without invalidating either one.

Different views of the same object

> *Syntactic rule: R:* ⟨if part⟩ × ⟨then part⟩
> *Operational rule:* R: matching_condition → executable_part
> *Semantic rule*: *R:* premise → action
> *Rule abstraction*: *R:* class_of_premise × class_of_action

In this case, a rule is typed differently depending on its use. The syntactic rule is the sense needed for parsing. The operational rule is the sense needed for the inference engine. The semantic rule is the sense needed for the knowledge base. The rule abstraction is the sense needed where the knowledge base itself reasons about its own rules.

This example has an implied abstraction which incorporates the different rule senses, for example:

Rule: Syntactic_form × Operational_form × Semantic_form × Data_form

The implied abstraction should be made explicit, and the appropriate form extracted where needed. This forces attention as to which rule sense subsequent domains must incorporate. It also identifies the parts of the system and allows their relationship to be made explicit.

3.2. DISADVANTAGES TO ONTOLOGICAL ANALYSIS

The SUPE-SPOON language provides the facility to enumerate basic types, compose new types, provide typing for functions which operate on domains, etc. However, it has several deficiencies.

(1) Types are not first-class objects

While types can be constructed and referenced, the type itself is not a value. Because the issue of typing is so closely involved in the abstraction process, types as values is particularly important.

(2) The type hierarchy is not available for inspection

This structure defines the existing abstraction environment and needs to be available for inspection, modification, etc.

(3) There is no operational component identified
The operations of a type are necessary for fully identifying a type. We have no way to define the behavior of an object, only its structure, which leads to:

(4) There is no facility for identifying inheritance
Subtypes are commonly identified so that types may inherit operations, structure, or other relevant aspects of the type.

(5) The abstraction process must allow for contradictory typing while the knowledge-level analysis is in progress.
Some of the issues mentioned on multiple domain equations arise because we use the multiple domain equations to represent the ongoing definition of the domains. As our knowledge becomes more precise, we create new (perhaps multiple) equations which must be reconciled.

3.3. THE NEXT GENERATION KNOWLEDGE-LEVEL ANALYSIS LANGUAGE

This preliminary knowledge-level analysis language has provided several pointers as to the next generation. The ultimate goal of knowledge level analysis is to identify the appropriate abstractions to the domain. While none of the above deficiencies is insurmountable, it is unlikely that they can be solved solely in a language. The solution to many of these problems must lie in a hybrid system of a formal language with a supporting computer environment.

The formal language and support environment must address the above disadvantages. In particular, our current thoughts are that an analysis system should include:

(1) Formal and/or mechanized support for abstraction creation. Types appear to be a convenient formal mechanism for abstraction. Using a type system as a formal base, tools can be created to support the abstraction process. For example, the maintenance of a type hierarchy and the incorporation of incremental type definitions;

(2) Support for managing change. Because the abstraction process is iterative, the system needs to provide support for changing abstractions, maintaining different versions, analysing the existing abstraction structure (type hierarchy), etc;

(3) Support for moving from the analysis stage (the type hierarchy) to a target representation language.

These areas are currently under investigation.

4. Conclusions

We have presented a technique, ontological analysis, that has provided us with much needed experience in a knowledge-engineering methodology. There are weaknesses with the Ontological Analysis technique as currently defined as discussed above. Even so, we have found the methodology useful for conceptualizing a knowledge engineering problem, and creating a forum for cogent discussion. We hope that methodologies of this type will release the discipline from *ad hoc* descriptions of knowledge and provide a principled means for a knowledge engineer and expert to analyse the elements of a problem space and communicate the analysis to others. The abstract level at which domain equations characterize the semantics of structures and procedures, without specifying too much detail, help in this regard.

The effectiveness of a technique depends critically on the formulation of more and better principles to guide its use as a well-founded language and support system. We are currently working on the formal language, tools, and environment. We invite other knowledge engineers to try this approach and relate their experiences.

References

ALEXANDER, J. H., FREILING, M. J., MESSICK, S. L. & REHFUSS, S. (1986). Knowledge level engineering: ontological analysis. *Applied Research Technical Report CR-86-16,* 1 April 1986. Tektronix, Inc., Beaverton, OR.

ALLEN, J. F. An Interval-Based Representation of Temporal Knowledge. *1981 International Joint Conference on Artificial Intelligence,* Vancouver, British Columbia, Canada, August, 1981.

CHEN, P. P. The Entity-Relationship Model—Toward a Unified View of Data. *ACM Transactions on Database Systems, 1,1,* March, 1976.

CODD, E. F. Extending the Database Relational Model to Capture More Meaning. *ACM TODS 4:4,* December 1979, 397–434.

ERICSSON, K. A. & SIMON, H. A., *Protocol Analysis.* MIT Press; Cambridge, MA, 1984.

FREILING, M. J., ALEXANDER, J. H., MESSICK, S. L., REHFUSS, S. & SHULMAN, S. Starting a Knowledge Engineering Project—A Step-by-Step Approach. *A.I. Magazine, 6,3,* Fall, 1985.

FREILING, M. J., ALEXANDER, J. H., FEUCHT, D. & STUBBS, D. GLIB—A Language for Describing the Behavior of Electronic Devices. Applied Research Technical Report CR-84-12, April 6, 1984. Tektronix, Inc., Beaverton, OR.

FREILING, M. J., REHFUSS, S., ALEXANDER, J. H., MESSICK, S. L. & SHULMAN, S. The Ontological Structure of a Troubleshooting System for Electronic Instruments. *First International Conference on Applications of Artificial Intelligence to Engineering Problems,* Southampton University, U.K., April, 1986.

GORDON, M. J. C. *The Denotational Description of Programming Languages.* Springer Verlag; New York, NY, 1979.

GUTTAG, J. & HORNING, J. J., *Formal Specification as a Design Tool.* Xerox PARC Technical Report CSL-80-1, January, 1980.

LOB, C. *RUBICC: A Rule-Based Expert System for VLSI Integrated Circuit Critique.* Electronic Research Laboratory Memo UCB/ERL M84/80, University of California, Berkeley, 1984.

NEWELL, A. The Knowledge Level. *Artificial Intelligence, 18,* pp. 87–127, 1982.

NEWELL, A. & SIMON, H. A. *Human Problem Solving.* Prentice-Hall; Englewood Cliffs, N.J., 1972.

REHFUSS, S., ALEXANDER, J. H., FREILING, M. J., MESSICK, S. L. & SHULMAN, S. J. *A Troubleshooting Assistant for the Tektronix 2236 Oscilloscope.* Applied Research Technical Report CR-85-34; Tektronix, Inc.; Beavertron, OR; September 25, 1985.

SIMON, H. A. *The Sciences of the Artificial.* The MIT Press; Cambridge, MA; 1981.

SHORTLIFFE, E. H. Details of the Consultation System. *Rule-based Expert Systems: The MYCIN Experiments of the Stanford Heuristic Programming Project,* Addison-Wesley; Reading, MA, 1984.

SMITH, J. M. & SMITH, D. C. P., Database Abstractions: Aggregation and Generalization, *ACM Transactions on Database Systems, 2:2,* June, 1977.

STALEY, J. L. An Intelligent Electronic Calendar: A Smalltalk-80® Application. *Tekniques,* in press, Information Display Group, Tektronix, Wilsonville, OR.

Appendix: an example ontological analysis: the Intelligent Electronic Calendar (IEC)

The IEC (Staley, in press) is a calendar system designed to automatically schedule meetings and rooms. A more complete description of the system and analysis can be found in Alexander *et al.* (1986). The following pages give a partial description of the static, dynamic, and epistemic ontologies.

STATIC ONTOLOGY

Person = ⟨atomic⟩
Persons = 2** Person
Project = ⟨atomic⟩
Department = ⟨atomic⟩
Scheduled_Meeting = (Meeting × Person)
Meeting_Room = ⟨atomic⟩
Name = ⟨string⟩
Group = ⟨atomic⟩

Meeting_Room_Accessory = (blackboard, screen, overhead_projector}
Chair_Arrangement_Type = {conference_table, classroom, auditorium}

Meeting = ⟨atomic⟩
Meetings = 2** Meeting
Required_Participations = [Meeting → Person_Description]
Purposes = [Meeting → Meeting_Purpose]

Meeting_Purpose = One_Time_Meeting_Purpose
   + Repetitive_Meeting_Purpose
One_Time_Meeting_Purpose = {discuss, plan, review} × Project
Repetitive_Meeting_Purpose = {staff, reading, project} × Department

Meeting_Proposal =
   Time_Proposal + Location_Proposal + Participant_Proposal

Time_Proposal = Time_Description
Location_Proposal = Location_Description
Participant_Proposal = Persons

Reflection = [Scheduled_Meeting → Meeting]

Person_Name = [Person → Name] = [Name → Person]
Person_Attribute =
   Name + [Name × Hierarchical_Link]
   + [{rep_of} × Group]
   + [{resp_rep_of} × Group]
   + [{head_of} × Group]
Person_Description = 2** Person_Attribute

Hierarchical_Link = {boss_of, subordinate_of}*
Organization_relation_of_Person = Hierarchical_Link

Concession_Type = {time, location, . . .}
Owes_Concession_To = [(Person × Person) → Concession_Type*]
negotiating_points:
   [(Person × Person × Concession_Type*
                  × Organization_Relation_of_Person) → INTEGER

Group_Contained_By = [Group → Group]
Member_Of_Group = [Person → Group]
Project_Name = [Project → ⟨string⟩]

Location_Description = {Room_Capacity} × INTEGER × {blackboard, no_board}
Room_Has = Meeting_Room → 2** Meeting_Room_Accessory
Room_Capacity = Meeting_Room → INTEGER
Chair_Arrangement_In_Room = Meeting_Room → Chair_Arrangement_Type
Building = ⟨atomic⟩
Campus = ⟨atomic⟩
Site = Building × Campus
At = [Meeting_Room → Site]

STATIC ONTOLOGY: TIME DESCRIPTION

Real_Time_Point = INTEGER
Time_Quantum = INTEGER; in quarter hours
Quarter = {00, 15, 30, 45}
Hour = {0 . . 24}
Date = {1 . . 31}
Month = {1 . . 12}
Year = {−BB . . +BB}
Cycle = {−BB' . . +BB'}
Year' = {000, 100, . . . , 900}
Ap = {1 . . 13}
Day = {1 . . 28}

Identified_Time_Interval = [Real_Time_Point→ INTEGER]
   ; interval 0 is 12 mid-12:15 on 1/1/1901
Calendar = [Real_Time_Interval→ Calendar_Interval]
Real_Time_Interval =
   [Real_Time_Point × Real_Time_Point]
   + [Real_Time_Point × {unbounded}]
   + [{unbounded} × Real_Time_Point]
   + [{unbounded} × {unbounded}]
Event_Description = Interval_Description × Meeting_Description
Interval_Description =
   [{between} × Calendar_Point × Calendar_Point]
   + [{before} × Interval_Description]
   + [{after} × Interval_Description]
   + [{before, after, during} × Event_Description]

Calendar_Region = Gregorian_Point + Japanese_Point
Calendar_Interval = Calendar_Point × Calendar_Point]
   + [{before} × Calendar_Point]
   + [{within} × Interval_Description]

Gregorian_Point = Year × Month × Day × Hour × Quarter
Japanese_Point = Era × Year × Month × Day × Hour × Quarter
express_as: [Calendar→ [Real_Time_Point→ Calendar_Point]]
interpret_as: [Calendar→ [Calendar_Point→ Real_Time_Point]]

Event = Scheduled_Meeting + Block_Schedule
Events = 2** Event
Assignments = [Event→ Real_Time_Interval]
Schedule = Events × Assignments
Block_Schedule = {read, errand, fill_out_form} × Time_Quantum

DYNAMIC ONTOLOGY

Meeting_Plan = [Meeting_Proposal→ Signoffs]
Signoffs = Persons
Arbitrator = Person
Reviewer = Person
Participant = Person
Old_Meeting_Plan = Meeting_Plan
New_Meeting_Plan = Meeting_Plan

State = Meetings × Purposes × Required_Participations
   × [Meeting→ Arbitrator] × [Meeting→ Reviewer]
   × [Meeting→ Meeting_Plan] × [Person→ Schedule]
   × [Room→ Schedule]

Operation = Heuristic_Operation + Algorithmic_Operation
  + Autonomous_Operation + {schedule_new_meeting}
Heuristic_Operation = {select_arbitrator, select_reviewer,
  select_meeting_to_act_on}
Algorithmic_Operation = {create_new_meeting, reserve, assimilate}
Autonomous_Operation = {signoff_or_propose, assent, arbitrate,
  initial_proposal}

schedule_meeting = (Purpose × Required_Participation) → [State → State]
create_new_meeting: (Purpose × Required_Participation) → Meeting
select_arbitrator: Meeting × Purpose → Arbitrator
select_meeting_to_act_on: State → Meeting
select_reviewer: Meeting → [State → Reviewer]

initial_proposal: [Arbitrator → Meeting_Plan]
signoff_or_propose: [Reviewer → [Old_Meeting_Plan → New_Meeting_Plan]]
arbitrate: (Old_Meeting_Plan × New_Meeting_Plan) → (Meeting_Plan × Continue)
Continue = BOOLEAN

assent: Meeting_Plan → [(Person + Room) → Schedule]
assimilate:
  ((Meeting × Meeting_Plan) +
  ((Person + Room) × Schedule) +
  Meeting × Arbitrator) +
  (Meeting × Reviewer)) →
    [State → State])

EPISTEMIC ONTOLOGY

Arbitrator_Selection_Rules =
  2^{**} (Purpose × Person_Description)
Meeting_Selection_Rules =
  2^{**} Meeting_Plan_Pattern
Reviewer_Selection_Rules =
  2^{**} (Meeting_Plan_Pattern × Person_Description)

Meeting_Plan_Pattern =
  ((Time_Pattern × Signoff_Pattern)
    (Location_Pattern × Signoff_Pattern)
    (participant_pattern × Signoff_pattern))

Time_Pattern = Time_Description + {anytime}

Location_Pattern = 2^{**} Location_Description + {anywhere}

Participant_Pattern = 2^{**} Person_Description + {anybody}

Signoff_Pattern = 2^{**} Person_Description + {anybody} +
  {nobody_but_proposer}

Expertise transfer and complex problems: using AQUINAS as a knowledge-acquisition workbench for knowledge-based systems

JOHN H. BOOSE AND JEFFREY M. BRADSHAW

*Knowledge Systems Laboratory, Boeing Advanced Technology Center 77–64,
Boeing Computer Services, P.O. Box 24346, Seattle, WA 98124, U.S.A.*

Acquiring knowledge from a human expert is a major problem when building a
knowledge-based system. Aquinas, an expanded version of the Expertise Transfer
System (ETS), is a knowledge-acquisition workbench that combines ideas from
psychology and knowledge-based systems research to support knowledge-acquisition
tasks. These tasks include eliciting distinctions, decomposing problems, combining
uncertain information, incremental testing, integration of data types, automatic
expansion and refinement of the knowledge base, use of multiple sources of
knowledge and providing process guidance. Aquinas interviews experts and helps
them analyse, test, and refine the knowledge base. Expertise from multiple experts
or other knowledge sources can be represented and used separately or combined.
Results from user consultations are derived from information propagated through
hierarchies. Aquinas delivers knowledge by creating knowledge bases for several
different expert-system shells. Help is given to the expert by a dialog manager that
embodies knowledge-acquisition heuristics.
Aquinas contains many techniques and tools for knowledge acquisition; the
techniques combine to make it a powerful testbed for rapidly prototyping portions of
many kinds of complex knowledge-based systems.

Obtaining and modeling expertise

EXPERTISE TRANSFER SYSTEM

The Expertise Transfer System (ETS) has been in use in Boeing for more than 3
years. Hundreds of prototypical knowledge-based systems have been generated by
ETS. The system interviews experts to uncover key aspects of their problem-solving
knowledge. It helps build very rapid prototypes (typically in less than 2 h), assists
the expert in analysing the adequacy of the knowledge for solving the problem, and
creates knowledge bases for several expert system shells (S.1, M.1, OPS5, KEE,
and so on) from its own internal representation (Boose, 1984, 1985, 1986).

The tools in ETS are now part of Aquinas, a much larger system. Aquinas was
developed to overcome ETS's limitations in knowledge representation and reasoning (Fig. 1). Due to these limitations, ETS was usually abandoned sometime during
the knowledge-acquisition process. Typically project approaches were explored or
feasibility was assessed for several days or a week, and then development continued
in some other expert system shell. While the use of the tool in this way saved
substantial time (typically 1 or 2 calendar months from a 12–24-month project), it
was desirable to explore new approaches for making the system more powerful.

39

Features of AQUINAS

Improved process efficiency:
  Rapid feasibility analysis;
  Multiple alternative testing with little resource expenditure;
  Expert enthusiasm;
  Easier to learn expert-system and knowledge engineering concepts;
  Group knowledge elicitation and decision making.
Faster knowledge-base generation:
  Very rapid prototyping;
  Vocabulary identification;
  Solution elicitation;
  Trait elicitation through triads and other methods;
  Hierarchies,
    Problem decomposition;
    Reasoning at varied levels of abstraction.
Improved knowledge-base quality:
  Embedded testing and feedback during the knowledge elicitation process;
  Multiple knowledge representations;
  Multiple methods for handling uncertainty based on needed precision, convenience;
  Tools for comparing knowledge from different experts to show similarities and differences;
  Consultation systems giving consensus and dissenting opinions from multiple sources of knowledge;
  Analytic tools.
Better knowledge-base maintenance and comprehensibility:
  Case-based and knowledge source-based elicitation, structure, analysis;
  Knowledge at higher levels of abstraction;
  Single central source generation of expert-system shell knowledge bases;
  Knowledge libraries.
Extensions to personal construct theory methods:
  Manipulation of rating grids in hierarchies;
  Multiple variable scale types;
  Many analytic tools in a single framework;
  Interactive testing and debugging of rating grid knowledge.

FIG. 1. Aquinas is a knowledge-acquisition workbench that provides a variety of capabilities.

AQUINAS TASKS AND TOOL SETS

Aquinas is a collection of integrated tool sets. They share a common user interface (the dialog manager) and underlying knowledge representation and data base (Fig. 2). Each set of tools addresses a general knowledge-acquisition task and embodies sets of strategies that support the task. Many of these strategies will be illustrated later.

TASK: ELICIT DISTINCTIONS

Gaines (in press) has characterized knowledge acquisition as: "the modeling of events enabling adequate prediction and action". In this view, a *distinction* is the primitive concept underlying the representation of knowledge and the formal theory of modeling. Systems that acquire problem-solving knowledge seek to establish qualitative and quantitative distinctions that lead to effective prediction and action, while weeding out distinctions that are redundant or inconsequential.

Eliciting distinctions with Aquinas

  Personal construct psychology. George Kelly's personal construct theory (Kelly, 1955) provides a rich framework for modeling the qualitative and quantitative

Dialog manager						
ETS Repertory grid tools	Hierarchical structure tools	Uncertainty tools	Internal reasoning engine	Multiple scale type tools	Induction tools	Multiple expert tools
Object-oriented DBMS						
CommonLoops/CommonLisp						

FIG. 2. The Aquinas workbench is a collection of integrated tool sets that support various knowledge-acquisition tasks.

distinctions inherent in an expert's problem solving knowledge. Expertise Transfer System (ETS) is a set of tools used by the expert to elicit, analyse, and refine knowledge as rating grids. In a rating grid, problem solutions—*elements*—are elicited and placed across the grid as column labels, and traits of these solutions—*constructs*—are listed alongside the rows of the grid (Fig. 3, taken from the Programming Language Advisor). Traits are first elicited by presenting groups of solutions and asking the expert to discriminate among them. Following this, the expert gives each solution a rating showng where it falls on the trait scale.

Many of the strategies used in building a rating grid are extensions of ideas in the work of Kelly and in the PLANET system (Gaines & Shaw, 1981; Shaw & Gaines, in press *a, b*). These strategies include triadic elicitation, corner filling, and multiple

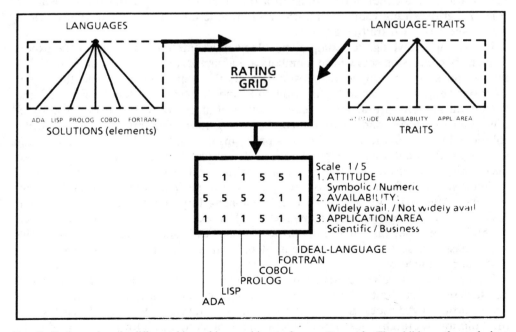

FIG. 3. Rating values in different hierarchies combine to form *rating grids*. The children of a node in a *solution hierarchy* supply the solutions along the top of the grid; the children of a node in a *trait hierarchy* supply the traits down the side of a grid.

analysis and display tools. Aquinas can analyse a rating grid in many ways to help the expert refine useful distinctions and eliminate those that are inconsequential or redundant. Distinctions captured in grids can be converted to other representations such as production rules, fuzzy sets, or networks of frames.

TASK: DECOMPOSE PROBLEMS

Experts building large knowledge bases face the task of decomposing their problem in ways that enhance efficiency and clarity. In our previous work using ETS, the difficulty of representing complex problems in a single rating grid became clear. First, a single rating grid can represent only "flat" relations between single solutions and traits. No deep knowledge, causal knowledge, or relationship chains can be shown. A second limitation was that only solutions or traits at the same level of abstraction could be used comfortably in a single grid. Finally, large single grids were often difficult to manipulate and comprehend.

Problem decomposition strategies in Aquinas

Hierarchies. Hierarchical tools in Aquinas help the expert build, edit, and analyse knowledge in hierarchies and lattices. These hierarchies allow the expert to break up complex problems into pieces of convenient size and similar levels of abstraction. Hierarchies in Aquinas are organized around *solutions, traits,* knowledge sources (i.e. *experts*), and *cases*.

Nodes in the four hierarchies combine to form rating grids. In the most simple case, the children of a node in a solution hierarchy supply the solutions along the top of a grid; the children of a node in a trait hierarchy supply the traits down the side of a grid. Rating values within the grid provide information about the solutions with respect to each trait (Fig. 3).

In eliciting knowledge for complex problems it is sometimes difficult for the expert to identify conclusion sets whose members are at similar, useful levels of granularity. For instance, in an engine diagnostic system, the expert may include the repair solutions "engine", "battery", "ignition coil" and "electrical system". "Engine" and "electrical system" are at more general levels of structural and functional abstraction than "battery" and "ignition coil". Mixing more general and more specific solutions in the same rating grid causes problems during trait elicitation, since traits useful in differentiating "engine" from "electrical system" problems are not necessarily those useful in discriminating "ignition coil" from "battery" problems.

Solution hierarchies. Solutions are grouped in specialization hierarchies within Aquinas. This structure aids experts in organizing large numbers of solutions that may exist at different levels of abstraction. For example, a solution class named "vehicle" is a superclass (parent or prototype) to "car" and "truck" subclasses. The "car" class can serve in turn as a parent to a class of specific car models or to a particular instance of a car.

Trait hierarchies. Characteristics of a particular level in the solution hierarchy can be structured in trait hierarchies. For instance, in a knowledge base for a Transportation Advisor, the solutions exist in hierarchies of vehicles. Each level in the solution hierarchy has a trait hierarchy that contains information needed to select solutions at that level. A trait hierarchy attached to the "vehicle" abstraction level of a solution hierarchy, for instance, may contain information about general use type, relative speed, cost, and so forth for the types of vehicles in the hierarchy. The "car" subclass is attached to a car trait hierarchy that contains information useful in selecting a particular car.

Two other hierarchies are formed in Aquinas (Fig. 4).

Expert hierarchies. Expert hierarchies represent multiple knowledge sources as structured groups. Each node in the expert hierarchy may represent an individual, an aspect of an individual, a group, or an independent knowledge source. Information from multiple experts may be independently elicited and analysed, then weighted and combined to derive joint solutions to problems. Analyses can be performed that show similarities and differences among experts. Experts each have their own solution and trait hierarchies, which may or may not overlap those of others. Each expert's unique problem-solving strategies and information are preserved.

Case hierarchies. Case hierarchies define subsets of the knowledge base appropriate to solving a particular class of problems. For example, in a knowledge base of information about vehicles, a user may want to include different knowledge for selecting a vehicle for going over land than for going over water. A land case and a water case may be created, each drawing on a subset of the expert pool knowledgeable in those areas. Additional levels may be created for short or long land trips, cost considerations, and so on. A hierarchy of cases allows the knowledge base to be developed, modified, and maintained based on specific classes of situations. Eventually the lower leaves in case hierarchies become specific consultation instances when the knowledge is tested and used to solve a specific problem.

From hierarchies to rating grids. A rating grid is built by combining values associated with nodes in each of the four basic hierarchies. Relationships between nodes do not have to be strictly hierarchical; lattices may be formed when more than

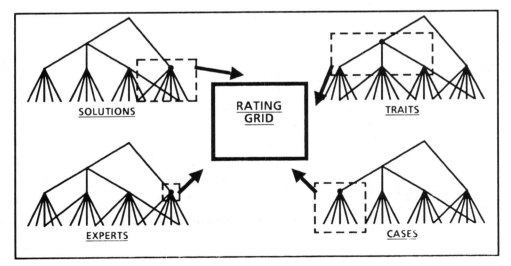

FIG. 4. Values from *expert* and *case hierarchies* as well as solution and trait hierarchies are combined in many ways to form rating grids. Relationships between nodes do not have to be strictly hierarchical; lattices may be formed when more than one parent points to the same child.

one parent points to the same child. The expert defines the current rating grid by selecting appropriate nodes in the hierarchies.

Figure 5 shows selected map nodes (case: K-ACQUISITION; expert: WEC; solution: WEC.ELEMENT; trait: WEC.ELEMENT.TRAIT) that define the rating grid of Fig. 3. Each different collection of nodes (at least one from each hierarchy) describes a rating grid. A rating grid could be a single column or row, or even a single cell. Inversely, each cell in a rating grid is uniquely described by its location in the four hierarchies.

In a sense, each rating grid is four-dimensional. Any two of these dimensions are shown at once as rows and columns in a given grid. Usually solutions and traits are shown, but sometimes it is useful to show other combinations. For instance, a grid could display the ratings of several experts across the top with particular solutions down the side. The associated trait and case nodes would be shown to the side of the grid. Often the ratings displayed summarize or generalize information from different nodes in the hierarchies; this issue is discussed later.

Techniques for defining and exploring hierarchies. Strategies for helping the expert build and refine hierarchies in Aquinas include laddering, cluster analysis, and trait value examination. Some of these strategies will be demonstrated in the section describing the Programming Language Advisor.

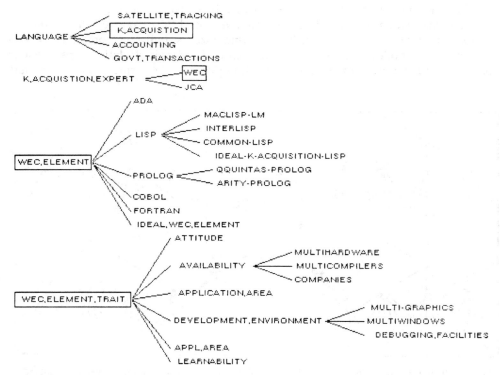

FIG. 5. Each cell in a rating grid is described by a unique set of four hierarchy nodes. Aquinas users specify rating grids by selecting sets of nodes (either the nodes themselves or their children).

TASK: SPECIFY METHODS FOR COMBINING UNCERTAIN INFORMATION
A major limitation of most current knowledge engineering tools is that they do not allow experts to specify how specific pieces of information should be combined (Gruber & Cohen, in press). Most tools either tend to use fixed, global numeric functions to compute values or restrict the expert to purely symbolic representations of uncertainty. Ideally, flexibility and comprehensibility could be achieved by allowing experts to specify how information should be combined locally either by selecting from a set of commonly accepted combining functions (e.g. as done by Reboh & Risch, 1986; Reboh, Risch, Hart & Duda, 1986) or by defining their own method.

Combining uncertain information in Aquinas
In Aquinas, uncertain knowledge, preferences, and constraints may be elicited, represented, and locally applied using combinations of several different methods. These methods may be classified into three main types: absolute, relativistic, and probabilistic.

Absolute reasoning. Absolute (categorical) reasoning involves judgments made with no significant reservations. It "typically depends on relatively few facts, its appropriateness is easy to judge, and its result is unambiguous" (Szolovitz & Pauker, 1978). For example, in selecting a programming language, users may be able to say with certainty that they would be interested only in languages that run on an Apple Macintosh or that they will not consider a language that costs more than $400, regardless of other desirable characteristics. Experts can also build these types of absolute constraints into the knowledge associated with an Aquinas rating grid.

Relativistic reasoning. Unfortunately, not all judgments can be absolute. Many involve significant trade-offs, where information and preferences from several sources must be weighed. Even if criteria for the ideal decision can be agreed on, sometimes it can be only approximated by the available alternatives. In these cases, problem-solving information must be propagated in a relativistic fashion. Aquinas incorporates a variety of models and approaches to relativistic reasoning, including MYCIN-like certainty factor calculus (Adams, 1985), fuzzy logic (Gaines & Shaw, 1985), and the Analytic Hierarchy Process (AHP, Saaty, 1980).

Probabilistic and user-defined reasoning. In the current version of Aquinas, some limited propagation of probabilistic information is made possible by allowing discrete distributions on rating values. Future versions of Aquinas will have more complete models for the elicitation (Alpert & Raiffa, 1982; Spetzler & Stal von Holstein, 1984; Wallsten & Budescu, 1983) and analysis of probabilistic information including Bayesian (Howard and Matheson, 1984; Cheeseman, 1985; Henrion, 1986; Pearl 1986; Spiegelhalter, 1986), Dempster–Shafer (Shafer, 1976; Gordon & Shortliffe, 1985), and other approaches (Shastri & Feldman, 1985). Users may also define their own methods for combining and propagating information.

The availability of different inference methods within a single workbench allows users and experts flexibility in adapting Aquinas to the problem at hand. Methods are currently selected based on the cost of elicitation, the precision of the knowledge needed, convenience, and the expert's preference. Future research will suggest heuristics for helping experts select appropriate methods and designs for particular types of questions (e.g. Shafer & Tversky, 1985). These heuristics will be incorporated into the Aquinas dialog manager.

TASK: TEST THE KNOWLEDGE
McDermott (1986) has emphasized the inseparability of acquired knowledge from the role it plays in problem solving. Within a given knowledge-acquisition tool, the problem method must be available to the expert as the knowledge base is being constructed so that incremental testing and refinement can take place.

Testing knowledge in Aquinas
A mixed-initiative reasoning engine within Aquinas supports consultations. The model of problem solving currently used in Aquinas is that of multiple knowledge sources (experts) that work together in a common problem-solving context (case) by selecting the best alternatives for each of a sequential set of decisions (solutions). Alternatives at each step are selected by combining relevant information about preferences (relativistic reasoning), constraints (absolute reasoning) and evidence (probabilistic reasoning).

For many structured selection problems, a more specialized version of this model seems adequate. After analysing several expert systems for classification, Clancey (1986) suggested that many problems are solved by abstracting data, heuristically mapping higher-level problem descriptions onto solution models, and then refining these models until specific solutions are found (Fig. 6). This is also similar to the establish-refine cycle used in CSRL (Bylander & Mittal, 1986; Chandrasekaran, 1986; Bylander & Chandrasekaran, in press). In the version of Aquinas described in this paper, data abstraction is carried out within hierarchies of traits, and solutions are refined as information is propagated through solution hierarchies.

While the current version of Aquinas works best on those problems whose solutions can be comfortably enumerated (such as those amenable to the method of heuristic classification), we are interested in generalizing Aquinas to incorporate synthetic (constructive) problem-solving methods such as those in SALT (Marcus, in press).

TASK: INTEGRATE DIVERSE DATA TYPES
Problem solving in knowledge-based systems often involves combining symbolic and numeric information. Qualitative and quantitative aspects are complimentary rather

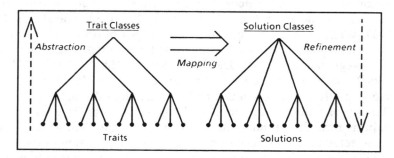

FIG. 6. Clancey (1986) studied structured selection systems and built an abstraction and refinement model. Inference in Aquinas typically occurs in a bottom–up fashion through the trait hierarchies and in top–down fashion through the solution hierarchies.

than opposing considerations, so knowledge-acquisition tools need to represent such information flexibily and conveniently. In our work with ETS, we found that it was inconvenient to represent certain types of problem-solving information solely using Kelly's constructs. Unordered variables, such as a set of computer types, had to be represented as a series of bipolar traits (VAX/NOT-VAX, IBM/NOT-IBM, and so on) when it would have been easier to combine them into a single nominal trait (a COMPUTER trait whose values are VAX, IBM, and so on).

Experts also apply different levels of precision at different points in the knowledge-acquisition process. For example, in some instances it might be sufficient to know that an object is hot or cold. At a later point, it may be important to know the exact temperature of the object. Levels of precision must also be appropriately flexible. ETS only dealt with ordinal ratings on a scale from 1 to 5, not probabilities or exact numeric values.

Integrating data types within Aquinas

In Aquinas, various trait (attribute) scale types can be elicited, analysed, and used by the reasoning engine. Traits are currently described according to the level of measurement of their rating scales, which is determined by the expert. The level of measurement depends on the presence or absence of four characteristics: *distinctiveness, ordering in magnitude, equal intervals,* and *absolute zero* (Coombs, Dawes & Tversky, 1970). These four characteristics describe the four major levels of measurement, or types of traits: nominal (unordered symbols), ordinal, interval, and ratio (Fig. 7). The additional information about trait types gives increased power to analytical tools within Aquinas and allows experts to represent information at the level of precision they desire.

Ratings may be generated through several methods:

(1) Direct. An expert directly assigns a rating value for a trait and an element. If an exact value is unknown, Aquinas helps the expert derive an estimate (Beyth-Marom & Dekel, 1985). If fine judgments are needed, Aquinas can derive a set of ratio scaled ratings from a series of *pairwise comparisons* (Saaty, 1980). Aquinas also contains tools for encoding of probability distributions on specific values. The value with the highest probability is displayed in the grid, but all appropriate values are used in reasoning and may be edited with graphic distribution aids.

(2) Derived. Incomplete grids can be automatically filled through propagation of

RATING SCALE	DESCRIPTION	EXAMPLES
Nominal	Unordered set	LANGUAGE: {ADA COBOL LISP}
Ordinal	Ordered set	COLD/HOT: {1 2 3 4 5}
		SIZE: {SMALL MEDIUM LARGE}
Interval	Ordered set with measurable intervals	SMALL-INTEGERS: {1 2 3 4 5 6 7}
		F-TEMP: {32 . . 112}
Ratio	Ordered set with measurable intervals and an absolute origin	HEIGHT: {0.0' 1.0' . .}

FIG. 7. Aquinas expands the knowledge representation capability of rating grids from personal construct theory by allowing the use of several types of rating scale values. Scale types are selected for convenience, precision, or efficiency of value entry.

rating values from another grid through the hierarchies (e.g. from lower-to higher-level grids, different experts, or different cases).

Precision and cost. Increased precision and specificity in knowledge acquisition allow increased problem-solving power but usually at some cost (Michalski & Winston, 1985). This cost is reflected in both the amount of work needed to elicit the additional information and increased complexity and greater number of steps in the reasoning process. Aquinas tries to minimize this cost by eliciting more precise information only when it is needed to solve critical portions of the problem. If, for example, Aquinas finds that it cannot sufficiently discriminate between solutions from simple rating values between 1 and 5, it may suggest that the user perform a series of pairwise comparisons to increase the sensitivity of judgments.

TASK: AUTOMATIC EXPANSION AND REFINEMENT OF THE KNOWLEDGE BASE
Knowledge-acquisition tools can increase their leverage by suggesting appropriate expansions and refinements of the knowledge based on partial information already provided by the expert. Michalski (1986) has discussed the advantages of incorporating learning strategies within conventional knowledge-acquisition tools.

Expanding and refining knowledge with Aquinas
Several types of tools make inductive generalizations about existing knowledge. Generalizations can be examined by the expert and used to refine the knowledge, and are used by the reasoning engine. Sometimes, Aquinas may suggest that traits be deleted after analysing the knowledge through a process that is similar to the simplification of decision tables (Hurley, 1983, Michalski, 1978) and decision trees (Quinlan, 1983).

Learning strategies in Aquinas include simple learning from examples (e.g. selective induction on lower level grids to derive values for higher level grids), deduction (e.g. inheritance of values from parents), analogy (e.g. derivation of values based on functional similarity of traits), and observation (e.g. constructive induction based on cluster analysis). The dialog manager (described below) also contains various learning mechanisms.

TASK: USE MULTIPLE SOURCES OF KNOWLEDGE
Future knowledge-acquisition systems can neither assume a single source of expertise nor a closed world. In ETS, we began experimenting with strategies for manually combining ETS knowledge from several domain experts (Boose, in press). Others in our laboratory have been involved in developing methods for cooperative problem-solving (Benda, Jagannathan & Dodhiawala, 1986).

Using multiple sources of knowledge in Aquinas
Knowledge from multiple experts (or other knowledge sources) can be analysed to find similarities and differences in knowledge, and the degree of subsumption of one expert's knowledge over another (Gaines & Shaw, 1981). Information from analyses can be used to guide negotiation among experts. The reasoning engine uses knowledge from user-specified and weighted sources and gives consensus and dissenting opinions.

TASK: PROVIDE KNOWLEDGE-ACQUISITION PROCESS GUIDANCE

As knowledge-acquisition tools become more sophisticated and knowledge bases grow larger, the complexity of the knowledge engineering task increases. One approach to managing this complexity is to implement some form of apprenticeship learning program that is available to the expert (e.g. Wilkins, in press).

Providing process guidance in Aquinas

A subsystem called the dialog manager contains pragmatic heuristics to guide the expert through knowledge acquisition using Aquinas. Its help is important in the use of Aquinas, given the complexity of the Aquinas environment and the many elicitation and analysis methods available to the expert. The dialog manager makes decisions about general classes of actions and then recommends one or more specific actions providing comments and explanation if desired. This knowledge is contained in rules within the dialog manager in Aquinas. A session history is recorded so that temporal reasoning and learning may be performed (Kitto & Boose, in press).

Using Aquinas: building a programming language advisor

Aquinas is written in Interslip and runs on the Xerox family of Lisp machines. Subsets of Aquinas also run in an Interslip version on the DEC Vax and a "C/UNIX"-based portable version. The Aquinas screen is divided into a typescript window, map windows showing hierarchies, rating grid windows, and analysis windows (Fig. 8). Experts interact with Aquinas by text entry or by mouse through pop-up menus.

Following are the steps in a Aquinas session in which an expert is building a Programming Language Advisor. Novice software engineers and project managers would use such a system to help select programming languages for application projects. Aquinas guides the expert in putting knowledge into Aquinas's knowledge base, and continues through the making of a knowledge base for the S.1 expert-system shell. These steps are:

(1) ELICIT CASES AND THE INITIAL GRID (SOLUTIONS, TRAITS AND RATINGS)

The expert is first asked to specify the behavior of Aquinas's dialog manager. Then the expert enters several problem test cases and selects one for analysis. The *knowledge-acquisition language* case is selected (satellite tracking, accounting and government transaction cases are also entered). The cases are added to the case hierarchy and appear in the *map window* (Figure 8; upper right corner). Eventually experts may be able to select and modify grids and cases from a library; we expect that in several years this library will contain hundreds of hierarchies of grids.

The expert chooses to think about a language for developing a knowledge acquisition testbed, and enters potential candidates (Fig. 9). After five languages are entered, Aquinas adds an *ideal language* for this problem. This would be an ideal solution for the knowledge-acquisition case. The languages are added to the solution hierarchy as children. Then Aquinas asks the expert to enter traits based on differences and similarities between languages. This is the heart of Kelly's interviewing methodology. Aquinas uses it in several different ways as knowledge is expanded through elicitation and analysis.

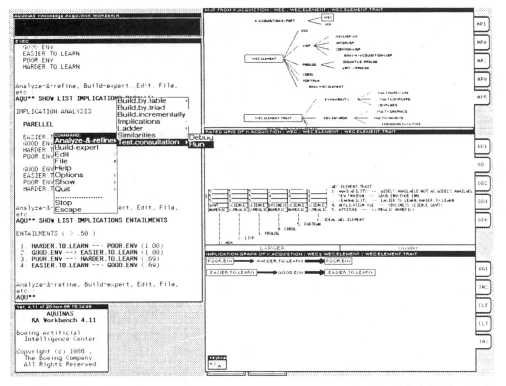

FIG. 8. Aquinas screen showing developing hierarchies for expert WEC, a rating grid, and an implication analysis graph of the grid.

Aquinas initially assumes that traits will be bipolar with ordinal ratings between 1 and 5. The expert is asked to rate each solution with regard to each trait, but the expert may specify different rating scales (unordered, interval, or ratio). Aquinas later assists in recognizing and changing types of rating scales.

Aquinas also elicits information about the importance of each trait. This knowledge is used later in the decision-making process.

(2) ANALYSE AND EXPAND THE INITIAL, SINGLE GRID

Once a grid is complete, an analysis is performed to show *implications* between various values of traits (see the lower right-hand window in Fig. 8). Implications are read from left to right, and the thickness of the arc shows the strength of the implication (HARDER TO LEARN implies POOR DEVELOPMENT ENVIRONMENT). A method similar to ENTAIL (Gaines & Shaw, 1985; Shaw & Gaines, in press) derives implications. Rating grid entries are used as a sample set and fuzzy-set logic is applied to discover inductive implications between the values. This method uncovers higher-order relationships among traits and later helps build trait hierarchies. The expert can also use an interactive process (implication review) to analyse and debug this information; the expert may agree or disagree with each implication. If the expert disagrees, the knowledge that led to the implication is

```
--- ELICITING ELEMENTS ---
Please enter a list of LANGUAGE elements for K-ACQUISITION, one to a line. When you're
done, enter a RETURN. Try to include at least one LANGUAGE that would NOT be good for K-
ACQUISITION (a counter example).
AQU** ADA
AQU** LISP
AQU** PROLOG
AQU** COBOL
AQU** FORTRAN
AQU** (CR)
Can you imagine a new ideal LANGUAGE for K-ACQUISITION?
AQU** YES
For now, it will be called IDEAL-K-ACQUISITION-LANGUAGE.

--- BUILDING TRAITS BY TRIADS ---
When answering the following questions, remember to keep the K-ACQUISITION case in
mind.

Think of an important attribute that two of ADA, LISP, and PROLOG share, but that the other
one does not. What is that attribute?
AQU** SYMBOLIC
What is that attribute's opposite as it applies in this case?
AQU** NUMERIC
What is the name of a scale or concept that describes
SYMBOLIC/NUMERIC?
AQU** ATTITUDE

Think of an important trait that two of LISP, PROLOG, and COBOL share, but that the other
one does not. What is that trait?
AQU** WIDELY AVAILABLE
What is that trait's opposite as it applies in this case?
AQU** NOT AS WIDELY AVAILABLE
What is the name of a scale or concept that describes WIDELY-AVAILABLE/NOT-AS-WIDELY-
AVAILABLE?
AQU** AVAILABILITY
        :

--- FILLING IN RATINGS ---
Please rate these things on a scale of 5 to 1, where 5 means more like SYMBOLIC and 1 means
more like NUMERIC. If neither one seems to apply, enter N(either). If both seem to apply, enter a
B(oth). If you would like to change the range or type of scale, enter C(hange scale)
SYMBOLIC(5) NUMERIC(1)
    ADA ** 5
    LISP ** 1
    PROLOG ** 1
    COBOL ** 5
    FORTRAN ** 5
    IDEAL-K-ACQUISITION-LANGUAGE ** 1
        :
```

FIG. 9. Aquinas asks the expert for an initial set of potential solutions to the first problem case. Then, the solutions are presented in groups of three, and the expert gives discriminating traits. Ratings are entered for each solution for each trait.

reviewed, and the expert can change the knowledge or add exceptions that disprove the implication (Boose, 1986). Certain types of *implication patterns* are also uncovered. Discovery of *ambiguous* patterns, for example, may mean that traits are being used inconsistently (Hinkle, 1965; Boose, 1986).

After the initial grid is complete, the dialog manager suggests a method to help the expert expand the grid. The method depends on the size of the grid, analysis of information in the grid, session history, and so on. The dialog manager inserts the appropriate command on the screen. The expert may change this recommendation or accept it by entering RETURN.

(3) TEST THE KNOWLEDGE IN THE SINGLE GRID

The dialog manager next recommends that the grid knowledge be tested by running a consultation. The expert is asked to provide desirable values for the traits associated with an instance of the case under consideration. These values may be appended with a certainty factor and/or the tag ABSOLUTE to show an absolute constraint. Consultation questions are ordered according to a computed benefit/cost ratio that depends on both the generated system (e.g. entropy of a given trait, Quinlan, 1983) and the specified expert (e.g. cost of obtaining information) parameters. The questions may also be ordered according to an arbitrary specification given by the expert. Performance is measured by comparison of experts' expectations with Aquinas consultation results.

Two methods are available in Aquinas for turning rating values in grids into solution recommendations. One approach for turning rating values in grids into solution recommendations involves mapping this information onto certainty factor scales. Each rating in the grid is assigned a certainty factor weight based on its *relative strength* (a 5 is stronger than a 4), the *relative weight* the expert has assigned to the trait, and any *absolute constraints* that the expert has specified for the trait. In the test consultation, EMYCIN's certainty factor combination method (Adams, 1985) is used to combine the certainty factors. The result is a rank-ordered list of solutions with certainty-factor assignments. These certainty factors are also used when rules are generated for expert-system shells.

Another approach available employs Saaty's Analytic Hierarchy Process to order a set of possible solutions. Grid information obtained through pairwise comparisons or through regular rating grid methods is mapped onto *judgment matrices*. The *principal eigenvector* is computed for each matrix; the eigenvectors are normalized and combined to yield a final ranking of the solutions. Each solution has a score between 0·0 and 1·0. In a knowledge base consisting of multiple grids, these values are propagated through the hierarchies.

(4) BUILD HIERARCHIES (STRUCTURED AS SOLUTIONS AND TRAITS IN MULTIPLE
     GRIDS) FROM THE FIRST GRID

Next, the dialog manager recommends that the expert expand the trait and solution hierarchies by performing a *cluster analysis* (Fig. 10). Aquinas uses a method of single-link hierarchical cluster analysis based on FOCUS (Shaw & Gaines, in press *a*) to group sets of related solutions or traits. The junctions in the clusters can be seen as conjectures about possible new classes of solutions or traits. These more general trait or solution classes may be named and added to the hierarchies.

Laddering is also used to find traits at varying levels of abstraction (Boose, 1986). "Why?" questions are used to find more general traits;

What is a new trait that says why you think GOOD-DEVELOPMENT-ENVIRONMENT should be true of a LANGUAGE for K-ACQUISITION? AQU** FASTER SYSTEM DEVELOPMENT.

"How?" questions help find more specific traits:

How could a language for K-ACQUISITION be characterized by WIDELY-AVAILABLE?
AQU** RUNS ON MULTIPLE HARDWARE
AQU** MANY COMPILERS AVAILABLE
AQU** MANY COMPANIES OFFER.

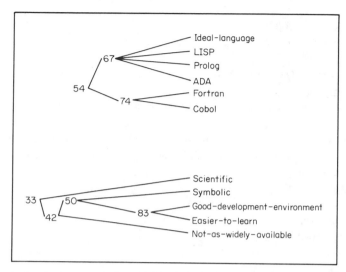

Fig. 10. Solution and trait clusters are formed from information in rating grids. The expert is asked to label nodes and expand clusters where possible; new traits are used to expand the hierarchies.

Experts stop expanding the trait hierarchies when they are able to provide direct grid ratings at these more specific trait levels. Ratings need not be explicitly given at each level of the trait and solution hierarchies, but can often be inferred from other grids in the knowledge base (e.g. induction from more specific examples or inheritance from more general ones) (Lieberman, 1986).

(5) USE SEVERAL RATING VALUE TYPES (TRANSFORM ORDINAL RATINGS TO
    NOMINAL AND INTERVAL RATINGS) TO REPRESENT KNOWLEDGE
Aquinas helps the expert convert a trait with ordinal values (DELIVERY-COST: HIGH-COST(5)/LOW-COST(1)) into a trait with ratio scaled rating values (DELIVERY-COST: (1500–60 000) DOLLARS-US). The expert re-rates the solutions in terms of the new values and these values appear on the grid Aquinas provides several forms of estimation help. Four estimation procedures are provided: START-&-MODIFY, EXTREME-VALUES, DECOMPOSITION, and RECOMPOSITION (Beyth-Marom & Dekel, 1985). In this instance, the EXTREME-VALUES procedure first asks for the least and greatest DELIVERY-COST one could imagine for the type of Lisp being considered. Through a series of questions, Aquinas helps shrink this range until a satisfactory estimate is given.

Aquinas also helps the expert change trait scale types by checking values associated with particular kinds of traits. For instance, bipolar traits that receive only extreme ratings (e.g. RUNS ON VAX/RUNS ON IBM) may be better represented with an unordered trait (e.g. COMPUTER TYPE).

(6) TEST KNOWLEDGE IN HIERARCHIES; TEST KNOWLEDGE FROM MULTIPLE
    EXPERTS
Another expert adds knowledge about programming language selection to the knowledge base and tests it. In the first consultation (Fig. 11), the user is interested

```
--- TEST CONSULTATION --

Would you like to run an EXISTING or NEW consultation?

AQU** EXISTING

What is the name of this existing consultation?

AQU** LISP-PROLOG-ADA-ONLY

This test consultation is named K-ACQUISITION LISP-PROLOG-ADA-ONLY.


Which K-ACQUISITION alternatives you would like to consider in this consultation (LISP-PROLOG-
ADA-ONLY). Enter them one to a line  If you wish all solutions to be considered, type ALL  When
done, press RETURN.

AQU** MACLISP-LM

AQU** INTERLISP

AQU** COMMON-LISP

AQU** QUINTUS-PROLOG

AQU** ADA-1

AQU** (CR)

The following experts know about MACLISP-LM, INTERLISP, COMMON-LISP, QUINTUS-PROLOG,
and ADA-1: WEC  JCA. Would you like to exclude or weight any of these experts?

AQU** NO


Please indicate the desired trait selection values for LISP-PROLOG-ADA-ONLY solutions. Press
RETURN to indicate agreement with the default values, or type in a new value  Values may be
appended with a certainty factor in the form '.8' and/or the word ABSOLUTE to indicate that the
value is an absolute constraint when selecting a type of LANGUAGE for K-ACQUISITION.

(WIDELY-AVAILABLE(5), 1 0)** (CR)

(GOOD-DEVELOPMENT-ENVIRONMENT(5), 1.0)** (CR)

(LOW-COST(<45000 DOLLARS-US), 1.0, ABSOLUTE) (NOTE: THIS INCLUDES HARDWARE FOR A
WORKSTATION) ** <30000 DOLLARS-US 1.0 ABSOLUTE

            :
```

FIG. 11. The expert tests the knowledge by running a consultation. The expertise of two experts is used
and consensus and dissenting solutions are given (see Fig. 12).

in selecting a particular version of Lisp, Prolog, or ADA for a knowledge
acquisition project. Because of the many potential solutions, the user is given the
opportunity to specify a subset for consideration. The solutions in this subset are
called *solution candidates*.

Aquinas then asks for a set of absolute and preferred trait values for this
consultation. The user enters an absolute constraint that only languages with a
delivery cost of less than $30 000 will be considered. Patterns of constraints may be
entered by using key words such as AND and OR. The user may accept default
values entered in a previous consultation by pressing the RETURN key. If a default
value has not been previously specified and the user types RETURN, the trait will
be ignored in the inference process for this consulatation. The user's preference for

HARDWARE type is partitioned among three manufacturers by pairwise comparison (Fig. 12), which generates a ratio scaled set of preferences (Saaty, 1980).

The results of the consultation are presented to the user. For each solution, the *consensus* recommendation of the experts consulted is presented, followed by the weight of each expert that contributed to the recommendation. With multiple experts, it may sometimes be useful to examine a set of recommendations from a *dissenting* expert or group of experts. Since WEC's recommendations differed most from the consensus, these are listed as a dissenting opinion.

A general model illustrating the inference propagation path was shown in Fig. 6. For each expert consulted and for each level in that expert's solution hierarchy, a

---

```
        :
(COMPANIES(VAX .33, IBM .33, ATT .33), 1.0)** PAIRWISE
Please compare these values of HARDWARE with regard to their importance in contributing to an
overall high score for a particular type of LANGUAGE for K-ACQUISITION in the context of LISP-
PROLOG-ADA-ONLY.
Please compare VAX and IBM. Enter.
VAX = IBM if VAX and IBM are equally important
VAX>IBM or VAX<IBM if one of the pair is weakly more important
VAX>>IBM or VAX<<IBM if one is strongly more important
VAX>>>IBM or VAX<<<IBM if one is demonstrably or very strongly more important
VAX>>>>IBM or VAX<<<<IBM if one is absolutely more important
AQU** VAX<IBM

Please compare VAX and ATT Enter:
VAX = ATT if VAX and ATT are equally important
VAX>ATT or VAX<ATT if one of the pair is weakly more important
VAX>>ATT or VAX<<ATT if one is strongly more important
VAX>>>ATT or VAX<<<ATT if one is demonstrably or very strongly more important
VAX>>>>ATT or VAX<<<<ATT if one is absolutely more important
AQU** VAX>>>>ATT
        :

Results for test consultation K-ACQUISITION LISP-PROLOG-ADA-ONLY:
 1: INTERLISP  (.47  (WEC .5, JCA  5))
 2: QUINTUS- PROLOG  ( 40: (WEC 1 0))

Would you like to see the dissenting opinion for this consultation?
AQU** YES

The following dissenting opinion was given by WEC
Overall agreement with consensus  .79
 1: QUINTUS PROLOG (.40)
 2: INTERLISP (.39)
```

FIG. 12. Test consultation (continued). The expert specifies "run-time" values for traits, entering an absolute cost constraint, and performing a pairwise comparison task to derive relative values for hardware. Consensus and dissenting opinions are given along with the weighted contributions of each expert.

partial problem model is constructed, evaluated, and abstracted in a bottom–up fashion through the trait hierarchy of that solution level. Through this process the solution is refined as the children of the best solutions are chosen for continued evaluation. Bottom–up abstraction takes place again in the trait hierarchy at the new solution level, and the cycle continues until all remaining solution candidates have been evaluated. Then an ordered list of solution candidates is obtained and combined with the results from other experts. This information from a single case may then be combined, if desired, with information from other cases to derive a final ranking of solution candidates. Users may override this general model of inference propagation by specifying explicit inference paths and parameters.

(7) EDIT, ANALYSE AND REFINE THE KNOWLEDGE BASE, BUILDING NEW CASES
Once the experts have entered information about one case, they describe additional cases. They could start from scratch by entering a list of relevant solutions and traits, but that would be inefficient if there were significant overlap in those required by a previously entered case and a new one (Mittal, Bobrow & Kahn, 1986). Aquinas allows an expert to copy pieces of hierarchies (and, optionally, their associated values) between cases. Information copied in this way can be modified to fit the new context. This facility may also be used to copy pieces of hierarchies between experts.

(8) FURTHER EXPAND AND REFINE THE KNOWLEDGE BASE
Hiearachies and rating grids continue to be used during the session to expand and refine the knowledge base. Work in progress is shown in Fig. 8. Aquinas contains a variety of other tools to help analyse and expand the knowledge base.

Comparison of experts (sources)
The MINUS tool (Shaw & Gaines, 1986) compares grids from different experts on the same subject and points our differences and similarities. This information has been used to manage structured negotiation between experts (Boose, 1986). SOCIOGRIDS features (Shaw & Gaines, in press *a*) will be available in the future to display *networks* of expertise. Nodes and relations in these networks show the degree of subsumption of one expert's grid over grids from other experts.

Incremental interviewing
Aquinas can use an incremental dialog to elicit new traits and solutions, one at a time, from the expert (Boose, 1986). This is useful when the expert does not have a list of solutions to start a grid and in other situations during knowledge refinement.

Trait value examination
New solutions can be identified by asking the expert to "fill in holes" in the values of trait ranges. For instance, no solution may exist with a rating of 2 on some ordinal trait scale; the expert is asked if one can be identified:

> What is a new LANGUAGE that would receive a value of 2 on the scale SCIENTIFIC(5)/BUSINESS(1)?

New traits can also be identified by forming triads based on ratings: if LISP and

PROLOG are rated 5 on SCIENTIFIC(5)/BUSINESS(1), and ADA is rated 4, the expert is asked:

What is a new trait having to do with SCIENTIFIC/BUSINESS that makes LISP and PROLOG similar yet different from ADA?

Trait range boundary examination
Important traits can frequently be identified by exploring the boundaries of trait ranges:

You said that the range of DELIVERY-COST for LISP for the K-ACQUISITION case was 1500 to 60 000 DOLLARS-US. Can you think of any conditions in the future that might make DELIVERY-COST LESS THAN 1500?
AQU** YES
Enter conditions in terms of traits , one to a line; enter a RETURN when done.
AQU** HARDWARE BREAKTHROUGH-LISP ON A CHIP
AQU** (CR)
Can you think of any conditions in the future that might make DELIVERY-COST GREATER THAN 60 000?
AQU** YES
Enter conditions in terms of traits, one to a line, enter a RETURN when done.
AQU** VERY POWERFUL HARDWARE
AQU** PARALLEL ARCHITECTURES AVAILABLE
AQU** (CR)

Completeness checking
A single grid can be used as a table of examples. If the table is incomplete, the expert is asked to fill in other examples (Boose, 1986).

Combine similar traits
Sometimes different labels are used for the same underlying concept. This can be discovered when a similarity analysis is performed (functionally equivalent traits with different labels may be uncovered). If the expert cannot think of a new solution to separate identical traits, then the traits may be combined into a single trait.

(9) GENERATE RULES FOR EXPERT-SYSTEM SHELLS
The expert is the judge of when the point of diminishing returns has been reached within Aquinas. When such a point is reached, a knowledge base is generated for an expert-system shell, and development continues directly in that shell. Similarity and implication analyses allow experts to determine whether traits or solutions can be adequately and appropriately discriminated from one another. The system provides correlational methods for comparing the order of Aquinas recommendations with an expert's rankings.

Aquinas can generate knowledge bases for several expert-system shells (KEE, KS-300/EMYCIN, LOOPS, M.1, OPS5, S.1, and others). The knowledge contained in grids and hierarchies is converted within Aquinas into rules, and the rules are formatted for a particular expert-system shell. Appropriate control knowledge is also generated when necessary. Rules are generated with screening clauses that partition the rules into subsets. An *expert clause* is used when expertise from multiple experts is weighted and combined together. A *case clause* controls the focus of the system during reasoning.

Four types of rules are generated:

(1) *Implication rules* are generated from arcs in the implication graph and conclude about particular traits. The conclusion's certainty factor is proportional to the strength of the implication. The use of implication rules restricts search and lessens the number of questions asked of users during consultations;

(2) *Solution rules* conclude about a particular solution class. The conclusion's certainty factor is derived from a combination of the *grid rating strength* and the *trait weight*;

(3) *Absolute rules* are generated when the expert places an absolute constraint on the value of a trait. Sometimes information about absolute constraints is included elsewhere when knowledge bases for expert system shells are generated;

(4) *Specialization/generalization rules* are derived from information in the hierarchies and are used to propagate hierarchical information.

Discussion

GENERAL ADVANTAGES AND DISADVANTAGES OF AQUINAS

Improved process efficiency and faster knowledge-base generation
Aquinas inherits the advantages of ETS: rapid prototyping and feasibility analysis, vocabulary, solution and trait elicitation, interactive testing and refinement during knowledge acquisition, implication discovery, conflict point identification, expert-system shell production, and generation of expert enthusiasm (Boose, 1986). It is much easier for users to learn knowledge-based system concepts through using Aquinas than through reading books or attending classes (i.e. rules are automatically generated and used dynamically in consultations; new vocabulary is incrementally introduced).

ETS, still in use at Boeing, has been employed to build hundreds of single-grid prototype systems. Single grids as large as 42×38 (1596 ratings) have been built. Alternative approaches may be tested with little expenditure of resources. Knowledge bases have been generated for expert-system shells that contain over 2000 rules. Typically, something on the order of a 15×10 grid is built that generates several hundred rules.

Over 30 prototype systems have been built during the development of Aquinas (an AI book consultant, and AI tool advisor, a course evaluation system, a customer needs advisor, a database management system consultant, an investment advisor, a management motivation analyser, a personal computer advisor, a personality disorder advisor, a product design and impact advisor, a robotic tool selector, a Seattle travel agent, and a wine advisor, among others). Some of these systems contain thousands of ratings arranged in hierarchical grids. The Programming Language Advisor session took less than 2 h with each of the two experts.

Improved knowledge-base quality
Aquinas offers a rich knowledge representation and reasoning environment. We believe that Aquinas can be used to acquire knowledge for significant portions of most structured selection expert-system problems. Hierarchies help the expert break down problems into component parts and allow reasoning at different levels of abstraction. Varying levels of precision are specified, with multiple types of rating scales when needed. Multiple methods for handling combining uncertain information are available based on needed precision and convenience. Knowledge from multiple experts may be combined using Aquinas. Users may receive dissenting as well as consensus opinions from groups of experts, thus getting a full *range* of possible solutions. Disagreement between the consensus and the dissenting opinion can be measured to derive a *degree of conflict* for a particular consultation. The system can be used for cost-effective group data gathering (Boose, in press).

Analytic tools help uncover inconsistencies and circularities in the growing knowledge base.

Better knowledge-base maintenance and comprehensibility
Elicitation, structuring, analysis, and testing of knowledge is based on specific cases. When knowledge in Aquinas is updated, it is done so with respect to a specific case. Addition of new knowledge in this way can be strictly controlled by the expert; the tendency for local changes to degrade other cases is thus curbed.

The expert builds and refines knowledge in rating grids and hierarchies—not directly in production rules. As a result, knowledge at this higher level of abstraction is more compact, comprehensible, and easier to maintain.

The growing collection of rating grids and case knowledge represents an important resource for building a variety of knowledge-based systems. Knowledge is stored explicitly with associated problem cases, making knowledge bases easier to update and maintain.

Currently, a user may copy and change any portion of the Aquinas knowledge base during a consultation. In the future, each expert will be able to protect areas of knowledge. The expert may believe protection is necessary because some knowledge should not be changed or because the knowledge has commercial value.

Extensions to personal construct theory methods
Aquinas significantly extends existing personal construct theory methods. Rating grid knowledge can be tested and used interactively to make decisions; rating grid information may be arranged and coupled in hierarchies; multiple rating scale types are available (not just bipolar ordinal scales); many grid analysis tools are available in a single workbench.

Process complexity
Aquinas is not as easy to use as was ETS using single grids. There are many elicitation and analysis tools for a novice to understand; the decision-making process and inference engine can be set up to work in several different ways. We expect that continuing improvements in the dialog manager will help make the system more comprehensible and decrease the learning time for new users.

THEORETICAL ISSUES—KNOWLEDGE ELICITATION

Personal construct psychology methods provide no guarantee that a *sufficient* set of knowledge will be found to solve a given problem. Aquinas attempts to expand the initial subset of solutions and traits based on problem-solving knowledge for specific cases. The goal is to solve enough cases to that the knowledge is sufficient to solve *new* cases. This is the methodology of knowledge engineering in general; Aquinas helps make the process explicit and manageable.

Hierarchical decomposition can be used to build intuitive, comprehensible models that seem to behave in reasonable ways. One disadvantage is that some problems do not easily fit the hierarchical model. It also may be true that a particular problem would best be represented by a *collection of conflicting hierarchies* (hierarchies for mechanical problems tend to model structure *or* function, not both, and both may be necessary).

The use of multiple rating value types provides more flexibility, convenience, and precision in representing knowledge. However, deciding a particular type of variable to use can be a complex task. The dialog manager offers some assistance, but the expert usually must learn appropriate usage of rating types through experience.

Experts develop Aquinas knowledge bases serially. In the future, we would like to build a participant system in which many experts could dynamically share rating grids and hierarchies (Chang, 1985).

ANALYSIS AND INFERENCE

Multiple analysis tools and elicitation methods in Aquinas help the expert think about the problem in new ways and tend to point conflicts and inconsistencies over time. Lenat (1983*a, b*) argues that knowledge representations should shift as different needs arise. This should lead to a better problem and solution descriptions, and, in turn, to better problem solving.

Inference in Aquinas is efficient because the problem space is partitioned. Information in the trait hierarchies is attached to particular levels of solutions. Although no formal studies have been conducted, consultation results using the methods described above seem reasonable.

Rule generation for expert-system shells is straightforward. Development of the knowledge base can continue in an expert system shell that may offer advantages of speed, specialized development and debugging facilities, and inexpensive hardware.

FUTURE DIRECTIONS

We intend to build a knowledge-acquisition environment that includes specific domain knowledge for specialized application areas and can acquire knowledge for synthetic problems, combining features from other knowledge acquisition tools such as MDIS (Antonelli, 1983), DSPL (Brown, 1984), MORE (Kahn, Nowlan & McDermott, 1985), MOLE (Eshelman, Ehert, McDermott & Tan, in press), and TKAW (Kahn, Breaux, Joeseph & De Klerk, in press).

Presently Aquinas works best on those problems whose solutions can be comfortably enumerated (*analytic* or *structured selection* problems such as classification or diagnosis) as opposed to problems whose solutions are built up from components (*synthetic* or *constructive* problems such as configuration or planning).

Simple classification can be thought of as a single-decision problem (handled by ETS). Complex structured selection problems may require a set of linked data abstraction/solution refinement decisions (Aquinas). The next step may be to generalize this process to acquire and represent knowledge for planning, configuration, and design problems where the order of linked decisions in solution hierarchies may represent precedence of events or goals rather than just solution refinement. In these problems hierarchies may be assembled at consultation time rather than constructed totally in advance as they are currently. Grid cells might sometimes contain an arbitrary computation rather than a rating. These would include results of functions (such as found in spreadsheets) or data base retrievals. Deeper models of the structure and function of physical systems could be modeled.

An important step in expanding the knowledge-acquisition workbench concept is the linking together of other specialized tools. At the Boeing Knowledge Systems Laboratory we are investigating ways of integrating diverse knowledge representations from different laboratory projects so that this may be more easily accomplished. In the domain of knowledge acquisition, we feel that the approach used in SALT (Marcus, McDermott & Wang, 1985; Marcus & McDermott, in press; Marcus, in press) is particularly promising. SALT is a system that interviews experts to build knowledge bases for certain types of constructive problems (its first use was to configure elevators). We are also interested in generating knowledge sources for BBB, a blackboard system that has been successfully applied to a variety of problems (Benda, Baum, Dodhiawala & Jagannathan, 1986).

Development of the Aquinas workbench will continue in an incremental fashion. Techniques will be continuously integrated and refined to build an increasingly more effective knowledge-acquisition environment.

Thanks to Roger Beeman, Miroslav Benda, Kathleen Bradshaw, William Clancey, Brian Gaines, Cathy Kitto, Ted Kitzmiller, Art Nagai, Doug Schuler, Mildred Shaw, David Shema, Lisle Tinglof-Boose, and Bruce Wilson for their contributions and support. Aquinas was developed at the Knowledge Systems Laboratory, Advanced Technology Center, Boeing Computer Services in Seattle, Washington.

References

ADAMS, J. (1985). Probabilistic reasoning and certainty factors. In BUCHANAN, B. & SHORTLIFFE, E., Eds, *Rule-Based Expert Systems. the MYCIN Experiments of the Standford Heuristic Programming Project*, Reading. Massachusetts: Addison–Wesley.

ALPERT, M. & RAIFFA, H. (1982). A progress report on the training of probability assessors. In KAHNEMAN, D., SLOVIC, P. & TVERSKY, A. Eds, *Judgment under Uncertainty: Heuristics and Biases*, New York: Cambridge University Press.

ANTONELLI, D. (1983). The application of artificial intelligence to a maintenance and diagnostic information system (MDIS). *Proceedings of the Joint Services Workshop on Artificial Intelligence in Maintenance*, Boulder, Colorado.

BENDA, M., BAUM, L. S., DODHIAWALA, R. T. & JAGANNATHAN, V. (1986). Boeing blackboard system. *Proceedings of the High-Level Tools Workshop*, Ohio State University, October 1986.

BENDA, M., JAGANNATHAN, V. & DODHIAWALA, R., On optimal cooperation of knowledge sources. *Workshop on Distributed Artificial Intelligence*, Gloucester, Massachusetts.

BEYTH-MAROM, R. & DEKEL, S. (1985). *An Elementary Approach to Thinking under Uncertainty*. London: Lawrence Erlbaum Associates.

BOOSE, J. H. (1984). Personal construct theory and the transfer of human expertise. *Proceedings of the National Conference on Artificial Intelligence,* Austin, Texas.

BOOSE, J. H. (1985). A knowledge acquisition program for expert systems based on personal construct psychology. *International Journal of Man–Machine Studies,* **23,** 495–525.

BOOSE, J. H. (1986). *Expertise Transfer for Expert System Design.* New York: Elsevier.

BOOSE, J. H. (1987). Rapid acquisition and combination of knowledge from multiple experts in the same domain. *Future Computing Systems Journal* In press.

BROWN, D. E. (1984). Expert systems for design problem-solving using design refinement with plan selection and redesign. Ph.D. Thesis, Ohio State University, CIS Department, Columbus, Ohio.

BYLANDER, T. & CHANDRASEKARAN, B. (1987). Generic tasks in knowledge-based reasoning: the "Right," level of abstraction for knowledge acquisition. *International Journal of Man–Machine Studies.* In press.

BYLANDER, T. & MITTAL, S. (1986). CSRL: a language for classificatory problem solving and uncertainty handling. *AI Magazine,* August.

CHANDRASEKARAN, B. (1986). Generic tasks in knowledge-based reasoning: high-level building blocks for expert system design. *IEEE Expert,* Fall.

CHEESEMAN, P. (1985). In defense of probability. *Proceedings of the Ninth International Joint Conference on Artificial Intelligence,* Los Angeles, California.

CLANCEY, W. (1986). Heuristic classification In KOWALIK, J. Ed., *Knowledge-Based Problem-Solving.* New York: Prentice–Hall.

COOMBS, C. H., DAWES, R. M. & TVERSKY, A. (1970). *Mathematical Psychology.* Englewood Cliffs, New Jersey: Prentice–Hall.

ESHELMAN, L. EHRET, D., MCDERMOTT, J. & TAN, M. (1987). MOLE: a tenacious knowledge-acquisition tool *International Journal of Man–Machine Studies.* In press.

GAINES, B. R. (1987). An overview of knowledge acquisition and transfer. *International Journal of Man–Machine Studies.* In press.

GAINES, B. R. & SHAW, M. L. G. (1987). New directions in the analysis and interactive elicitation of personal construct systems. In SHAW, M. L. G. Ed., *Recent Advances in Personal Construct Technology.* New York: Academic Press.

GAINES, B. R. & SHAW, M. L. G. (1985). Induction of inference rules for expert systems. *Fuzzy Sets and Systems.*

GORDON, J. & SHORTLIFFE, E. (1985). The Dempster–Shafer theory of evidence. In BUCHANAN, B. & SHORTLIFFE, E. Eds, *Rule-Based Expert Systems: the MYCIN Experiments of the Stanford Heuristic Programming Project.* Reading, Masachusetts: Addison–Wesley.

GRUBER, T. & COHEN, P. (1987). Design for acquisition principles of knowledge system design to facilitate knowledge acquisition. *International Journal of Man–Machine Studies.* In press.

HENRION, M. (1986). Propagating uncertainty by logic sampling in Bayes' networks. *Proceedings of the Second Workshop on Uncertainty in Artificial Intelligence,* Philadelphia, Pennsylvania.

HINKLE, D. N. (1965). The change of personal constructs from the viewpoint of a theory of implications. *Ph. D. Thesis,* Ohio State University, Ohio.

HOWARD, R. A. & MATHESON, J. E. (1984). Influence diagrams. In HOWARD, R. A. & MATHESON, J. E. Eds, *Readings on the Principles and Applications of Decision Analysis,* Menlo Park, California: Strategic Decisions Group.

HURLEY, R. (1983). *Decisions Tables in Software Engineering,* New York: Van Nostrand Reinhold.

KAHN, G., NOWLAN, S. & MCDERMOTT, J. (1985). MORE: an intelligent knowledge acquisition tool. *Proceedings of the Ninth Joint Conference on Artificial Intelligence,* Los Angeles, California.

KAHN, G. S., BREAUX, E. H., JOESEPH, R. L. & DEKLERK, P. (1987). An intelligent mixed-initiative workbench for knowledge acquisition. *International Journal of Man–Machine Studies.* In press.

KELLY, G. A. (1955). *The Psychology of Personal Constructs,* New York: Norton.

KITTO, C. & BOOSE, J. H. (1987). Heuristics for expertise transfer: the automatic management of complex knowledge-acquisition dialogs. *International Journal of Man–Machine Studies*. in press.

LENAT, D. (1983*a*). The nature of heuristics. *Artificial Intelligence,* **19,**

LENAT, D. (1983*b*). The nature of heuristics. *Artificial Intelligence,* **21.**

LENAT, D., PRAKASH, M. & SHEPARD, M. (1986). CYC: using common sense knowledge to overcome brittleness and knowledge acquisition bottlenecks. *AI Magazine,* **6.**

LIEBERMAN, H. (1986). Using prototypical objects to implement shared behavior in object-oriented systems. *Proceedings of the Object-Oriented Programming Systems, Languages, and Applications Workshop,* Portland, Oregon

MARCUS, S., MCDERMOTT, J. & WANG, T. (1985). Knowledge acquisition for constructive systems. *Proceedings of the Ninth Joint Conference on Artificial Intelligence,* Los Angeles, California.

MARCUS, S. & MCDERMOTT, J. (1987). SALT: a knowledge acquisition tool for propose-and-revise systems. *Carnegie–Mellon University Department of Computer Science technical report.* In press.

MARCUS, S. (1987). Taking backtracking with a grain of SALT. *International Journal of Man–Machine Studies.* In press.

MCDERMOTT, J. (1986). Making expert systems explicit. *Proceedings of the IFIP Congress,* Dublin, Ireland.

MICHALSKI, R. S. (1978). *Designing Extended Entry Decision Tables and Optimal Decision Trees Using Decision Diagrams.* Urbana, Illinois: Intelligent Systems Group, Artificial Intelligence Laboratory, Department of Computer Science, University of Illinois.

MICHALSKI, R. S. & WINSTON, P. (1985). Variable precision logic. *MIT AI Memo,* Artificial Intelligence Laboratory, Masachusetts Institute of Technology, 857.

MICHALSKI, R. S., *Machine Learning.* Plenary talk at the *AAAI Knowledge Acquisition for Knowledge-Based Systems Workshop,* Banff, Canada, November, 1986.

MITTAL, S., BOBROW, D. & KAHN, K. (1986). Virtual copies: at the boundary between classes and instances. *Proceedings of the Object-Oriented Programming Systems, Languages, and Applications Workshop,* Portland, Oregon.

PEARL, J. (1986). Fusion, propagation and structuring in belief networks. *Technical report CSD-850022, R-42-VI-12,* Cognitive systems Laboratory, Computer Science Department, University of California, Los Angeles, California.

QUINLAN, J. R. (1983). Learning efficient classification procedures and their application to chess end games. In MICHALSKI, R. S., CARBONELL, J. G. & MITCHELL, T. M. Eds, *Machine Learning—An Artificial Intelligence Approach,* Vol. 1. Tioga: Palo Alto, California.

REBOH, R. & RISCH, T. (1986). SYNTEL: knowledge programming using functional representations. *Proceedings of National Conference on Artificial Intelligence (AAAI-86),* Philadelphia, Pennsylvania.

REBOH, R., RISCH, T., HART, P. E. & DUDA, R. O. (1986). Task-specific knowledge representation: a case study. *Proceedings of the High-Level Tools Workshop,* Ohio State University.

SAATY, T. L. (1980). *The Analytic Hierarchy Process.* New York: McGraw–Hill.

SHAFER, G. (1976). *A Mathematical Theory of Evidence.* Princeton: University Press.

SHAFER, G. & TVERSKY, A. (1985). Languages and designs for probability judgment. *Cognitive Science,* **9,** 309–339.

SHASTRI, L. & FELDMAN, J. (1985). Evidential reasoning in semantic networks: a formal theory. *Proceedings of the Ninth International Joint Conference on Artificial Intelligence,* Los Angeles, California.

SHAW, M. L. G. & GAINES, B. R. (1987*a*). PLANET: a computer-based system for personal learning, analysis, negotiation and elicitation techniques. In MANCUSO, J. C. & SHAW, M. L. G. Eds, *Cognition and Personal Structure: computer Access and Analysis.* Praeger Press. In press.

SHAW, M. L. G. & GAINES, B. R. (1987*b*). Techniques for knowledge acquisition and transfer. *International Journal of Man–Machine Studies.* In press.

SPETZLER, C. & STAL VON HOLSTEIN, C. (1983). Probability encoding in decision analysis. In HOWARD, R. & MATHESON, J. Eds, *Readings on the Principles and Applications of Decision Analysis,* Vol. 2. Palo Alto, California: Strategic Decisions Group.

SPIEGELHALTER, D. J. (1986). Probabilistic reasoning in predictive expert systems. In KANAL, L. N. & LEMMER, J. Eds, *Uncertainty in Artificial Intelligence.* Amsterdam: North-Holland.

SZOLOVITZ, P. & PAUKER, S. (1978). Categorical and probabilistic reasoning in medical diagnosis. *Artificial Intelligence,* **11,**

WALLSTEN, T. & BUDESCU, D. (1983). Encoding subject probabilities: a psychological and psychometric review. *Management Science,* **29**.

WILKINS, D. C. (1987) Knowledge base debugging using apprenticeship learning techniques. *International Journal of Man–Machine Studies.* In press.

The application of psychological scaling techniques to knowledge elicitation for knowledge-based systems

NANCY M. COOKE† AND JAMES E. MCDONALD
Computing Research Laboratory and Department of Psychology, New Mexico State University, Las Cruces, NM 88003 U.S.A.

A formal knowledge-elicitation methodology that incorporates psychological scaling techniques to produce empirically derived knowledge representations is discussed. The methodology has been successfully applied in several domains and overcomes many of the difficulties of traditional knowledge-elicitation techniques. Research issues pertaining to the use of scaling techniques as knowledge-elicitation tools are outlined and a particular issue, the elicitation of levels of abstraction in knowledge representations, is discussed in detail. Results from a study on the elicitation of knowledge about levels of abstraction for a set of Unix commands from experienced Unix users indicated that the representations obtained using this methodology can be used to obtain more abstract (i.e. categorical) representations of that knowledge.

Introduction

Currently, the process of eliciting knowledge from human experts for the purpose of transferring this knowledge to an expert, or knowledge-based, system suffers from numerous problems. Not only is the process time consuming and tedious, but the weak methods often used (i.e. interviews and protocol analysis) are inadequate for eliciting tacit knowledge and may, in fact, lead to inaccuracies in the knowledge base. Much expert knowledge is not available to conscious introspection (i.e. it is automatic or compiled) and consequently, experts may give erroneous or incomplete accounts of their knowledge (Nisbett & Wilson, 1977). Indeed, Ericsson and Simon (1984) contend that information must be in the focus of attention (i.e. short-term memory) in order to be verbalized. One approach to these problems has been to formalize interview and protocol analysis techniques (e.g. Ericsson & Simon, 1984; Hoffman, in press; Johnson, Zualkernan & Garber, 1987). Alternatively, several investigators have suggested that psychological scaling techniques, such as cluster analysis and multidimensional scaling, be used as a means of eliciting knowledge from domain experts for the purpose of building expert systems (Butler & Corter, 1986; Cooke & McDonald, 1986; Gammack & Young, 1985). It is generally believed that these techniques are more objective and formal than traditional knowledge-elicitation methods.

We (Cooke & McDonald, 1986) have proposed the development of a tool kit of scaling techniques that could be used to elicit and represent core components of knowledge from an expert or group of experts. The core knowledge-base would consist of basic concepts, relations, facts, rules, and procedures that are at the heart of the domain and could be used to either guide subsequent knowledge elicitation (i.e. interviews, protocol analysis, or more scaling techniques) or act as a starting

---

† Requests for reprints should be sent to Nancy M. Cooke, Department of Psychology, Rice University, P.O. Box 1892, Houston, Texas 77251.

65

KNOWLEDGE-BASED SYSTEMS Vol. 2
ISBN 0-12-115920-5

point for an automated system which continually refined the knowledge-base.† In the following sections we discuss some of the scaling techniques comprising the tool kit.

Scaling techniques

There are several psychological scaling techniques that produce structural representations of knowledge based on human judgments. All of the scaling techniques discussed here require as input a matrix of distance estimates for all pairs of items in a set to be scaled. The techniques differ largely in the types of structural representations they produce. For instance, multidimensional scaling procedures (e.g. Kruskal, 1977; Kruskal & Wish, 1978; Shepard, 1962a,b) generate spatial representations in which concepts are located in an n-dimensional space, where each dimension might represent a particular feature (e.g. size, ferocity, predacity). Alternatively, hierarchical cluster analyses (e.g. Johnson, 1967) produce taxonomic representations. Whereas hierarchical representations might be adequate for representing some types of knowledge, they are inadequate for representing knowledge that is not strictly hierarchical in nature. Recently, a network scaling technique (Pathfinder: Schvaneveldt & Durso, 1981; Schvaneveldt, Durso & Dearholt, 1985) has been developed that produces graphs which are constrained to hierarchical relationships.

MULTIDIMENSIONAL SCALING

Multidimensional scaling (MDS) is an elaborate least-squares fitting technique. Most MDS programs require that the user input a symmetrical distance matrix and specify the number of dimensions to which the data should be fit. The algorithm then attempts to fit the data to the specified number of dimensions by minimizing the amount of "stress", or deviation from the optimal fit, in an iterative fashion. There are several types of MDS analyses available, the most common variables being whether they are metric or non-metric (i.e. whether they assume interval or ordinal data) and weighted or non-weighted (i.e. whether individual subject matrices are considered or only a single composite matrix). In general, non-metric techniques are to be preferred to metric, since it is often difficult to insure that the data have interval properties. Also weighted techniques are more robust than non-weighted (i.e. they tend to reduce the problems associated with local minima and are claimed to be nonrotatable). The MDS solution consists of a set of dimensionless points (one for each item in the set) in an n-dimensional space. While the relative positions of

---

† We believe that it is important to distinguish *knowledge elicitation* (the topic of this paper) from *knowledge acquisition*. The latter term is quite general, often ambiguous, and includes knowledge-elicitation techniques, as well as machine learning approaches. The machine learning approach is one possible solution to the problem of acquiring knowledge for knowledge-based systems. An alternative solution is to improve upon the techniques available for extracting knowledge from human experts. We use the term *knowledge elicitation* to refer to this approach. We feel that the two approaches complement each other in many ways. Knowledge elicitation techniques could be used to produce the core knowledge-base and machine learning techniques could be used to augment and refine this core knowledge. In fact, one can think of knowledge elicitation as a special case of learning, i.e. learning by being told.

items can be considered optimal, the orientation of the space itself is arbitrary (i.e. it is rotatable). Thus, it is often difficult to identify the dimensions (if they are in fact meaningful) or to determine the correct number of dimensions to use.

CLUSTER ANALYSIS

There are numerous clustering techniques (e.g. hierarchical, overlapping, disjoint), but hierarchical clustering schemes (HCS) are the most common. Furthermore, there are several HCSs, the most common being the minimum (connected) and maximum (diameter) methods. HCS is conceptually simple and consists of repetitively combining the two closest objects in the data matrix into a single cluster. Once formed, distances to this new cluster must be computed and can either be the minimum or maximum of the distances from each of the objects (the average is also occasionally used). The output of the HCS is a "tree" with connections between items and clusters at various levels. The number of clusters ranges from n (each item is a separate cluster) to 1 (all items in a single cluster). One of the difficulties in employing HCS for knowledge representation is deciding on an appropriate cutoff level, that is, when to stop grouping items together. Unfortunately, this decision must be left to experimenter judgment.

PATHFINDER

The networks generated by Pathfinder consist of nodes representing concepts (or objects or actions), and links between some pairs of nodes, representing relationships between those concepts. Pathfinder, like other scaling techniques, requires estimates of relatedness or distance for all possible pairs of concepts in a set. Basically, the Pathfinder algorithm determines whether or not a link will be present between each pair of concepts. Links are assigned weights (distances in the data matrix) corresponding to their strength. A link is added if the minimum distance between the concepts based on all existing paths (chains of one or more links) is greater than the distance estimate for that pair.

Pathfinder allows for systematic variation in the complexity (number of links) of the resulting networks as parameters of the method are varied (i.e. r and q). The parameter r is based on the Minkowski r-metric. Its value can range from 1 to ∞ and determines how path length is computed. While continuously variable, simple interpretations exist only for r equal to 1 (all links in the path are added), 2 (the Euclidean distance is computed), and ∞ (the longest link in the path is computed). The q parameter determines the maximum number of links that can be included in a path. When $r = \infty$ and $q = n - 1$ the network is minimally connected and the data are assumed to be ordinal. For these reasons, $r = \infty$, $q = n - 1$ are generally the preferred values for these parameters. Regardless of the values specified for r and q, the resulting network solution is inherently *not* dimensional and is difficult to represent graphically. While nodes and connecting links are specified, no real limitations are placed on the location of nodes in the n-dimensional space. Further, links are at most weighted arcs, since no information about the meaning of links is supplied as part of the analysis.

APPLICATIONS OF SCALING TECHNIQUES

In general, scaling techniques such as those described above have been used in cognitive psychology to study the organization of concepts in memory (e.g. Rips, Shoben & Smith, 1973; Shoben, 1983). Cooke, Durso, and Schvaneveldt (1986) found that lists of words organized according to either the Pathfinder or multidimensional scaling representations of those concepts were easier to learn that unorganized lists. Further, they found that a list organized according to the Pathfinder representation was easier to learn than a list organized according to the multidimensional scaling representation. These results provided evidence for the psychological validity of scaling representations in that the representations were predictive of learning time.

Scaling techniques have also been used to investigate cognitive structures underlying human expertise in domains such as air-to-air flight maneuvers (Schvaneveldt, Durso, Goldsmith, Breen, Cooke, Tucker & DeMaio, 1985) and computer programming (Cooke and Schvaneveldt, 1986). Information gained from such studies can be applied to design, training, and selection problems. For example, Cooke and Schvaneveldt (1986) had expert, intermediate, novice, and naive computer programmers judge the relatedness of all possible pairs of a set of abstract programming concepts (e.g. *algorithm, global variable, debug*). These data were used to empirically derive Pathfinder network representations of programmer knowledge of these concepts. In Figs 1 and 2 the average naive- and expert-programmer network representations are displayed. Results indicated that the representations varied depending on programming experience and that the changes were systematic with expertise, providing evidence for evolution of the structures. The networks also revealed some critical associations of expert programmers and some misconceptions of naive programmers.

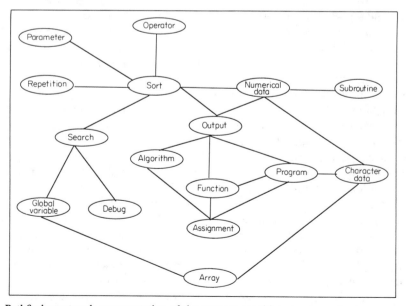

FIG. 1. Pathfinder network representation of the average cognitive structure of naive programmers.

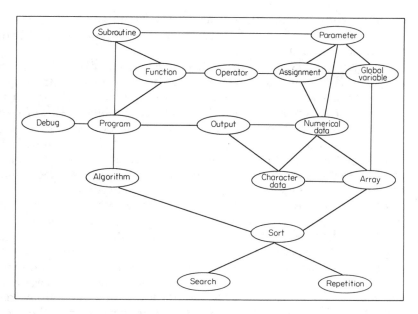

FIG. 2. Pathfinder network representation of the average cognitive structure of expert programmers.

In addition, scaling techniques have been applied to the design of the human–computer interface (McDonald, Dayton & McDonald, 1987; McDonald, Dearholt, Paap & Schvaneveldt, 1986; McDonald, Stone, Liebelt & Karat, 1982; Roske-Hofstrand & Paap, 1986b; Tullis, 1985). McDonald *et al.* (1986) have proposed a formal interface design methodology based on user knowledge. One of the applications they discussed involved the development of an indexing aid for the Unix on-line documentation system (the "man" system). Their approach was to derive a model of the Unix operating system empirically from experienced users of the system, then to base the design of the index on this model. During the model-building phase of their study, McDonald *et al.* (1986) first used a sorting methodology to obtain estimates of distance for approximately 200 basic Unix commands (section 1 of the man system) from 15 experienced Unix users. They then performed Pathfinder and cluster analyses on the obtained proximity matrix. These analyses formed a base-level Unix user's model. Some of the specific results of this study are summarized later in this paper.

ADVANTAGES OF SCALING TECHNIQUES AS KNOWLEDGE-ELICITATION TOOLS

As previously mentioned, scaling techniques can overcome many of the criticisms of knowledge elicitation techniques such as interviews and protocol analysis. In addition to facilitating knowledge elicitation, scaling techniques provide information concerning the structure of knowledge that might serve as a basis for representing that knowledge in the system. For example, the organization inherent in the scaling representation might suggest an organization of a set of production rules that would facilitate search. More generally, we believe that our knowledge elicitation methodology will allow the development of empirically derived knowledge-bases in which the information elicited determines the content and architecture of the system, as opposed to the traditional approach in which the elicitation of knowledge is guided by an existing or proposed system architecture.

Traditionally, knowledge-elicitation methodologies have involved interviews with one or more experts. The use of multiple experts tends to increase the opportunity for conflicts in the knowledge-base, which might simply be a reflection of the fact that there are several different, yet correct, solutions to problems. However, it is not clear how idiosyncrasies among different experts should be coded in a knowledge base. One advantage to the use of scaling techniques is that they can be applied to group, as well as individual data. The resulting group solution can be thought of as a prototypical representation of expert knowledge. Thus, scaling techniques also provide a means of combining knowledge from multiple experts.

In summary, the scaling approach to knowledge elicitation has a number of advantages over traditional knowledge-elicitation techniques. Psychological scaling techniques require less introspection on the part of the expert than traditional interviews in which the expert is asked: "tell me what you know and how you know it". Scaling techniques require experts to make judgments rather to introspect and verbalize about how they do what they do. Ericsson and Simon (1984) have noted that appropriate cues are necessary in order to retrieve knowledge from long-term memory. Consequently, some of the problems of verbal reports might be avoided by providing experts with specific cues in the form of the concept set. Scaling techniques also offer a more formal, as well as more objective, means of eliciting knowledge than traditional techniques. Scaling solutions are standard, in the sense that given a set of distance estimates and a specific scaling technique two different researchers/knowledge engineers will independently produce identical representations. On the other hand, the same two individuals may have radically different interpretations of the same protocol. Finally, the scaling approach can handle, and is in fact well-suited to, elicitation of knowledge from multiple experts.

Research issues concerning the use of scaling techniques as knowledge-elicitation tools

Whereas there are many foreseeable advantages to using scaling techniques for knowledge elicitation, the application to this particular domain raises several methodological issues. In general, the scaling techniques themselves are well specified, but there are other aspects of the methodology as a whole (e.g. method of data collection) that require investigation. Thus, the issues outlined in this section are aimed at formalizing the methodology from start to finish. By formalizing all aspects of the methodology, its application will be simplified and subject to less interpretation on the part of the researcher/knowledge engineer.† Recently, there have been several studies conducted that addressed one or more of the research issues. In fact, the development of a knowledge-elicitation tool kit can be thought of as a series of studies designed to answer questions and solve problems related to the application of scaling techniques to knowledge elicitation. In the following sections

---

† It should be pointed out that many of these issues are relevant for other applications as well (e.g. interface design and studies investigating expertise).

the major issues are presented, along with a brief summary of research directed at each particular issue. The issues are organized according to the three major phases involved in scaling analysis: (1) data collection; (2) scaling; and (3) interpretation. It should be emphasized that the fact that clearly delineated phases and research issues can be identified attests to the formal qualities already present in this approach.

DATA COLLECTION

All of the scaling techniques discussed require as input a matrix of distance estimates for all pairs of items to be scaled. It is assumed that a relatedness estimate for a pair of items is indicative of the distance between the corresponding concepts in memory. According to the distance metaphor of memory, concepts that are semantically related are closer in memory than concepts that are less related. The scaling solutions all represent the notion of distance in different ways. Two concepts that are judged to be highly related will generally be close in the spatial solution of MDS, appear in the same cluster in cluster analysis, or be joined by a link in a Pathfinder network. The four issues that follow have to do with the collection of distance estimates for a set of items.

Obtaining a set of items to be scaled
The first step in the data-collection phase of these techniques involves the selection of a set of items (concepts, objects, actions) to be represented. It is usually appropriate to limit the number of items in the set in order to simplify data collection and interpretation of the resulting solution. Therefore, it is important to avoid including items that are irrelevant to the domain and at the same time attempt to capture all (or at least most) of the critical items of a domain. Unfortunately, no satisfactory techniques exist for identifying the important items in a domain or for selecting a subset of the important items once they have been identified. In some cases a pre-defined set of items exists (e.g. the set of all Unix commands), however, the set may be inappropriate. For instance, McDonald *et al.* (1986) found in their study of the Unix system that only 44 of the 219 commands in the set were known by all of the experienced users. In addition, event records of command usage collected from experienced Unix users indicated that out of 235 different commands used, only 112 were from the original set of 219. Typically, researchers select a set of items based on their intuitions about the domain or the intuitions of a domain expert. Because it is often difficult to introspect and to verbally express mental processes (Nisbett & Wilson, 1977), this set of intuitively derived items may be incomplete or inappropriate.

Research has been conducted on various methods for eliciting domain-related information from experts (Cooke & McDonald, 1986). The goal of this work was to develop a methodology for identifying the core set of ideas in a particular domain. It should be noted that this goal differs from the general goal of knowledge elicitation in which not only ideas are needed, but also relations, rules, and facts connecting the ideas. Cooke and McDonald (1986) investigated four idea elicitation tasks that were given to domain experts: (1) listing critical domain concepts; (2) listing steps involved in a domain-related task; (3) listing chapter titles and subtitles for a hypothetical book on the domain; and (4) extracting critical ideas from an interview with an expert. Results indicated that the four methods differed in terms of the number of ideas that were generated as well as the types of knowledge (concepts, facts, general rules) generated. Interestingly, less that ten percent of the ideas took the form of "if-then" rules, suggesting that knowledge (at least in this domain) is not naturally conveyed in this form.

Contextual effects

The selection of an appropriate set of items is important for several reasons. An obvious ramification of selecting an incorrect or incomplete set of concepts is a resulting knowledge representation that is also incorrect or incomplete. However, there is another not-so-obvious reason that the set of items plays an important role. The distance estimates supplied by the subjects are affected by the context or frame supplied by the rating environment (Tversky, 1977; Murphy & Medin, 1985). Murphy and Medin (1985) have argued that theories underly similarity judgments and that different theories are appropriate in different contexts. Consequently, context changes, such as subtle differences in instructions, can affect relatedness judgments. For example, Murphy and Medin (1985) suggested that judgments of relatedness between concepts such as *children, jewelry,* and *photograph albums* would change given the context of a burning house. Like instructions, the specific concepts that make up the concept set provide a context for relatedness judgments. For example, *penguin* is very similar to *bird* when the other concepts are types of vegetables, but not so similar when the other concepts are types of birds. Therefore, the particular concepts chosen to make up the concept set have nontrivial consequences for the outcome of the psychological scaling representations. Research is being conducted that investigates the effects of different contexts on the scaling representation of a set of items (Roske-Hofstrand & Paap, 1986a). Results thus far have indicated that relatedness estimates are indeed affected by the addition or deletion of items in a given set.

Methods of collecting distance estimates

Distance estimates between all possible pairs of items can take the form of a matrix in which the rows and columns designate specific items in the set. Such matrices may be symmetrical (i.e. the distance from A to B is equal to the distance from B to A) or asymmetrical (i.e. the distance from A to B is not equal to the distance from B to A), although none of the current scaling techniques except Pathfinder make use of this information.

Distance estimates can be obtained through paired comparisons, sorting, listing, event record analysis, and the repertory grid technique. In the paired-comparison task judges are required to rate the relatedness or similarity of all $n(n-1)/2$ pairs of items. Distance estimates are computed as the inverse of the relatedness ratings. Theoretically, asymmetrical distances can be obtained using this technique, but it is a time consuming task—extremely so for large sets of items.

Sorting entails having judges sort items into piles based on shared relationships. For a group of judges, distance estimates are the inverse of the frequency with which pairs of items are placed in the same pile. This technique is considerably less time consuming than the method of paired comparison.

Distance estimates can be obtained from lists of relevant domain concepts by computing the conditional probability that one item follows another in the lists.

However, this technique does not insure that estimates of distance for all items of interest are obtained. Alternative methods for computing distance from lists are available, for instance, number of intervening items in the list. Similar techniques can be applied to event records where the lists consist of actions recorded as experts perform domain-related tasks.

Estimates of distance can also be obtained using the repertory grid technique which has its roots in personal construct theory (Kelly, 1955). Elements are rated according to various bipolar constructs or dimensions. The distance between two elements can be obtained by computing the distance between the two corresponding rating vectors (Hart, 1986). The main disadvantage of the repertory grid approach is that the relevant constructs, as well as the elements must be known. However, if the constructs are known, then the technique offers a solution to the "effect of instructions" problem discussed below. It should be noted that the repertory grid technique (often in combination with cluster analysis) has been applied by several researchers to the knowledge-elicitation problem (Boose & Bradshaw, in press; Shaw, 1984).

Research is needed that compares these various data collection methods in terms of the distance estimates that they produce. Representations may differ depending on the method used to obtain the distance estimates. The advantages and disadvantages of each method need to be addressed explicitly and the appropriate applications for a given method should be identified. As a preliminary step toward resolving this issue, Roske-Hofstrand and Paap (1986a) have compared scaling representations derived for the same set of items using either the paired-comparison method or the sorting method.

The effect of instructions
Concepts can be related along a variety of dimensions (e.g. *apple–fire truck, bird–robin, hamburger–french fries, pen–type writer*) and as a result, it is difficult to decide what instructions should be given to the judges concerning relatedness. Typically, general "relatedness" instructions have been given under the assumption that judges will choose the most relevant dimensions on which to compare the items. We have observed, however, that this lack of guidance can lead to difficulties when the data are scaled (e.g. uninterpretable dimensions using MDS) or even later when the results of the scaling analysis are applied. For example, if raters are asked to judge the relatedness of a set of editor functions that occur together in task sequences (e.g. *find* and *change* might be frequently used together) and that also have featural similarities (e.g. *insert* and *delete* might require similar command sequences), then judges may use different dimensions for different pairs of functions, rather than weighing each pair on the same set of dimensions. McDonald, Dayton, and McDonald (1987) found that quite different scaling representations were obtained by giving instructions to either judge the similarity of items or to judge how well items go together. In general, the relatedness instructions should be carefully considered in the data collection phase of this methodology.

SCALING

As part of the process of deciding how the estimates of distance are to be obtained, the scaling analysis to be used should also be considered. These two stages (obtaining distance estimates and scaling) may interact, since certain data collection methodologies emphasize (or allow) certain characteristics of the data to emerge (such as hierarchical arrangement) while other methods do not. Furthermore, once a particular scaling technique has been selected, decisions must be made concerning the particular algorithm (e.g. maximum or minimum hierarchical cluster analysis) and/or parameters (e.g. q and r for Pathfinder) for that technique.

Selection of a scaling technique

We believe that multiple scaling techniques should be used in combination to elicit knowledge. Each of the techniques emphasizes different features in the data. For instance, Pathfinder captures information about local relations (pairs of items that are highly related), whereas multidimensional scaling captures information about global relations among the item set as a whole (i.e. dimensions). Furthermore, the techniques differ in terms of the type of representation (e.g. spatial, network, hierarchical) that they generate. A particular representation or combination of representations might be desirable for a particular application. Research is needed that compares the scaling techniques in terms of psychological validity and the type of knowledge elicited. Given this information, a mapping could be derived between features of specific domains and scaling techniques. In one study that investigated this issue, Cooke *et al.* (1986) compared the multidimensional scaling technique with the Pathfinder technique and found that Pathfinder was superior in terms of the elicitation of knowledge that was related to recall.

Selection of a particular solution

Given a particular scaling technique, the choice of parameters can greatly influence the resulting solution. There are several criteria that can be used to select a particular solution. A solution may be selected because it is an intuitively appealing representation of the domain. However, this criterion is subject to the same criticism as introspective techniques. A more objective approach is to select the solution that corresponds most closely to behavioral measures such as recall or categorization performance. The criterion that is most often used to choose among various solutions concerns "goodness of fit". The solution is selected that best fits the original data (i.e. distance estimates). Of course, the more parameters in the solution (e.g. links, dimensions) the better the fit, but because the general goal of this approach is to reduce the original set of data, it is desirable to select the solution in which fit is maximized while number of parameters is minimized. It should be noted that use of the fit criterion assumes that the original distance estimates accurately reflect knowledge. It could be that the best representation is one that least resembles the original ratings. Generally, the criteria are heuristics, not formal rules. Research is needed to make these notions more precise and to evaluate solutions resulting from varying parameters. In the Cooke *et al.* (1986) study, a comparison was also made among various multidimensional scaling representations and various network representations of the same data. Results indicated that some representations generated by the same general technique were better at predicting recall than representations with slightly different parameters.

INTERPRETATION OF THE SOLUTIONS

Once scaling solutions have been generated they must be mapped onto the particular application. For example, in the interface design application mapping can consist of taking the output of the scaling analysis selected and projecting it rather directly onto the organization of the interface. Even with this simple approach, there is ample room for interpretation. If hierarchical clustering is used, for example, there are numerous ways of emphasizing the inter- and intra-cluster relationships, ranging from a traditional dendrogram to a spatial arrangement of items (cf. McDonald, Stone & Liebelt, 1983). In the knowledge elicitation application, scaling solutions need to be mapped onto a knowledge base. This mapping can occur indirectly, by using the solutions to guide structured interviews which in turn generate information for the knowledge-base, or by transforming the solutions into a format compatible with a particular knowledge base architecture (e.g. production rules). The scaling solutions could also be directly mapped into the knowledge base of a system capable of interpreting it. In any case, the scaling solutions require some form of interpretation before they can be used by a knowledge-based system.

Because the interpretation process is not formalized, it is subject to numerous biases. Thus, the identification of dimensions in a multidimensional scaling analysis, a cluster level cutoff point in a hierarchical clustering solution, and link labels in a Pathfinder network are not specified by the scaling techniques, yet the interpretation of the resulting representation is highly dependent on this type of information. For example, Pathfinder networks only become semantic networks with the interpretation of links. Without link labels, caution must be exercised in interpreting and comparing links in the networks. In the knowledge engineering application, it is necessary to know not only *that* two concepts are related, but *how* they are related as well. In order to provide the Pathfinder network with semantics, the links must be interpreted or labeled. Cooke and McDonald (1986) have taken some preliminary steps towards a formal methodology for classifying and labeling links according to semantic relationships.

The identification of semantic relations or dimensions is one means of providing the scaling representations with semantics. Another is through the identification of levels of abstraction in these structures. In any domain there are some concepts that are superordinate categories of other concepts or that are simply more general than other concepts. Knowledge concerning levels of abstraction enables inferences to be drawn about concepts at one level of abstraction based on concepts at a higher (i.e. more general) level of abstraction. One could envision a multi-leveled scaling representation in which each successive level contained concepts that were increasingly abstract. In the study that follows, a technique is investigated for identifying abstract concepts or categories in a set of Unix commands.

We have suggested that scaling representations can be used as a starting point for further knowledge elicitation or machine learning approaches. On the other hand, it is possible that the scaling approach could eventually result in a complete knowledge base. If the representation is to be complete, however, a way of interpreting it is needed (Hayes, 1985). That is, even if the details of a representation (i.e. link labels, dimensions) are identified, it is still necessary to determine how to make use of the representation. The representations themselves are not capable of making inferences, answering questions, making decisions, or solving problems. For instance, a production system could be used to reason over facts in a semantic network knowledge-base (cf. Anderson, 1983). Some preliminary work has been done on reasoning over Pathfinder networks using principles of spreading activation in a connectionist fashion (R. W. Schvaneveldt, pers. comm.). This approach to interpretation eliminates the need for semantic link labels.

The elicitation of levels of abstraction

In the previous section several research issues were outlined along with some efforts toward resolving these issues. In this section we elaborate on the issue of levels of abstraction and discuss a study designed to build representations with multiple levels of abstraction.

As previously mentioned, scaling techniques require interpretation in order to apply them to many real-world situations. One potentially useful type of information not explicitly conveyed in scaling solutions concerns the differentiation among concepts according to levels of abstraction. For instance, Pathfinder networks are "flat" in the sense that relations between concepts at the same level (e.g. property relations such as *bird–feathers* or *robin–red*) and relations between concepts at different levels (e.g. superordinate relations such as *bird–robin* or *animal–bird*) are not distinguished. Whereas hierarchical clustering schemes do produce multilevel structures, the levels do not necessarily correspond to actual levels of abstraction due to possible error in the data and the fact that the resulting solution needs to be completely connected. In fact, hierarchical clustering schemes may generate a multileveled structure even when the concepts are all from the same level. In order to concretize these issues and provide necessary background for the subsequent study on abstraction, results from the McDonald *et al.* (1986) study on Unix commands are summarized below.

The purpose of the McDonald *et al.* (1986) study was to elicit knowledge about Unix commands from experienced users and to employ this knowledge in the development of an Interactive Documentation Guide for the Unix on-line documentation system. Each of 219 Unix commands was printed on an index card and 15 experienced Unix users were each asked to sort the cards based on the functions of the commands. Subjects also indicated whether or not they were familiar with the commands. A matrix of distance estimates was obtained by counting for each pair of commands the number of subjects that placed that pair in the same pile and subtracting this value from 16. A conditional probability matrix was then created by dividing each of these co-occurrence values by the smaller of the two frequencies (number of judges familiar with each item) for that pair. This procedure tends to reduce the relative distances between pairs in which one or both items are less common. Only 44 of the 219 commands were sorted by (and thus were familiar to) all 15 experienced Unix users. Of these, 37 commands were identified as "core" Unix commands by eliminating those commands which were not grouped with one

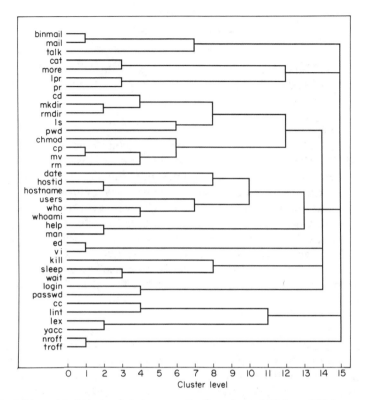

FIG. 3. A hierarchical cluster (maximum method) analysis of 37 "core" Unix commands.

or more of the other 43 commands by at least half of the raters. While scaling analyses were performed on the data from all 219 commands, for the sake of simplicity the hierarchical cluster analysis (maximum method) of the 37 core commands is shown in Fig. 3.

In Fig. 3 a cluster level of 1 indicates that all 15 experienced Unix users grouped the commands in that cluster. The higher the level, the fewer subjects who sorted the connected commands together. Even though there are 15 cluster levels, it is unlikely that there are 15 meaningful levels of abstraction for this set of commands. Thus it becomes important to distinguish between clusters that form because of categorical associations and clusters that form because of variability in the data. Additionally, the cluster analysis provides no information concerning the category labels for particular clusters. In fact, the nameability of each cluster might differentiate meaningful clusters from clusters that are artifacts. Clusters that are easily named are probably more meaningful than clusters that are not easily named. The purpose of the following study was to elicit information about levels of abstraction of the Unix commands from experienced Unix users in the form of "goodness of cluster" ratings and cluster names.

METHOD

Subjects
Four experienced Unix users from New Mexico State University voluntarily participated in this study. These subjects had also participated in the first Unix study.

Materials
Materials consisted of 83 clusters of two or more Unix commands taken from the original set of 219. The clusters were obtained as follows. A minimum cluster analysis was performed on the 152 commands that at least eight of the 15 experienced Unix users were familiar with. A cluster level cutoff value of 10 or more in this particular solution resulted in a total of 83 clusters (some of these were nested in that a small cluster may also be included in a larger cluster). Thus, the 83 clusters contained commands that at least half of the experienced Unix users were familiar with and that belonged together, that is, at least five judges felt that the items belonged with one of the other 151 commands. Because seven of the 152 commands did not cluster in the solution at the cluster level of ten, they did not appear at all in the 83 clusters.

Procedure
Each subject was seated in front of a CRT upon which each of the 83 clusters was randomly presented one at a time. For each cluster the subject was asked to respond by pressing the "0" key if there were one or more items in the cluster that were unfamiliar. If the subject responded with a "0" the next cluster was presented. Otherwise, the subject was asked to rate the "goodness" of the cluster by entering a rating of "1" through "5". A response of "1" indicated that the cluster was very bad and a response of "5" indicated that the cluster was very good. Following the rating, subjects were asked to assign a name to the cluster. After the cluster was named, the next cluster was presented. Trials continued in this fashion until all 83 clusters had been presented.

RESULTS AND DISCUSSION

In general, the four subjects tended to agree on goodness of category ratings for the 83 clusters (mean interjudge correlation—r (81) $= 0.97$, $p < 0.001$). Ratings of "0" through "5" occurred 4.2, 9.0, 7.2, 14.5, 22.0, and 43.1% of the time, respectively. Thus, the distribution of the ratings was skewed with the higher ratings of "4" or "5" occurring most frequently suggesting that the cluster analysis did indeed produce mostly meaningful categories.

For each of the clusters, the "goodness" ratings were averaged over the four subjects. In addition, if the subjects agreed on a name (or a significant part of a name) for a cluster then that name was assigned to the cluster. In many cases, names tended to migrate from smaller clusters to a larger superset cluster. That is, subjects often assigned the same name to a subset of commands as they did to the larger superset. In this case the smaller subset clusters were collapsed and the name was assigned to the superset cluster. The name migration criterion, along with

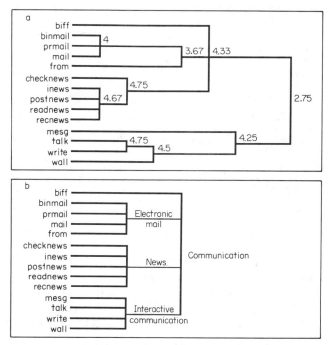

FIG. 4. Hierarchical cluster analysis (minimum method) with average judged "goodness" (a) and after reduction based on naming (b).

changes in the "goodness" rating allowed the elimination of many clusters resulting in a simpler, but more meaningful, representation. An example of this procedure for a subset of 14 of the 152 commands is presented in Fig. 4. In Fig. 4a the original cluster analysis (minimum method) for this subset is presented along with the average "goodness" ratings. In Fig. 4b the clusters are collapsed and labeled. It should be noted that for this particular subset, name migration was responsible for all of the collapsing since all of the clusters were judged to be quite good. That is, subjects labeled *talk* and *write* as *interactive communication* as well as *talk, write, wall* and *talk, write, wall, mesg*. Thus, in this example, information about category names, reduced the number of clusters from 10 to five.

There are, however, some anomalies in the resulting representation. For instance, the command *biff* (which informs the system whether or not you want to be notified when mail arrives during the current terminal session) does not cluster in the hierarchical cluster analysis with the other four electronic mail commands until later when it also clusters with the commands related to news. We are currently working on methods for extracting information about categories from Pathfinder network solutions. A Pathfinder representation of the same subset of commands is shown in Fig. 5. The three main categories are also apparent in this representation and can be identified by rich interconnections among items within the same category. We are in the process of quantifying such information so that it can be used to define category boundaries. Note that in this representation of the data, the *biff* command appears to be part of the mail commands.

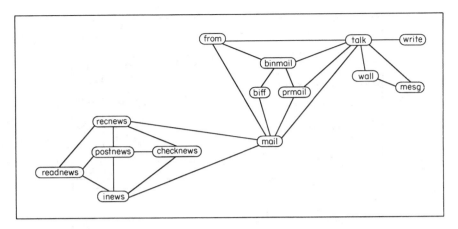

FIG. 5. Pathfinder solution for communication commands ($r = \infty$, $q = n - 1$).

These results suggest that information about levels of abstraction can be obtained as a second step in the representation process. Both naming and rating appear to provide information that aids in the identification of "real" categories. The resulting representation appears to be more complete as a characterization of experienced user knowledge.

Conclusions

We feel that the psychological scaling approach to knowledge elicitation has numerous advantages over traditional knowledge elicitation techniques, notably the formalization of the elicitation process. Results that have been obtained in other areas using this same approach have been quite promising. These techniques have been successful in the elicitation of knowledge from experts in domains such as computer programming, flight maneuvers, and the Unix operating system. However, there are several issues that should be addressed in order to refine this methodology so that it is most useful for knowledge elicitation.

A long-term goal of our research is to develop a system that embodies the knowledge-elicitation tool kit along with expertise concerning the appropriate use of the tools. Thus, this knowledge-elicitation expert system would be able to elicit a set of domain-related items, select an appropriate data collection methodology, choose appropriate scaling techniques, carry out the scaling, select a particular scaling solution, and interpret the resulting solution. The formalization of all aspects of this methodology is needed in order to develop such a system.

On the other hand, the application of this methodology is not at a stand-still until these issues are resolved. Indeed, it has already been applied to several problems and results have been encouraging. The resolution of the issues would serve to formalize many of the aspects of this methodology that are currently left to the judgment of the experimenter or knowledge engineer. At any rate, we believe that even in its current state, this methodology constitutes a more formal and objective approach to knowledge elicitation than other existing techniques.

The authors would like to acknowledge Donald Dearholt, Kenneth Paap, and Roger Schvaneveldt for their valuable contributions to this paper. Thanks also to the experienced Unix users who participated in the abstraction study.

The first author is now at Rice University. Requests for reprints should be sent to Nancy M. Cooke, Department of Psychology, Rice University, P.O. Box 1892, Houston, Texas, 77251.

References

ANDERSON, J. R. (1983). *The Architecture of Cognition*. Cambridge, MA: Harvard University Press.

BOOSE, J. H. & BRADSHAW, J. M. (1987). Expertise transfer and complex problems: Using AQUINAS as a knowledge acquisition workbench for expert systems, *International Journal of Man–Machine Studies*, **26**, 000–000.

BUTLER, K. A. & CORTER, J. E. (1986). The use of psychometric tools for knowledge acquisition: a case study. In GALE W. Ed., *Artificial Intelligence and Statistics*. Reading, MA: Addison–Wesley.

COOKE, N. M. & SCHVANELDT, R. W. (1986). The evolution of cognitive networks with computer programming experience. Paper presented at the *Workshop on Empirical Studies of Programmers*, 5–6 June 1986, Washington, D.C.

COOKE, N. M., DURSO, F. T. & SCHVANELDT, R. W. (1986). Recall and measures of memory organization. *Journal of Experimental Psychology: Learning, Memory, and Cognition*, **12**, 538–549.

COOKE, N. M. & McDONALD, J. E. (1986). A formal methodology for acquiring and representing expert knowledge. *IEEE Special Issue on Knowledge Representation*, **74**, 1422–1430.

ERICSSON, K. A. & SIMON, H. A. (1984). *Protocol Analysis: Verbal Reports as Data*. Cambridge, MA: MIT Press.

GAMMACK, J. G. & YOUNG, R. M. (1985). Psychological techniques for eliciting expert knowledge. In BRAMER, M. A. Ed., *Research and Development in Expert Systems*, pp. 105–112. London, UK: Cambridge University Press.

HART, A. (1986). *Knowledge Acquisition for Expert Systems*. New York: McGraw–Hill.

HAYES, P. J. (1985). Some problems and non-problems in representation theory. In BRACHMAN, R. J. & LEVESQUE H. J. Eds, *Readings in Knowledge Representation*, pp. 3–22. Los Altos, CA: Morgan Kaufmann.

HOFFMAN, R. R. (1987). The problem of extracting the knowledge of experts from the perspective of experimental psychology. *AI Magazine*, **26**, 000–000.

JOHNSON, P. E., ZUALKERNAN, I. & GARBER, S. (1987). Specification of expertise: knowledge acquisition for expert systems. *International Journal of Man–Machine Studies*, **26**, 000–000.

JOHNSON, S. C. (1967). Hierarchical clustering schemes. *Psychometrika*, **32**, 241–254.

KELLY, G. A. (1955). *The Psychology of Personal Constructs*. New York: Norton.

KRUSKAL, J. B. (1977). Multidimensional scaling and other methods for discovering structure. In ENSLEIN, RALSTON & WILF Eds, *Statistical Methods for Digital Computers*. New York: Wiley.

KRUSKAL, J. B. & WISH, M. (1978). Multidimensional Scaling. *Sage University Paper series on Quantitative Applications in the Social Sciences*, #07-011. London: Sage Publications.

McDONALD, J. E., DAYTON, J. T. & McDONALD, D. R. (1987). Adapting menu layout to tasks. *International Journal of Man–Machine Studies*. In press.

McDONALD, J. E., DEARHOLT, D. W., PAAP, K. & SCHVANELDT, R. W. (1986). A formal interface design methodology based on user knowledge. *Proceedings of Human Factors in Computer Systems, CHI '86*, pp. 285–290.

McDONALD, J. E., STONE, J. D., LIEBELT, L. S. & KARAT, J. (1982). Evaluating a method for structuring the user–system interface. *Proceedings of the 26th Annual Meeting of the Human Factors Society*.

McDONALD, J. E., STONE, J. D. & LIEBELT, L. S. (1983). Searching for items in menus: the effects of organization and type of target. *Proceedings of the 27th Annual Meeting of the Human Factors Society.*

MURPHY, G. L. & MEDIN, D. L. (1985). The role of theories in conceptual coherence. *Psychological Review,* **92,** 289–316.

NISBETT, R. E. & WILSON, T. D. (1977). Telling more than we can know: verbal reports on mental processes. *Psychological Review,* **8,** 231–259.

RIPS, L. J., SHOBEN, E. J. & SMITH, E. E. (1973). Semantic distance and the verification of semantic relations. *Journal of Verbal Learning and Verbal Behavior,* **12,** 1–20.

ROSKE-HOFSTRAND, R. J. & PAAP, K. R. (1986a). Cognitive JNDs: implications for scaling techniques. Paper presented at the *27th Annual Meeting of the Psychonomic Society,* New Orleans, November. 1986.

ROSKE-HOFSTRAND, R. J. & PAAP, K. R. (1986b). Cognitive networks as a guide to menu organization: An application in the automated cockpit. *Ergonomics,* **29,** 1301–1312.

SCHVANEVELDT, R. W. & DURSO, F. T. (1981). Generalized semantic networks. Paper presented at the *Meetings of the Psychonomic Society.*

SCHVANEVELDT, R. W., DURSO, F. T. & DEARHOLT, D. W. (1985). Pathfinder: scaling with Network Structures. *Memorandum in Computer and Cognitive Science, MCCS-85-9,* Computing Research Laboratory, New Mexico State University.

SCHVANEVELDT, R. W., DURSO, F. T., GOLDSMITH, T. E., BREEN, T. J., COOKE, N. M., TUCKER, R. G. & DeMAIO, J. C. (1985). Measuring the structure of expertise. *International Journal of Man–Machine Studies,* **23,** 699–728.

SHAW, M. L. G. (1984). Knowledge engineering for expert systems. *Interact 332.*

SHEPARD, R. N. (1962a). Analysis of proximities: multidimensional scaling with an unknown distance function. I. *Psychometrika,* **27,** 125–140.

SHEPARD, R. N. (1962b). Analysis of proximities: multidimensional scaling with an unknown distance function. II. *Psychometrika,* **27,** 219–246.

SHOBEN, E. J. (1983). Application of multidimensional scaling in cognitive psychology. *Applied Psychological Measurement,* **7,** 473–490.

TULLIS, T. S. (1985). Designing a menu-based interface to an operating system. *Proceedings of Human Factors in Computing Systems (CHI '85) Conference.*

TVERSKY, A. (1977). Features of similarity. *Psychological Review,* **84,** 327–352.

KRITON: a knowledge-acquisition tool for expert systems

Joachim Diederich, Ingo Ruhmann and Mark May

Research Division "Expert Systems", Institute for Applied Information Technology, German Research Institute for Mathematics and Data Processing, Schloß Birlinghoven, Postfach 1240, D-5205 Sankt Augustin 1, West Germany

A hybrid system for automatic knowledge acquisition for expert systems is presented. The system integrates artificial intelligence and cognitive science methods to construct knowledge bases employing different knowledge representation formalisms. For the elicitation of human declarative knowledge, the tool contains automated interview methods. The acquisition of human procedural knowledge is achieved by protocol analysis techniques. Textbook knowledge is captured by incremental text analysis. The goal structure of the knowledge elicitation methods is an *intermediate knowledge-representation language* on which frame, rule and constraint generators operate to build up the final knowledge bases. The intermediate knowledge representation level regulates and restricts the employment of the knowledge elicitation methods. Incomplete knowledge is laid open by pattern-directed invocation methods (the intermediate *knowledge base watcher*) triggering the elicitation methods to supplement the necessary knowledge.

1. Introduction

The KRITON system for knowledge acquisition is designed to meet the requirements of practical knowledge engineering tasks. The starting point in developing the system was the assumption, that no single acquisition method will be powerful enough to overcome the so called knowledge-acquisition bottleneck in knowledge engineering. To fill that gap, it requires *hybrid knowledge-acquisition tools,* employing several knowledge-acquisition methods to capture different kinds of human knowledge. Within the domain of expert systems, two major knowledge sources are available, in principle:

(1) The human expert with his declarative and procedural knowledge of the domain in question. This knowledge has been obtained in long practice and is often turned to account without sufficient meta-knowledge about the way it is used. To model problem solving processes mounting on these, often incomplete and unstructured, knowledge chunks is the task assigned to expert systems.

(2) Well-structured static knowledge, fixed in the traditional mode of knowledge representation: natural-language documents, text books, technical descriptions and instructions.

Depending on the actual application, all of the above mentioned knowledge sources may become important and a knowledge-acquisition tool should be able to meet these requirements.

KNOWLEDGE-BASED SYSTEMS Vol. 2
ISBN 0-12-115920-5

The aim of the present paper is to put forward an integrated methodological approach, which takes into consideration different types of expert knowledge (declarative knowledge vs procedural knowledge) combining so far divergent methods to a modular knowledge acquisition system, each submethod being able to acquire information on specific aspects of the problem-solving process and to transform the gained information into a knowledge-representation formalism.

The KRITON-approach for automatic and semi-automated knowledge acquisition integrates methods of artificial intelligence with those of cognitive science. One of the important strategies of knowledge engineering is the interview, i.e. the dialogue between knowledge engineer and expert to inquire about important terms and concepts of an application domain (Newell & Simon, 1972) and their interdependence.

From cognitive science we adopted the method of protocol analysis, i.e. processing and transformation of texts gained by transcribing protocols of loud thinking during a problem-solving process. In AI, the analysis of thinking-aloud protocols has been automated quite early (Waterman & Newell, 1971, 1973).

The analysis of texts with respect to syntactic, semantic and pragmatic criteria also goes back to cognitive science. Although content analysis has developed into a standard method in the social sciences, it still represents a not much used option for knowledge acquisition on the basis of natural-language texts. KRITON uses a form of incremental text analysis to take advantage of these valuable knowledge sources.

Figure 1 shows the basic architecture of the KRITON system. In short: three knowledge elicitation methods are employed, namely an automated interview, text analysis and protocol analysis. After a completion process and a consistency check

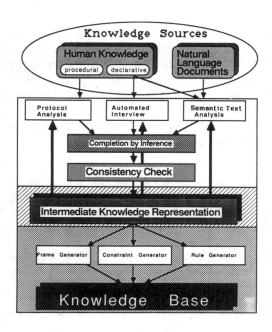

FIG. 1. The basic KRITON architecture.

the elicited information is transformed into an intermediate knowledge-representation language consisting of a descriptive language for functional and physical objects, and a propositional calculus.

Frame, rule and constraint generators operating on the intermediate representation level are finally used to build up the destination knowledge base. On the other side, the already acquired knowledge guides the employment of the elicitation methods to complete the knowledge bases incrementally.

2. Methods for knowledge elicitation

On its first processing level our model makes use of three different knowledge elicitation methods, to be outlined in this chapter.

2.1. INTERVIEW
One of the most important strategies of knowledge engineering is the interview. Grover (1983) distinguishes four different interview techniques for rule acquisition:
(1) *Forward scenario simulation*
An applicational situation within a problem domain is selected and investigated under laboratory conditions. The expert reports on the relevant terms and concepts and describes the steps in problem-solving, i.e. his or her own reasoning to achieve a goal.
(2) *Goal decomposition*
The knowledge engineer divides the overall problem into subgoals and asks the expert to describe paths for achieving the subgoals.
(3) *Procedural simulation*
Grover (1983) uses this umbrella term for protocol analysis. In his opinion controlling interventions by the knowledge engineer are absolutely necessary.
(4) *Pure reclassification*
Expert statements are further differentiated and classified into specific objects and relations between objects by means of a dialogue between knowledge engineer and expert. As a result of the interview, object-relations may be reclassified and new taxonomic relations eventually discovered. An interview techniques not mentioned in Grover's classification is:
(5) *Laddering*
The expert is asked to name important concepts of the problem domain in question. These concepts are then used as basis for the interview to follow. Especially supertypes and instances of generic concepts are inquired about, allowing the derivation of a taxonomic structure.

2.1.1. Interview methods in KRITON
In the KRITON system, interview techniques are completely automated, that is to say, the expert interacts directly with the system. A combination of the repertory grid technique, forward scenario simulation and laddering is used to explore the relevant concepts of a problem domain.

The top-level technique is the repertory grid approach: triples of semantic related concepts are presented to the expert in form of natural-language sentences and the expert is asked for attributes two of the concepts share distinguishing them from the third.

If the expert is not able to name discriminating attributes, the system switches into laddering mode to explore taxonomic relations between the concepts. The expert may either answer with a single word, denoting a specific concept, or can enter free text, which is analysed through morphologic–syntactic techniques to detect the relevant concepts.

The interview produces structured objects at the intermediate knowledge representation level. These objects incorporate the explored taxonomic relations and attributes.

2.2. PROTOCOL ANALYSIS

Protocol analysis refers to the automated or semi-automated analysis of thinking-aloud protocols, that is, tape-recorded utterances of an expert during a problem-solving episode. The result of the protocol analysis can be considered as a path through successive knowledge states representing the sequence of the problem solving events. In case that an expert system uses this sequence of knowledge states (e.g. in consultation) a surface modeling of the human problem-solving process takes place.

Although automatic protocol analysis has been suggested as an adequate method for knowledge acquisition in expert systems for some time now, fully developed systems are rare. A consistent approach to protocol analysis is described by Kuipers & Kassirer (1983, 1984), their approach aiming at both, a structural description of the problem domain and a qualitative simulation of the transitions between knowledge states during the problem solving process. A constraint language is used to fill up incomplete protocol segments. The power of protocol analysis quite decisively depends on the quality of the protocol recording. Only if the protocol is actually one of loud thinking during a problem-solving process and only if this protocol has been correctly transcribed, automatic analysis will be successful. As the success of any protocol analysis depends on the quality of the recorded information, detailed and adequate instructions with respect to the attainment of protocol recordings of verbal utterances during the problem-solving process are of great importance. In any case, it requires psychologically trained manpower to achieve a constant cognitive load of the thinking-aloud expert (for a comprehensive review on problems with verbal data, see Ericsson & Simon 1980, 1984).

Granularity of expert knowledge has turned out to be a serious and not easy to handle problem. Even the most careful employment of protocol analysis will not avoid problem-irrelevant knowledge elements to be acquired. As soon as not directly problem-relevant concepts are uttered by the expert, they are contained in the verbal material and hence are fed into the analysis. For example, this can be the case when the expert starts commencing upon, explaining or evaluating his thoughts or actions.

The other extreme, however, might as well occur, namely an expert communicating his "compiled knowledge" to the system. That is to say, that the expert over his extended learning process has combined inference steps so that the verbal report on the problem-solving process is incomplete. The expert skips, more or less small, nonetheless essential inference steps. Even if this does not necessarily affect the efficacy of the future expert system, it will reduce the explainability of the problem-solving process.

2.2.1. Protocol analysis in the KRITON system

Protocol analysis as a knowledge elicitation method is used in the KRITON system in order to get hold of procedural human knowledge. Ideally, knowledge that was part of text analysis or some previous interview is observed "in action" during the protocol recording. Goal structure of the protocol analysis is the propositional part of the intermediate knowledge representation level. In KRITON protocol analysis is accomplished in five steps. First the transcribed protocol is partitioned into segments on the basis of the experts speech pauses during recording. The second step is the semantic analysis of the segments, creating propositions for each segment. In a third step, the appropriateness of the selected operators and arguments is checked upon. Next, a knowledge-base matching is attempted to instantiate variables inside the propositions (variables are inserted if appropriate references for pronouns etc. cannot be found). In a last step, propositions are arranged according to their appearance in the natural language protocol.

2.3. TEXT ANALYSIS

Knowledge engineering phase models recommend the knowledge engineer to start off with studying manuals and documents on the problem domain in question. This can be very time-consuming, particularly if the knowledge engineer is supposed to become an expert on the topic before beginning his or her actual work.

For about 40 years content analysis has been concerned with analysing texts, especially newspaper articles. Since the 1950s, programs for automatic content analysis are available (Krippendorff, 1980; Merten, 1983). Utilization of these methods for constructing knowledge-based systems have, in the best case, been outlined in the published literature. Nishida, Kosaka & Doshita (1983), for example, analyse hardware manuals by means of action–event models. Frey, Reyle & Rohrer (1983) use discourse representation structure (DRT, by H. Kamp) as "intermediate level" between the natural-language text (a fragment of German language) and a data basis.

2.3.1. Incremental text analysis in KRITON

KRITON supports the knowledge engineer in incremental content analysis. The knowledge engineer can ask for statistical information on keyword frequencies in a selected text. If a text seems expedient for knowledge acquisition, the user can define the size of a text-fragment surrounding the keywords, to be used for the generation of basic propositions in a similar manner to that in protocol analysis.

The resulting propositional structures are sometimes faulty and therefore not appropriate for inference processes. The goal structures as part of the intermediate knowledge representation are to be constructed in an interactive process, where possible objects and relations are presented to the user in a menu and window system. Appropriate items can be selected by mouse operations and the corresponding knowledge structures are set up.

3. Utilization of acquired knowledge

The employment and use of the already acquired knowledge has major advantages and is an important task for knowledge acquisition tools. In KRITON, the already captured knowledge is used in several ways, depending on the amount and quality of the existing knowledge.

Moreover, existing knowledge is completed by *acquisition knowledge bases* (AKBs) for better guidance of the ongoing acquisition process. These acquisition knowledge bases are viewed as an integral part of the KRITON system. In every stage of the acquisition process, the user can use these knowledge bases in addition to existing knowledge for better employment of the KRITON facilities for knowledge-based knowledge acquisition. AKBs contain a set of structured objects defining important concepts of the domain. They are predefined declarative deep models of a domain with the sole purpose of optimizing the ongoing acquisition process.

Depending on the richness and quality of the existing knowledge, the already acquired knowledge is used in the following ways:

guidance of the acquisition process through discovery of incompleteness (see also section 5);
completion of domain-dependent deep models (AKBs);
employment as an Interpretation Model for the discovery of new situations (see also Breuker & Wielinga, 1985).

4. Intermediate knowledge representation level

In our system, all output from the mentioned above techniques is translated into an intermediate knowledge-representation system. This representation system has two subparts: a descriptive language for functional and physical objects, representing the generic concepts, and a propositional calculus representing the transformation path of these concepts during the human problem-solving process.

The description language consists of structured objects, their features and interrelations in a semantic net. The semantic net is the goal language for the methods interview and text analysis and serves as the basis for the frame-generation process.

The second part of the intermediate knowledge representation language is a propositional calculus, using semantic primitives to describe the basic relations of concepts detected by protocol analysis. The set of semantic primitives is not complete and will have to be updated for each application domain (e.g. technical applications).

The intermediate knowledge representation level allows integration of different knowledge sources and supplies the tool with openness towards elicitation methods currently not available. Moreover, it can be used for the generation of various knowledge bases for different expert system shells and knowledge-representation systems taking advantage of the facilities of interactive knowledge-base generation.

From this point of view, Intermediate Knowledge Representation has at least six different purposes:

openness for extensions (possible integration of currently unknown elicitation methods);
knowledge acquisition for different knowledge representation tools;
storage of incomplete knowledge for the ongoing elicitation process;
integration and employment of *acquisition knowledge bases*;
maintaining information closer to the sources (e.g. expert utterances);
management of knowledge bases with varying degrees of completeness in different knowledge representation languages.

5. Dealing with incomplete knowledge: knowledge-guided knowledge elicitation

The use of knowledge elicitation methods depends not only on decisions of the knowledge engineer but also on requirements the KRITON system detects on the basis of the already acquired knowledge.

A significant role in dealing with *incomplete knowledge* is played by the *watcher*. The watcher is an always active demon controlling the intermediate knowledge representation for missing components. For example, the user (the knowledge engineer or the expert) might have generated several objects during the incremental text analysis without any relation to the taxonomic organization of the objects of the corresponding domain (i.e. no information about the inheritance paths, part-of relations or instance relations was given). The watcher checks all objects at the intermediate knowledge representation level for missing, but possible or indispensable, links (every object has to be placed in a taxonomic organization), sends a message to the user and recommends the employment of an elicitation method to complete the knowledge base. The watcher is also invoked if an elicitation method starts, informing the user about incomplete parts of the knowledge base. Furthermore, the user can delegate the selection of concepts to be used in an interview to

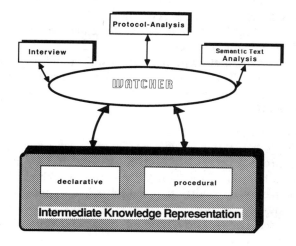

FIG. 2. Interaction between intermediate knowledge representation and elicitation methods.

the watcher. In this case the demon looks for semantic related but incomplete objects and triggers an interview further exploring that domain.

6. Knowledge-base generation

As mentioned above, the intermediate knowledge representation is the blackboard for frame, rule and constraint generation.

The task of the frame generator is to translate the information stored in structured objects and their relation into a frame language. In principle, this is a simple syntactic transformation process. After frame generation, the user can interactively correct the translation process with a structure editor.

The output of the protocol analysis is the input for the rule generator. A subset of propositional clauses, extracted from adjacent segments in the thinking-aloud protocol, is offered to the user for rule generation. The user can either reject the proposal or use it for rule generation. Rule junctors and rule actors are inserted by selection from pop-up menus, premises and actions by entering the corresponding proposition number. Again, a rule editor can be called to correct for shortcomings of the automated protocol analysis.

Thus far, frame and rule generator build knowledge bases using the BABYLON frame and rule language (Di Primio & Brewka, 1985).

If the user, through interaction with the system, detects global value restrictions, the constraint generator is used to represent these global restrictions in a constraint language (Guesgen, unpubl.).

7. Steps in knowledge engineering with KRITON

The following is a description of phases in automatic knowledge acquisition using the KRITON methodology. These steps are not strongly chronological. Especially through the influence of the knowledge-guided elicitation process, loops (cyclic and alternating employment of the different KRITON submethods) are probable and for applications of considerable size can be considered necessary.

There is no doubt, that in certain cases the exclusive employment of single submethods of KRITON will be successful.

The technique of incremental content analysis will be described in more detail in forthcoming publications. The overall knowledge-acquisition process consists of three levels: *knowledge elicitation, intermediate knowledge representation* and *knowledge base generation*.

(I) *Definition of the domain*
   The actual knowledge domain defined by the situation, in which human problem-solving process occurs, is initially investigated by means of interview techniques. The definition of the domain and the breaking down of the experts extensive knowledge into proportionate subparts is an important precondition for the automated acquisition process.

(II) *Elicitation of declarative knowledge by automated interview techniques and incremental content analysis*
   The important terms and concepts of a concrete knowledge domain to be investigated by means of automated protocol analysis or other acquisition

methods for procedural knowledge are inquired about and entered into the computer-based analysis system. Interview and text analysis are employed in a cyclic manner until the network of structured objects reaches a significant size.

(III) *Guided protocol recording*

A protocol of loud thinking is tape-recorded. This requires a careful guidance to secure constant verbalization of the expert during the problem-solving work. It will take quite a few protocols if the problem domain is not to be restricted to a single problem-solving path.

(IV) *Transcription*

The recorded protocol is transcribed. While punctuation is not used, speech pauses are supplemented. The protocol is entered into the analysis system.

(V) *Protocol segmentation*

The protocol is automatically divided into numbered segments, the speech pauses determining the length of the segments.

(VI) *Search for the knowledge elements in the segmented protocol*

The segmented protocol is searched for the various knowledge elements of the problem space. Concepts that are detected are stored together with the segments they are contained in.

(VII) *Semantic analysis of the segmented protocol*

By comparison with the available lexicon entries, all words contained in the segments found by V. are examined whether they include:

(a) *ordinal relations,* e.g. A is smaller than B or X is equal to Y or;

(b) *tendencies,* e.g. The state of X is stable. The value of Y continues to increase.

(VIII) *Propositionalization*

If such elements are found, the knowledge elements together with the operators interconnecting them are set down in a propositional calculus.

(IX) *Completion of propositions*

The system tries to find knowledge elements, which allow a completion of the above mentioned propositions. This is first done within the same segment, subsequently in the neighbouring segments.

(X) *Knowledge base matching*

The method described under VIII does not allow the identification and solution of references, especially over longer distances. In case of a proper realization of protocol recording, however, complex syntactic constructions are not to be expected. By way of trial, the completion of propositions is accomplished by searching for complete propositions displaying the components already extracted. The missing arguments are taken from these propositions.

(XI) *Intermediate knowledge representation*

All output from the protocol analysis is integrated in the intermediate knowledge representation system. This language supplies a propositional language as a goal for the protocol analysis. Each proposition consists of an operator, i.e. a semantic deep case representing the basic relation between the acquired concepts, a segment marker, i.e. a pointer to the origin of the proposition in the natural language protocol, and the relevant concepts.

(XII) *Checking for completeness in the network of structured objects*

Usually, protocol analysis will exhibit voids in the network of structured objects. This is always the case, when concepts used during the thinking-aloud procedure are not sufficiently defined. In this case, interview and text analysis should be repeated.

(XIII)   *Frame generation*

Structured objects in the semantic net of the intermediate knowledge representation level are translated into frame format, i.e. the BABYLON frame representation language. In general, frame generators for several other languages can be added, using the intermediate knowledge representation as a blackboard.

(XIV)   *Rule generation*

Rule generation is an interactive process realized by mouse-operations for the selection of propositions to be used on the left- or right side of rules. Corrective actions can be taken by calling a structure editor. The organization of rule sets as well as the selection of control strategies, for the present, remains a task of the knowledge engineer.

(XV)   *Constraint generation*

If global dependencies between data are discovered while using KRITON, these relations are encoded in a constraint language. The selection of data and their relations proceeds by mouse interaction.

8. Comparison with other systems of automatic knowledge acquisition

None of the so far developed systems for automatic knowledge acquisition has reached product features. Most systems are experimental in character. Though the approaches are often very different and based on different theoretical assumptions, some common features are identifiable. The efforts center around the construction of a conceptual structure by means of an interactive system.

Nevertheless, there is no system that handles multiple knowledge-representation formalisms or makes use of several different knowledge sources to acquire both declarative and procedural knowledge. Some systems, for instance ROGET, have no elicitation component and are primarily used for purposes of knowledge base extension.

KADS (Breuker & Wielinga, 1985) is an interactive system using a set of different functions in support of the knowledge engineer. This includes assistance in planning problems, data interpretation and consistency check. KADS was mainly based on a KL-ONE implementation in PROLOG provided with a simple rule interpreter, the rules being part of a network. This knowledge based system, containing task-dependent and domain-independent information, is used for the interactive analysis of a knowledge domain. Analysis is controlled by interpretation models that are typical for specific problem-solving processes (e.g. in a diagnostic task domain). In principle, KADS can be considered as a library containing different elicitation methods.

ROGET (Bennett, 1985) directly interacts with an expert to construct a rule base that is understood as fundamental conceptual structure of the knowledge domain. ROGET itself was developed in the context of EMYCIN and supports only systems of this type. A ROGET consultation is used for the following tasks:

(1)   definition of problem-solving type;

(2)   acquisition of conceptual structure;
(3)   analysis of conceptual structure;
(4)   operationalization of conceptual structure for a specific knowledge engineering environment (of the EMYCIN type).

ETS (Boose, 1984, 1985) is another interactive system for generation of knowledge bases of the EMYCIN and OPS 5 types. The heart of the system consists of an on-line implementation of the repertory grid test by Kelly (1955). Factor analytical methods are applied for an investigation of semantic distance between concepts and possible implicational relations. ETS only supports rule-base generation.

9. Implementation

So far, all components described in this paper are implemented in a preliminary form on a XEROX-1108 machine in INTERLISP-D using object-oriented features from LOOPS. The structured object representation of the intermediate knowledge representation language is realized in form of LOOPS-objects. Protocol and text analysis make use of a lexicon for "closed class" words. Detection of word-stem works by means of an analysis of inflection, which itself is part of the lemmatization component. Lemmatization is to some extent lexicon-based and partly rule-based. The hit rate is well above 90% and in so far comparable to that of other systems. A first application of the system is planned for the second half of 1986. Application domain is an expert system for planning and configuration of bureau equipment.

10. Conclusions

We are aiming at an integrated, modular system-tool for knowledge acquisition in expert systems. On the one hand the system should be of high supportive value for the acquisition of declarative and procedural expert knowledge. On the other hand it should be open, in the sense, that it provides facilities for its own extension and elaboration. At the present stage of the systems development the protocol and the text analysis still work inaccurately and sometimes erroneously. For the present, these shortcomings in automatic text analysis are compensated by the use of appropriate editors, through which the employment and testing of the system in applied industrial fields is guaranteed.

To sum up: the approach presented here to automated knowledge acquisition not only has the potency of taking advantage of developments in hybrid knowledge representation formalisms, but also is hybrid in the sense that it makes use of information from different knowledge sources. In our opinion, the guaranteed openness for future extensions is a most promising feature of the knowledge acquisition tool presented here, supplying it with a remarkable amount of applicability for various industrial fields.

References

BENNETT, J. S. (1985). ROGET: a knowledge-based system for acquiring the conceptual structure of a diagnostic expert system. *Journal of Automated Reasoning*, **1**, 49–74.

Boose, J. (1984). Personal construct theory and the transfer of the human expertise. *Proceedings of the National Conference on Artificial Intelligence,* Austin, Texas 1984.

Boose, J. (1985). A knowledge acquisition program for expert systems based on personal construct psychology. *International Journal of Man–Machine Studies,* **23,** 495–525.

Breuker, J. & Wielinga, B. (1985). KADS: structured knowledge acquisition for expert systems. *Proceedings of Expert Systems and their Applications,* Vol. 2, 887–900.

Di Primio, F. & Brewka, G. (1985). BABYLON: kernel system of an integrated environment for expert system development and operation. *Proceedings of the Fifth International Workshop "Expert System and their Applications",* Avignon, France, May 1985.

Ericsson, K. A. & Simon, H. A. (1980). Verbal reports as data. *Psychological Review,* **87,** 3.

Ericsson, K. A. & Simon, H. A. (1984). Protocol analysis. Verbal reports as data. Cambridge, Massachusetts: MIT Press.

Frey, W., Reyle, U. & Rohrer, C. (1983). Automatic construction of a knowledge base by analyzing texts in natural language. *International Joint Conference on Artificial Intelligence,* **83,** 727–729.

Grover, M. D. (1983). A pragmatic knowledge acquisition methodology. *International Joint Conference on Artificial Intelligence,* **83,** 436–438.

Kelly, G. (1955). *The Psychology of Personal Constructs.* New York: Norton.

Krippendorff, K. (1980). *Content Analysis. An Introduction to its Methodology.* Beverly Hills: Sage.

Kuipers, B. & Kassirer, B. (1983). How to discover a knowledge representation for causal reasoning by studying an expert physician. *IJCAI* **83,** 49–56.

Kuipers, B. & Kassirer, B. (1984). Causal reasoning in medicine: analysis of a protocol. *Cognitive Science,* **8,** 363–385.

Merten, K. (1983). *Inhaltsanalyse.* Opladen: Westdeutscher Verlag.

Newell, A. & Simon, H. A. (1972). *Human Problem Solving.* Englewood Cliffs, New Jersey: Prentice–Hall Inc.

Nishida, T., Kosaka, A. & Doshita, S. (1983). Towards knowledge acquisition from natural language documents—automatic model construction from hardware manuals. *International Joint Conference on Artificial Intelligence,* **83,** 482–486.

Waterman, D. A. & Newell, A. (1971). Protocol analysis as a task for artificial intelligence. *Artificial Intelligence,* **2,** 285–318.

Waterman, D. A. & Newell, A. (1973). PAS II: An interactive task free version of an automatic protocol analysis system. *International Joint Conference on Artificial Intelligence,* 431–445.

MOLE: a tenacious knowledge-acquisition tool

Larry Eshelman, Damien Ehret, John McDermott & Ming Tan

Department of Computer Science, Carnegie Mellon University, Pittsburgh, Pennsylvania 15213, U.S.A.

MOLE can help domain experts build a heuristic problem-solver by working with them to generate an initial knowledge base and then detect and remedy deficiencies in it. The problem-solving method presupposed by MOLE makes several heuristic assumptions about the world, which MOLE is able to exploit when acquiring knowledge. In particular, by distinguishing between covering and differentiating knowledge and by allowing covering knowledge to drive the knowledge-acquisition process, MOLE is able to disambiguate an under-specified knowledge base and to interactively refine an incomplete knowledge base.

1. Introduction

MOLE (Eshelman & McDermott, 1986) is an expert-system shell that can be used in building systems that do heuristic classification. It is both a performance system which interprets a domain-dependent knowledge base and a knowledge-acquisition tool for building and refining this knowledge base. MOLE the performance system presupposes that the task can be represented as a classification problem: some object is selected from a set of pre-enumerable candidates (e.g. faults, diseases, components) on the basis of weighted evidential considerations (e.g. symptoms, cues, requirements) (Clancey, 1984, 1985; Buchanan & Shortliffe, 1984). MOLE the knowledge-acquisition tool builds a knowledge base by eliciting knowledge from the domain expert guided by its understanding of how to represent the knowledge required by its problem-solving method, and discovers missing knowledge and refines the knowledge base guided by its understanding of how to diagnose what knowledge the problem-solving method might be missing.

MOLE belongs to a family of knowledge-acquisition tools which get their power by paying close attention to the problem-solving method used by their performance systems (McDermott, 1986, Gruber & Cohen, in press). Examples of such systems are TEIRESIAS (Davis & Lenat, 1982), ETS (Boose, 1984), MORE (Kahn, Nowlan & McDermott, 1985*a,b*), KNACK (Klinker, Bentolila, Genetet, Grimes & McDermott, in press), SALT (Marcus, McDermott & Wang, 1985), and SEAR (van de Brug, Bachant & McDermott, 1985). MOLE resembles the first three systems in that its method can be described as a variant of heuristic classification. It differs from them in that its problem-solving method incorporates certain explicit assumptions about the world which, along with several assumptions about how experts express themselves, are exploited during the knowledge-acquisition process.

Our goal has been to make MOLE smart—i.e. to enable it to build a reasonable knowledge base with a minimal amount of information elicited from the expert. Our research strategy has been to overly restrict (or so it seems at first) the information

95

KNOWLEDGE-BASED SYSTEMS Vol. 2
ISBN 0-12-115920-5

that MOLE can elicit from the expert and then to search for heuristics that will enable it to build from this limited information a knowledge base that can perform the given task reasonably well. In this paper we shall describe the results of this strategy. In section 2 we describe the method presupposed by MOLE and the set of knowledge roles imposed by the problem-solving method. In section 3 we describe how MOLE's knowledge of its performance system's method is exploited in knowledge acquisition.

2. MOLE's method

MOLE the knowledge-acquisition tool gets its power from its knowledge of the problem-solving method of MOLE the performance system. In this section we shall describe the method used by MOLE the performance system. MOLE's problem-solving method is a variant of heuristic classification. MOLE selects or classifies candidate hypotheses on the basis of "rules" associating the candidates with various evidential considerations. However, unlike some heuristic classification systems such as MYCIN, these rules are not just arbitrary implications among arbitrary facts about the world (Szolovits & Pauker, 1978). By making certain assumptions about the world and interpreting the rules or associations in light of these assumptions, MOLE is able to obtain considerable leverage for its knowledge acquisition. MOLE's problem-solving method consists of the following steps:

(1) ask what symptoms need to be explained;
(2) determine what hypotheses will explain or cover these symptoms (Covering Knowledge);
(3) determine what information will differentiate among the hypotheses covering any symptom (Differentiating Knowledge);
(4) ask for that information;
(5) if any differentiating knowledge needs to be explained, go to 2;
(6) pick the best combination of viable hypotheses that will explain all of the symptoms (Combining Knowledge)
(7) if there is information that will affect the viability of some combination of hypotheses, ask for that information, and go to 2;
(8) display the results.

Central to MOLE's method is the distinction between evidence that needs to be explained or covered by some hypothesis and evidence that helps differentiate among hypotheses. The former, Covering Knowledge, reflects two basic assumptions that MOLE makes about the world:

(1) exhaustivity: every abnormal finding has an explanation—i.e. some candidate hypothesis will account for it;
(2) exclusivity: explanations should not be multiplied beyond necessity—i.e. do not accept two hypotheses if one will do.

The exhaustivity assumption enables MOLE to interpret the hypothesis–symptom associations in its domain model causally. Every symptom is assumed to have a cause. If a symptom is not explained by one hypothesis, it must be explained by another. The exclusivity assumption is a version of Occam's razor: all other things being equal, parsimonious explanations should be favored. As a general rule of thumb, the types of events represented by hypotheses are fairly rare, so it is unlikely that several occur simultaneously. (Of course, two such events might be interrelated, but then this should be represented by combining knowledge).

An important corollary follows from the exhausivity and exclusivity assumptions: accept the best candidate relative to its competitors—i.e. a candidate may "win" by ruling out competing candidates. Because symptoms must be explained by some hypothesis (exhausivity), one of the hypotheses must be true. And because only one hypothesis is likely to be true (exclusivity), we can drive up the support of one hypothesis by driving down the support of its competitors or vice versa. This provides the basis for MOLE's second kind of knowledge role, Differentiating Knowledge.

Differentiating Knowledge enables MOLE to evaluate the relative likelihood of hypotheses explaining the same symptom. MOLE understands four types of differentiating knowledge:

Anticipatory Knowledge;
Circumstantial Knowledge;
Refining Knowledge;
Qualifying Knowledge.

In all four cases, the knowledge helps differentiate which hypothesis is the most likely explanation of a symptom. Anticipatory Knowledge is closely tied to Covering Knowledge. Given the Covering Knowledge that event E_1 explains event E_2, Anticipatory Knowledge is the additional information that the presence of E_1 is likely to lead to E_2, or alternatively, that the absence of E_2 tends to rule out E_1. Circumstantial Knowledge, like Covering Knowledge, associates evidence with hypotheses. But unlike Covering Knowledge, the evidence does not have to be explained or covered. Circumstantial Knowledge is merely correlated—positively or negatively—with the hypothesis. Such evidence indicates that the hypothesis is more or less likely to be true, but there is no presumption that one of the hypotheses with which it is associated must be true. Refining Knowledge points to distinguishing features of a symptom which indicate that a proper subset of the hypotheses covering it are more likely to contain the correct explanation. By refining the symptom, MOLE is able to differentiate among the hypotheses that might explain the unrefined symptom. Qualifying Knowledge is any background condition which qualifies the strength of an association. A qualifying condition may either strengthen an association or weaken (or completely mask) an association.

MOLE the performance system seeks to explain all the symptoms which are present. Covering Knowledge and Differentiating Knowledge are used to determine local explanations. Combining Knowledge, on the other hand, is instrumental in integrating the local explanations into a global explanation. Once the hypotheses which best cover or explain each symptom that needs to be covered have been discovered, Combining Knowledge is used to select the best combination of hypotheses that will explain all the symptoms that are present: More specifically, Combining Knowledge overrides MOLE's default method for combining hypotheses. MOLE classifies active hypotheses in one of three categories: accept, reject, or indeterminate. Hypotheses that are clearly better than any of their competitors at explaining some symptom are tentatively accepted. Hypotheses which are not accepted and are not needed to explain any symptoms because these symptoms are explained by some accepted hypothesis are rejected. All other active hypotheses are classified as indeterminate. Among the indeterminate hypotheses MOLE tries to find the smallest viable set that will explain all the unexplained symptoms. Combining Knowledge overrides MOLE's default procedure and recommends a less parsimonious combination of hypotheses.

We have mainly used MOLE to build knowledge bases for diagnostic tasks. However, we have described MOLE's method so that no particular type of domain is presupposed, for we suspect that there is a much wider range of tasks for which MOLE would be useful. For example, MOLE might be used in a domain whose task is component selection. Covering Knowledge would link the components (hypotheses) with requirements that must be met (symptoms). Differentiating Knowledge would be information indicating what tradeoffs can be made between various components. Combining Knowledge would be heuristics suggesting how to select a combination of components if no single component met a set of overlapping requirements.

Since most of our research has involved diagnostic problems, we will illustrate MOLE's method and the knowledge roles presupposed by its method with an example of a system which diagnoses problems in a coal-burning power plant. The knowledge base built by MOLE the knowledge-acquisition tool enables MOLE the performance system to diagnose problems connected with the boiler, the central unit in a power plant. The problems rarely prevent the boiler from functioning, but they are a major source of inefficiency. A boiler that is functioning inefficiently can waste millions of dollars of fuel as well as dump tons of pollutants into the atmosphere.

Suppose, for example, the operator notices that there is a loss in gas and that the ash leaving the boiler is dark. These are two symptoms that need to be covered or explained. The loss in gas has two potential explanations: (1) a high gas temperature; (2) high excess air. The other symptom, dark ash, has three potential explanations; (1) high excess air; (2) low excess air; (3) large fuel particles. For each symptom present, MOLE tries to differentiate among the potential causes. For example, when there is high excess air, there is a strong expectation (anticipatory knowledge) that there will be a high fly ash flow. If this expectation is not met, support for the high excess air hypothesis is driven down. Consequently, support for the competing explanation, high gas temperature, is driven up and becomes the likely explanation for the loss in gas. Since high excess air is also a potential explanation for the dark ash, support for its competitors, low excess air and large fuel particles, is also driven up. MOLE tries to differentiate further between these two hypotheses. For instance, if the flame temperature is not low, contrary to what one would expect if there is low excess air, then support for the low excess air hypothesis is also driven down, leaving large fuel particles as the most likely explanation for the dark ash. Once MOLE has finished locally differentiating the hypotheses covering each symptom that is present, MOLE looks at what combination of hypotheses will best explain all the symptoms. In this case MOLE will accept two hypotheses, high gas temperature and large fuel particles, since the only hypothesis which will explain all the relevant symptoms has been ruled out by the absense of a high fly ash flow. Having accepted these two hypotheses, MOLE next sees whether they, in turn, can be treated as symptoms that are explained by higher-level hypotheses. In this case, they both have higher-level explanations. For example, the large fuel particles can be explained by either the setting of the pulverizer or by a malfunction of the pulverizer. Knowing that the grinder had recently been maintained would provide circumstantial evidence that a malfunction is unlikely and thus drive up the likelihood that the setting of the pulverizer is the explanation for the large fuel particles. MOLE continues until it has attempted to explain every event that can be explained.

In the next section we will draw from our experiences with the power-plant diagnosis task to illustrate how MOLE uses its knowledge of its method to guide the knowledge-acquisition process both when generating the initial knowledge base and when refining it.

3. Knowledge acquisition

Usually it is not a very hard to elicit knowledge from an expert. The hard problem is eliciting the right sort of knowledge. Knowledge needs to be in such a form that it will be applied to the problem in the right way at the right time. The first step in satisfying this need is to identify explicitly the appropriate problem-solving method for the task and the types of knowledge roles relevant for this method. Once this is done, it is fairly easy to build a knowledge collector. However, if the ultimate goal is to replace the knowledge engineer with an automated system, rather than providing the knowledge engineer with a programming tool, then two troublesome features of the knowledge-acquisition process must be addressed:

(1) indeterminateness: when specifying associations between events, the expert is likely to be fairly vague about the nature of these associations and events;
(2) incompleteness: the expert will probably forget to specify certain pieces of knowledge.

The indeterminateness problem reflects the fact that experts are not accustomed to talking about the associations between events in a way that precisely fits the problem-solving method's pre-defined knowledge roles. Since our ultimate goal is to develop a knowledge-acquisition tool that replaces the knowledge engineer, the burden is upon the knowledge-acquisition system to make sense of whatever information the domain expert is willing to provide. Although the expert can be encouraged to be as specific as possible, a smart knowledge acquisition tool must be able to tolerate ambiguity and indeterminateness.

The incompleteness problem is the problem of how to identify missing or incorrect knowledge. The expert, no matter how qualified and thorough he may be, is going to forget to mention certain special circumstances. And sometimes the expert will make mistakes. Thus, a smart knowledge-acquisition tool needs to be able to incrementally add knowledge to the knowledge base, refine existing knowledge, and sometimes correct existing knowledge.

The indeterminateness problem and the incompleteness problem dominate the two phases of knowledge acquisition: (1) the gathering of information for constructing the initial knowledge base; and (2) the iterative refinement of this knowledge base. During the first phase, MOLE mainly relies upon static techniques of analysis.

MOLE examines specific associations and events in light of the context provided by the surrounding structures. MOLE concentrates on disambiguating the information provided by the expert, although MOLE also tries to recognize areas where the knowledge is obviously incomplete. During the second, dynamic phase, MOLE and the expert interact in order to refine the knowledge base. The expert gives MOLE a test case and tells MOLE the correct diagnosis. If MOLE the performance program comes to an incorrect conclusion, MOLE the knowledge-acquisition tool tries to determine the source of the error and recommends possible remedies. Typically, this means adding knowledge or qualifying existing knowledge, but sometimes the interpretation provided in the previous phase needs to be revised.

In the following two subsections, we shall discuss the techniques MOLE uses during both the construction and refinement phases of knowledge acquisition.

3.1. CONSTRUCTING THE INITIAL KNOWLEDGE BASE

MOLE initiates the knowledge acquisition process by asking the expert to list the events—i.e. hypotheses and evidence—that are commonly relevant to the expert's domain and to draw associations between pairs of events. This information is easy to elicit from the expert, although the expert will often overlook certain associations or events. However, in order for MOLE to be able to fashion this network of events and associations into a knowledge base suitable for diagnosis, four additional pieces of information are needed.

(1) the type of event (i.e. whether observed or inferred);
(2) the type of evidence an association provides (e.g. covering evidence, anticipatory evidence);
(3) the direction of an association (e.g. does E_1 explain E_2 or vice versa);
(4) the numeric support value attached to an association.

MOLE understands that experts are not very good at providing such information and so does not require that the expert provide a fully specified network of associations. Instead, MOLE relies on its expectations about the world and how experts enter data in order to mold an under-specified network of associations into a consistent and unambiguous knowedge base.

The most critical piece of information is the association type. Both the direction and support value of an association are dependent upon its type. The problem with directly asking the expert for the association type is that it is hard to convey to the expert what these types mean. The distinction between covering and circumstantial evidence, for example, is part of MOLE's jargon, not the expert's. But the problem is not simply a matter of finding a translation from MOLE's jargon into terminology that the expert can understand. The indeterminacy is deeper than this. Not only does the expert have difficulty distinguishing among types of evidence, often he cannot decide whether an event should be classified as evidence rather than a hypothesis. He may not even be sure whether he should say it is observed or inferred. Perhaps it can be observed, but only with difficulty. For example, one of the causes of a misbalance of convection is the presence of fouling. Whether the operator can see signs of fouling depends upon what part of the boiler it is occurring. On those occasions when he cannot observe fouling, he still may be able to infer fouling. Furthermore, even if an event is observed, it can function as a hypothesis. Suppose that fouling can be observed and that a low heat transfer needs to be explained. A misbalance of convection competes with a misbalance of radiation as explanations of a low heat transfer. If fouling is discovered before the explanation of a low heat transfer has been resolved, then fouling serves as evidence for a misbalance of radiation. On the other hand, if it has already been ascertained that there is a misbalance of radiation, then the fouling provides the explanation.

After several unsuccessful attempts to find ways of unambiguously eliciting the association types from the expert, we discovered that we are looking for the solution in the wrong place. In the three domains that we have explored most extensively, the only associations that the experts have ever spontaneously entered are covering and anticipatory associations. Instead of having to worry about identifying half a dozen knowledge roles, we only have to worry about two. In a sense there is no identification problem at all, since every anticipatory association can be interpreted as a covering association and vice versa. However, the anticipatory strengths of some covering associations are so weak that they can be ignored in practice. So the problem is to identify which covering associations provide significant anticipatory evidence. We shall return to this question when we discuss how MOLE determines the support values of associations.

On reflection, it is not very surprising that the initial knowledge-acquisition process generates just these two types. The starting point in diagnosis is a set of events that need to be explained. MOLE asks for the names of these events and their potential explanations, and then for explanations of these explanations. The knowledge-acquisition process is driven by covering knowledge and to a lesser extent anticipatory knowledge. Other types of knowledge are secondary and tend to be overlooked by the expert. For example, given that low excess air needs to be explained, the most common explanations will occur to the expert—e.g. the fan power has been exceeded or there is a leak in the duct. While he is thinking about fan power it may occur to him that if he knows that a valve is malfunctioning, he will anticipate that the fan power has been exceeded. On the other hand, it is unlikely to occur to him that the installation date of the duct is a relevant circumstance for determining the likelihood of a leak. When providing covering knowledge, the expert is biased toward thinking of events causing other events. He tends to overlook circumstances or states that are correlated with an event except in the context of some actual test case.

Given the expert's bias toward providing only covering associations, finding out the direction of these covering associations would seem to be a straightforward matter. All we need to do is ask the expert whether E_1 explains E_2 or vice versa. Unfortunately, about 20% of the time experts reverse the direction. When the expert says that E_1 explains E_2 what he may mean is that E_1 explains why he would accept E_2, not that E_1 is the physical explanation of E_2. The same confusion occurs with cause and effect language. Sometimes the expert will say that E_1 causes E_2 and mean that the occurrence of E_1 "caused" him to think of E_2 as the explanation of E_1. We have found that the most reliable directional information that can easily be elicited from the expert is an association's temporal direction—i.e. which event occurs first. MOLE assumes, all things being equal, that the temporal direction is a reliable indicator of the explanatory direction. If, for example, the expert says that E_2 supports E_1 and that E_1 precedes E_2, MOLE assumes that E_1 explains E_2.

However, if the expert indicates that he is not sure about the temporal direction, MOLE will try to elicit more information in order to clarify the nature of the association. It could be that the association is circumstantial, or, more likely, that one event is really a direct indication of the other event. For instance, a small, red flame is a direct indication of a low flame temperature. Although MOLE interprets the flame temperature as explaining the flame size and color, the expert may be reluctant to put a temporal direction on this relationship.

The final type of information that MOLE needs in order to fashion the initial network of associations into a knowledge base is each association's support value. However, experts do not like providing numeric support values and are not very good at it. In our experience, when experts are asked to indicate the degree of support of some piece of evidence for a hypothesis by selecting a number within a fixed range, they will think about the question for a while and then almost inevitably choose some number near the middle of the range. Fortunately, it turns out that the support values do not have to be very accurate, and that on the basis of a few simple assumptions MOLE can assign default support values that are just as good, if not better, than those assigned by the expert. (They subsequently can be adjusted by MOLE during dynamic analysis).

MOLE's method for assigning support values for covering evidence follows directly from MOLE's exhaustivity and exclusivity assumptions. The assumption that every symptom can be explained by some hypothesis plus the assumption that only one of the covering hypotheses is likely to be the explanation suggests that the positive support provided by the presence of a symptom should be distributed among the hypotheses and should sum to $1 \cdot 0$. Since MOLE initially has no information how this support should be distributed, it makes the default assumption that the support values for any symptom should be equally divided among the hypotheses which explain it.

The method for assigning support values for anticipatory evidence has a weaker rationale. MOLE assumes that if an expert spontaneously mentions a piece of anticipatory knowledge, then it is the sort of information that is likely to have a significant impact; thus, a relatively high support value is assigned. The problem, then, is to determine when an expert is spontaneously entering anticipatory evidence. As was explained earlier, covering evidence and anticipatory evidence are closely linked. They enable MOLE to reason in both directions between two events. If E_1 explains E_2, then the occurrence of E_2 provides some evidence for E_1. If in addition there is a strong anticipatory connection between the events, then the occurrence of E_1 increases the likelihood of E_2. MOLE pays attention to the direction of this supporting relationship. If the expert indicates that E_1 supports E_2 and that E_1 is temporally prior, then MOLE will infer that the expert is spontaneously entering an anticipatory association. MOLE will also assume that there is a covering association between the two events. On the other hand, if the temporal and supporting directions are different—e.g. if E_1 supports E_2, and E_2 is prior to E_1—MOLE assumes that the expert is entering a covering association, and assumes, until evidence to the contrary, that there is no strong anticipatory association.

MOLE has one other opportunity to identify anticipatory associations in the initial phase of knowledge acquisition. MOLE monitors the static knowledge base and notes any symptoms which have hypotheses that cannot be differentiated. MOLE assumes that if the expert provides several explanations for some event, then he probably can provide knowledge that will differentiate among them. For example, suppose that MOLE learns during the initial construction of the knowledge base that low excess air can be explained by either the fan power being exceeded or by a leak in the duct, but is not told about any evidence that would help differentiate between these hypotheses. MOLE will ask the expert how he can tell which hypothesis is the cause of low excess air. The expert may indicate that if there is no loud noise coming from the wind box, then MOLE can rule out that there is a leak. This will enable MOLE, at least in principle, to differentiate the two hypotheses.

Before discussing the second phase of knowledge acquisition, something should be said about the absence of any stress on qualifying knowledge during the first phase. Based on the descriptions of other diagnostic systems, one might expect that for a system to perform adequately most associations would need a large number of qualifications. If MOLE did not distinguish between covering and differential knowledge and simply tried to build rules associating evidence with hypotheses, then, no doubt, its initial network of associations would require many qualifications. However, because of the emphasis that MOLE puts on covering knowledge, MOLE tends to build multi-layered networks with sparse connections rather than flat networks where several layers of information need to be compiled into one rule. By asking for the explanations of a symptom rather than the conditions for accepting a hypothesis, MOLE naturally discovers intermediate events which mediate between the bottom-level symptoms and the top-level hypotheses. The knowledge base for diagnosing boiler problems, for example, consists of eight levels of explanation and has as much depth as it has breadth.

However, there is a price to pay for the heavy reliance on intermediate events. There is the danger that redundant pathways are drawn between events. MOLE needs to check for duplicate pathways. For example, in one session MOLE was told that the two explanations for a misbalance of convection are fouling and low excess air. However, in a later session MOLE learned that low excess air can be explained by the fan power being exceeded which, in turn, can be explained by fouling. Thus, there is a direct path from fouling to misbalance of convection and an indirect path through fan power being exceeded and low excess air. The question is whether the direct path is an actual causal path or whether it represents a compiled version of the longer path. MOLE has no way of knowing the answer, but it is important that MOLE notice such occurrences and ask the expert about them.

3.2. REFINING THE KNOWLEDGE BASE

In the previous section, we mentioned that MOLE checks to make sure that hypotheses can in principle be differentiated. If they cannot, MOLE tries to elicit knowledge from the expert that will enable it to differentiate among them. However, such static techniques of refinement are quite limited. The expert typically needs a richer context to remind him of missing knowledge, and MOLE needs a richer context in order to be able to distinguish a wider range of association types. The needed context is provided by feedback from the expert during dynamic analysis. The expert gives MOLE a test case and tells MOLE the correct diagnosis.

If MOLE the performance system has come to an incorrect diagnosis, MOLE the knowledge-acquisition tool tries to determine the source of the errors and recommends possible remedies.

In the remainder of this section we will discuss MOLE's techniques for doing synamic analysis. These techniques reflect the three types of knowledge roles understood by MOLE: Covering Knowledge, Differentiating Knowledge, and Combining Knowledge.

3.2.1. Differentiating knowledge

If MOLE's diagnosis does not match that supplied by the expert, MOLE first determines whether or not the diagnosis would have been reachable if the hypotheses had been differentiated differently. If it is so reachable, then MOLE looks for missing differentiating knowledge which will shift the support among the hypotheses. An important consideration, when looking for differentiating knowledge, is whether the needed shifts can be accomplished globally or locally. A global solution may be possible if the raising or lowering of some hypothesis's likelihood will affect the explanations of several symptoms in the right direction and so have a global effect. If a global solution is not possible, then the shifts must be made locally by shifting support among hypotheses which explain the same symptom. (Sometimes what looks like a global problem is actually a collection of several local problems).

Anticipatory Knowledge. If a global solution appears possible, MOLE will first focus on identifying anticipatory knowledge. As was explained in our discussion of static analysis, if the expert spontaneously enters a covering association, MOLE cannot tell whether the two events are also linked by an anticipatory association, so it only generates a covering association. MOLE now examines whether there are any inactive covering associations which would have the desired effect if they were also interpreted as anticipatory assumptions.

For example, knowing that a loss in gas is explained by either a high gas temperature or high excess air, and that a high fly ash flow is explained by either very small fuel particles or high excess air, and not having any information to differentiate between these pairs of hypotheses, MOLE will accept high excess air as the explanation for both symptoms and reject the other two hypotheses. MOLE's reasoning is that since it does not have any reason to favor the other two hypotheses over high excess air, high excess air is the best choice because it alone can explain both symptoms. However, when given this case, the expert told MOLE that it was wrong—it should have rejected high excess air and accepted high gas temperature and very small fuel particles. MOLE recognized that if there was some evidence that could drive down the likelihood of high excess air, then the likelihood of the other two hypotheses would be driven up. Noting the absence of an event which provides covering evidence (a high oxygen reading) which would have been explained by high excess air, MOLE reasoned that if these two events were also linked by anticipatory knowledge, then the absence of a high oxygen reading would tend to rule out the high excess air hypothesis. MOLE asked the expert whether the absence of a high oxygen reading ruled out high excess air. The expert confirmed that it did.

Circumstantial Knowledge. If a global solution appears possible, and no anticipatory knowledge is discovered, MOLE focuses on circumstantial knowledge. One reason that circumstantial knowledge is given less priority than anticipatory knowledge is that we have found that anticipatory knowledge is more common. But a more important reason is that anticipatory knowledge is tied to covering knowledge and so the existing covering knowledge provides the richer context which MOLE tries to exploit first. Even when MOLE interprets a piece of knowledge as circumstantial, it does so tentatively, keeping in mind that in another example it may learn that it should be interpreted as anticipatory knowledge.

In our previous example, if MOLE had not known anything about the relevance of a high oxygen reading and the expert had entered it for the first time, then MOLE would have interpreted it as circumstantial evidence. If MOLE later learned that a high oxygen reading needs to be explained by high excess air, then it would add a covering association and reinterpret the circumstantial association as an anticipatory association.

Refining Knowledge. If the problem is local to a symptom (i.e. the hypotheses which need to be differentiated explain a common symptom), MOLE will ask the expert whether there are many features of the symptom which narrow the set of the hypotheses that are the likely causes.

So far in the power-plant domain we have not found any occasion for refining a symptom. However, in other domains refinement has been useful. For example, in a system that diagnoses automobile problems the symptom that the car would not start was refined to include the feature of whether or not the engine cranked. This feature is used to distinguish the hypothesis that the battery is dead from alternative explanations for the car not starting such as being our of gas, faulty spark plugs, and carburetor problems.

Qualifying Knowledge. Qualifying knowledge can adjust existing anticipatory, circumstantial, and refining knowledge. If such knowledge exists but its support is in the wrong direction, or in the right direction but is too weak, MOLE asks if there is any background condition which would strengthen or weaken the existing association in the right direction. In addition qualifying knowledge can be added in conjunction with an anticipatory association. This, in effect, adds a condition which strengthens a potential anticipatory association into one that has a significant impact.

For example, when trying to acquire knowledge that would lead it to accept that the fan power is being exceeded as the explanation for low excess air, and so reject a leak in an air duct as the explanation, MOLE looked for potential anticipatory knowledge. It knew that there was evidence of fouling and that this could cause the fan power to be exceeded, but discovered that the link was too weak to have the needed effect. This suggested to MOLE that it should ask the expert whether there was any condition which would make it very likely that the fan power would be exceeded when there was fouling. The expert confirmed that fouling almost always leads to the fan power being exceeded when there is a heavy load.

Adjusting Support Values. If the expert fails to provide any special knowledge which will differentiate among the hypotheses in the needed fashion, then there are three possibilities: (1) there is a need for combining knowledge; (2) the numeric support values are wrong and need to be adjusted; (3) a combination of locally differentiating evidence is needed, instead of a single globally differentiating piece of knowledge. MOLE's choice of what to explore first will depend on the "maturity" of the network and the reliability of feedback from the expert. It is easier for the expert to understand and respond to questions about locally differentiating evidence, so this option is usually tried first, provided the network is mature.

However, early in the refinement phase the most likely possibility is that the support values are wrong. After all, the support values are simply MOLE's guesses based on the structure of the network. The most common change is a shift of a symptom's support from some of its hypotheses to others. For example, there are only two hypotheses explaining the fan power being exceeded—fouling and a malfunction of a valve—so MOLE initially set the support value of each association to 0·5. However, fouling is much more likely than a valve malfunction, unless the fan has not been maintained for a long time. In a test case where the fan power had been exceeded and there was no further evidence for favoring fouling over a malfunction of a valve, MOLE could not decide between the two hypotheses. The expert indicated, however, that MOLE should have picked fouling. After failing to elicit any knowledge from the expert that would help it differentiate between these two causes, MOLE decided that its apportionment of support between the two hypotheses must be mistaken and shifted support from the malfunction of a valve hypothesis to the fouling hypothesis.

3.2.2. Covering knowledge
So far we have examined the case where MOLE would have reached the correct diagnosis if it has differentiated among the hypotheses differently. If differentiation is not the problem, then MOLE looks for missing covering knowledge. There are two possible cases: (1) a hypothesis should be rejected but cannot be because it is needed to explain some otherwise unexplained symptom; (2) a hypotheses should be accepted, but it was rejected because it is not needed to explain any symptom.

If a hypothesis fails to be rejected because it is needed to explain some symptom, then MOLE asks the expert for an alternative explanation of the symptom. For example, MOLE discovered that low excess air was a possible explanation of dark ash after being told in a test case that both of the hypotheses that it considered possible explanations for the dark ash should be rejected. MOLE reasoned that dark ash must have an explanation that it did not know about, and asked the expert for this explanation.

Suppose the expert had told MOLE that there is no alternative explanation; yet, the two explanations that it knows about are incorrect. MOLE considers two possibilities: (1) the symptom report is mistaken; (2) the evidence is not really a symptom—i.e. it has misinterpreted the event as covering evidence. MOLE would first inquire whether it is possible that the reported observation that there is dark ash could be mistaken. If it can be, MOLE would lower the default certainty for the report of this event. Then if it is again faced with a situation where there is evidence against both the explanations for this symptom, it will reject them both and suggest that a mistaken report (or mistaken observation) is the most likely explanation for the reported symptom. On the other hand, if the expert is quite certain about this reported event, then MOLE would examine how it can most coherently reinterpret the association—e.g. interpret the association as a circumstantial association instead of a covering association.

If a hypothesis is mistakenly rejected because it is not needed to explain anything, then MOLE asks the expert if there is some symptom that is present which can be explained by this hypothesis. For example, MOLE learned about the high stack gas temperature reading in a test case where it wrongly rejected high gas temperature as an explanation for loss in gas. MOLE the performance system had reasoned that since high excess air was needed to explain high fly ash and could also explain loss in gas, the high gas temperature was not needed. However, upon being informed that it should not have rejected high gas temperature, MOLE the knowledge-acquisition tool reasoned that there must be some piece of evidence that high gas temperature explained which was not explained by any other hypothesis. MOLE asked the expert for this information, and was told that the missing piece of evidence was the fact that the stack gas temperature reading was high.

3.2.3. Combining knowledge

But what if the expert indicates that there is no missing evidence that needs to be explained by the rejected hypothesis? MOLE reasons that it is probably missing some combining knowledge. If its hypotheses are properly differentiated locally and there is no missing piece of evidence for the hypothesis to explain, then this must be a case where the best explanation for some symptom is the combination of several hypotheses. It should be stressed that MOLE's default strategy will accept several explanations for a set of symptoms, provided each hypothesis is the best explanation of at least one symptom. What distinguishes the case where combining knowledge is needed is that several hypotheses are needed to explain one symptom. MOLE, with the guidance of the expert, acquires a rule for handling this special case.

For example, a misbalance of radiation and a misbalance of convection are alternative explanations for low heat transfer. Furthermore, the misbalance of convection hypothesis is only needed to explain the low heat transfer. When MOLE has reason to accept a misbalance of radiation as the explanation of low heat transfer, its default combining strategy will dictate that it reject the misbalance of convection hypothesis as unneeded. When told that this diagnosis was wrong, MOLE first looked for some symptom which a misbalance of convection explains but a misbalance of radiation does not. Upon learning that there are was no such symptom, MOLE reasoned that it must be missing a special combining rule, and asked the expert for the circumstances that lead him to accept both misbalance of radiation and misbalance of convection. In this case, it is the presence of low excess air.

As MOLE has evolved, dynamic analysis has increasingly taken on a more important role. By not insisting that the expert identify an event's type or an association's direction during the construction phase if he is uncertain about its value, the knowledge base used in the refinement phase is less determinate than it would otherwise be. These indeterminate associations provide MOLE with variable pieces of information when doing dynamic analysis. Whenever MOLE learns that it has made an incorrect diagnosis and has located the portions of the network where there is likely to be missing knowledge, indeterminate associations in these parts of the network are prime candidates for the missing knowledge. And since MOLE knows something about these associations—e.g. what events they connect—it can be quite certain how they should be interpreted even if the expert is not.

4. Conclusion

MOLE illustrates how much power a knowledge-acquisition tool can obtain from a set of domain independent heuristics about the knowledge-acquisition process and the nature of the world as it relates to diagnosis. MOLE plays the role of an experienced knowledge engineer who is able to work in conjunction with a domain expert and build a diagnostic system, even though the knowledge engineer has little or no knowledge of the domain. Like such a hypothetical knowledge engineer MOLE begins with no knowledge of the target domain nor any understanding of the domain's vocabulary. By interpreting its assumptions about the world in terms of explicit knowledge roles that guide heuristic classification and by exploiting a few heuristics about how domain experts are likely to express themselves, MOLE is able to extract intelligently from the expert information relevant for building a reasonable knowledge base for performing the given diagnostic task.

We want to thank Gary Kahn and Sandra Marcus for helpful suggestions in the development of MOLE. We also would like to thank Holger Sommer for serving as MOLE's expert in the power plant domain and for the useful feedback that he provided in the development of MOLE.

References

BOOSE, J. (1984). Personal construct theory and the transfer of human expertise. In *Proceedings of the National Conference on Artificial Intelligence.* Austin, Texas, 1984.

BUCHANAN, B. & SHORTLIFFE, E. (1984). *Rule-based Systems: the Mycin experiments of the Stanford Heuristic Programming Project.* Reading, Massachusetts: Addison–Wesley.

CLANCEY, W. (1984). Classification problem solving. *Proceedings of the National Conference on Artificial Intelligence,* Austin, Texas, 1984.

CLANCEY, W. (1985). Heuristic classification. *Artificial Intelligence,* **27,** 289–350.

DAVIS, R. & LENAT, D. (1982). *Knowledge-Based Systems in Artificial Intelligence.* McGraw-Hill.

ESHELMAN, L. & McDERMOTT, J. (1986). MOLE: a knowledge acquisition tool that uses its head. *Proceedings of the National Conference on Artificial Intelligence,* Philadelphia, Pennsylvania, 1986.

GRUBER, T. & COHEN, P. (1987). Design for acquisition: designing knowledge systems to facilitate knowledge acquisition. *International Journal of Man–Machine Studies.* In press.

KAHN, G., NOWLAN, S. & McDERMOTT, J. (1985a). Strategies for knowledge acquisition. *IEEE Transactions on Pattern Analysis and Machine Intelligence,* **7,** 511–522.

KAHN, G., NOWLAN, S. & McDERMOTT, J. (1985B). MORE: an intelligent knowledge acquisition tool. *Proceedings of Ninth International Conference on Artificial Intelligence,* Los Angelos, California, 1985.

KLINKER, G., BENTOLILA, J., GENETET, S., GRIMES M. & McDERMOTT, J. KNACK— report-driven knowledge acquisition. *International Journal of Man–Machine Studies.* In press.

MARCUS, S., McDERMOTT, J. & WANG, T. (1985). Knowledge acquisition for constructuve systems. *Proceedings of Ninth International Conference on Artificial Intelligence,* Los Angelos, California, 1985.

McDERMOTT, J. (1986). Making expert systems explicit. *Proceedings of 10th Congress of the International Federation of Information Processing Societies,* Dublin, Ireland, 1986.

SZOLOVITS, P. & PAUKER, S. (1978). Categorical and probabilistic reasoning in medical diagnosis. *Artificial Intelligence,* **11,** 115–144.

VAN DE BRUG, A., BACHANT, J. & McDERMOTT, J. (1985). Doing R1 with Style. *Proceedings of the Second IEEE Conference on Artificial Intelligence Applications,* Miami, Florida, 1985.

Knowledge-based knowledge acquisition for a statistical consulting system

WILLIAM A. GALE

AT & T Bell Laboratories 2C278, 600 Mountain Avenue, Murray Hill, NJ 07974, U.S.A.

Knowledge-based knowledge acquisition means restricting the domain of knowledge that can be acquired and developing a conceptual model of the domain. We have built a prototype knowledge-based knowledge acquisition system for the domain of data analysis. A critique of the prototype has led to a design for a possibly practical data analysis knowledge acquisition system.

1. Introduction

Daryl Pregibon and I built our first statistical consultation system, REX, using standard expert system techniques (Gale, 1986a; Pregibon & Gale, 1984). REX is a consultation program in regression analysis, a statistical technique for data analysis. It demonstrated the feasibility of using expert system techniques to construct data analysis consultation systems. It had an active life as a demonstration system, running weekly about for a year.

We then faced the problem of building consultation systems for other analytic techniques, which brought home the inadequacies of the knowledge-acquisition methods used in building REX. The next (second) section reviews the shortcomings of standard expert system construction methods as we experienced them in a statistical application. Similar shortcomings have been noted in many application areas, leading to a wide-spread perception of need for better knowledge-acquisition methods.

REX made two major contributions to subsequent work. The first is a viewpoint for thinking about data analysis as a diagnostic problem. Briefly, one should list model assumptions (analogous to possible diseases), test the data set at hand for violations of the assumptions (analogous to symptoms), and if found select a transform of the data (analogous to treatment). The success of this approach depends on the representation of statistical knowledge. This is the second major contribution of REX. REX has a set of statistical primitives including tests, plots, assumptions, and transforms, which can be implemented as frames with slots containing procedures, or as objects (classes) with instance variables and methods. The hierarchical structure of the network of frames directs the interpretation of the statistical knowledge.

We refer to the statistical knowledge as *strategy*. A hand held calculator can do (some) regression *calculations*. But the assumptions behind this calculation, how they can be examined, when they should be examined, and how they can be remedied if found require considerably more expressive power than even such elaborate calculators as modern statistical packages.

109

KNOWLEDGE-BASED SYSTEMS Vol. 2
ISBN 0-12-115920-5

Student was subsequently designed to allow expert statisticians working alone to build and test strategies (Gale, 1986*b*). It was conceived of as a program by example system, because of the key role that examples seemed to play in the construction of REX. We built a prototype that acquired knowledge from a *first* example in a new data analysis area. The third section describes the knowledge-acquisition techniques used in the prototype, and the fourth criticizes them.

One successful part of the Student prototype is knowledged-based knowledge acquisition. The key to this technique is restricting the domain for which knowledge can be acquired. Just as domain restriction allows domain specific knowledge to be used in a knowledge-based *consultation system,* domain restriction allows domain specific knowledge to be used in a knowledge-based *knowledge-acquisition system.* The domain-specific knowledge essential for knowledge-based knowledge acquisition is a conceptual framework for the domain. The framework must specify the types of primitive entities to be used, how each primitive will be represented, acquired, and modified, and how the primitives can be combined and displayed. The fifth section discusses the issues that must be resolved in order to use knowledge-based knowledge acquisition.

At the risk of redundancy, let me define *knowledge-based knowledge acquisition* as the approach to knowledge acquisition which: (1) restricts the domain of knowledge which can be acquired; and (2) builds a conceptual model of the restricted domain.

The sixth section discusses the generality of knowledge-based knowledge acquisition. It is a practical tool for widening the knowledge-acquisition bottleneck when several similar consultation systems must be built.

2. A critique of knowledge acquisition in REX

Developing a strategy for use in REX was a labor-intensive process. Two phases can be distinguished. In the first phase the statistician responsible for the strategy, Daryl Pregibon, chose a half dozen regression examples that clearly showed some frequent problems. He then analysed them using interactive statistical software with an automatic trace. After analysing the group of examples, he studied the traces and abstracted a description of what he was doing. We coded this as a strategy for REX and tried it on a few more examples. He revised the strategy completely at this point, and the second phase began.

In the second and longer phase, one of us would select one additional regression example and run REX interactively on the chosen example. Since we selected the example knowing what would stretch REX, REX usually reported a severe problem that it didn't know how to fix. Then we would modify the strategy so that the example would be handled. This process was iterated through about three dozen more examples.

Based on this experience, and on a feeling that it was typical of other techniques, we do not believe it is possible to construct a data analysis strategy without working through many examples. One must make many decisions to construct a strategy, and there is no literature simplifying the task. Therefore the only available defense of a strategy is to demonstrate performance, which requires working many examples more than those used to construct the system. On the other hand, our experience also leads us to believe that it is easy to generalize from data analysis examples. The basis for generalization is usually a statistical test which statisticians can provide. Generalization then consists of determining the range of values of the test for which the demonstrated technique holds.

However, the way in which we worked examples for REX was far from ideal. The first difficulty with our method was assuring ourselves that a strategy modified to work one additional example still worked all previous examples. We could by brute force run REX in batch mode on all previous examples and see if the performance was the same. Usually we reasoned that most of the previous examples could not be affected, and checked the few that might be affected by hand. Naturally, the more examples worked, the more severe this problem became. The need to check consistency in batch mode for a system designed to be interactive reduced the flexibility of the strategy developed.

Second, the method used was the epitome of the currently standard two-person development of expert systems. I built the inference engine used while Daryl was responsible for the strategy developed. Whenever Daryl wanted to do something he had not done before, we had to huddle, as Daryl was learning a language he would only use to construct one program. In a department with twenty professional statisticians and one person intimately familiar with the inference engine, it was not clear how many additional data analysis techniques could be handled by this two-person approach.

Third, it would be difficult to modify the strategy in REX. Modifiability is important because a growing literature on strategy (Gale, 1986c; Haux, 1986; Darius, 1986) can be expected to suggest desirable changes. It is also important because users will probably want to modify strategies to their particular needs. Statistics is a discipline that is applied in other, "ground" domains. Current knowledge representation and language-generation techniques are not adequate to produce a tool that will speak physics with physicists and psychology with psychologists. An alternative to one broad tool is a tool that is readily specialized. However, the first two problems would make this difficult: to specialize the program a local statistician would have to learn a language used by no other program in the world, and the modifications made might inadvertently destroy some capabilities of the strategy.

The contribution of REX to subsequent work was stated in the introduction. It provided us with the beginnings of a conceptual framework for data analysis: a data analysis consists of a desired calculation, assumptions required for the calculation to be meaningful, tests for the violation of the assumptions, and transformations to ameliorate the violations. The classes of frames used in REX provided us with an initial list of classes of primitives that has remained useful and has been expanded.

3. Knowledge acquisition in a Student prototype

The necessity of working examples to construct a data-analysis strategy suggested the possibility of acquiring strategies directly through that process. A system should assist the teacher in establishing consistency across all examples worked, and should not force a statistician to learn an obscure language. It appeared that examples might provide a language suitable for communication between statisticians and computers.

The first issue encountered in designing Student was how to learn from the *first* example. In a system without knowledge, there is simply no basis for use of information provided in working an example. By providing Student with the conceptual framework induced from REX, we have built a prototype that can deal meaningfully with an example even when it has seen no previous examples. This step was only possible because the system was limited to data analysis.

The prototype was implemented on a Symbolics 3670 communicating with a statistics program on a Vax 750.

The conceptual framework used in the Student prototype had the ten classes of primitives shown in the following table. Each instance of a primitive was represented by a frame. In the table, indentation indicates that names of instances of the primitive indented occurred as values in some slot of the superordinate primitive. That is, the relation shown by indentation is "uses information from".

```
        input variables
                    data types
        assumption testing
                    plot
                                        generic plot
                    test
                                        generic test
    action
                    question discriminator
                    predicate discriminator
```

Each primitive has a set of slots, which are also chosen to reflect the structure of data analysis. As an example, perhaps the simplest primitive is the input variable frame, which had only a few slots:

input variable
    external name of input
    required or optional
    default if optional
    data type
    variable name

The content of the instances of these primitives is the information that a consultation system must have. For instance, when asking a consulting client for a specific input, it is necessary to know the common name of the input. Likewise, the system must know whether to insist upon having a given input variable before beginning the analysis (required or optional), and what default to use if the user does not have one of the optional input. The system must also know what data type is required for the input in order to determine if submitted data is possible. Since we do not want to overwrite input data with later calculations, we need a standard variable name to copy the input to.

Gale (1986*b*, *c*) discusses the formalization of data analysis used in Student in more detail. Here it is sufficient to note that the work stands as an example of how the conceptual framework from one consultation system (REX) can be generalized and formalized.

Knowledge-based knowledge acquisition in this context means specifying how the contents of each slot will be acquired. In the case of the input variable primitive, each slot could be acquired by asking the teaching statistician. Most of them could also be acquired more actively. The internal name could be created from the external name and perhaps a unique number. Acceptable data types could be inferred from the data types of the inputs to the set of examples provided. Optional variables and their defaults could be inferred as those with repeated inputs. In fact, it seemed better in each of these cases to ask the teaching statistician and then use the information to check inputs to teaching examples.

Thus, subsidiary techniques designed for the specific knowledge will be chosen. The Student prototype used three subsidiary techniques: interviewing, limits induction, and Monte Carlo learning.

The preponderance of cases were handled by interviewing. Knowing what is needed, and having a statistician at hand, it is easy just to ask. Even so, exactly how to ask for the information varied between menus, fill in the blank, multiple simultaneous choice, and free response. And of course the prompts varied for each item.

Monte Carlo learning was used to establish initial notions of the distributions for test results. The distributions were used in turn to set initial cut points, or *limits* for distinguishing severe, mild and insignificant cases of assumption violations.

Limits induction is inference of limits on test ranges from test results and action (transform) or non-action by the statistician. Let v_i be the value of a test on the ith data set, and a_i be T or F as the statistician acted or didn't act in the situation covered by the test. Then set the upper cut point as $\max(v_i \mid a_i = F)$ and the lower cut point as $\min(v_i \mid a_i = T)$. Then for test values above the upper cut point, the statistician has always acted, and for values below the lower cut point, the statistician has never acted. This simple scheme is slightly modified to include the Monte Carlo results. Limits induction was programmed in the prototype, but with only single examples, it was not tested.

Knowledge-based knowledge acquisition has several advantages. First, the information in each slot is necessary for a consultation program. Systematizing the knowledge to acquire from a statistician speeds construction because the system won't forget what is needed.

Another advantage of knowledge-based knowledge acquisition can be shown in the acquisition of an input variable. It is almost always appropriate to run a number of tests on each input variable by itself. Without knowledge-based knowledge acquisition each time a new variable is given, a battery of tests must be specified by the teaching statistician. However, it is easy to keep track of what tests have been used for all input variables by data type, and to suggest these to the statistician. Since the tests are based only on knowing the data type of the input, they will often be appropriate in many different data analysis procedures. The domain knowledge we are using here is that the tests are similar in many different analysis types, and that they are reasonably organized by data type.

As another example, a statistician may notice after some time of programming that an optional input variable is possible. One would then back up and increase the generality of numerical procedures to accommodate the extra variable. With knowledge-based knowledge acquisition, the statistician is encouraged to think of optional inputs at the beginning of the construction process, thus avoiding the costs of reprogramming. This encouragement may not be effective in all cases, but it can only work in the direction of reducing the problem. In short, by providing a framework for data analysis, the statistician is encouraged to think in previously successful terms.

A system that acquires first examples does not address all the problems in building a knowledge acquisition system. However, the domain restriction is expected to be useful for extending a given body of knowledge as well as initiating it. Extension of knowledge for a given data analytic technique involves demonstrating more assumptions, how to detect their violation, and how to fix them. The same techniques used for initial acquisition suffice here. However, it is also necessary to check consistency for previously worked examples.

Consistency means that after incorporating information on a new assumption, the recommended analyses of all previously worked examples are not changed. This is a requirement analogous to logical monotonicity. Some changes can be proved consistent by using domain knowledge. The domain knowledge consists of a theorem, and the proof consists of verifying the hypotheses of the theorem, so this is not automatic theorem-proving. The proof may use data that could be specified and collected when the previous examples were demonstrated. This will be more efficient than rerunning examples. Other cases, such as showing that a new test is not passed for an old example, require new calculations. Domain knowledge may be able to specify data to save which will make such checking faster than completely reworking an example.

Of course, the check may find that a change is inconsistent. That is, that the recommended analysis for at least one previous example has changed. Then the statistician will need to *revise* the existing body of knowledge. This might just consist of blessing the revised analysis for the inconsistent examples. Or it may require revising the strategy, perhaps revising the assumption just added. This can be assisted by domain knowledge encoded as editing procedures.

4. A critique of knowledge acquisition in student

Interviewing is useful. A knowledge-based interview is easy to write, since one knows exactly what to acquire. Interview procedures attached to slots are easy to keep track of, so that it is easy to see if all slots can be acquired.

A research issue is how much can and should be acquired by interviewing, and how much must or should be provided as initial knowledge. The prototype tested this by attempting to acquire everything by interviewing. It appeared that everything *could* be acquired this way. However, experience with this extreme approach led to deciding to provide some items as initial knowledge. The collected reasons used to justify initial provision of an item were:

(1) distractingly frequent requests for information;
(2) need for richly structured information;
(3) need for careful control of the generality of information; and
(4) stable and non-controversial information.

For example, data types (vectors, matrices, time series, . . .) will be built in for reasons 2 and 4. An initial core of technical definitions will be provided for reasons 1 and 4. The domains of functions (so that no attempt will be made to take logs of negative numbers) will be built in for reasons 3 and 4. Reason 4 is cited in each case and appears to be necessary.

Programming by example is possible, but slow and clumsy. There is, however, key information in the examples. And, as argued, examples are necessary. It is useful when describing a plot or test to have an example to do the operations on immediately.

The lisp machine was a successful prototyping environment. However, our consultation systems must use a statistical package for their specialized computations. Therefore, a practical system will probably have to be built on the same machine as the package for reliability of delivery.

The Student prototype assumption testing frames need to be generalized. First, arguments are needed. The prototype was built to redo REX so it copied the REX organization of assumptions. REX had explicitly represented "checking the dependent variable for outliers", and "checking the independent variable for outliers". Thus the Student prototype is only prepared to learn about ground-level assumption violations such as "dependent-outlier" and "independent-outlier". Clearly, acquiring a variable-containing entity to represent "checking the input variable for outliers" would be more powerful. Second, the assumption-testing notion needed to be generalized to the notion of "feature", which might never lead to a transformation, but which might lead to a report item.

We found in building REX that the most powerful explanations in statistics were not verbal, but graphical. Thus we programmed before and after plots for each transformation. Student is able to construct these automatically from plots acquired in the course of being shown how to detect an assumption violation. This is a convenience. Generic plots may be another example of knowledge best provided initially. But it may be best to include the capability to acquire them even if it is rarely used.

Monte Carlo learning seems like a technique with much wider applicability for statistical systems to learn about statistical tests. Limits induction is apparently a useful idea although it has not been tested. It can describe what a statistician has actually done, possibly pointing out a poorly worked example, or a poor test. It can be used to alert statisticians to taking an action that is not consistent with previous actions, but can be changed easily if they insist.

5. Issues for knowledge-based knowledge acquisition

DOES THE RESTRICTED DOMAIN HAVE A USEFUL GENERALITY?

Restriction to the point that one can provide a framework necessarily sacrifices generality. If only one expert system can be made within the restrictions, building a special tool to assist in its construction will be unproductive. Snee (1980) reports a survey result that a dozen data analysis techniques will cover the bulk of data analysed. So perhaps this many systems would be needed for standard forms of analysis. There are also, however, many specialized forms, practiced in only one industry or one company. After building S (Becker & Chambers, 1984), it was observed that S was being used frequently to construct specialized analytic environments. This suggests a need for many statistical expert systems.

WHAT IS THE CONCEPTUAL FRAMEWORK FOR THE DOMAIN? SPECIFICALLY...
What classes of primitives are needed?
Probably the most efficient way to develop a conceptual framework is to build one expert system in the domain. The classes of primitives used are highlighted if one uses a frame-based programming approach. The different classes of primitives have different slots and different control procedures. REX was programmed using a system allowing either rules or frames. It turned out that the frames were more useful. A side effect was to identify the classes of primitives used. The Student prototype was built to use frames, and thinking in terms of the classes of primitives made its structure clearer from the start.

How are the primitives structured?
Slots in frames which refer to other frames induce a network structure on a collection of frames. This structuring is easy to implement, and has been sufficient for representing assumptions using plots, tests, and transforms in slots. It has not been sufficient for representing a strategy using assumptions, because control concepts (branch and loop) turned out to be necessary. But the additional structure was easy to add.

How is the knowledge validated?
This will be highly dependent on the domain. Validation needs to be supported as much as possible, however. In our case, the knowledge is validated by the coincidence of machine-generated analyses of specific examples and expert analyses of the same examples. Therefore Student is designed to collect and display examples and their analyses. It can then check the required coincidence automatically.

What background knowledge will be supplied?
This will also depend strongly on the domain. Knowledge at the periphery of the domain, such as knowledge of mathematics as required for statistics, is likely to have the required stability and to be non-controversial. The background knowledge identified in our case consists of knowledge about data types, functions, plot types, and vocabulary.

How is the knowledge communicated?
We are trying to build systems that will allow subject matter experts to construct a consultation system. The conceptual framework must be communicated clearly to the expert using the system. Indeed, the expert must be actively encouraged to think in the specific terms provided by the framework, even if it is a natural one.

Probably the most important area to communicate is the structuring of primitives. We have found graphical displays of the hierarchy to be useful here.

6. The generality of knowledge-based knowledge acquisition

The issues raised in the previous section lead directly to an assessment of the generality of knowledge-based knowledge acquisition.

First, it is clear that it applies to areas where more than one expert system is to be built. It will, in fact, usually be necessary to built at least one expert system manually before it is clear what a conceptual framework for a domain might be. My impression is that many expert systems built to date are representatives of similar ones that might also be built. For instance, medical diagnosis and mineral-deposit detection have many specific diseases and minerals to deal with. Thus there may be many domains with both sufficient generality and sufficient restriction.

Second, a conceptual framework is necessary. In building a first, ground-level, system it will help to seek regularity and common cases. A frame based programming system helps to identify these commonalities. But, if the first system has a myriad of types of rules or frames, a generalized framework is unlikely.

Third, the framework must be readily presentable. The subject matter specialists may need to be encouraged to think within the specific framework provided, even if it is natural. For hierarchically organized knowledge, graphs are an attractive communication medium. Some restriction in expressiveness may be appropriate to get easier communication.

DeJong's (1983) method of explanatory schema acquisition is another example of the possibility of one-shot learning that is possible with domain knowledge. His approach has more detailed and explicit domain knowledge than ours, and learns independently of human assistance. His technique has not been used for knowledge acquisition for a consulting system, but might be extended that way.

Mark Musen's OPAL (Musen, 1986) is the most similar approach at this conference. The representation of entities and relations in OPAL uses the same approach as the representation of primitives in Student. The result in his case is also to reduce the knowledge acquisition problem to that of filling in the blanks. The approach of SALT (Marcus, 1986) while less similar is still related. The domain of SALT is broader, its domain-knowledge weaker than for OPAL and Student.

7. Summary

Knowledge-based knowledge acquisition is possible when the domain of knowledge acquisition can be restricted and a conceptual framework for the restricted domain provided. It is useful when the restricted domain still allows constructing a variety of expert systems. We have demonstrated the feasibility of using knowledge-based knowledge acquisition in one domain, data analysis, by building a prototype. The method should be usable in other domains. The principal requirements on the domain are: (1) that several independent consulting systems are needed; and (2) that the conceptual framework from one consultation system can be formalized.

References

BECKER, R. A. & CHAMBERS, J. M. (1984). *S: an Interactive Environment for Data Analysis and Graphics*. Belmont, California: Wadsworth.

DARIUS, P. (1986). Building expert systems with the help of existing statistical software: an example. *Proceedings COMPSTAT86*, Physica-Verlag, Vienna, Austria, p. 277.

DEJONG, G. (1983). Acquiring schemata through understanding and generalizing plans. *Proceedings Eighth IJCAI*, Morgan Kauffman, Los Altos, California, p. 462.

GALE, W. A. (1986a). REX review. In GALE, W. A. Ed., *Artificial Intelligence and Statistics*, Massachusetts: Addison-Wesley, Reading, Chapter 9.

GALE, W. A. (1986b). Student Phase 1: a report on work in progress. In GALE, W. A. Ed., *Artificial Intelligence and Statistics*. Reading, Massachusetts: Addison-Wesley, Chapter 11.

GALE, W. A. (1986c). A comparison of representations for statistical strategies. *Proceedings of Statistical Computation Section*, ASA, Washington, D.C.

MARCUS, S. (1986). Taking backtracking with a grain of SALT. *Proceedings of the Knowledge Acquisition for Knowledge-Based Systems Workshop*, Banff, Canada, 1986.

MUSEN, M. A., FAGAN, L. M., COMBS, D. M. & SHORTLIFFE, E. H. (1986). Using a domain model to drive an interactive knowledge editing tool. *Proceedings of the Knowledge Acquisition for Knowledge-Based Systems Workshop*, Banff, Canada, 1986.

PREGIBON, D. & GALE, W. A. (1984). REX: an expert system for regression analysis. *Proceedings COMPSTAT84*, Physica-Verlag, Vienna, Austria, p. 242.

HAUX, R. Ed. (1986). *Expert Systems in Statistics*. Stuttgart: Gustav Fischer Verlag.

SNEE, R. D. (1980). Preparing statisticians for careers in industry. *The American Statistician*, May 1980, v. 34, pp. 65–75.

A conceptual framework for knowledge elicitation

Chaya Garg-Janardan and Gavriel Salvendy†

School of Industrial Engineering, Purdue University, West Lafayette, Indiana 47907, U.S.A.

This paper includes a statement of the knowledge-elicitation problem and argues that the problem is two-fold: to outline a conceptual framework and to develop and validate a knowledge extraction methodology. Required and desirable attributes of a knowledge elicitation methodology are discussed. A conceptual framework that may be used to derive a knowledge elicitation methodology is outlined. This conceptual framework is established by extending Newell's and Simon's (1972) problem space concept and integrating it with Kelly's (1955) theory of personal constructs. This framework provides guidelines regarding the kind of knowledge to be elicited, and the sequence and format in which this should be done. It also elicits knowledge that is used subconsciously and in unique ways by the expert.

1. Knowledge elicitation

Knowledge elicitation is a critical first step in the construction of expert systems, since the time required by this phase affects the cost-effective development of expert systems. Also, the performance of the expert system in terms of the systems reliability, validity and utility depends on the reliability, validity and accuracy of the elicited knowledge. It is thus of great concern that knowledge elicitation poses a significant bottleneck to the process of building expert systems. Knowledge elicitation is the process by which facts, rules, patterns, heuristics, and operations used by humans to solve problems, in the particular domain are elicited. Besides humans, knowledge may be elicited from several sources including books, journals, reports, manuals, databases and case studies. However, knowledge elicitation from humans is the major thrust here since the intuition, experience and heuristics used by humans in problem solving are rarely stated explicitly in the literature.

1.1. IMPORTANT ISSUES IN KNOWLEDGE EXTRACTION

A concise and formal statement of the problem of knowledge elicitation precludes the possibility of making explicit the many diverse but interacting factors that contribute to it. To this effect, the statement of the problem is preceded by an examination of issues identified as important to this problem. These include: (a) what knowledge should be elicited; and (b) what attributes should a knowledge elicitation methodology possess? Each of these issues is discussed below.

---

† The writing of this paper and development of the concepts herein were made possible due to fellowships to the first author by NEC Corporation and IBM Corporation and by the NEC Corporation professorship to the second author.

119

What knowledge to elicit?

Two kinds of knowledge: process and content, may be elicited from humans. *Process knowledge* is defined as the strategies and procedures used in problem solving. *Content knowledge* represents the actual facts and rules used by the human in solving problems. The two kinds of knowledge cannot be divided into mutually exclusive classes. Process knowledge includes the methods by which a subset of the content knowledge is accessed, combined and used to solve problems. Combinations of content and process knowledge and heuristics may be used successfully so often that they become automated and stored as chunks by the human. As soon as the human recognizes a pattern in a given problem, the associated chunk is executed. These chunks form as an individual's experience and expertise level increases and render the process–content distinction more ambiguous. In the context of knowledge extraction, it may be impossible for the knowledge engineer to assert that only one of process or content knowledge will be elicited. This is because, as stated above, the two kinds of knowledge cannot be divided into mutually exclusive classes. Despite this ambiguity, definition of the kind of knowledge that is of primary interest provides a framework within which to elicit knowledge, helps evaluate the completeness of the elicited knowledge and prevents the development of methods that elicit random samples of domain-specific knowledge. The kind of knowledge that is of primary interest may vary from domain to domain. Elicitation of content knowledge may be the chief concern in analysis type domains; whereas, in synthesis type domains elicitation of both process and content knowledge may be equally important. Analysis problems are those where all possible solutions can be enumerated ahead of time. Synthesis problems are those where unique solutions may be built from components of inputs. In synthesis problems it is not possible to enumerate all possible solutions, at the very outset.

Attributes of a knowledge-elicitation methodology

A first step in the formulation of an effective and efficient knowledge elicitation methodology is the enumeration of its attributes (both required and desirable). The methodology *should rest on a theoretical framework,* i.e. the procedure used by the methodology should derive from this theoretical framework. A valid theoretical framework facilitates delineation of what knowledge to elicit, provides a bases against which to validate the methodology and the elicited knowledge, and structures the procedure used by the methodology. The methodology should be such that it almost *ferrets* information out of the human. This is because humans have difficulty in expressing the actual information and strategies used in problem-solving. A methodology is needed which draws attention to various aspects of the problem and prompts expression. Instead of eliciting random subsets of knowledge, the methodology should attempt to elicit *deep, causal, strategic, and nearly complete* knowledge. The methodology should not employ procedures that are task specific and vary widely from domain to domain and researcher to researcher. Instead procedures used should be *applicable to a class of problem domains.*

A knowledge-elicitation tool should objectively check for *inconsistencies and conflicts* in the elicited data. Such checks are necessary because humans in their perceptual, response and decision-making process are subject to several sources of bias and inaccuracy (Tversky & Kahneman, 1974; Moray, 1985). Checks for conflicts are particularly necessary when eliciting expertise from multiple sources. Expertise Transfer System's (ETS, Boose, 1986) method of presenting knowledge in multiple forms to the expert facilitates the detection of conflicts but does not guarantee it. The tool should have a system for *combining information elicited from multiple experts* and for resolving conflicts in expertise collected from multiple sources or from a single source. ETS incorporates a method to achieve this.

Appropriate *quantitative and qualitative methods* should be used to analyse the elicited data, so that any implicit relations, trends and patterns in the elicited knowledge are made explicit. A first step towards the use of quantitative techniques in analyzing data is ENTAIL (Gaines & Shaw, 1981; Boose, 1986). Graesser and Clark (1985) suggest the identification of conceptual graph structures in the elicited information as an effective way of imposing structure and making explicit much of the implicit information. Such analyses will facilitate outputting the elicited data in a structured format. Any hidden relations identified may be used to chunk and establish links in network and frame based representations. The tool should provide facilities using which the elicited data may be *examined and modified* by the expert. Systems which currently provide this facility include TEIRESIAS (Davis, 1979), ETS (Boose, 1986) and XPLAIN (Swartout, 1984). The format in which the subject responds should be *flexible*. There should be a trade off between flexibility offered and running the risk of permitting the human to ramble on as in undirected 'think aloud' protocol analysis. The individual may be given the option of choosing one of several response formats.

In essence the problem is two-fold: to outline a conceptual framework and develop and validate a tool for knowledge acquisition. Both problems need to be solved in light of the above specifications regarding *what* knowledge to elicit, and *how* to elicit this knowledge. This paper includes a solution to the first part of the problem. A solution to the latter part is currently being developed and validated. Prior to outlining a solution to the former part, a brief discussion on the existing methodologies for knowledge elicitation is included.

2. Current methodologies for knowledge elicitation

2.1. PROTOCOL ANALYSIS AND RELATED METHODS

Protocol analysis is the collection of information from subjects by having them "think aloud" or introspect and verbalize. Nisbett and Wilson (1977) caution researchers about the pitfalls of protocol analysis. Removal in time, a priori theories (correctly or incorrectly formed), mechanics of judgment, context, non-events and discrepancy between the magnitude of cause and effect are listed by Nisbett and Wilson as the factors which affect the availability and representativeness of events and stimuli in individuals. These in turn affect the consistency and accuracy of the verbal reports that emerge.

Ericcson and Simon (1984) provide a critical but comprehensive discussion on methods used to collect and analyse protocols and factors that users of protocol analysis should be aware of. Ericcson and Simon list timing of verbalizations, directedness and content of verbilizations and amount of intermediate processing required as factors that affect the consistency and completeness of verbal reports. Thus, while analyzing protocols it is very essential to account for the influence of the above mentioned factors.

Knowledge-extraction techniques derived using protocol analysis include Grover's (1983) three-phase metholology, delphi (Jagannathan & Elmaghraby, 1985), Crawford Slip Method (Rusk & Krone, 1984) and Smith's and Baker's (1983) idea of presenting experts with novel problems and recording their problem-solving process. The common denominator underlying these techniques is an emphasis towards structuring and systematizing the knowledge-elicitation process. Despite its weaknesses protocol analysis has been used to elicit knowledge in the construction of a majority of the expert systems. Sufficient knowledge may be elicited using protocol analysis only at the expense of large investments of time, effort and money. This has led many knowledge engineers to conclude that the knowledge-extraction phase has significantly stymied the building of expert systems. Grover's method while more structured and streamlined than protocol analysis is subject to all the shortcomings attributed to protocol analysis. This is because protocol analysis is largely resorted to for information elicitation. The development of interactive methods to elicit expertise evidenced a movement aways from protocol analysis.

Several methods that elicit expertise interactively have been developed including MDIS (Antonelli, 1983); PLANET (Shaw, 1984); MORE (Kahn, Nowlan and McDermott, 1985); SALT (Marcus, McDermott and Wang, 1985); CAP (Koubek, Salvendy and Dunsmore, 1986); ETS (Boose, 1986), and Student (Gale, 1986).

2.2. INTERACTIVE METHODS FOR KNOWLEDGE ELICITATION

Expertise Transfer System (ETS) is an interactive grid-based method for eliciting knowledge (Boose, 1986). The repertory grid technique was developed for use as a psychotherapeutic tool by George Kelly in 1955 based on his personal constructs theory. Application of this grid approach to diverse domains for information elicitation and several quantitative methods for the analysis of grids are outlined in Shaw (1980, 1981). In fact, PLANET (Shaw, 1984) is an integrated set of computer programs, that offers several alternative approaches for the elicitation and analysis of repertory grids, from one or more people. It provides programs for the analysis of a single grid as well as for comparison and analysis of data across several grids. In ETS Boose first applied the grid technique to knowledge extraction for building expert systems.

ETS is a particularly effective knowledge-elicitation tool in analysis type domains, due to the many features it provides, including generation of entailment graphs, intermediate and conclusion rules; combination of expertise from multiple sources; presentation of elicited data to the expert in multiple forms; and a system for tracing through the knowledge base of elicited data. NeoETS (Bradshaw & Boose, 1986), a new version of ETS incorporates ideas from Saaty's (1980) Analytic Hierarchy Process (AHP) and uses hierarchies as well as rating grids with multiple variable types to represent knowledge. Hierarchies not only help the expert break down problems into component parts but also permit reasoning at different levels.

MORE (Kahn *et al.*, 1985) is an automated knowledge-acquisition system that helps refine an existing knowledge base. The builders of this system based on their experience in hand-crafting MUD, a drilling fluid diagnostic and consultant, developed a qualitative model of causal relations and identified a set of strategies that they found useful in refining (manually) the MUD knowledge base. This causal model and set of strategies are used by MORE to guide the interview process. Given a model of the domain knowledge and the set of strategies this system appears to be particularly effective in refining an existing knowledge base.

SALT (Marcus *et al.*, 1985) is one of the first systems developed for knowledge acquisition in synthesis-type domains, i.e. domains where problems are solved by constructing solutions. In particular, SALT was developed as a knowledge-acquisition tool for VT, an elevator system configurer. To accomplish this, SALT's problem-solving shell draws on three kinds of knowledge (method, constraint and fix schemas) that are elicited and represented using the two subsystems (the interviewing and the rule-generation subsystems) within SALT. Based on the input, data-driven procedures are used to determine each piece of the configuration and the values for each piece. Knowledge which helps identify constraint violations is drawn upon to spot constraint violations by identifying and checking constrained values. Next, knowledge which indicates "fixes" for constraint violations is used to "fix" potential constraint violations. It appears that the problem solving shell used by SALT facilitates knowledge acquisition in synthesis-type domains.

In summary, the existing methods for knowledge elicitation are reviewed. The PLANET set of programs provide a convenient and structured format to elicit and analyse responses from a single individual as well as compare responses across several individuals. PLANET's suitability as a tool for knowledge extraction may be dramatically improved by incorporating in it a scheme to draw attention to various aspects of the domain and a method to detect conflicts in the elicited data. ETS is very appropriate for eliciting knowledge in analysis-type domains; however, in synthesis type domains its inability to elicit "causal knowledge, procedural knowledge or strategic knowledge", (Boose, 1986) mitigates its usefulness. The methods used in both SALT and MORE may be borrowed to improve significantly existing tools for knowledge extraction. For example, the strategies used in MORE may be used to effect rapid and accurate refinement of the elicited knowledge. The knowledge-elicitation techniques described above do not specifically address the problem of outlining a conceptual framework which may be used to derive a knowledge extraction methodology. Below, one such framework is described.

3. A conceptual framework for knowledge elicitation

The conceptual framework (Fig. 1) outlined here is established by extending a well-known theory of problem-solving and integrating it with a theory which explains how individuals construe themselves and their environment. The former is Newell's and Simon's (1972) theory of problem-solving and the latter is Kelly's (1955) theory of personal constructs. In the following section, the two theories are described, and the integration of the two theories, is brought out.

3.1. THE PROBLEM SPACE CONCEPT

In this paper, the authors extend Newell's and Simon's (1972) concept of a problem space. To clarify and illustrate certain concepts, an arbitrary domain is chosen, the

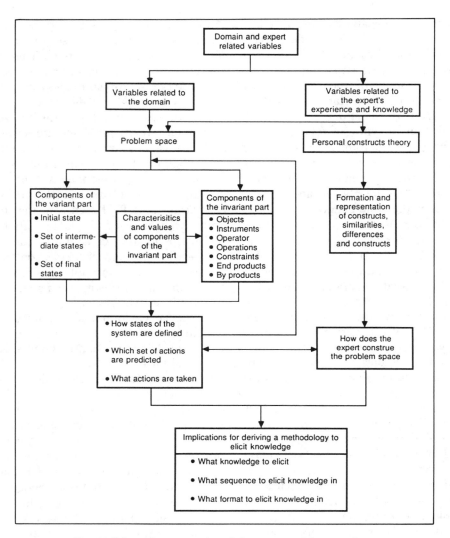

FIG. 1. Schematic presentation of the conceptual framework.

control and monitoring of a Flexible Manufacturing System (FMS), by a supervisor. It is asserted that the problem space of any problem consists of an invariant part and a variant part. Further, the authors contend that the invariant part is comprised of the following components: objects, instruments, operator, operations, operating conditions, end products, by products and certain constraints. The variant part is comprised of a set of states. Each of the two parts is described before the relationship between the parts is brought out.

3.1.1. The invariant part of the problem space

Definition of each component of the invariant part. The *object* is the inputs given to the problem which is being solved. The *instruments* are the tools, machines and aids which may be used by the operator to perform operations on the given object. The *operator,* though a part of the problem space, has an overview of it. The operator not only knows what problem is being worked on, but is also aware of what the end products and by products should be, what resources are available or unavailable and under what constraints the work has to proceed. The *end products* and *by products* are what would result if the problem is solved successfully. *Operations* are the actions which may be taken by the operator and which may bring about changes in the other invariant and variant components of the problem space. The invariant components do not change *per se,* but the values of their characteristics undergo change. This is discussed later, in this paper. *Constraints* are imposed on the problem space and the operations which the operator may use not only due to the characteristics of the invariant components of the problem space but also due to indirect sources. In a manufacturing situation, factors such as inventory level, batch size and the availability of manpower are some of the direct constraints that affect the operations that an operator may perform. For instance, they may influence the operator's decision to replace a tool. Indirect constraints are imposed on the problem space due to the thought and perceptual process of the operator. How and why this is a constraint is clarified when bringing out the relationship between the variant and the invariant parts of the problem space.

Characteristics and values. Given a problem, each of the components of the invariant parts of the problem space may be defined by a set of characteristics. These characteristics reflect the nature of the component, influence the problem-solving process used, and reflect how well the problem is solved. These characteristics may take on one of a range of values. The values may be numeric or alphanumeric and may fall in the normal expected range or may lie beyond the limits of this range; thereby, indicating some malfunction in the state of the system. Several or pairs of these values are closely related to each other, i.e. changes in the value of one characteristic may bring about or be accompanied by changes in the values of other characteristics. This is due to the interrelationships between the characteristics. Interrelationships between values may also impose constraints on the sets of values that may or may not appear together. Such constraints may constitute the preconditions that have to satisfied for the occurrence (or non-occurrence) of sets of values.

3.1.2. The variant part of the problem space

Definition and its relation to the invariant part. The variant part of the problem space consists of a set of states. This set is comprised of an *initial state,* a *set of intermediate states* and a *set of final states.* For every final state there exists a set of intermediate states. A *state* is defined by the values and the interrelationships between the values which are taken up by the characteristics of the components of the invariant part of the problem space. This definition of a state brings out the relationship between the invariant and the variant parts of the problem space. Although it is always possible to define the initial state only a subset of the intermediate and final states can be defined at the beginning. This is because it is not even possible to enumerate all the elements of the set of intermediate and the set of final states, at the beginning. However, a state can always be defined, once it is attained. A state n changes to state $n + 1$ when some action or operation is performed on state n by the operator.

Ideally, there should exist an initial state, a set of defined intermediate and final states and a set of actions. However, in practice this is not true, due to the infinitely many combinations in which the values of the characteristics may appear and due to the presence of the human operator in the problem space. This is because the action performed on each state n to reach state $n + 1$ is determined by the operator's perception (patterned or otherwise) of state n. In other words, the action taken and hence the new state reached depends upon the operator's definition, perception and interpretation of state n.

The second kind of constraint comes into play now. This constraint is due to the perceptual style of the operator. By perceptual style is implied the operator's perception of the characteristics and values (in patterns and schemas vs single discrete characteristics) and the meanings attached to the values. Thus the definition of a state by an operator may be affected by the operator's perceptual style. The set of values and characteristics used by an operator to define a state need not be totally subsumed in the set of actual values which define the state. However, this does not imply that the intersection of two sets is empty. The operator's interpretation of a state refers to the *set of outcomes* (*expected, slightly expected and precluded outcomes*), that are predicted by the operator for the given state. The operator then chooses the operation or action to be performed on the given state, in order to reach the most preferred outcome (an outcome at the current step becomes a state at the next step). Performing of an operation merely implies that the values of certain characteristics are changed.

To summarize, it is asserted here that all knowledge required in solving a problem (not the process of problem solution), may be derived by eliciting all characteristics and values associated with each part of the problem space, i.e. objects, instruments, end products, by products, operators, operations and constraints; the set of states which the problem may terminate in and how each of these states which the problem may terminate in are reached (intermediate states, actions). In other words, it is contended that problem-solving knowledge may be elicited from an individual by determining how the individual construes the given problem space. Towards this end, the theory of personal constructs is used.

3.2. THE THEORY OF PERSONAL CONSTRUCTS

Kelly's (1955) theory of a personal scientist or theory of personal constructs indicates that each individual seeks to predict and control events by forming theories, testing hypotheses and weighing evidence. Kelly asserted that individuals' perception of the world, other events, individuals and situations was represented in the form of constructs in the individual. A construct is defined as an internal bipolar scaled dimension which brings out the similarity of a set of elements and the difference of this set of elements from other elements. Thus a construct implies both similarity and contrast. According to Kelly, anticipated outcomes depend on the individual's interpretation of past similar events. This generalization which causes anticipation is based on similarities and differences perceived in events that have already taken place and also on when events are perceived as beginning and ending. This dependence on personal experience accounts for why unique responses may be given by individuals even when the same set of elements is used for each individual.

Constructs may also be represented as hierarchies, i.e. with some superordinate constructs subsuming other subordinate constructs.

Personal constructs theory was first applied by Kelly (1955) to elicit the client's perception of individuals who played an important part in his (the clients) life. Since then the theory has been applied to many a setting (Shaw, 1980, 1981), from helping determine the causes for strained employer employee relations to knowledge extraction for building expert systems (Boose, 1986).

3.3. INTEGRATION OF THE THEORY OF PROBLEM SOLVING AND THE THEORY OF PERSONAL CONSTRUCTS

From Kelly's theory that people think in terms of constructs, it is inferred that people can perceive similarities and differences. It is asserted that people can perceive similarities and differences only because they associate characteristics at certain values with given states, events and situations (Fig. 1). Individuals anticipate a set of intermediate and final outcomes based on the characteristics which they perceive in a given initial situation, event or state. The choice of action or operation to be performed on the given state (call it *state 1*), by the individual is determined by the element in the set of anticipated outcomes that the individual wants to reach. This outcome (call it *outcome 1*) becomes a state (*state 2*) and the individual performs another action or operation to reach *outcome 2,* which is *state 3*. The only distinction between *state 2* and *outcome 2* (which is state 3) is that the values of certain characteristics are different. It follows that the set of anticipated outcomes will be different for the two states. This continues until the desired final state (equivalently the final outcome) is reached.

In essence, it is asserted that an individual's definition, perception and interpretation of a state is determined largely by the characteristics (and the values of the characteristics) which the individual associates with the state. Thus an ability to elicit from the individual the characteristics, values of these characteristics, the inter-relationships between the values, expectations of outcomes and choice of actions for each of the components of the given problem space, should yield detailed problem-solving knowledge. This amounts to eliciting how an individual construes his problem space. Different individuals will construe the same problem space differently based on personal experience. Reasons to believe that this framework facilitates the elicitation of detailed knowledge and the derivation of a knowledge-elicitation methodology are discussed below.

4. Implications of the above conceptual framework

Several direct and indirect benefits accrue from the conceptual framework presented in section 3. This framework facilitates the derivation of a knowledge elicitation methodology that possesses several of the attributes listed in section 1.1. This methodology is currently being developed and validated. In developing the methodology this framework provided guidelines regarding what knowledge to elicit and the sequence and format that should be used to elicit this knowledge (Fig. 1). Knowledge that should be elicited includes characteristics of components of the problem space, ranges of values of these characteristics, intercorrelations between the characteristics, sets of characteristics that may or may not occur together (and the constraining factors), states of the system, the set of predicted outcomes and the actions that allow realization of a desired outcome, given a particular state.

The repertory grid technique developed by Kelly permits the elicitation of knowledge in a structured format. Elicitation of knowledge in such a structured format reduces significantly the time required to analyse the elicited data. Further, it permits the use of statistical methods (for example, distance-based clustering techniques) for analysing the elicited data. Boose (1986) and Shaw (1980, 1981) have successfully demonstrated that the repertory grid technique and existing clustering algorithms may be used to elicit and analyse knowledge, respectively.

The components of the invariant part of the problem space may enable the knowledge engineer to draw the expert's attention to various components of problem solving knowledge that the expert may be using (consciously or subconsciously) to solve problems in the domain. This facilitates the elicitation of knowledge that is used subconsciously. Use of Kelly's personal constructs theory makes possible the elicitation of any unique approaches and heuristics that the expert may be employing to solve problems. This is possible because the emphasis is on eliciting how the expert construes the problem space. Although it remains to be demonstrated, there is reason to believe that this conceptual framework may be used to elicit knowledge in both analysis and synthesis type domains; the latter because the methodology emphasizes elicitation of sets of characteristics that may or may not occur together. Implicit here is the elicitation of factors that constrain the simultaneous occurrence of certain sets of characteristics and values.

Indirect benefits accruing from this framework include the scope for gaining insight into the generic components of knowledge within and across domains. Analysis of data using quantitative and qualitative methods and classification of the elicited knowledge based on the components of the invariant part of the problem space may yield valuable insight into the relations, patterns and structures implicit in the elicited data. This may be used to chunk knowledge and establish links between and across the chunks of knowledge in network and frame-based representations.

References

ANTONELLI, D. (1983). The application of artificial intelligence to a maintenance and diagnostic information system (MDIS). In *Proceedings of the Joint Services Workshop on Artificial Intelligence in Maintenance,* Boulder, Colorado.

BOOSE, J. (1986). *Expertise transfer for expert system design.* New York: Elsevier.

BRADSHAW, J. M. & BOOSE, J. H. (1986). NeoETS. *Proceedings of the North American Personal Constructs Network Second Biennial Conference* University of Calgary: Department of Computer Science, pp. 27–41.

DAVIS, R. (1979). Interactive transfer of expertise: Acquisition of new inference rules. *Artificial Intelligence,* **12,** 121–158.

ERICCSON, K. A. & SIMON, H. A. (1984). *Protocol Analysis: Verbal reports as Data.* Massachusetts: The MIT Press.

GAINES, B. R. & SHAW, M. L. G. (1981). New directions in the analysis and interactive elicitation of personal construct systems. In SHAW, M. L. G. Ed., *Recent Advances in Personal Construct Technology,* pp. 147–180. New York: Academic Press.

GALE, W. A. (1986). Knowledge based knowledge acquisition for a statistical consulting system. *Proceedings of the Knowledge Acquisition for Knowledge-Based Systems Workshop* Banff, Canada, pp. 15.0–15.9.

GRAESSER, A. C. & CLARK, L. F. (1985). *Structures and Procedures of Implicit Knowledge.* New Jersey: Ablex.

GROVER, M. D. (1983). A pragmatic knowledge acquisition methodology. *Proceedings of the Eighth International Joint Conference of Artificial Intelligence,* Karlsruhe, West Germany, pp. 436–438.

JAGANNATHAN, V. & ELMAGHRABY, A. S. (1985). MEDKAT: multiple expert delphi-based knowledge acquisition tool. *Technical Report,* University of Louisville, Engineering, Mathematics and Computer Science Department, Louisville.

KAHN, G., NOWLAN, S. & McDERMOTT, J. (1985). Strategies for knowledge acquisition. *IEEE Transactions on Pattern Analysis and Machine Intelligence, PAMI-7 (3),* 511–522.

KELLY, G. A. (1955). *The Psychology of Personal Constructs.* New York: Norton.

KOUBEK, R. J., SALVENDY, G. & DUNSMORE, H. (1986).CAP: a knowledge extraction methodology for computer programming. In *Proceedings of the Human Factors Thirtieth Annual Meeting,* Human Factors Society, Dayton, Ohio, pp. 492–496.

MARCUS, S., McDERMOTT, J. & WANG, T. (1985). Knowledge acquisition for constructive systems. In *Proceedings of the Ninth International Joint Conference on Artificial Intelligence* Los Angeles: CA, pp. 637–639.

MORAY, N., (1985). Sources of bias and fallibility in humans. In *Proceedings of the Workshop on Knowledge Engineering in Industry,* University of Toronto, Toronto, Canada.

NEWELL, A. & SIMON, H. A. (1972). *Human Problem Solving.* New Jersey: Prentice–Hall, Inc.

NISBETT, R. E. & WILSON, T. D. (1977). Telling more than we can know: verbal reports on mental processes. *Psychological Review,* **84,** 231–259.

RUSK, R. A. & KRONE, R. M., (1984). The Crawford slip method (CSM) as a tool for extraction of expert knowledge. In SALVENDY, G. Ed., *Human–computer Interaction,* pp. 279–282. New York: Elsevier.

SAATY, T. L. (1980). *The Analytic Hierarchy Process.* New York: McGraw–Hill.

SHAW, M. L. G. (1980). *On Becoming a Personal Scientist.* New York: Academic Press.

SHAW, M. L. G. (1981). *Recent Advances in Personal Construct Technology.* New York: Academic Press.

SHAW, M. L. G. (1984). Interactive knowledge elicitation. In *Proceedings of the Canadian Information Processing Society Annual Conference,* Calgary, Canada.

SMITH, R. G. & BAKER, J. D. (1983). The DIPMETER advisor system. In *Proceedings of the Eighth International Joint Conference on Artificial Intelligence* Karlsruhe, West Germany, pp. 122–129.

SWARTOUT, W. R. (1984). Explaining and justifying expert consulting programs. In CLANCEY, W. J. AND SHORTLIFFE, E. H. Eds, *Readings in Medical Artificial Intelligence: the First Decade,* pp. 382–398. Reading, MA: Addison–Wesley.

TVERSKY, A. & KAHNEMAN, D. (1974). Judgment under uncertianty: heuristics and biases. *Science,* **184,** 1124–1131.

Design for acquisition: principles of knowledge-system design to facilitate knowledge acquisition

THOMAS R. GRUBER AND PAUL R. COHEN

Experimental Knowledge Systems Laboratory, Department of Computer and Information Science, University of Massachusetts, Amherst, Massachusetts 01003, U.S.A.

The problem of knowledge acquisition is viewed in terms of the incongruity between the representational formalisms provided by an implementation (e.g. production rules) and the formulation of problem-solving knowledge by experts. The thesis of this paper is that knowledge systems can be designed to facilitate knowledge acquisition by reducing representation mismatch. Principles of *design for acquisition* are presented and applied in the design of an architecture for a medical expert system called MUM. It is shown how the design of MUM makes it possible to acquire two kinds of knowledge that are traditionally difficult to acquire from experts: knowledge about evidential combination and knowledge about control. Practical implications for building knowledge-acquisition tools are discussed.

1. Introduction

Knowledge acquisition is the process of gathering knowledge about a domain, usually from an expert, and transforming it to be executed in a computer program. It is a part of the knowledge-engineering process, which includes defining a problem, designing an architecture, building a knowledge base, and testing and refining the program. Knowledge acquisition is regarded as the bottleneck in this process. Our thesis is that the design of a knowledge system should anticipate the acquisition process. By analogy with "design for testability," in which digital hardware is designed to be easily tested (Bennetts, 1984), our aim is *design for acquisition:* designing knowledge systems to facilitate knowledge acquisition.

The first advance on the knowledge acquisition problem was the invention of *general architectures:* knowledge representation techniques and accompanying interpreters that allow the programmer to encode domain knowledge in a knowledge base separate from the algorithm that interprets it. The EMYCIN architecture is paradigmatic (van Melle, 1979; see also Buchanan & Shortliffe, 1984). Its essential architectural features are a rule formalism with conjunctive premises, certainty factors, and an exhaustive backward-chaining control strategy.

With the general architectures came tools to help the knowledge engineer and expert transform knowledge into the available formalisms. Experts were insulated from the Lisp implementation by rule editors and pseudo-natural language interfaces (Shortliffe, 1976). In TEIRESIAS, Davis (1976) demonstrated that a knowledge-acquisition program can use knowledge about the architecture, such as the structure of rules and the effect of backward chaining, to help users refine and debug the knowledge base. With ROGET, Bennett (1985) showed that information

131

about the kinds of domain knowledge likely to be useful for a task could be used by a system to help acquire the initial "conceptual structure" of a domain.

Recently, knowledge systems research has emphasized the power of less general, more task-specific architectures (Chandrasekaran, 1986; Clancey, 1985; McDermott, 1983). Many systems share common problem-solving methods, despite differences in implementation. When the task can be characterized at a level independent of the implementation, an architecture can be designed to capture the task-specific problem-solving knowledge. For example, the HERACLES architecture (Clancey, 1986) is designed to do *heuristic classification,* a common task for knowledge systems.

Knowledge acquisition tools for task-specific architectures can apply knowledge about the kind of problem that the task addresses and the problem-solving methods it provides. For example, ETS (Boose, 1984) is a method of acquiring knowledge for hierarchical classification tasks. It applies a psychological theory of how to elicit classification hierarchies from people. SALT (Marcus, McDermott & Wang, 1985) assists in knowledge acquisition for iterative design tasks such as configuration. The architecture for SALT identifies three kinds of domain knowledge used by its problem-solving strategy, and SALT uses knowledge about their form and purpose to focus and constrain the knowledge-acquisition dialog. In both cases, the knowledge-acquisition method is driven by demands of the task (e.g. classification or configuration) rather than the implementation formalisms (e.g. rules).

Both ETS and SALT acquire knowledge for well-characterized problem solving methods, with corresponding architectures. However, the space of methods (and even tasks) for knowledge-based systems has surely not been fully explored. For those problems without suitable task-specific methods, knowledge systems and tools to build them must be *designed.* Design means choosing knowledge representations and control strategies that can bring expert knowledge to bear on the problem. Careful attention to the design of a problem solving architecture can make knowledge acquisition easier both for knowledge engineers and automatic knowledge-acquisition tools.

This paper presents principles for designing knowledge systems to facilitate knowledge acquisition. In section 2, we introduce three general principles of design for acquisition. In section 3, we show how these principles have been applied in the design of an architecture for managing uncertainty in medicine. The architecture makes it possible to acquire two kinds of knowledge that are traditionally difficult to acquire: knowledge about evidential combination and knowledge about control. In section 4 we show how the principles of design for acquisition imply a hierarchical organization of tools for implementing knowledge-system architectures, emphasizing the integration of knowledge-acquisition support.

2. Principles of design for acquisition

This section presents three principles that should be considered during the design of a knowledge system architecture. They may be familiar to knowledge engineers as heuristics for knowledge representation. We emphasize the goal of making it easy for *experts* to express their knowledge.

PRINCIPLE 1: DESIGN TASK-LEVEL REPRESENTATIONAL PRIMITIVES TO CAPTURE IMPORTANT DOMAIN CONCEPTS DEFINED BY THE EXPERT

This principle prescribes that the knowledge engineer provide a language of task-level terms. It addresses a fundamental obstacle to knowledge acquisition, the *representation mismatch* between the way that an expert formulates domain knowledge and the way the knowledge is represented in an implementation (Buchanan *et al.*, 1983). Representation mismatch typically occurs when the knowledge engineer imposes implementation-level primitives on the expert. For example, knowledge acquisition in a strictly rule-based architecture is ultimately *rule* acquisition, and if it is difficult for an expert to express problem-solving expertise as rules, then it is hard to acquire the knowledge. The problem is that rules are implementation-level primitives.

An example of a *task-level* primitive is the notion of a "trigger"—a special relation between data and hypotheses such that when the data are found, a hypothesis is immediately activated. Trigger is natural construct for diagnosticians. For the cardiologist, a 45-year-old man complaining of chest pain with exercise "brings to mind" the hypothesis of angina. If it is a representational primitive for the system, then acquiring triggering relations from the expert is straightforward. If instead one must achieve the effect of a trigger by, say, "tuning" the certainty factors of rules or the weights on links, then it will be difficult to acquire, explain, and modify this knowledge.

PRINCIPLE 2: DESIGN EXPLICIT, DECLARATIVE REPRESENTATIONAL PRIMITIVES

From the standpoint of knowledge acquisition, declarative knowledge representations are preferable to procedures. The meaning of declarative representations can be "read" directly, whereas the meaning of procedures can only be had by executing the procedure or simulating its execution. For experts to understand procedural representations of their knowledge they must first understand the algorithm that interprets them. Even when knowledge seems naturally represented with procedures (e.g. control knowledge), formulating it declaratively can facilitate acquisition, explanation, and maintenance. Furthermore, the requirement of explicitness means that when a new primitive is needed to express some domain concept or expert strategy, its purpose and operational definition must be made public; this is important when multiple experts and programmers work on a system.†

In section 3.3 we show how designing declarative primitives for control knowledge allows one to represent expertise in deciding what to do next under conditions of uncertainty. By making the knowledge explicit and declarative, the expert can examine the assumptions underlying his or her control decisions. In section 4 we show how representing task-level terms declaratively allows the use of conventional "form-filling" user interface technology in knowledge-acquisition tools.

† Neches, Swartout and Moore (1985) emphasize the advantages of this principle for explainability and maintainability, and Clancey (1983) argues for the explicit representation of control knowledge to facilitate explanation, knowledge engineering, and tuning. Our point here is that "good engineering" is also good for knowledge acquisition.

PRINCIPLE 3: DESIGN REPRESENTATIONS AT THE SAME LEVEL OF
GENERALIZATION AS THE EXPERT'S KNOWLEDGE

This principle can be summarized with two caveats:

Do not force experts to generalize except when necessary;
Do not ask experts to specify information not available to them.

Generalization is one of the dimensions of representation mismatch, the distance between the expert's formulation and the implementation.† A representation and its referent in the world are at different levels of generalization if there are distinctions in the world that the representation fails to capture or the representation makes artificial distinctions. An example of overgeneralization is forcing a large range of values into a small set of categories. The expert interpreting blood pressure considers the full range of systolic/diastolic ratios, while the knowledge engineer may want to categorize it as **high**, **normal**, or **low**, to make it easier to implement. Conversely, the knowledge engineer may ask the expert to specify more knowledge than he or she has, again to suit the implementation. For example, the expert may be asked to supply degrees of belief with far more precision that is justified by his or her knowledge.

3. A case study of design for acquisition

In this section we illustrate the principles of design for acquisition in the context of a medical expert system. We show how the design of the system facilitates the acquisition of two kinds of knowledge that are traditionally hard to acquire: knowledge about how to combine evidence and knowledge about how to control the order of actions. The ability to capture this expertise gives the system a unique ability to *manage uncertainty* by selecting or planning actions that will minimize uncertainty or its effects.

3.1. TASK DOMAIN: PROSPECTIVE DIAGNOSIS

MUM is an knowledge system that Manages Uncertainty in Medicine, currently in the domains of chest and abdominal pain. (See Cohen *et al.*, 1987, for details.) Physicians make a distinction between *retrospective diagnosis,* in which all the evidence is known in advance and the goal is to make the correct diagnosis, and *prospective diagnosis,* which emphasizes the proper management of the patient through the *workup,* a diagnostic sequence of questions and tests. In prospective diagnosis, uncertainty about the patient's condition is managed by gathering evidence in the best order (e.g. to maximize diagnostic information and therapeutic effectiveness and to minimize cost and discomfort). MUM's task is prospective diagnosis; it uses expert knowledge about evidence and control to generate an intelligent workup for a patient.

The knowledge-acquisition task for MUM includes not only eliciting *heuristic associations* (Clancey, 1985) between evidence and diseases ("What are the symptoms of angina?"), but also *combining knowledge* ("What is the effect of risk

---

† Another dimension is *operationalization,* converting advice to procedures (Mostow, 1983).

factors like smoking on the hypothesis of angina when there has only been one episode of pain?"), and *control knowledge* ("Under what conditions should an angiogram be given?").† The expert for MUM has a wealth of combining and control knowledge, central to his expertise as a physician. This knowledge is difficult to represent, and thus acquire, in current architectures. We designed MUM in accordance with the principles discussed above to make it easy to acquire combining and control knowledge.

3.2. DESIGN FOR ACQUISITION OF COMBINING KNOWLEDGE

Combining knowledge specifies how belief in several pieces of evidence is combined to support a single conclusion. Remarkably, knowledge engineers rarely ask experts how they combine evidence. Instead, fixed, global numeric functions that compute degrees of belief are built into the architecture (Duda, Hart & Nilsson, 1976; Shafer, 1976; Shortliffe & Buchanan, 1975; Zadeh, 1975). Although the numeric representations and functions are a convenient implementation formalism, they make it surprisingly difficult for experts to express their knowledge about how they manage uncertainty (Cohen & Gruber, 1985; Szolovits & Pauker, 1978).

MUM's design does three things to facilitate the acquisition of combining knowledge. First, it replaces the real-valued numeric representation of uncertainty with symbolic *states of belief* that are meaningful in domain terms. Second, it provides an explicit representation for *clusters of evidence,* to encapsulate diagnostically significant subsets of evidence. Third, it replaces the global numeric function with *local combining functions,* specified by the expert, for each cluster of evidence.

MUM represents belief as ordinal values that characterize the expert's evaluation of evidential support. Seven states of belief are defined by the expert: **confirmed, disconfirmed, supported, detracted, strongly supported, strongly detracted,** and **unknown**. They are primitives at the task level; each has diagnostic or therapeutic significance.

MUM represents combinations of evidence with *clusters,* frames that represent diagnostically significant groupings of evidence. With respect to evidential support, diseases are clusters. Clusters also represent intermediate results, such as common groupings of clinical findings and definitional data abstractions (Clancey, 1985). For example, the cluster **chest-pain-when-eating** illustrated in Fig. 1 describes a situation in which the chief complaint of a patient is pain or pressure in the chest that begins after eating. This cluster *triggers* the disease classic-esophageal-spasm. **crescendo-pain-long-duration** in Fig. 1 represents the situation where the pain has been increasing in intensity for more than 10 min. The cluster discriminates between angina and esophageal spasm: pain from the former usually lasts less than 10 min.

MUM represents evidential combination with *local combining functions,* symbolic functions mapping states of belief in evidence to states of belief in a conclusion. Each cluster has its own combining function, and there are no global combining functions. Combining functions are acquired from the expert, usually as a set of rules, but they can also be acquired in a tabular or graphical form. The combining function for the first cluster in Fig. 1 is a simple example; if an episode of chest pain

---

† An angiogram is an expensive, invasive test for coronary artery blockage, usually given only after other tests show positive results.

Cluster: chest-pain-when-eating
Combining-function:
    IF (and (or (confirmed episode-chief-complaint=pain)
              (confirmed episode-chief-complaint=pressure))
         (confirmed episode-chief-complaint-location=chest)
         (confirmed episode-incited-by-eating))
    THEN confirmed

Cluster: crescendo-pain-long-duration
Combining-function:
    IF (and (or (confirmed episode-chief-complaint=pain)
              (confirmed episode-chief-complaint=pressure))
         (confirmed episode-chief-complaint-frequency=crescendo)
         (confirmed episode-chief-complaint-duration>10min))
    THEN confirmed

FIG. 1. Two clusters for diagnosing chest pain. Clusters represent diagnostically significant combinations of evidence. They might play a part in a diagnostic scenario like this: A patient reports an episode of chest pain incited by eating (**chest-pain-when-eating**); this combination of findings is relevant to many diagnoses. (For instance, it *triggers* **classic-esophageal-spasm**, shown in Fig. 2). The physician then asks about the duration and time course of the pain. If the report matches the situation characterized here as **crescendo-pain-long-duration**, the cluster is confirmed. This cluster of symptom descriptions is useful in differential diagnosis; for instance, it *supports* **classic-espohageal-spasm** and *detracts* **classic-angina**). In these examples, the combining functions specify necessary and sufficient conditions for clusters to be confirmed; no other belief state (such as *supported*) is relevant.

(which may also be described as pressure) is incited by eating then this is a confirmed case of **chest-pain-when-eating**. No other combination of states of belief in evidence has any affect on belief in that cluster. Diseases, also represented as clusters, typically have more complex combining functions. For example, the frame for **classic-esophageal-spasm**, with the set of rules that define its combining function, is shown in Fig. 2.

The representation of combining knowledge in MUM is unconventional, but not novel. (Similar designs are used in PIP (Pauker, Gorry, Kassirer & Schwartz, 1976), MDX (Chandrasakeran, Mittal & Smith, 1982), and the "criteria tables" of Kingsland and Lindberg (1986).) It was, however, designed to facilitate knowledge acquisition, in accordance with the principles of design for acquisition. First, applying Principle 1, the ordinal states of belief are chosen to be sufficient to characterize diagnostically significant situations, and nothing more. Since the expert defines these terms, there is no problem of "getting numbers from experts". The expert can state categorically the implications of a subset of findings, instead of relying on the system to calculate a partial match to a set of possible findings, as in INTERNIST (Pople, 1977). Second, symbolic combining functions are explicit, declarative representations of decisions about evidential support, whereas the belief in a conclusion given belief in evidence is only implicit in global, numeric combining functions. Adhering to Principle 2 in this case means representing evidential *judgments,* rather than representing degrees of belief and *computing* the result. Third, symbolic, local combining functions represent specific combinations; only a subset of possible evidence is considered for each cluster, and only some of the belief states in each constituent piece of evidence are specified. This contrasts with the situation where *no* local combining function is specified, and *every* possible

---

Cluster: classic-esophageal-spasm
Isa: disease
Triggered-by: (confirmed chest-pain-when-eating)
Combining function:
   IF (or (confirmed barium-swallow=spasm)
        (confirmed manometrics))
    THEN confirmed
   IF (or (confirmed vasodilator-tx)
        (confirmed nitroglycerin-tx))
    THEN strongly-supported
   IF (confirmed crescendo-pain-long-duration)
    THEN supported
   IF (disconfirmed nitroglycerin-tx))
    THEN detracted
   IF (confirmed chest-pain-short-duration))
    THEN detracted
   IF (disconfirmed barium-swallow=spasm)
    THEN disconfirmed

FIG. 2. Part of a disease frame for classic esophageal spasm. The evidential combining function for this disease is made up of rules; each *IF* part specifies conditions on the state of belief in clusters, and each *THEN* part asserts a state of belief for the disease. "tx" means trial therapy; for example, nitroglycerin-tx is confirmed if pain goes away when the patient takes a nitroglycerin tablet. Manometrics and barium swallow are tests; barium-swallow=spasm is a cluster that is confirmed when the barium-swallow shows a spasm. The triggering function has the same syntax as the left hand sides of rules in the combining function. In this example, when the cluster **chest-pain-when-eating** (Fig. 1) is confirmed, the disease **classic-esophageal-spasm** is triggered. These combining and triggering functions were elicited by a knowledge engineer working with a physician, in the context of actual cases.

From inspecting the combining function, a planner can infer that the tests (manometrics and barium swallow) are most diagnostic, since they can confirm and disconfirm the diagnosis of this disease. In the frames representing these tests, however, one will find that they are invasive and therefore costly—to be avoided. Slightly less diagnostic information (strongly-supported, detracted) can be obtained from trial therapies, and even less (supported, detracted) from reports of episodes of pain given by the patient.

combination of belief is possible. In accordance with Principle 3, the expert is not asked for information (e.g. probabilities) that can be used to make distinctions (e.g. in levels of belief) that he or she does not endorse.

We have found that having to specify the combining knowledge explicitly and locally makes knowledge acquisition more efficient when maintenance and knowledge base refinement are considered. Combinatorial problems are avoided because the space of combinations is very sparse; not *every* combination of belief in every piece of evidence is relevant in the chest-pain domain. This holds advantages for knowledge base refinement and testing. First, every combination of evidence is justified. Second, when test cases are found for which combining knowledge is inadequate, the omission is easily localized to the cluster where the combining function is underspecified. If combining functions produce conflicting belief states for the same cluster, it indicates a case that the expert had not considered, an error of omission. Thus the design helps experts, knowledge engineers, and knowledge acquisition tools address the credit assignment problem.

3.3. DESIGN FOR ACQUISITION OF CONTROL KNOWLEDGE

A major part of expertise in *prospective* medical diagnosis is the ability to gather data in the proper order, omitting unnecessary tests, asking only those questions that pertain to relevant hypotheses, and prescribing preliminary or exploratory treatment before all of the manifestations of a disease are present.† This is *control knowledge* about what to do, rather than what to believe. Traditionally, domain knowledge is acquired without troubling the expert to think about control. Simple control strategies such as forward chaining are implicit in the interpreter, separated from the domain knowledge base, and selected by the knowledge engineer. When these weak methods are inadequate, the knowledge engineer coerces the interpreter to do something more complicated, perhaps by ordering rules or having rules communicate via control flags. Other techniques for specifying control, such as procedural attachment in frame-based systems, are, again, designed and implemented by knowledge engineers largely without consulting experts. But experts have useful domain-specific knowledge about *how* to solve problems that should be acquired.

The problem we faced in MUM was how to represent control knowledge so we could acquire it from the expert. The solution is to ask the expert for the parameters of a domain that affect control decisions, and then ask him to formulate control knowledge in terms of these control parameters. For example, some diseases are more *dangerous* than others; some clinical tests are very *costly*; and some evidence is more *diagnostic*. Control knowledge is easier to acquire in these *task-level* terms, in contrast to *implementation-level* parameters, such as the priorities of tasks on an agenda, or the order of clauses in a rule. Since task-level control parameters are declarative they can be reasoned about by a knowledge-based system, and more to the point, they can be acquired.

Control parameters are a vocabulary for describing situations in which the expert knows what to do. *Control rules* (Davis, 1976), acquired from the expert in terms of control parameters, represent the decision points in diagnosis. Given the evidence that has already been acquired, and the hypotheses it suggests, the diagnostician selects some action, typically to gather evidence for a suspected hypothesis, sometimes by prescribing trial therapy. MUM was designed to represent this decision-making process, so that the expert could specify how it should proceed.

Some control rules specify preferences among alternative actions. For example:

Control rule: prefer-cheap-to-confirming
Conditions: $action_1$ is potentially-confirming, and
$action_2$ is potentially-supporting, and
$action_1$ costs more than $action_2$
Strategy: prefer $action_2$

The effect of this rule is to cause the system to favor cheaper actions and sacrifice a little support.‡ Other control rules specify focusing strategy:

Control rule: focus-on-dangerous-supported-hypos

---

† Prospective diagnosis is concerned with gathering evidence for diagnosis and treatment, and is fundamentally different from retrospective diagnosis which concentrates on the classification of data already available.

‡ Features of evidence like *potentially confirming* are derived from descriptions of the actions and the clusters for which they serve as evidence. An action (e.g. running a test) is *potentially confirming* if it can result in evidence that contributes to a *confirmed* state of belief in a cluster (e.g. a disease).

Conditions: hypothesis$_1$ is supported, and
hypothesis$_2$ is supported, and
hypothesis$_1$ is more dangerous than hypothesis$_2$
Strategy: focus on hypothesis$_1$

This rule directs the attention of the system to the most dangerous hypothesis (e.g. a life-threating disease) that has support. That is, the system will search for evidence for and against the more dangerous hypothesis first.

Just as the design of clusters and combining functions give structure to the expert's descriptions of evidential belief, control parameters and control rules organize the expert's strategic knowledge. Control parameters define a space of diagnostic situations, called the *control space,* distinct from the *belief space* of evidential support for hypotheses. In accordance with Principle 1, both the control space and the belief space are constructed from task-level terms. The representation of the control space is designed to facilitate knowledge acquisition from experts rather than forcing them to abide by implementation decisions that they often do not understand. As recommended by Principle 2, MUM selects actions based on declarative control rules; they describe control decisions in terms of explicit control parameters, rather than as unexplainable procedures. In accordance with Principle 3, the design of MUM does not ask the expert to generalize beyond the diagnostic situations with which he or she is familiar.

As combining functions prescribe local combinations of evidence, control rules represent local control decisions. Local control rules have the same relation to global conflict resolution strategies (e.g. "choose the most specific rule") as local combining functions have to their global counterparts (e.g. Bayes' rule). Again the local context facilitates acquisition and makes errors of omission more transparent. When control rules conflict, the cause is missing control knowledge in a particular context. For example, the **prefer-cheap-to-confirming** rule resolves the conflict between more general preference rules, one that says "prefer actions that are potentially confirming" and the other that specifies "prefer actions that cost less." The tradeoff is acquired from a particular diagnostic situation.

4. Implications for the design of architecture support tools

In the previous section we emphasized the design of knowledge *representations* to facilitate knowledge acquisition, but the principles in section 2 also have practical implications for the design of software support for knowledge *engineering*. Specifically, the principles guide the design of *task-specific architectures*. A task-specific architecture integrates particular knowledge representation formalisms and problem-solving strategies to perform a well-defined task, such as hierarchical classification.† The point for knowledge acquisition is that task-specific architectures can provide a language of task-level terms to the expert and a way for knowledge engineers to implement these terms declaratively and at the appropriate level of generality, hiding the implementation.

---

† Task-specific architectures have been designed for many familiar tasks. Among them are varieties of classification and diagnosis (Bylander & Mittal, 1986; Clancey, 1985) and design and configuration (Brown 1985; Howe, Dixon, Cohen & Simmons, 1986; Marcus *et al.*, 1985).

This section presents a hierarchy of knowledge engineering tools for an architecture called MU that is a generalization of MUM. Figure 3 illustrates some of the structure of task-level constructs that MU generalized from MUM; for example, triggering and evidential combination are instances of *inferential relations,* which automatically propogate values through a symbolic inference net.

Table 1 shows the organization of software support for the MU architecture. The three tiers correspond to functional levels. The left column shows the hierarchical relationship among tools. The knowledge-acquisition interface is constructed from functionality supplied by the shell, which is built on top of implementation primitives supplied by an AI toolbox. The center column shows the objects that a user would work with at each level; experts would use application-specific terms that are instantiations of task-level constructs, which are in turn implemented using primitives provided by the AI programming environment. The right column lists some of the services provided by software at each level.

At the base of the hierarchy are the implementation level tools. Instead of Lisp, the primitives are AI programming constructs: frames and slots with inheritance and attached procedures, "worlds" for assumption-maintenance, and graphical displays. The software support is standard technology; we currently use the commercial product KEE.† The primary user of these tools is the knowledge engineer. Figure 4

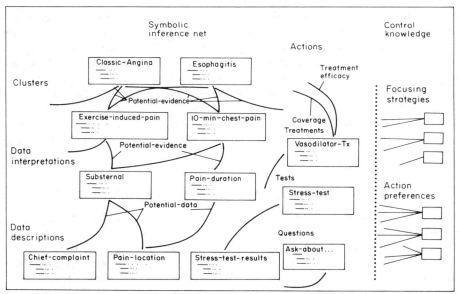

FIG. 3. The structure of a MU knowledge base. In the MU architecture, objects in a symbolic inference net are connected by *inferential relations* that propagate symbolic values. For example, the **potential-evidence** relation propagates *belief states,* such as **supported** and **confirmed**. At each node, a local *combining function* determines the belief state of the current node as a function of the belief states of nodes contributing potential evidence. The control knowledge is used to focus (e.g. decide which clusters to concentrate on) and to choose among possible actions (such as prescribing a test), given the state of the objects in the net and characteristics of actions (tests and treatments are actions).

† Which is, of course, a trademark and product of IntelliCorp.

TABLE 1

A hierarchy of knowledge engineering tools to support the MU architecture

Tool	Objects in user's view	Software support
Knowledge acquisition interface	*Application-specific terms*	*(Meta-)knowledge-based utilities*
	Diseases, tests, treatments, questions, intermediate diagnoses, criticality of diseases, cost of tests, efficacy of treatment	Language-specific editors and form-filling interfaces, inferential consistency analyser, graphical display for objects and relations
Virtual machine (shell)	*Task-level constructs*	*Task-specific reasoning mechanisms*
	Clusters and combining functions	Value propagation functions
	Control parameters	Interface to the inference net
	Control rules	Rule-based planner
	Preference rankings	Decision-making support
AI toolbox (KEE)	*Implementation primitives*	*AI programming techniques*
	Rules, pattern matching language frames and slots	Rule interpreter Knowledge base bookkeeping, Inheritance mechanisms,
	Lisp objects and functions	Assumption maintenance
	Windows and graphic objects	Demon and message passing support Window system

shows an implementation-level view a fragment of the knowledge base for MUM, reimplemented in MU.

The middle level is the shell—the software that implements a "virtual machine" that operates on task-level constructs. Supporting a virtual machine level is a natural application of Principle 1. The shell is a set of tools, some that support runtime operations, such as propagating the effects of data through an inference net, and others that provide an interface for customizing task-level terms (defined by the architecture) for a specific application. Task-level constructs are implemented as objects using the AI toolbox, but can be viewed by the user as primitives.† For instance, one can relate data to hypotheses with an evidential relation or a triggering relation without thinking about how those relations are implemented. Figure 5 shows a virtual machine view of the evidential support relation for MUM.

The top tier is the knowledge acquisition interface, a set of tools that together present a "user illusion" (Kay, 1984) of a language of application-specific instantiations of constructs provided by the architecture. For example, **classic-angina** is an instantiation of a cluster, and it is presented to the expert as an object related to other clusters and data by links in a graph of evidential support (such as Fig. 5). The primary function of the knowledge-acquisition interface is to make it easy for experts to formulate their expertise in the available language. A practical effect of applying Principle 1 is that the language is restricted to task-level terms. This allows one to build a knowledge-acquisition tool that can apply specific heuristics for acquiring them, as is done in SALT (Marcus, in press).

† In our implementation, they are represented as class frames, slots, slot facets, attached demons, and method functions.

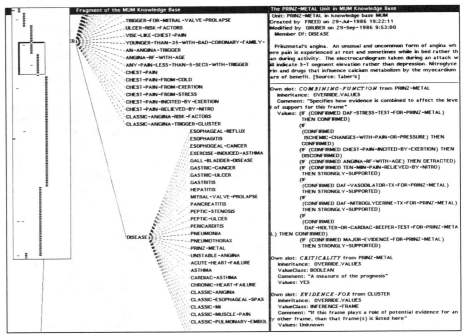

FIG. 4. The implementation-level view: a fragment of the MUM knowledge base as displayed by KEE. The objects in the user's view are implementation-level objects: frames, annotated slots, and inheritance relationships. The graph shows a fragment of a hierarchy of frames. They are organized by their implementation. The window on the left shows some of the clusters and diseases (a subclass of clusters) of MUM. The window on the right shows a KEE display of a disease frame. The semantics of slots are defined by the architecture; for example, all clusters have a slot for combining-function, defined in the **clusters** class frame. **prinz-metal** is a kind of cluster, and it instantiates its own combining function.

When task-level terms are represented declaratively as objects, meta-knowledge (Davis & Buchanan, 1984) about how to acquire task-level terms can be represented as annotations to those objects. This straightforward application of Principle 2 allows one to use simple syntactic techniques to improve the user interface for knowledge acquisition. A surprising amount of leverage can be achieved by using conventional data entry techniques, which we will call *form-filling*, to elicit knowledge from experts. Form filling is a generalization of the "fill in the blank" style of data entry, where each "blank" is labeled and presented in a context. The legal input values are highly constrained and possible values are enumerated when known. On-line help is conveniently accessible, in the form of descriptions of the expected input and examples. For instance, choosing from a menu is a simple kind of form filling (for a single "blank"). A more sophisticated example is the rule editor shown in Fig. 6, a kind of "language-specific editor" for acquiring rules of various kinds in MU. It uses descriptions of task-level objects to restrict the user's input to semantically valid choices. This technique is similar to the menu-based approach to natural language interfaces described in (Tenant, Ross, Saenz, Thompson & Miller, 1983). A better example is OPAL (Musen, Fagen, Combs & Shortliffe, 1987) the knowledge acquisition interface for the ONCOCIN expert system, which uses form-filling to acquire the *majority* of the expert knowledge used in specifying treatment plans for cancer therapy. Form filling is a viable knowledge-

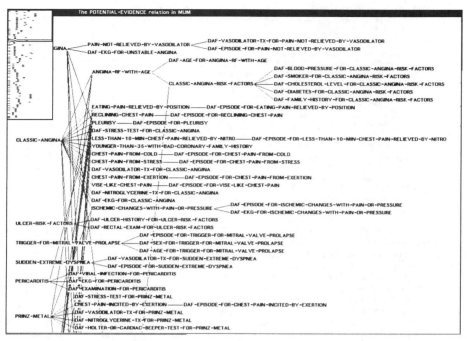

FIG. 5. The architectural view: a fragment of the evidential support relation in MUM. This lattice shows one kind of inferential relation in MUM, the evidential support relation (**potential-evidence**). The nodes in the lattice represent assertions that may be believed. The links represent the inference paths that evidence may take; belief in one node is propagated (i.e. from right to left) to other nodes for which it is evidence (that it may support or detract). The expert or knowledge engineer can select nodes to edit them or add new nodes, and the graph displays the evidential context. Similar graphs are available for other inferential relations provided by the MU architecture, such as triggering and treatment efficacy, and each relation may be viewed in both directions. This view of the knowledge base differs from the frame hierarchy of Fig. 5 in that the structure represents evidential rather than hierarchical relationships—i.e. the structure of the knowledge rather than the implementation.

acquisition technique because the terms that the expert instantiates (e.g. the "blanks" in a form) are explicit and declarative, so that each primitive can be annotated with meta-level descriptions to constrain and validate input. Furthermore, integrating the representations used by knowledge-acquisition tools with the shell and the implementation environment is possible because the design of the system anticipated acquisition.

5. Towards automated knowledge acquisition

If the problem of knowledge acquisition is viewed as representation mismatch, the primary contribution of design for acquisition is to make the notation for expressing knowledge more comprehensible and accessible to those with the knowledge. An analysis of successful knowledge acquisition tools (Bennett, 1985; Boose, 1984; Davis, 1976; Eshelman & McDermott, in press; Kahn, Nowlan & McDermott, 1984; Marcus *et al.*, 1985) suggests that they satisfy two requirements: to identify the kinds of knowledge to expect from the user, and to provide a functional mapping from user input to implementation primitives. When the underlying architecture supports

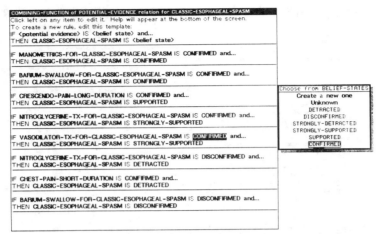

FIG. 6. The expert's view: a knowledge-based rule editor for acquiring a combining function. The rule editor is a sophisticated instance of conventional data entry technology: form-filling. Each term in the rule editor can be selected with a mouse; they are the "blanks" to fill. In the example, the set of rules comprises a symbolic combination function, computing the belief in the diagnosis **classic-esophageal-spasm** as a function of several sources of evidence. The syntax of the rules is supplied as a parameter to the editor, and can be seen in the rule template at the top of the window. In this case, the left hand side of a rule is a statement about belief in one of the clusters which serve as **potential-evidence** for this disease, and the right-hand side is always a statement about belief in the diagnosis. The user has selected a belief term from the left-hand side of a rule. The meta-level description of combining functions for **potential-evidence** tells the editor that only members of a class called **belief-states** are allowed for this term, and so a menu is presented. If the user chooses to create a new **belief-state**, a form for creating new instances of that class is invoked.

task-level primitives, the first is accomplished and the second is simplified. Thus design for acquisition facilitates knowledge acquisition by both human and machine.

Yet the problem of knowledge acquisition can go beyond representation and implementation issues. It may be that for some kinds of expertise, it is difficult to design *any* notation comprehensible to the expert that can also be executed. If an expert diagnostician is not accustomed to formalizing his or her expertise, there may be no *natural* notation other than the *cases* with which he or she works. For this kind of expertise, induction from examples can be an appropriate acquisition methodology. An inductive learning program can transform knowledge in the form of examples, which alone are inadequate to drive a knowledge system, into more general knowledge of the sort useful to the system.†

Acquiring control strategies is an example where a knowledge-acquisition methodology can profit from augmenting a good design with induction techniques. Experts who are not familiar with programming may have difficulty writing general control rules, even if they are specified in a comprehensible language of control parameters. Experience with MUM has shown that a good way to acquire these rules is by analysing physicians' workups on actual patients.‡ This suggests a

---

† If the system only knew about a set of examples, and had no generalizations, it would be the extreme of "brittleness": it would reduce to a lookup table.

‡ Workups are a natural representation of diagnostic procedure for physicians; they are often published in medical journals. Specific workups for a set of patients can be be merged to produce a *workup graph*, which is a compact form of a decision tree.

knowledge acquisition tool that asks about control parameters in the context of decision trees (in the sense of Hannan & Politakis, 1985). Each node in the decision tree corresponds to a decision about what to do next (e.g. test to perform); each arc represents a possible outcome (e.g. test result). The tree contains a wealth of *implicit* control knowledge, in the choice of actions and the order they are prescribed. The role of the acquisition tool is to elicit example decision trees, and to walk the expert through hypothetical cases (paths in the tree) asking for control parameters pertinent to each decision. It could ask questions such as "What factors influenced your decision to do action X instead of Y?" The decision tree is then annotated with these *reasons* for action, and inductive techniques are used to find patterns for generating plausible control rules. The success of the induction still depends, however, on the description language for generalizations [i.e. the *bias* (Utgoff, 1986)]. Thus integrating induction with "interviewing" style knowledge acquisition ultimately requires that the proper task-level terms, in this case control parameters, be designed.

6. Conclusions

We described three principles of design for acquisition and demonstrated their appplication in an architecture where knowledge about evidential combination and knowledge about control can be acquired from an expert. We conclude that proper design of knowledge representation primitives can reduce the representation mismatch between implementation-level and task-level formalisms and thereby facilitate knowledge acquisition. We also conclude that emphasizing knowledge *acquisition* in the design of an architecture is consistent with good knowledge *engineering*; if knowledge-acquisition tools are designed with the architecture, they can be integrated with runtime and implementation-level software. The function of knowledge-acquisition interfaces is made easier when the underlying architecture supports "acquirable" primitives. Finally, we proposed a technique to address a fundamental limitation of the "intelligent interface" approach to automating knowledge acquisition. When the expert cannot formulate the necessary knowledge in any notation, then expert-guided induction may facilitate generalization from examples of problem solving. However, the success of induction still depends on whether the knowledge engineer can devise the proper language of generalizations—the right task-level terms.

We are indebted to the researchers on the MUM project: Dan Suthers, Rick Kjeldsen, Mike Greenberg, Jeff Delisio, and David Day, and to Dr Paul Berman, of the University of Massachusetts Medical School. Our thanks for insightful comments go to Kevin Ashley.

This research was funded by National Science Foundation grant IST 8409623 and DARPA/RADC Contract F30602-85-C-0014.

References

BENNETT, J. S. (1985). ROGET: a knowledge-based consultant for acquiring the conceptual structure of a diagnostic system. *Journal of Automated Reasoning*, **1**, 49–74.
BENNETTS, R. G. (1984). *Design of Testable Logic Circuits*. Reading, Massachusetts: Addison–Wesley.
BOOSE, J. H. (1984). Personal construct theory and the transfer of human expertise.

Proceedings of the National Conference on Artificial Intelligence, Austin, Texas, pp. 27–33 (August).

BROWN, D. C. (1985). Capturing mechanical design knowledge. *Proceedings of the 1985 International Computers in Engineering Conference,* ASME, Boston, Massachusetts, (August).

BUCHANAN, B. G., BARSTOW, D. K., BECHTEL, R., BENNETT, J., CLANCEY, W., KULIKOWSKI, C., MITCHELL, T. & WATERMAN, D. A. (1983). Constructing an expert system. In HAYES-ROTH, F., WATERMAN, D. A. & LENAT, D. B. Eds, *Building Expert Systems,* Reading, Massachusetts: Addison-Wesley.

BUCHANAN, B. G. & SHORTLIFFE, E. H., Eds (1984). *Rule-Based Expert systems: the MYCIN Experiments of the Stanford Heuristic Programming Project.* Reading, Masscahusetts: Addison-Wesley.

BYLANDER, T. & MITTAL, S. (1986). CSRL: A language for classificatory problem solving and uncertainty handling. *AI Magazine,* **7,** 66–77.

CHANDRASAKERAN, B. (1986). Generic tasks in knowledge-based reasoning: high-level building blocks for expert system design. *IEEE Expert,* **1,** 23–30.

CHANDRASAKERAN, B., MITTAL, S. & SMITH, J. W. (1982). Reasoning with uncertain knowledge: the MDX approach. *Proceedings of the Congress of American Medical Informatics Association,* San Francisco, pp. 335–339.

CLANCEY, W. J. (1983). The advantages of abstract control knowledge in expert system design. *Proceedings of the National Conference on Artificial Intelligence,* Washington, D.C., pp. 74–78 (August).

CLANCEY, W. J. (1985). Heuristic classication. *Artificial Intelligence,* **27,** 289–350.

CLANCEY, W. J. (1986). From GUIDON to NEOMYCIN and HERACLES in twenty short lessons. *AI Magazine,* **7,** 40–60.

COHEN, P. R. & GRUBER, T. R. (1985). Reasoning about uncertainty: a knowledge representation perspective. *Pergamon Infotech State of the Art Report.* Also COINS Technical Report 85–24, Department of Computer and Information Science, University of Massachusetts.

COHEN, P., DAY, D., DELISIO, J., GREENBERG, M., KJELDSEN, R., SUTHERS, D. & BERMAN, P. (1987). Management of uncertainty in medicine. *Proceedings of the IEEE Conference on Computers and Communications,* Phoenix, Arizona February 25–27, 1987, pp. 501–506. Published by the IEEE Computer Society Press, Washington, D.C.

DAVIS, R. (1976). Applications of meta-level knowledge to the construction, maintenance, and use of large knowledge bases. *Doctoral dissertation,* Computer Science Department, Stanford University. Reprinted in DAVIS, R. & LENAT, D. B. Eds, *Knowledge-Based Systems in Artificial Intelligence.* New York: McGraw–Hill.

DAVIS, R. & BUCHANAN, B. G. (1984). Meta-level knowledge. In BUCHANAN, B. G. & SHORTLIFFE, E. H. Eds, *Rule-Based Expert Systems: the MYCIN Experiments of the Stanford Heuristic Programming Project.* Reading, MA: Addison–Wesley.

DUDA, R. O., HART, P. E. & NILSSON, N. J. (1976). Subjective Bayesian methods for rule-based inference systems. *Proceedings of the 1976 National Computer Conference.* (AFIPS Conference Proceedings), Vol. 45, pp. 1075–1082.

ESHELMAN, L. & MCDERMOTT, J. (1987). MOLE: a tenacious knowledge acquisition tool. *International Journal of Man–Machine Studies.* In press.

HANNAN, J. & POLITAKIS, P. (1985). ESSA: an approach to acquiring decision rules for diagnostic expert systems. *Proceedings of the Second Conference on Artificial Intelligence Applications,* Miami Beach, Florida, 11–13 December 1985, pp. 520–525.

HOWE, A. E., DIXON, J. R., COHEN, P. R. & SIMMONS, M. K. (1986). DOMINIC: a domain-independent program for mechanical engineering design. *International Journal for Artificial Intelligence in Engineering,* **1,** 23–29.

KAHN, G., NOWLAN, S. & MCDERMOTT, J. (1984). A foundation for knowledge acquisition. *Proceedings of the IEEE Workshop on Principles of Knowledge-base Systems,* Denver, Colorado, 89–98 (December).

KAY, A. (1984). Computer software. *Scientific American,* **251,** 52–59.

KINGSLAND, III, L. C. & LINDBERG, D. A. B. (1986). The criteria form of knowledge representation in medical artificial intelligence. *Proceedings of the Fifth Conference on Medical Informatics,* Washington, D.C., pp. 12–16 (October 26–30).

MARCUS, S., McDERMOTT, J. & WANG, T. (1985). Knowledge acquisition for constructive systems. *Proceedings of the Ninth International Joint Conference on Artificial Intelligence,* Los Angeles, CA, pp. 637–639 (August).

MARCUS, S. (1987). Taking backtracking with a grain of SALT. *International Journal of Man–Machine Studies.* In press.

McDERMOTT, J. (1983). Extracting knowledge from expert systems. *Proceedings of the Eighth International Joint Conference on Artificial Intelligence,* Karlsruhe, West Germany, pp. 100–107 (August).

MOSTOW, D. J. (1983). Machine transformation of advice into a heuristic search procedure. In MICHALSKI, R. S., CARBONELL, J. G. & MITCHELL, T. M. Eds, *Machine Learning: an Artificial Intelligence Approach,* pp. 243–306. Palo Alto: Tioga.

MUSEN, M. A., FAGEN, L. M., COMBS, D. M. & SHORTLIFFE, E. H. (1987). Use of a domain model to drive an interactive knowledge editing tool. *International Journal of Man–Machine Studies.* In press.

NECHES, R., SWARTOUT, W. R. & MOORE, J. (1985). Enhanced maintenance and explanation of expert systems through explicit models of their development. *Transactions on Software Engineering,* **SE-11,** 1337–1351.

PAUKER, S. G., GORRY, A., KASSIRER, J. P. & SCHWARTZ, W. B. (1976). Towards the simulation of clinical cognition: taking a present illness by computer. *American Journal of Medicine,* **60,** 981–996.

POPLE, H. (1977). The formation of composite hypotheses in diagnostic problem solving—an exercise in synthetic reasoning. *Proceedings of the Fifth International Joint Conference on Artificial Intelligence,* Cambridge, Massachusetts, pp. 1030–1037.

SHORTLIFFE, E. (1976). *Computer-based Medical Consultations: MYCIN.* New York: American Elsevier.

SHORTLIFFE, E. H. & BUCHANAN, B. G. (1975). A model of inexact reasoning in medicine. *Mathematical Biosciences,* **23,** 351–379.

SHAFER, G. (1976). *A Mathematical Theory of Evidence.* Princeton, New Jersey: Princeton University Press.

SZOLOVITS, P. & PAUKER, S. G. (1978). Categorical and probabilistic reasoning in medical diagnosis. *Artificial Intelligence,* **11,** 115–144.

TENANT, H. R., ROSS, K. M., SAENZ, R. M., THOMPSON, C. W. & MILLER, J. R. (1983). Menu-based natural language understanding. *Proceedings of the Association for Computational Linguistics,* Massachusetts Institute of Technology, pp. 151–158 (June).

UTGOFF, P. (1986). Shift in bias for inductive concept learning. In MICHALSKI, R. S., CARBONELL, J. G. & MITCHELL, T. M. Eds, *Machine Learning: an Artificial Intelligence Approach,* Vol. II. Los Altos, California: Morgan Kaufmann.

VAN MELLE, W. (1979). A domain independent production rule system for consultation programs. *Proceedings of the Sixth International Joint Conference on Artificial Intelligence,* pp. 923–925, Tokyo, Japan (August).

ZADEH, L. A. (1975). Fuzzy logic and approximate reasoning. *Synthese,* **30,** 407–428.

Structured analysis of knowledge

S. A. Hayward

STC Technology Ltd, Six Hills House, London Road, Stevenage,
Herts, SG1 1YB, U.K.

B. J. Wielinga and J. A. Breuker

University of Amsterdam, Herengracht 196, 1016 BS Amsterdam, The Netherlands

Traditional approaches to Expert Systems development have emphasized the use of exploratory programming techniques and moving as quickly as possible from conceptualisation to code. Our research demonstrates that implementation independent domain modelling is feasible and useful within the context of a methodology which aims at supporting good software engineering principles as applied to Expert Systems.

Introduction

The work reported here is part of a collaborative research project entitled "A Methodology for the Development of Knowledge Based Systems".† It aims to consider the whole of the lifecycle for development of knowledge-based systems from the perspective of providing "structured techniques" to support the development process. The work to date has given most attention to the knowledge analysis and acquisition process, but the project is now also moving on to consider requirements specification and design of system architecture for knowledge-based systems.

The project has so far produced a theoretical basis for the modelling of domain expertise in an implementation independent way and developed tools to support this process. The techniques and tools are currently being applied to a number of experimental system development activities within the project and also for commercial clients.

The rationale for the research

The traditional approach to the development of knowledge-based systems has been essentially experimental. This is in keeping with its roots in the scientific field of artificial intelligence research. Thus, for knowledge-based systems, an application area is chosen because it is hoped that it will shed light on capabilities and techniques of application of AI methods. Development is progressed as far as interest and research budgets permit.

When it then comes to the attempt to apply the technology to commerical systems

---

† This project is part funded by the European Community's Esprit Programme. The partners are STC plc, Scicon Ltd., SCS GmbH, Cap Sogeti Innovation, The University of Amsterdam and the KBSC (Polytechnic of the South Bank, London). The research on knowledge acquisition and analysis is based on ideas originated at the University of Amsterdam.

KNOWLEDGE-BASED SYSTEMS Vol. 2
ISBN 0-12-115920-5

development there is a clash of objectives. In this case the primary concern is to achieve a system with a prespecified level of capability, and preferably within time and cost budget constraints. In other words we expect to apply the normal criteria for any commercial software development. An experimental methodology cannot expect to satisfy these criteria. This point in fundamental and simply recommending "simpler" applications and labelling the methodology "rapid prototyping" does not overcome it. Doubtless science can be converted to engineering by the gradual accretion of experience, but we would like to achieve the transfer more rapidly and more efficiently. In particular in this case one might hope to learn something from the history of other types of software.

Apart from these pragmatic concerns there are other, more theoretical, reasons for dissatisfaction with a wholly unstructured approach to knowledge-based systems development. There is a huge conceptual gap between knowledge as expressed by an expert and the encoding of expertise in a software system. This is not in any way to denegrate achievements in knowledge representation theory and languages. These achievements have made the gap bridgeable, but it is still wide. The attempt to transform data from protocols, for example, direct to an implementation language is doomed to misinterpretation or underinterpretation.

In our research we have adopted two related ideas in an attempt to advance our capability. The first is that the separation of software development into phases is applicable to knowledge-based systems, in particular that one should undertake analysis prior to commitments to implementation detail. This implies that the results of the analysis can be expressed in a way which is independent of decisions concerning system implementation. The second is that knowledge can be analysed at a number of levels and that analysis at an epistemological level is necessary to achieve a full understanding of a domain and to manage the transition from knowledge expressed by an individual (or set of individuals) to knowledge embodied in a software system.

The primary concern of the project in the area of knowledge acquisition and analysis has therefore been to provide techniques and support for such an epistemological analysis. The product of this analysis is then precisely the implementation independent representation required to satisfy our software engineering predilections.

It is perhaps interesting to note that when this project started (about three years ago) this approach was somewhat unusual; Bennett's work on ROGET (Bennett, 1983) was one of the few early pointers for us, together with work in the cognitive modelling tradition. However there are a number of instances where other researchers appear to share similar insights, notably Clancey who has also explicitly championed implementation independent analysis (Clancey, 1983, 1985), together with work of perhaps more pragmatic origins (tackling the "knowledge-acquisition bottleneck" e.g. Marcus, McDermott & Wang, 1985; Khan, Nowlan & McDermott, 1985) which has found value in abstracting away from implementation details to representation of "higher-level" structures in a domain. More recently we have noted the work of a research group at Tektronix who appear to be developing ideas similar to our own, though from a background in algebraic modelling in the formal software engineering tradition rather than cognitive modelling and knowledge representation (Freiling, Refuss, Alexander, Messick & Shulman, 1986).

Levels of knowledge analysis

We view the process of knowledge acquisition as one of "interpretation": verbal data (e.g. from interviews with experts or textbooks) is interpreted or mapped onto other representations and structures. Classically in knowledge-based systems development the attempt has been made to map directly from the verbal data to rules or some such implementation formalism. This is difficult and dangerous (in the sense that misinterpretation or underinterpretation is almost inevitable). We suggest that one can explicitly identify levels of analysis and in so doing provide a basis for supporting the interpretation process.

Sloman (1980) suggests four degrees of depth at which questions about knowledge can be asked: questions at the *individual* level, at the *conceptual* level, at the level of a particular *formalism* and at the level of *mechanisms* that implement a formalism. These levels closely correspond to the levels of representational primitives for different kinds of knowledge that Brachman (1979) distinguishes: *implementational, logical, epistemological, conceptual* and *linguistic* knowledge.

For the purpose of mapping verbal data onto knowledge we propose five levels representing a synthesis between Sloman's classification and Brachman's representational levels.

KNOWLEDGE IDENTIFICATION

This level of analysis corresponds to simply recording what one or more experts report on their knowledge. Although the result may be in a formalized form, the representational primitives on which this formalisation is based are linguistic (in the sense that Brachman uses this term). The same knowledge from different experts may have to be represented differently, because they use different terminology, or because their knowledge is structured in a different way.

KNOWLEDGE CONCEPTUALIZATION

Aims at the formalization of knowledge in terms of conceptual relations, primitive concepts and conceptual models. The knowledge of different experts, and possibly of different subdomains, is unified within one conceptual framework.

EPISTEMOLOGICAL ANALYSIS

At the epistemological level the analysis uncovers structural properties of the conceptual knowledge, formalised in an epistemological framework. Such a framework is based on epistemological primitives representing types of concepts, types of knowledge sources, structuring relations (such as hierarchical relations, inheritance), and types of strategies.

LOGICAL ANALYSIS

The level of analysis applied to the formalism in which the knowledge on higher levels is expressed and which is responsible for inference making.

IMPLEMENTATIONAL ANALYSIS

At this level of analysis, mechanisms are uncovered on which higher levels are based. The representational primitives are the ones which are normally used when an implementation of an AI programme is described (e.g. matching, testing, slot-filling, etc.).

The products of analysis

Knowledge analysis undertaken within the framework we propose produces as its major output a four layer model of expertise:

(1) DOMAIN LEVEL

Definition of the domain concepts and their static relations—primarily ISA but others may be relevant, e.g. consists_of, dependent_upon etc. This could extend to definition of causal relationships in some domains.

(2) INFERENCE LEVEL

Definition of relationships arising in a task context. These are conceived of as dynamic and are expressed in an inference structure. This structure describes only what inferences *can* be made, not which and how they are made in particular instances of problem solving. The inference structure is defined in terms of meta-classes, which describe the role of domain concepts (e.g. hypothesis, data) and "knowledge sources" i.e. the knowledge elements required to make inferences from concepts in one meta-class to another.

(3) TASK LEVEL

Specification of how the available inferences can be used to undertake a particular task—defined in terms of the goals of the task. There may of course by many task layers specified on a given inference structure, defining methods to achieve different goals or different methods for the same goal.

(4) STRATEGIC LEVEL

Definition of how the task level may be controlled e.g. changing task plans if an impasse is reached. We have conducted relatively little analysis of this level, but in general it would appear to consist of a plan, monitor, repair cycle. We anticipate that even sophisticated Expert Systems will often use a fixed task structure and this layer is defined more for conceptual completeness than practical necessity. It does however, help to indicate why certain naive assumptions about Expert Systems may not be realised e.g. graceful degradation at the limits of performance will depend on substantial modelling and implementation of this level, it does not arise from expertise *per se*.

The following section illustrates such a model.

A conceptual model for insurance underwriting†

This model describes one activity within an insurance company involving the underwriting of risks on export sales i.e. insurance for the supplier against the

---

† Massoud Davoodi (STL) played a major role in undertaking the analysis described here.

possibility of default by a foreign customer. The information provided here is clearly not sufficient to understand the domain in any detail but is rather intended to be illustrative of the output produced by the modelling techniques described above.

DOMAIN LEVEL

A full lexicon and glossary is not included but major domain concepts are shown in an ISA hierarchy in Fig. 1. The ISA relationship is particularly relevant in this domain since decision making involves consideration of sets of related factors. The creation of this hierarchy was in fact a highly non-trivial task and major category errors were made in early versions. This fact helps to illustrate that even an apparently simple structuring of domain knowledge is not without value.

Other major domain relations are: quantative (e.g. in formulas to calculate parameters), consist-of (e.g. between policy holder/buyer company property and market/business securities), empirical (e.g. between market sector and financial attributes).

INFERENCE LAYER

The inference structure is shown in Fig. 2. A full specification of the meta-classes and knowledge sources cannot be given here but Table 1 illustrates the domain concepts relevant to the meta-classes.

Given this general description of the inferences in the domain, the problem-solving of the expert may be informally described as follows.

In the first instance, the client submits an application in which he expresses the need for a guarantee; the need to reduce risk in export business implied by the application is expressed in the form of the meta class "problem". The expert is expected to provide a "solution" to this, in the form of the type of policy to be awarded. The type of policy may be determined in terms of credit limit, duration, and terms of payment.

Before applying the solution, the potential risks have to be assessed to ensure that the underwriting "norm" is not violated. The norm in this case consists of a set of conditions, some of which will need to be present as part of the "parameter" before a positive answer can be given. A norm, in our case, might consist of:

buyer_honesty is high;
buyer_exposure and buyer_market_condition are not both below certain threshold & p/h_competence is above average;
if buyer_exposure & buyer marker_condition are both marginal, then buyer_competence is above average; and
p/h_competence is high.

The "Parameter" requiring similar attributes as that of "norm" may consist of:

buyer_honesty;
buyer_competence;
buyer_exposure;
p/h_competence;
buyer_market_condition.

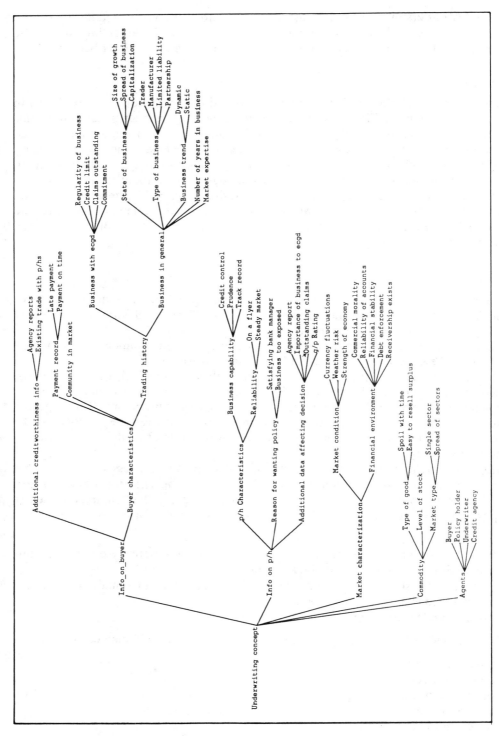

FIG. 1. ISA hierarchy of underwriting concepts.

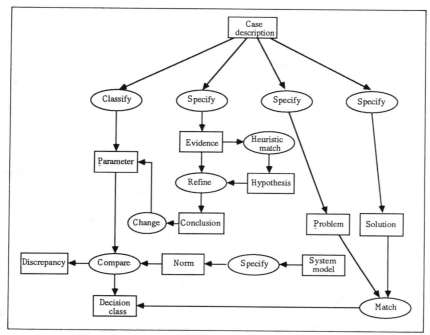

FIG. 2. Inference structure for underwriting.

The attributes of the "parameter" will have to be combined using and/or connectives to enable comparison against their counterpart clauses in the "norm".

The detailed specification of the knowledge sources shows how for example the values of parameters are derived from the raw data provided by the case description or how such parameters are to be evaluated against the norms.

TABLE 1

Meta classes for underwriting

Meta class	Domain concepts
Case description	Buyer attributes, p/h attributes, market attribute, commodity, agency reports.
System model	Underwriting policies
Problem	Risk reduction
Solution	Type of policy, terms of policy
Parameter	Buyer_honesty, buyer_competence, buyer market condition, ...
Norm	Risk levels
Decision class	Yes/no/refer
Evidence	Additional info on buyer/market condition, etc.
Hypothesis	Unreliability of data
Conclusion	Correction value
Discrepancy	Difference between 'parameter', and 'norm'

TASK LAYER

The expert follows an overall problem-solving strategy in which there is room for manoeuvre in individual cases.

When an application is submitted, the underwriter has to make a judgement on whether or not to insure the client. The underwriter cannot exercise much flexibility in providing a guarantee (solution). This is due to the nature of the type of insurance involved; namely, the client needs to have a large enough credit guarantee over a fixed period of time to cover his business. The underwriter is, therefore, required to assess the financial merits of a case very carefully. However, certain data (or a combination of them) on the client and the buyer in particular can have a near to conclusive effect on a decision being made. On the buyer's side, documents such as "letter of credit", or characteristics like "good business morality" are the kinds of data which can greatly influence the underwriter in giving a positive answer. In short, if the underwriter can make a clear yes/no decision based on the initial data supporting a case, then he is likely to do so without considering other potential "evidence" likely to have a marginal effect.

On the other hand, in a marginal cases the underwriter needs to rely on his other sources (agencies, embassy reports, . . .) to gather enough evidence (or show lack of it) to correct errors of judgement which might have inflated the 'parameter' in either direction. The diagnosis part of the inference structure is then used extensively to generate the measure of error ("conclusion") needed to adjust the "parameter".

The task structure (Fig. 3) combines inferences shown in Fig. 2 in order to achieve the objectives described in this strategy.

```
assesss(case, decision_class)
        obtain(case_description)
        match(solution, problem)
                specify(problem)
                specify(solution)
        assess(risk)
                compare(parameter, norm)
                        specify(norm)
                        clasify(case description)
                while discrepancy unacceptable
                        confirm_or_deny(hypothesis)
                        specify(evidence(discrepancy))
                                obtain(new case data)
                        heuristic_match(evidence)
                        refine(hypothesis, evidence)
                        change(parameter)
```

FIG. 3. Task structure for underwriting.

If issues bearing on a decision remain very marginal after all branches of the task structure have been considered, then a system would make no recommendation and refer the case to an expert. The more information is required for assessment of risks, the deeper the branches are evaluated.

The process of analysis

The application of these ideas in practise is not as complex as might be imagined. (This perhaps provides some supportive evidence for the methodology in that a "natural" process may be difficult to describe or characterize but will be easy to use).

Fundamental to our approach is that the knowledge engineer should not have to conduct the analysis in a wholly bottom-up fashion; this is very laborious and probably error-prone. In particular the creation of models as described above is very difficult; a process of top-down refinement is less demanding. This, of course, requires the predefinition of generic categories to act as a starting point.

The notion of meta-classes and knowledge sources already incorporates a high level of abstraction. We believe that these can be used to create prototypical inference structures which we term "interpretation models" (because of their role in interpreting the verbal data deriving analysis by postulating a certain model on the basis of an initial survey of the domain). The model can then be used as a basis for data gathering, since one has a view of the categories one is looking for. As the analysis proceeds the model may be modified or changed, where the data is found not to match. However, the process is one of top-down refinement and thus provides cognitive support, making it more manageable and controllable.

The analysis process overall is defined as consisting of three phases. In the initial phase, which we have called "orientation", the knowledge engineer becomes acquainted with the domain (and the expert). The major concepts in the domain are identified, together with the scope and complexity of the tasks undertaken. At this stage the knowledge engineer is identifying rather than interpreting data and the analysis is kept to a very general or global level. The main outputs of orientation are a statement of potential system boundaries (there may be more than one) and an estimate of the feasibility of the system(s). A start will also have been made on creating the domain lexicon (listing key concepts) and an initial interpretation model will be selected or constructed. The latter at this point is nothing more than a weak hypothesis. This first phase may be regarded as a preparation for knowledge acquisition proper.

Once the scope of the system has been specified, this defines in broad terms the function(s) of the system and its users. The aim is then to construct a detailed specification of the function the system has to perform. This specification includes the knowledge and strategies employed in the expertise. At this stage, processing of data becomes mainly model-driven. After a definition of the main- and sub-tasks involved in the performance of the system's functions, the interpretation model may be refined and moves towards becoming the inference structure for the particular domain/task of interest. This involves fully specifying the meta-classes in terms of domain concepts, and knowledge sources using domain relations; plus defining the task structure adequate for the performance of the desired functionality.

With an interpretation model identified, data can be collected and interpreted from expertise-in-action. Thinking aloud protocols may provide these data more adequately than interviews. Such on-line protocols are preferred to interviews or retrospective data, because there is ample evidence that experts do not necessarily employ the types of strategies and knowledge they may claim to use.

The interpretation model is used in such a way that the data from the domain and expert can be fitted within the structures provided by the model, thus producing a fully specified description of the expertise in a domain. However, the data may also "refute" the selected/constructed model, which may motivate revisions of the model. For instance, it may turn out that data obtained from early interviews on the strategies the expert claims to use, are not confirmed by more detailed and valid data collected from analysis of expertise in action. However it may also be noted that one may adopt a more synthetic approach to the definition of the task level, since the available inferences in the domain may be manipulated in a way which does not directly mirror their use by an expert. This may be the primary distinction between cognitive modelling and expert-system building. Of course the criteria for assessing the adequacy of the model become harder to define if one takes this approach, but this may be compensated by conceptual simplicity at this level.

These stages are described as problem identification and problem analysis. The basic distinction here is between identification of the various components in the domain, notably the domain concepts, but also such things as the roles and functions of user(s) and expert(s) in the domain; and the analysis of the problem solving behaviour in terms of describing these components within a coherent model. These two "phases" are in no way sequential. In practise one observes a highly iterative cycle, but the separation is useful in a normative or didactic sense because it enables the processes of identification (e.g. of behavioural components in a protocol) to be distinguished from the fitting of the identified elements within the framework of a model.

It should be noted that the analysis process must also include an analysis of the environment for the proposed system and of the characteristics of the intended users. These are not emphasized here because we have little to add at present beyond normal good software engineering practice. However it should be noted that user characteristics will impact on the model of expertise, particularly with regard to the task level, and in that area the user and expert analyses are effectively indistinguishable. Nevertheless there is a component of analysis which should cover the normal concerns of user analysis for defining the required man–machine interface, exception handling, explanation and so on.

The result of all this is full analysis documentation covering models of expertise, user and environment. We believe one should then be ready to proceed to issues of system architecture and design. These issues can now be considered on the basis of a full specification of the domain and the role of the proposed system, and without the need to backtrack over major parts of the knowledge-acquisition exercise.

Support tools

The techniques described above cannot realistically be carried out without computerised support. We have developed a system for this purpose, known as KADS (for Knowledge Acquisition and Documentation Structuring). This system is built on KL-ONE, which is used not only to record the domain concepts and their relationships but also to record the analysis concepts as defined by the methodology. A large part of a domain analysis is then guided and documented by instantiating these concepts and providing values for their attributes. Other components of the system allow the maintenance of lexicons and glossaries, the production of diagrams, and the analysis of interview transcripts. An illustration of the facilities provided is given by the screen shown in Fig. 4. The system is currently implemented in Quintus Prolog on Sun workstations.

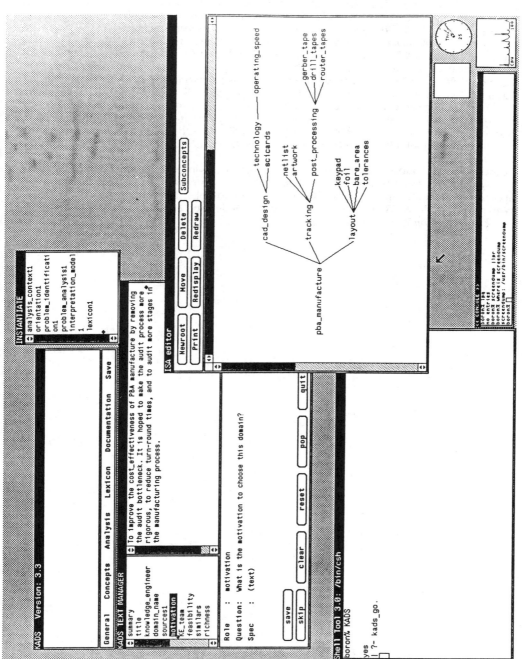

FIG. 4. A typical KADS screen display.

References

BENNETT, J. S. (1983). ROGET: a knowledge-based consultant for acquiring the conceptual structure of an expert system. *Stanford University Memo HPP-83-24.*

BRACHMAN, R. J. (1979). On the epistemological status of semantic networks. In FINDLER, N. V. Ed., *Associative Networks.* New York: Academic Press.

CLANCEY, W. J. (1983). The epistemology of a Rule Based Expert System—a framework for explanation. *Artificial Intelligence, 20, 3,* 215–25.

CLANCEY, W. J. (1985). Heuristic classification. *Artificial Intelligence 27, 3,* 289–350.

FREILING, M. J., REFUSS, S., ALEXANDER, J. H., MESSICK, S. L. & SHULMAN, S. J. (1986). The ontological structure of a troubleshooting system for electronic instruments. *1st International Conference on Application of AI in Engineering Problems,* Southampton.

KAHN, G., NOWLAN, S. & McDERMOTT, J. (1985). MORE: an intelligent knowledge acquisition tool. *Proceedings of the 9th International Joint Conference on Artificial Intelligence.*

MARCUS, S. McDERMOTT, J. & WANG, T. (1985). Knowledge acquisition for constructive systems. *Proceedings of the 9th International Joint Conference on Artificial Intelligence.*

SLOMAN, A. (1980). The Computer Revolution in Philosophy. Harvester.

WEILINGA, B. J. & BREUKER, J. A. (1986). Models of expertise. *Proceedings of the European Conference on AI,* Brighton.

A mixed-initiative workbench for knowledge acquisition

Gary S. Kahn, Edwin H. Breaux, Peter DeKlerk and Robert L. Joseph†

Carnegie Group Inc., 650 Commerce Court, Station Square, Pittsburgh, Pa 15219, U.S.A.

The TEST‡ Development Environment (TDE) enables knowledge engineers and trained domain experts to interactively build knowledge bases representing troubleshooting knowledge. **TEST** is an application shell, providing a domain-independent diagnostic problem solver together with a library of schematic prototypes. **TDE** provides both system-directed interrogation and a user-directed editor for building up the knowledge base. Novice users of **TDE** rely heavily on the guidance offered by system prompts, while experienced users tend to use the direct manipulation of graphic items as a preferred method. This paper examines four facets of **TDE**: first, the core concepts of the underlying diagnostic system; second, the knowledge acquisition mechanism; third, workbench functions for knowledge-base modification; and finally debugging support within the workbench.

1. Introduction

Expert system developers typically find that their knowledge acquisition techniques change with the course of system development. In first approaching a new problem, knowledge acquisition tends to be exploratory. The goal is not only to acquire knowledge but, more importantly, to identify a representational format and control strategy of sufficient power to capture domain-specific problem-solving behavior and domain-specific knowledge. Once this is done, knowledge acquisition becomes constrained by the target architecture. At this point, the rate at which knowledge can be 'pumped into' the system changes dramatically. However, it is still a time-consuming process to interview and code a knowledge base.

Diminishing the 'knowledge acquisition bottleneck' thus requires two interlocked solutions—first, a packaged problem-solving architecture which allows developers to focus on knowledge acquisition, rather than on knowledge base design and problem-solving control, issues of typically greater complexity; and secondly, a high-productivity workbench aimed at reducing the time it takes to build and maintain knowledge bases. In this vein, **TEST** provides an application shell for troubleshooting systems, while **TDE** provides the high-productivity workbench domain experts use to build and maintain knowledge bases.

TDE continues a line of research initiated by several previous systems, including ROGET (Bennett, 1985), ETS (Boose, 1984), and more recently, MORE (Kahn *et al.*, 1985), and SALT (Marcus *et al.*, 1985). These systems have looked at ways to

---

† The authors acknowledge Rajiv Enand, Wayne Homren, Al Kepner, Jeff Pepper and Bill Richer, all of whom have made key contributions to the development of the system described. The implementation effort has also benefited from the contributions of several others.

‡ An acronym for Troubleshooting Expert System Tool, TEST is an internal name for software in use at Carnegie group Inc.

KNOWLEDGE-BASED SYSTEMS Vol. 2
ISBN 0-12-115920-5

interrogate experts under the assumption that a chosen underlying architecture can solve the problems of interest. **TDE** differs from its predecessors in two important ways. First, it uses a problem-solving strategy that is more comprehensible to domain experts in the manufacturing and customer service domains. Unlike generic rule-based approaches to knowledge-base representation, **TDE** knowledge bases model the causal consequences of component and functional failures (failure-modes), as well as problem-solving methods specific to troubleshooting tasks. Second, **TDE** addresses the need for knowledge acquisition systems to conform to a developer's desire to provide information as it comes to mind. As a mixed-initiative workbench, **TDE** enables developers to provide information as they wish, while at the same time offering guidance and direction as it is needed. **TDE** thus avoids appearing rigid and tedious in its interrogation technique, a problem for several earlier systems.

The following sections examine four facets of **TDE**: first, the core concepts of the underlying diagnostic system; second, the knowledge acquisition mechanism; third, workbench functions for knowledge-base modification; and finally debugging support within the workbench†.

2. The problem-solving architecture

Knowledge acquisition is largely a matter of mapping the knowledge which supports expert decision-making into the representations required by a problem-solving system. When there is a conceptual correspondence between these representational units and the terms with which experts understand their task and domain, mapping becomes a straightforward operation. In addition, conceptual correspondence makes direct-manipulation techniques readily available, and permits the system to easily guide users engaged in knowledge base development.

2.1. TEST CONCEPTS

Unlike rule-based diagnostic systems that have evolved from the Emycin perspective (Van Melle *et al.*, 1981), **TEST** uses a semantic network of schematic objects, or frames, to represent its key concepts. **TEST** comes with a library of prototype schemata, called 'object types' within **TDE**. Each schema corresponds to a concept ordinarily important to expressing troubleshooting expertise. The domain expert builds a knowledge base by creating instances of these prototypes. Most critical, for example, is the **failure-mode**. A failure-mode represents a deviation of the unit under test from its standard of correct performance. Within **TEST**, the failure-mode prototype describes the characteristics which must be provided for each failure-mode instance, such as a broken cooling unit, in our example below.

Failure-modes are arranged in a hierarchy. At the top of the hierarchy are observable failures of the entire unit, e.g. hot air out of an air conditioner (CC-HOT-AIR), as shown in the top panel of Fig. 1. At the bottom of the hierarchy are failure-modes of individual components, e.g. a burned out motor (FM-MOTOR-

---

† Several **TEST** applications are currently in development or field test. A version of **TDE** with most of the features discussed is in use. However, at the time of writing, a small number of features are still to be implemented.

BURNED-OUT). Intermediate failure-modes typically represent functional failures which are causal consequences of component failures. Both taxonomic hierarchies, as in CSRL [Bylander *et al.*, 1983], and causal paths, as in CASTER (Thompson & Clancey, 1986), may be represented in this fashion. Many levels of intermediate failure-modes are common. Typical **TEST** networks have 4 to 10 levels of failures, though much deeper networks occur on occasion.

Other prototype objects within **TEST** include **questions**, **tests**, **test-procedures**, **repair-procedures**, **rules**, **decision-nodes**, and **parts**. Each of these concepts has an obvious mapping into the troubleshooting domain. Questions are simply queries to users which result in factual responses. Tests represent manual or sensor-based tests. Test-procedures describe sequences of tests, each of which must be carried out before the diagnostic significance of the overall procedure can be evaluated. Repair-procedures describe corrective actions to pursue upon determining the occurrence of a failure-mode. Rules represent a variety of contingent actions rather than evidence/belief propositions alone, as is typical in Emycin-like diagnostic systems. Parts provide descriptors of parts that are associated with component failures or with repairs.

Decision-nodes provide a mechanism for integrating conventional diagnostic decision logic into the otherwise failure-mode oriented knowledge base. Although **TEST** can generate its own decision logic from the failure-mode knowledge base, domain experts often prefer to provide the decision logic directly. This may be done by building a decision-node network. Each decision-node represents a test together with branches to other tests contingent on the result of the first. Decision-node networks typically terminate with the failure-modes that could cause the problem associated with the network's entry point.

Knowledge base maintenance is facilitated by clustering information around failure-modes. Inspection of a failure-mode provides direct access to associated tests, repairs and documentation, as well as to forward and backward causal links to other failure-modes in the network. Since the failure-mode is the key concept in most troubleshooting tasks, such aggregates provide an easily understood and readily accessible structure.

2.2. THE DIAGNOSTIC PROBLEM SOLVER

Domain-specific knowledge bases represent pre-compiled search spaces and serve as input to the problem solver. Given the failure-mode hierarchy and other auxiliary information, the problem solver searches for a diagnostic conclusion, interactively prompting a technician, or sampling sensors and databases as necessary to obtain evidence to proceed with the diagnostic session. The search space can be dynamically altered by rules sensitive to information acquired during a diagnostic session. Knowledge engineers can also choose the appropriate level of granularity for the representation of causal chains, thus constraining the depth of search required prior to hypothesizing a particular failure. Moreover, the preferred order in which to consider candidate causes may be easily specified.

In general terms, the problem solver pursues a depth-first recursive strategy starting with an observed or determined failure. It seeks the cause of an occurring failure-mode considering candidate causes (other failure-modes) referenced in the *due-to* slot of this failure-mode. Candidate causes can have three states: confirmed, disconfirmed, and unknown. Failure-modes are confirmed when the problem solver determines that they have occurred.

If a candidate cause is disconfirmed, the problem solver moves on to consider another possibility. If a candidate cause is confirmed, the problem solver will consequently seek to determine its causes. This procedure continues until a terminal failure-mode is identified. Terminal failures, those without instantiated *due-to* slots, are typically repairable faults.

A domain-specific knowledge base is used as input to the **TEST** diagnostic problem solver. Following the example in the top panel of Fig. 1, let us assume that hot air was blowing out of the unit (CC-HOT-AIR). In this case, the problem solver would first consider low freon (FM-LOW-FREON) as the cause of the hot air. If this were ruled out, it would proceed to consider if the cooling unit were broken (FM-BROKEN-COOLING-UNIT). If this were to be confirmed, or was unknown, the problem solver would proceed to consider its causes—a burned out motor (FM-MOTOR-BURNED-OUT) or a bad compressor relay (FM-BAD-COMPRESSOR-RELAY).

As a new failure-modes come up for consideration, the problem solver chooses a method of confirmation provided by the knowledge-base developer. It may be a direct test, a rule-based inference procedure, or the disconfirmatory recognition (*modus tollens*) that a necessary consequent of the failure-mode had not occurred. If the failure-mode cannot be confirmed or disconfirmed, the problem solver will nevertheless proceed to examine potential causes. If a failure-mode can have multiple causes, the diagnostic analysis will not terminate until all potential candidate causes are evaluated. The interested reader can find a further description of **TEST**'s problem-solving behavior in (Kahn, 1987).

3. Knowledge acquisition

TDE provides both system-directed interrogation and a graphic-oriented editor for building up the knowledge base. Novice users of **TDE** rely heavily on the interrogation techniques, while experienced users prefer to use the direct manipulation of graphic items representing knowledge-base objects. These methods support each other. For the novice user, a graphic map of the knowledge base is displayed and incrementally augmented as **TDE**'s questions are answered. The experienced user can directly manipulate the graphic representation, as well as activate the interrogator by selecting menu options and mouse clicking on relevant portions of the graphics display.

TDE interfaces are designed for modeless operation, enabling the user to move smoothly between operations, as well as to request system guidance. Commands may be invoked by typing the textual command, by bringing up a menu and selecting the command from that menu, or by striking a short-hand control-key sequence. Many commands let the user browse or directly manipulate the graphic representation of the knowledge base. Other commands permit the execution of a diagnostic session based on the evolving knowledge base. Diagnostic sessions are run as a separate task, which may be paused allowing resumption of the knowledge-base editor.

3.1. USING DIRECT MANIPULATION

A key problem for direct-manipulation techniques is that of determining and displaying relevant objects and object relations in a manner that's focused around the needs of the user's task. Within **TDE**, **TEST** provides a natural tripartite representational structure for constraining the display and manipulation of the knowledge base.

Primary, secondary, and tertiary information can be distinguished within a **TEST** knowledge base. The primary core of a **TEST** knowledge base is a failure-mode tree, as described above. Other secondary information in the knowledge base—including tests, repairs, and rules associated with the selected failure-mode—is clustered around each failure-mode. At the tertiary level, each of these objects has itself numerous attributes, or *properties,* providing further descriptive and control information.

TDE takes advantage of this tripartite division. A global view or window provides a filtered perspective of the knowledge base. Here failure-modes and the causal relations between them are displayed. A second window gives the user a local perspective into the secondary objects clustered around a selected failure-mode. Finally, objects selected within these windows can be displayed with their full attributive detail in a third window.

Figure 1 shows the three views into a knowledge base regarding air condition failures. In the global view, the failure-mode hierarchy is displayed. The *hot-air* concern is shown to be *due-to low-freon* or a *broken-cooling-unit*. The *hot-air* concern has been selected for further examination. Consequently, secondary information local to it is displayed in the lower right. It is shown to have an associated *question*. If other secondary information, such as rules, had been associated with this concern they would be displayed here as well. All attributes of the selected object are displayed in a structured text-editing window to the lower left.

TDE provides a straightforward mechanism for creating knowledge bases. A user can select the add operation by clicking the mouse on the Add 'button' on the screen. A graphic cursor (resembling a small tree node) helps the user choose a place to position to object. A failure-mode, for instance, may be graphically linked to another indicating that it is a cause of the latter problem. **TDE** then asks for a name and object type (failure-mode or whatever). Acceptable responses are restricted to those valid, given constraints on the knowledge-base architecture. Networks built in this way may also be edited using copy, move, and delete operations available within the workbench.

3.2. SYSTEM-DIRECTED USE

TDE also exploits the inherent tripartite structure of a **TEST** knowledge base to provide guidance to developers. Each perspective delineates a natural line of interrogation. Before asking detailed questions, **TDE** will first seek out the overall structure of the knowledge base as reflected in the global window. It will then seek to fill in detail at the level reflected in the local view. Finally, as necessary, **TDE** will cycle through the attribute slots of each object, completing the full picture. For example, **TDE** would have asked first about potentially observable air conditioner

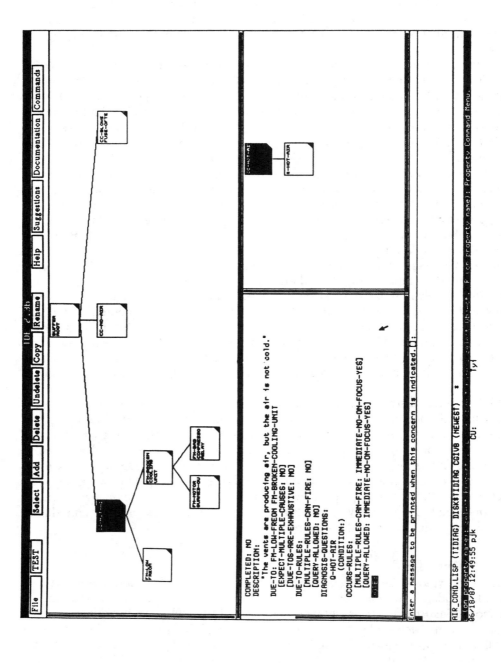

Fig. 1. The **TDE** interface.

problems that would signify some kind of malfunction. For each of these, it would attempt to find out their possible causes, as they would be considered by a technician engaged in troubleshooting the initial concern. Once this is done, **TDE** would inquire about associated diagnostic tests and repairs for each of these failure-modes. It would then attempt to get additional attributive information on all the specified failure-modes, repairs, and tests, as required.

As information is provided in response to prompts, **TDE** represents it graphically. Thus, the user can both see the system's interpretation of the information provided and follow the developing context in which further questions are asked.

3.3. EXAMPLES

For the purposes of demonstration, we have chosen a non-proprietary example of a knowledge base. The partial knowledge base which we use is for the on-site diagnosis of central air conditioning systems, as shown in the top panel of Fig. 1.

3.4. A SESSION WITH A NOVICE

When a user enters **TDE** the graphic windows show only a single node of the tree that is about to be built. That node represents the buffer itself, so that everything can be graphically 'attached' to the buffer. Unless told otherwise, **TDE** starts off in system-directed mode, providing extra assistance and commentary for the benefit of novices.

Prompts start to appear in the prompt window and an initial dialogue begins. **TDE** first elicits a list of symptomatic problems, or 'customer concerns'.

TDE: Please list all customer concerns to be diagnosed in this portion of the knowledge base.

User: Hot-Air No-Air

TDE: [Graphically displays customer concerns **Hot-Air** and **No-Air**. **Hot-Air** is in reverse video, indicating that it is now being selected as the basis for further questioning. A copy of **Hot-Air** is placed in the local view, but since **Hot-Air** has no definition yet, nothing else appears within the local view.]

Because the knowledge acquisition process must be constrained by the interviewee's knowledge and intended focus, **TDE** is flexible about the way it obtains its information.

TDE: Unless you indicate otherwise, we will proceed to complete the knowledge base by first asking for the structure of the knowledge base. Afterwards, we will go back and obtain more detailed information, such as descriptions of the tests and repair procedures. Finally, we will go back and fill in all remaining detail.
Please describe in words what the customer concern Hot-Air indicates.

User: The vents are producing air, but the air is not cold.

TDE: What are the possible causes of Hot-Air?

User: Low-Freon Broken-Cooling-Unit

TDE: What questions should be asked when the technician selects this concern?

User: Hot-Air
[Note that the name **Hot-Air** may be used for both the question and the concern. **TDE** distinguishes the two by putting a unique prefix on the front, in this case making the names CC-Hot-Air and Q-Hot-Air.]

In the above interaction, **TDE** has focused on eliciting the essential structure of the knowledge base: namely, the failure mode hierarchy, and the names of associate tests, questions, and repairs. **TDE** proceeds in a depth-first, partially elaborative manner. After **Hot-Air** is selected as the focus, **TDE** asks for basic structural information: its causes and the contingent background questions to ask. Following this, rather than fill out the detail on **Hot-Air**, **TDE** completes the basic structure of the knowledge base, first asking about **Low-Freon**, one of the causes of **Hot-Air**.

As information is provided, **TDE** represents it graphically. The customer concerns are displayed under the buffer node. Their proximal causes are represented in the global window as they were provided. Similarly, questions, tests, repairs, and rules are displayed in the local view as they are attached to the focal global object. The global object is highlighted in the global view to remind the user of the context in which additional information will be interpreted. With graphic cues such as these, the user can both see the system's interpretation of the information provided and follow the developing context in which further questions are asked. This latter point can significantly increase the user's ability to stay with a line of questioning.

The interrogator seeks to complete each object or concept that it knows about by filling in values for all the attributes. To perform its task, the interrogator uses the detailed attribute view mentioned above. This view is called the *textual view,* since the display is textual and the user interacts by typing text rather than by manipulating graphics with the mouse. As the user is being prompted for a given attribute, the interrogator displays that attribute within the textual view, if it is not already there, and then it highlights the attribute name. The user is then prompted using the prompt associated with that attribute. While the attribute is terse, the prompt is sufficiently descriptive for novices. Thus the novice learns attribute names by watching the interrogator highlight each name in turn as it asks its questions.

Interrogation is controlled by a script which may be modified by the user to change the order in which the information is collected by **TDE**. For example, the user can request that the information in the knowledge base be collected by expanding the tree breadth first instead of depth first. He may also request the immediate collection of detailed attribute information.

Because, as we shall see below, an experienced user can alter the flow of control, it is possible that questions in the script might be passed without being answered or even asked. The system keeps track of such questions and tries to get back to them whenever it can. At any time, **TDE** can help the user locate information that has not yet been provided.

There are several advanced features in the interrogator, such the editing of the previous value in response to the current question, which are available to experts and novices alike. A list of these features is readily accessible via online documentation.

3.5. A SESSION WITH AN EXPERIENCED USER

Using **TDE** over time is a learning experience. By providing reactive graphics, **TDE** teaches the user the graphic manipulations that can be performed to accomplish what had initially been done by answering questions as they arose. By suggesting, from time to time, where the user can override system control, **TDE** informs users of the flexible functionality that is at their disposal.

More advanced users move easily between graphics manipulation and reliance on the system to provide guidance through promoting. When they are first learning to take control, users tend to suspend **TDE** interrogation only temporarily. A user may do so simply by invoking a command instead of answering the pending question. This is useful for such activities as selecting another failure mode as a focus of attention. If the new failure mode does not exist yet, the user may create it and then select it. Of course the user may also issue any other command he chooses, including commands for browsing, editing, or changing control parameters. This technique of gaining temporary control is illustrated below:

TDE: If there are any exception rules, please list the names of the rules here.

User: [Clicks the mouse on the **Add** icon to activate the **ad object** command.]

TDE: Place the object using the mouse, then click left.

TDE: [Creates a dummy object on the screen near where the mouse currently sits and attaches it to the nearest object in either the global or local tree. (As the user moves the mouse, the dummy object moves also, always attaching itself to the closest global or local object.)]

User: [Positions the dummy object as the rightmost child under the buffer node and then clicks the mouse.]

TDE: What is the name of the object you are adding?

User: Blows-Fuse-Often

TDE: [Presenting the user with a menu:]
Is Blows-Fuse-Often a failure-mode, failure-mode-class, or decision-node?

User: [Selecting from the menu:]
failure-mode

TDE: [Displays the actual failure mode, labeled **Blows-Fuse-Often**, at the appropriate location on the screen, redisplaying the screen to keep the tree 'balanced'. Since the command is now complete, the interrogator once again resumes control:]

Please describe in words what the failure-mode Low-Freon indicates.

User: [Clicks on the **Blows-Fuse-Often** failure mode, once again interrupting the interrogator. This activates the **select object** command, with **Blows-Fuse-Often** as its argument.]

TDE: [Acts on the user command, then returns control to the interrogator. Since the **Blows-Fuse-Often** failure mode has been selected, and since neither the interrogator nor the user has filled in any information for that failure mode, the interrogator continues by asking the first question in the script for failure modes:]

Please describe in words what the failure-mode Blows-Fuse-Often indicates.

Note that the interrogator's behavior has effectively been altered by the actions of the user. Questions that would have been asked according to the script have, at least temporarily, been bypassed.

After a while, many users will find system-directed interactions to be annoying, even though the user can always override the system's requests. Such users can turn the system control off. When the user does so, the computer will immediately inform him as to how to turn control back on. If desired, the user may use the **fill object** command to ask the system to go into system-directed mode for just that object. After answering all questions for that object, the user is again given control. System-directed mode may be resumed on request or automatically with the next use of the **fill object** command.

4. Knowledge-base modification

In addition to facilities for building up a knowledge base, **TDE** offers further editing support. As developers make enhancements to pre-existing systems, they need special tools to help avoid errors which frequently lead to flawed knowledge bases. Typical errors include redundancy, incompleteness, and inconsistency. **TDE** helps by providing the user with the ability to browse quickly for information already in the knowledge base, and by detecting certain kinds of hard or suspected errors. The explicit representation of causal and classificatory information in **TEST** enables approaches that would be precluded by classical rule-based diagnostic systems.

4.1. BROWSING

Object classification, relational networks, and the maintenance of back-pointers within **TEST** enable multiple search techniques as well as efficient retrieval. As a result, **TDE** can offer developers string search, network browsing, and schematic pattern matching. Browsing facilities, such as these, are required when the user wants to confirm that a new (to be added) failure-mode is not already in the knowledge base, find a similar failure-mode which can be copied and edited to create the new object, or simply understand the content of what is already there. In a large knowledge base, it is impractical to browse without a means of directing attention to relevant segments of data.

Within **TDE**, string search is used to match against the names of knowledge base objects. Search of this kind is constrained by allowing the user to specify the type (class) of object (failure-mode, test, etc.). Network browsing is used to examine objects within the knowledge base that are in a specified relation to a specified object (e.g. 'has-test' voltage-meter). Pattern matching is used to find objects with attribute values specified in the search template. In additon, inverse links maintained in the knowledge base enable **TDE** to quickly point users to parts of the knowledge base that may be impacted by their modifications.

4.2. ERROR WARNINGS

When developing a knowledge base, the user may unknowingly duplicate a failure-mode by using a different name to refer to one already known. While this cannot be entirely prevented, the availability of richly structured information in a **TEST** knowledge base enables **TDE** to use heuristics to identify suspects. **TDE**, for instance, monitors for failure-modes which have similar causes and consequents, or those that share the same test and repair procedure. Isomorphic nodes within the knowledge-base network are typically unexpected and thus constitute grounds for suspicion.

TDE monitors for several other kinds of errors, as well. Of particular interest are objects that are not properly linked into the knowledge base. In addition, failure-modes without causal, test, or repair information are noticed. Violations of type restrictions associated with the attribute slots of each **TEST** object are also flagged.

5. Debugging support

In order to ease debugging by non-programmers, the **TEST** problem solver is designed to use the knowledge base in much the way an informed technician would proceed with fault isolation. This is made possible by structuring problem solving around the high-order concepts represented in the knowledge base. The trouble-shooting task proceeds by focusing on an observed or suspected failure-mode. An attempt is made to determine whether the failure-mode has occurred in the unit under test. If the failure-mode has occurred, or if its status remains unknown, then the possible causes of the failure-mode are investigated to see if they have occurred.

5.1. DEBUGGING TECHNIQUES

5.1.1. Breakpoints
In debugging knowledge-based systems, it is desirable to have access during execution to everything the system has already concluded or come to know, as well as to its current hypotheses, planned tests, and queries. This allows the developer to notice when the system is failing to conclude inferable information, is preparing to determine needless information, or acting incorrectly on known information. The **TEST** interpreter can provide this information on demand as the entire knowledge base is at its disposal.

In order to get at information at the right time, it is necessary to allow breakpoints at conceptually relevant junctures. Within the **TDE** environment, it is desirable to pause as particular failure-modes become the focus of attention. Since the problem-solver uses the knowledge base directly, developers can set breakpoints simply by toggling desired failure-modes. When the system is paused, the current state of the entire knowledge base can be browsed to determine how the diagnostic search is being conducted.

5.1.2. Tracing
A **TDE** execution can trace significant events in terms of the process described above. This includes the conclusions reached with respect to possible failure-modes,

changes in diagnostic focus, and rule-firings. The developer can trace all events of a particular type, or single out particular knowledge-base objects. When these are considered by the problem solver a trace message is printed. Problems recognized through an inspection of the trace window can be corrected by returning to the knowledge-base editor.

Reference in the trace window to knowledge-base objects are selectable. On selection they are opened up for inspection within the knowledge-base editor.

5.1.3. Message editing

During diagnostic problem-solving, errors may appear in the text displayed to the user. This might include descriptions of failure-modes, procedural information in regard to test or repairs, or prompts used to query the user. Rather than force return to the editor, **TDE** allows the user to select text strings for editing. The knowledge base is updated appropriately, as **TDE** maintains an association between displayed strings and their knowledge base source.

5.2. EXAMPLE

The following example demonstrates how some of the facilities described above can be used to extend the air conditioning knowledge base. In particular, the example illustrates the use of multilple browsing techniques, breakpointing, determining current knowledge and goals, and in-place correction of text.

Sam, a new knowledge engineer is assigned the task of adding in more failure-modes to the knowledge base. He wants to add the failure-mode **compressor-motor**, but is not sure if it is already in the knowledge base. He does a string search on motor, broken, and cooling across failure-mode names, but does not find the failure-mode that he wants. In order to assure himself that the failure-mode is not there, he uses string search to look for a test with compressor in its name. Finding **compressor-circuit test**, he uses the network browser to look at all the failure-modes linked to it by the **test-for** relation. This turns up the failure-mode **compressor-engine**, which turns out to be what Sam had in mind. Sam then links it to the broken-cooling-unit. In this example, the use of multiple browsing techniques has provided for successful identification of a failure mode already in the knowledge base, thus preventing unintended duplication.

In order to determine the effect of this addition, Sam sets a breakpoint on **compressor-engine** and then runs the knowledge base to see how it functions. When this failure-mode becomes the focus of attention, the system pauses. At this point, Sam wants to know what information the system knows. The system pops up a window indicating that it is trying to determine if there has been a compressor engine failure, and that it has determined that the air being produced is hot, that freon levels are ok, and that the cooling unit is not broken.

From this, Sam realizes that the system does not know if the thermostat works. He notes that a failure-mode is missing so he goes back and adds that failure-mode to the knowledge base, by placing an icon in the global window and answering prompt information provided by the system.

Sam then continues to run the example. The compressor engine is determined not to work. The repair procedure is then displayed in the window but there is a mistake. Sam selects the repair text and corrects it without stopping the diagnostic session. This correction is then made in the appropriate file.

6. Conclusion

By providing a mixed-initiative multi-task environment, **TDE** allows knowledge engineers and domain experts the option of directing or being directed by the underlying knowledge acquisition system. By providing a graphic interpretation of the underlying knowledge base as it changes with respect to user input, users are provided with a context in which to understand the impact of replies to system prompts. **TDE** supports knowledge base enhancement by providing tools that support knowledge-base browsing, modification and debugging.

The **TEST** architecture greatly aided the development of the **TDE** workbench. In particular, the choice of a schematic as opposed to rule-based representation led to a knowledge base characterized by the use of domain-familiar concepts, and sufficient conceptual structure to facilitate several **TDE** features. While much of **TDE** has been implemented, there is still much to do. During its continued development, users will be evaluating evolving prototypes. Because knowledge-engineering needs cannot be fully predicted, we expect to learn of many new requirements.

References

BENNETT, JAMES S. (1985). Roget: A knowledge-based system for acquiring the conceptual structure of a diagnostic expert system. *Journal of Automated Reasoning*, **1**(1), 49–74.

BOOSE, J. (1984). Personal construct theory and the transfer of human Expertise. In *Proceedings of the National Conference on Artificial Intelligence*. Los Altos, CA: William Kaufmann, pp, 27–33.

BYLANDER, T., MITTAL, S., & CHANDRASEKARAN, B. (1983). CSRL: A language for expert systems for diagnosis. In *Proceedings of the Eighth International Joint Conference on Artificial Intelligence*. Los Altos, CA: William Kaufmann, pp, 218–221.

KAHN, G. S. (1987). TEST: A model-driven application shell. In *Proceedings of AAAI-87*. Los Altos, CA: William Kaufmann, pp, 814–818.

KAHN, G. S., NOWLAN, S., MCDERMOTT, J. (1985). MORE: An intelligent knowledge acquisition tool. In *Proceedings of International Joint Conference on Artificial Intelligence*. Los Altos, CA: William Kaufmann, pp, 581–584.

MARCUS, S., MCDERMOTT, J., WANG, J. (1985). Knowledge Acquisition for Constructive Systems. In *Proceedings of International Joint Conference on Artificial Intelligence*. Los Altos, CA: William Kaufmann, pp, 637–639.

THOMPSON, T. & CLANCEY, W. J. (1986). A qualitative modelling shell for process diagnosis. *IEEE Software* **3**(2), 6–15.

VAN MELLE, W., SCOTT, A. C., BENNETT, J. C. & PEAIRS, M. A. (1981). The Emycin manual. *Technical Report,* Stanford University Computer Science Department.

Heuristics for expertise transfer: an implementation of a dialog manager for knowledge acquisition

Catherine M. Kitto and John H. Boose

Knowledge Systems Laboratory, Boeing Advanced Technology Center, Boeing Computer Services, P.O. Box 24346, Seattle, WA 98124, U.S.A

One of the most difficult and time-consuming activities in constructing an expert system is the process of knowledge acquisition. Our objectives are to identify a set of heuristics for *expertise transfer* and *modeling* based on our experience in knowledge acquisition for expert systems, and to formalize this knowledge as rules. Aquinas, a knowledge-acquisition workbench, contains tools that interview experts; analyse, test, and refine knowledge; and generate knowledge bases for expert system shells. A set of heuristics for knowledge acquisition has been defined and incorporated in the *Dialog Manager* sybsystem of Aquinas to provide guidance in the knowledge acquisition process to domain experts and knowledge engineers.

The implementation of the Dialog Manager is described, and an example transcript shows the interaction of Aquinas, the Dialog Manager, and the expert. A preliminary classification for knowledge acquisition heuristics is proposed. Finally, issues in formalizing strategies for knowledge acquisition and a plan for future research are presented.

Introduction

Aquinas is a knowledge-acquisition workbench consisting of an integrated set of tools for automated knowledge acquisition, representation, and reasoning (Boose & Bradshaw, in press). One of these tools, the *Expertise Transfer System* (ETS), interactively interviews an expert, analyses the information entered, assists the expert in refining that knowledge, and generates a production-rule knowledge base. Vocabulary, conclusions, problem-solving traits, trait structures, trait weights, and inconsistencies are elicited. This problem-solving knowledge is stored in a *rating grid* (shown later in Fig. 4). Problem solutions (*elements*) are requested and displayed across the top of a grid, while solution traits (*constructs*) are listed down the side of the grid as bipolar scales.

The interviewing methodology used to construct the rating grid is derived from Personal Construct Psychology (Kelly, 1955; Gaines & Shaw, 1981; Shaw & Gaines, in press). The expert supplies traits that discriminate between groups of problem solutions. Each element is given a *rating* by the expert showing where it falls on the trait scale. Production rules are generated from the ratings in the grid and can be tested in end-user consultations. Knowledge bases can be created for a number of expert-system shells (e.g. KEE, S.1, M.1, OPS5) from the common internal representation in Aquinas (Boose, 1985, 1986).

More than 500 knowledge-based system prototypes have been generated by ETS during the three years of its use at the Boeing Company. A typical prototype can be constructed in less than 2 h.

175

Aquinas extends the problem solving and knowledge-representation capabilities of ETS by allowing experts to structure information in hierarchies using multiple-variable types. Several methods exist for representing and reasoning about uncertainty, and dozens of tools related to building and maintaining the knowledge base are available.

A novice Aquinas user is led through an initial interview but can then be overwhelmed by the large number of alternative knowledge development and refinement methods. To assist novice and intermediate users in using Aquinas effectively, a *Dialog Manager* was created (Kitto & Boose, 1986). The Dialog Manager is a subsystem of Aquinas that contains heuristics for the modeling of expertise and for the use of Aquinas during knowledge acquisition.

Approach

Our goal was to identify heuristics used by experts and knowledge engineers in constructing a knowledge base using Aquinas. We were concerned with how and why users decide to invoke Aquinas commands in specific situations.

Another objective was to identify differences between strategies used by the novice user of Aquinas and the experienced user who has acquired skill in using the tool. Could the successful strategies of the experienced Aquinas user be captured and used to guide a novice through a knowledge-acquisition session? Could these heuristics be presented to the novice in an explanatory or tutoring capability? Would strategies that prove successful for a particular expert in a specific problem-solving domain be equally successful with a different expert and different domain?

As a starting point, a knowledge engineering development effort using ETS was examined in depth. A team of knowledge engineers had developed a knowledge-based financial consultant (Financial Advisor) to select appropriate investments for a client. The team maintained a journal summarizing discussions with the domain expert and their experience in using the ETS knowledge-acquisition tool.

This detailed account of applied knowledge acquisition was a productive source of heuristics for knowledge acquisition and strategies for the use of ETS. It was supplemented by transcripts and interviews with the domain expert and knowledge-engineering team. We reconstructed the interaction between ETS and the domain expert from the stored transcripts. The version of ETS in use at this time did not contain the Dialog Manager, so all the documented heuristics dealing with the use of ETS and the knowledge-acquisition process stemmed directly from the knowledge engineers and the domain expert. These heuristics were embedded in the Dialog Manager in the form of rules and procedures.

Next, we re-entered the Financial Advisor's knowledge base, this time using Aquinas. We were able to compare the performance of the Dialog Manager in selecting Aquinas operations with the original transcripts using ETS without the Dialog Manager. We identified differences in knowledge-acquisition strategies and areas where the Dialog Manager's heuristics could be improved.

Implementation of the Dialog Manager

The Dialog Manager has been implemented as an expert system. Its domain knowledge is the effective use of Aquinas. A rule-based approach to implementation was selected because of its flexibility, maintainability, and modifiability. Heuristics are encoded as rules directly within the Aquinas system.

OPTIONS FOR DIALOG MANAGER ASSISTANCE

The Dialog Manager offers a mixed-initiative environment with three modes of interactive assistance: *automatic, assist,* or *off.* It supports mixed-initiative system development much like the TKAW system (Kahn, Breaux, Joseph & DeKlerk, in press) with a continuum of control options, easy transfer between options, and ability to vary options depending on experience and task difficulty.

In the *automatic* mode, the Dialog Manager applies knowledge-acquisition heuristics to determine the best Aquinas operation to be performed next within the context of the current state of the knowledge base and the characteristics and preferences of the expert. The Dialog Manager displays the recommended command sequence, an explanation of what it is doing, and the reason it has chosen that option. This mode is most commonly used for new Aquinas users, particularly in the initial interview when they may be unfamiliar with Aquinas commands and desire guidance. The expert may interrupt the Dialog Manager to regain control.

The Dialog Manager also provides limited guidance to the expert in an *assist* mode in which the Dialog Manager again applies heuristics to suggest several suitable command alternatives and display its recommendation. However, experts may overrule the Dialog Manager by replacing the recommendation with their own command choices.

If the user overrides a proposed suggestion, the Dialog Manager asks for a textual explanation to be stored in a file accessible to Aquinas developers for later analysis. The recommendation of the Dialog Manager and the command preferred by the user are noted in the permanent history and flagged for the Dialog Manager learning facility.

Finally, experts may prefer to use Aquinas with the Dialog Manager in *off* mode. The Dialog Manager makes no suggestions to the expert, although it continues to record a history of selected operations. The *off* mode is typically used for brief demonstrations or by experienced Aquinas users who require little guidance.

Users can also select the level of prompting and explanatory information provided by the Dialog Manager. Three levels, *verbose, concise* and *terse,* permit users to select detailed or abbreviated explanations and justifications for Dialog Manager recommendations. Table 1 explains the levels of assistance and prompting in this mixed-initiative environment.

DATA STRUCTURES FOR REPRESENTATION OF KNOWLEDGE-ACQUISITION HEURISTICS

It was necessary to develop special data structures to capture information used in the knowledge acquisition heuristics. Because many heuristics for knowledge acquisition involve temporal reasoning or user characteristics, three types of data structures were defined to record and represent this information:

The *recent events list,* a mechanism for retaining Aquinas command sequences with associated time stamps. As a new command is entered, it is added to the recent events list, and the least recent is removed. This list is kept cached in memory.

TABLE 1
Dialog manager mixed-initiative environment

Dialog Manager modes		
Control	*off*	No recommendations; record keeping only
	assist	Offers recommendations; user may override
	automatic	Automatically implements recommendations
Explanation Level	*verbose*	Paragraphs of explanation
	concise	Medium level of explanation (sentences)
	terse	Little or no explanation of recommendations

The *permanent history,* a file containing the complete chronology of Aquinas commands entered by the expert for the current knowledge base. This is stored as a file that is loaded when the expert enters Aquinas.

The *user model profile,* a file containing information concerning individual Aquinas domain expert users and classes of Aquinas users.

Example typescript

The following example illustrates how the Dialog Manager employs its heuristics for knowledge acquisition to guide an expert in developing the Database Management System (DBMS) Advisor and how it explains its strategies. In the figures recommendations from the Dialog Manager are in bold type and preceded by [**DM**], while an Aquinas user entry is in underlined bold type.

In Fig. 1, the expert has specified that the Dialog Manager run in *automatic* mode, supplying *concise* explanations of alternatives and suggested actions. In this mode,

```
--- AQUINAS SYSTEM ---
Would you like to work on an OLD knowledge base, or create a NEW one?
AQ**NEW

Would you like help using AQUINAS from the DIALOG MANAGER?
AQ**YES

Would you like the DIALOG MANAGER to make suggestions (ASSIST) or
    run automatically (AUTOMATIC)?
AQ**AUTOMATIC

When giving advice, should the DIALOG MANAGER be VERBOSE,
    CONCISE, or TERSE?
AQ**CONCISE

Please give a short description of the problem you are trying to solve.
AQ**DBMS SELECTION
```

FIG. 1. Aquinas interviews an expert to obtain problem-solving knowledge with the Dialog Manager to guide the interaction automatically.

```
-- [DM] Enter a set of solutions for the DBMS domain
   -- ELICITING ELEMENTS --
Please enter a list of DBMS elements, one to a line. When you're done,
      enter a RETURN.
AQ**IMS
AQ**SIR
AQ**RIM
AQ**SQL/DS
AQ**IDMS
AQ**TOTAL
AQ**EASYTRIEVE
AQ**(CR)


--[DM]Now define a set of traits that discriminate between problem
   solutions.
   Solutions will be considered three at a time.


-- BUILDING TRAITS BY TRIADS --
Think of an important attribute that two of IMS, SIR, and RIM share, but
   that the other one does not. What is that attribute?
AQ**HIERARCHICAL
What is that attribute's opposite as it applies in this case?
AQ**NOT HIERARCHICAL

Think of an important attribute that two of SIR, RIM, and SQL/DS share,
   but that the other one does not. What is that attribute?
AQ**RELATIONAL
What is that attribute's opposite as it applies in this case?
AQ**NOT RELATIONAL
               •
               •
               •
```

FIG. 2. AQUINAS asks the expert for an initial set of potential solutions.

the Dialog Manager will control the interaction between expert and Aquinas, prompting the expert when domain knowledge is needed. The user may regain control of the dialog by escaping to the executive after any Aquinas prompt.

Next, in Fig. 2, Aquinas asks the expert for an initial set of DBMS problem solutions. The solutions are then combined into triads (sets of three), and the expert is asked to identify discriminating traits. The Dialog Manager automatically guides the user in this interaction. Prior to each step, the Dialog Manager displays a concise explanation of the activity to be performed.

The Dialog Manager continues to guide the user, prompting the user in Fig. 3 to rate each DBMS solution on each trait scale. In this case, the Dialog Manager suggests several appropriate alternatives, chooses EDIT FILL IN RATINGS, and briefly explains why that option was chosen. Figure 4 illustrates a partial Aquinas screen showing this initial DBMS knowledge base. The top window depicts the developing case, expert, solution, and trait hierarchies in a *hierarchy map*. The lower window shows the DBMS *rating grid*. The Dialog Manager automatically displays these graphs after the expert has entered solutions, trait pairs, and ratings.

In our example, the Dialog Manager has been operating in *automatic* mode with *concise* explanations. At this point the Dialog Manager applies the following

```
---[DM] Do you want to add elements, add traits, or fill.in ratings for each
   DBMS solution on each trait scale. I recommend you fill in grid
   ratings to keep the knowledge base simple for initial testing.
AQ**EDIT FILL.IN RATINGS

-- FILLING IN RATINGS --
Please rate these things on a scale of 1 to 5, where 1 means more like
   HIERARCHICAL and 5 means more like NOT.HIERARCHICAL. If neither
   one applies, enter N(either). If both apply, enter a B(oth).

HIERARCHICAL (1) / NOT HIERARCHICAL(5)
   IMS**1
   SIR**1
   RIM**5
   SQL/DS**5
   IDMS**3
   TOTAL**3
   EASYTRIEVE**5

Please rate these things on a scale of 1 to 5, where 1 means more like
   RELATIONAL and 5 means more like NOT RELATIONAL. If neither
   applies, enter N(either). If both apply, enter B(oth)

RELATIONAL(1)/NOT RELATIONAL(5)
   IMS**5
      •
      •
      •
```

FIG. 3. The Dialog Manager displays the possible next steps and suggests that the expert *fill in ratings*.

heuristic:

>*if fill-in-rating-grid-complete and*
>   *all-displays-current and*
>   *current-command-state = exec and*
>   *dialog-manager-mode = automatic and*
>   *user-AQUINAS-experience = high and*
>   *no-of-current-command-choices > 7*
>*then recommendation = OPTIONS DIALOG MANAGER ASSIST*
>*Because "you are an experienced AQUINAS user and*
>   *many knowledge base refinement commands are appropriate here"*

This is an example of a Dialog Manager heuristic based on used experience and current state of knowledge-base development. The expert has now entered the initial DBMS rating grid and the Dialog Manager is operating in *assist* mode (Fig. 5).

Once an initial set of elements, traits, and trait ratings is entered, as in our DBMS example above, the expert may choose from more than 180 alternative command leaves on menus and submenu hierarchies in Aquinas. These commands enable the following activities: applying analytic techniques to the knowledge base; editing cases, experts, elements, traits, and ratings; displaying grids, maps, and implications; setting options; and managing hierarchies of experts, cases, elements, and traits. Even an experienced knowledge engineer may be puzzled about which technique to attempt next. The Dialog Manager examines heuristics to identify a set of alternatives for the given state of the knowledge base and recommends the strategy of greatest potential value, determined by accumulated rule priorities.

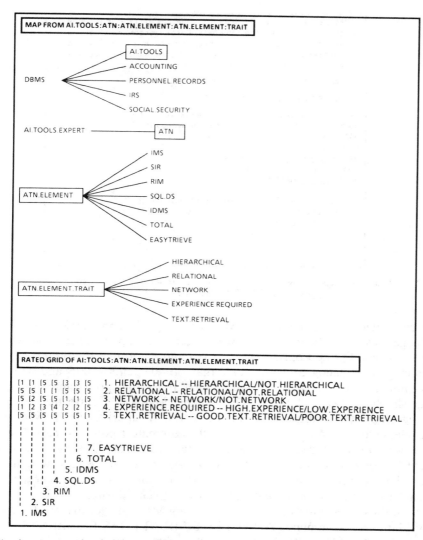

FIG. 4. Aquinas screen, showing the developing hierarchies and the rating grid for the DBMS knowledge base.

---CHANGING DIALOG-MANAGER OPTIONS --
---[DM]Now changing Dialog Manager options to *Assist* since you are an experienced AQUINAS user and many knowledge base refinement commands are appropriate here.
AQ**OPTIONS DIALOG-MANAGER ASSIST (CR))

FIG. 5. The Dialog Manager, still in "*automatic*" mode, applies a heuristic to automatically switch to assist mode.

```
---[DM] Do you want to add elements, add traits, test the knowledge,
   or correct problems in the knowledge base? I recommend that you
   correct problems by analyzing similarities elements since there are
   fewer than 6 traits and there is a high degree of similarity between
   two elements. Analyze similarities to distinguish them.

AQ**ANALYZE SIMILARITIES ELEMENTS (CR)        (user confirms)

---SIMILARITIES ELEMENTS ANALYSIS---

The two elements IDMS and TOTAL are matched at the 100% level. Can
 you think of a trait that distinguishes between them?
AQ**YES
What is that trait?
AQ**GOOD REPORT WRITER
What is that trait's opposite?
AQ** POOR REPORT WRITER

What is the name of a scale or concept that describes
 GOOD.REPORT.WRITER / POOR.REPORT WRITER?
AQ** REPORT WRITER
   •
   •
   •
```

FIG. 6. The Dialog Manager, now in *"assist"* mode, presents an array of command alternatives and suggests ANALYZE SIMILARITIES ELEMENTS.

We continued to use the Dialog Manager to guide construction of the DBMS knowledge base. As before, the Dialog Manager applies knowledge-acquisition heuristics to identify appropriate alternatives and determine the preferred strategy. In this case, the Dialog Manager finds that the elements IDMS and TOTAL are highly similar (100% match), indicating that the rating grid cannot meaningfully distinguish these two solutions. The Dialog Manager's heuristics specify that analysing element similarities and adding a trait to discriminate between the two similar elements would be the strategy with the greatest potential payoff to correct the problem. (This heuristic is illustrated later in Fig. 11). Heuristics dealing with correcting problems detected in the knowledge base are usually weighted more heavily than other command options. When more than one knowledge-base problem exists, the one with greatest severity is given priority.

Figure 6 illustrates interaction with the Dialog Manager in *assist* mode. When the Dialog Manager recommends ANALYZE SIMILARITIES ELEMENTS, it pauses until the expert confirms its recommendation with a carriage return or overrules it by erasing the line and entering a new command. The confirmation (or overruling) is recorded on the recent events list and permanent history for analysis by the learning facility.

Next, the Dialog Manager applies an heuristic based upon complexity of the knowledge base. As shown in Fig. 7, the Dialog Manager recommends that the expert use cluster analysis to analyse the knowledge base, since the rating grid is large, having more than 40 grid cells. The number of rating grid cells is just one measure of knowledge base size and complexity used in the Dialog Manager heuristics. As there is also a weak link in the element clustering relationship, the Dialog Manager recommends that the expert SHOW CLUSTERS ELEMENTS to perform a cluster analysis on knowledge base elements. The expert agrees with the recommendation and confirms it with a carriage return. After the DBMS element

---[DM] Do you want to add elements, add traits, analyze the knowledge, make hierarchies, or test the knowledge? I recommend you analyze the knowledge base by performing a cluster analysis, since there are more than 40 cells in the rating grid and there is a weak clustering relationship between element groups.
AQ**SHOW CLUSTERS ELEMENTS **(CR)**   *(user confirms)*

---[DM] Do you want to add elements, add traits, analyze the knowledge, make hierarchies, or test the knowledge? I recommend you MAKE HIERARCHIES by splitting the rating grid on elements because the grid has more than 5 traits and 40 cells and a weak element clustering link.
AQ**EDIT SPLIT GRID BY ELEMENTS **(CR)**   *(user confirms)*

---SPLITTING GRID BY ELEMENTS---
Do you want to use the element clusters?
AQ**__YES__
What is a class name for IDMS, TOTAL, SIR, IMS?
AQ**__HOST LANGUAGE DBMS__
What is a class name for EASYTRIEVE, SQL/DS, RIM?
AQ** __FOURTH GENERATION TYPE__

FIG. 7. The Dialog Manager, in "*assist*" mode, recommends SHOW CLUSTERS ELEMENTS and EDIT SPLIT GRID BY ELEMENTS using a heuristic based on knowledge base complexity.

cluster analysis is graphically displayed (Fig. 8), the Dialog Manager proceeds (Fig. 7) to suggest that the rating grid be split by element clusters since there is a clustering link of only 60% between the two groups (IDMS, TOTAL, SIR, and IMS) and (EASYTRIEVE, SQL/DS and RIM). The expert identifies a class name "Host Language DBMS" for the first group and "Fourth Generation Type DBMS" for EASYTRIEVE, SQL/DS, and RIM. This results in the addition of two new element classes and another level of abstraction in the element hierarchy.

Our expert continued to use the Dialog Manager to assist in the construction of the DBMS knowledge base. Figure 9 illustrates the hierarchy map for the completed DBMS knowledge base.

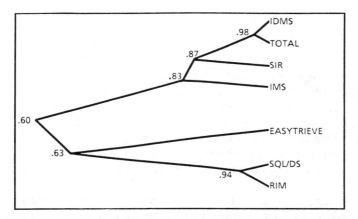

FIG. 8. Based on the recommendation of the Dialog Manager, the expert requested SHOW CLUSTERS ELEMENTS for the DBMS knowledge base. The two major clusters are (IDMS, TOTAL, SIR, IMS) and (EASYTRIEVE, SQL/DS, and RIM).

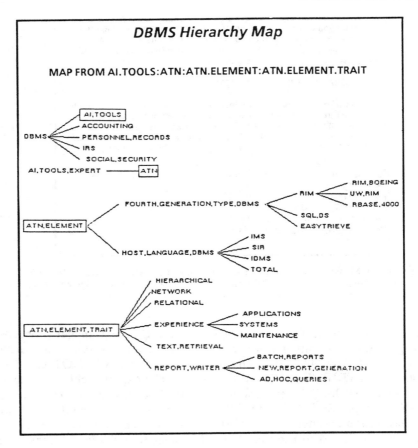

FIG. 9. The completed hierarchy map shows 10 DBMS elements, 12 trait pairs, two levels of traits, and three levels of elements.

Discussion

STRENGTHS AND WEAKNESSES OF APPROACH

Our experience with the Dialog Manager has demonstrated that it is possible to define a knowledge acquisition environment and to formalize knowledge about the transfer of expertise in a rule-based representation. Probably the most valuable result of the implementation of the Dialog Manager is the collection of heuristics for knowledge acquisition and the effective use of Aquinas. In the following section, a classification scheme is proposed that reflects the variety of heuristics that we encountered.

Our research effort focused on the knowledge-acquisition process and improved our understanding of how expertise can be transferred effectively. We were surprised at the number of different strategies practiced by individual experts and knowledge engineers. Our attempt to capture these strategies and formalize this knowledge in the Dialog Manager is an important step in understanding knowledge acquisition.

One disadvantage of the Dialog Manager is that individual experts may (at least initially) disagree with the strategies suggested by the Dialog Manager. It may be that the heuristics used are not appropriate for certain classes of problem or types of idiosyncratic behavior. As the scope of the Dialog Manager's heuristics expands to encompass a variety of strategies, we anticipate that this weakness may be alleviated. A learning capability has been incorporated in the Dialog Manager. Its strengths and weaknesses are discussed later in this section.

We have encouraged users to operate in the *assist* mode, as it provides feedback to the Dialog Manager and system developers for both cases where the user *agrees* with the recommendation of the Dialog Manager and where the user *disagrees* and overrules the decision. However, some experts object to having to erase the Dialog Manager entry and replace it with their own selection. Users have also criticized the occasionally excessive detail in the Dialog Manager's explanations and prompts.

A PROPOSED CLASSIFICATION OF HEURISTICS FOR EXPERTISE TRANSFER

As we developed the Dialog Manager, it was apparent that the heuristics for knowledge acquisition and expertise transfer could be classified. We began to detect certain patterns in the various heuristics for knowledge acquisition. We also observed that the components of these heuristics tended to fall into specific categories. This led to an attempt to define a preliminary classification of heuristics for knowledge acquisition and the transfer and modeling of expertise, summarized below.

Heuristics based on temporal reasoning

Heuristics considering the "recency" of some event:
Recent in some absolute sense of time or a fixed interval—"within the last 10 minutes";
Recent in a "relative" sense—"within the last 10 commands entered";
Recency may be defined differently by different experts and depend on the speed with which they perform various tasks.

Heuristics concerned with a specific order of events (may include functional dependencies):
Whether an event occurred prior to another event;
Whether a specific sequence of multiple events occurred in some pre-defined order;
Events that must automatically trigger the execution of some other command.

Heuristics based upon user preferences

Individual preferences:
Options for interaction selected in the past;
Degree of interactive assistance from Dialog Manager;
Level of Dialog Manager explanatory detail.
Patterns of command sequences repeated frequently by a user;

Repeated patterns in which the user overrules a specific Dialog;
Manager command with another;
Repeated past actions of expert to confirm Dialog Manager's suggestions.
User group or categorical preferences:
Inherited preference characteristics;
Default options for user group.

Heuristics related to the complexity of the knowledge base in terms of the relationships between:
Number of elements in rating grid;
Number of traits in grid;
Number of rating grids;
Number of experts developing the knowledge base;
Number of cases considered;
Number of implications between traits;
Complexity of the hierarchies;
Presence of multiple variable types.

Heuristics based upon the problem domain
Structure selection (Analysis);
Constructive problems (Synthesis);
Qualitative causal models for diagnostic problems.

Heuristics that depend on current state
Current state of interaction between user and Aquinas;
Current state of knowledge base;
Current state of Dialog Manager;
Current state of user history.

Heuristics based on knowledge-base problems

Heuristics derived from implication analysis or ambiguous relationships in knowledge base;
Heuristics derived from similarity analysis measures;
High similarity between traits;
High similarity between elements.
Heuristics derived from anomalies in solution and trait hierarchies;
Heuristics based on inconsistencies and circularities.

Heuristics based upon expertise or experience of user/user group

Number of knowledge bases created;
Number of Aquinas sessions performed;
Number of unique Aquinas commands used;
Complexity of knowledge bases:
Average size rating grid;
Maximum size rating grid;
Average number of rating grids;

Examples of dialog manager heuristics based on complexity of the knowledge base

If number-of-implications > 0 and
  number-of-traits / number-of-implications < 0.2
then recommendation = (ANALYSE IMPLICATIONS ALL)
because
  "there is a high number of implications in proportion to
  the number of traits in the grid".

if number-of-implications > 0 and
  number-of-implications / number-of-gridcells > 0.833
then recommendation = (ANALYSE IMPLICATIONS ALL)
because
  "there is a high number of implications in proportion to
  the size of the rating grid".

FIG. 10. Two examples of Dialog-Manager heuristics based on complexity of the knowledge base.

Maximum number of levels of abstraction.
Number of times Aquinas used with Dialog Manager off;
Level of prompt detail requested.

Heuristics for prioritization of command alternatives

Heuristics based on past problem-solving performance (measured by rank correlation with expert);
Heuristics based on severity of some problem in the knowledge base;
Heuristics based on expected benefits of command;
Default heuristics (to be applied when no others are appropriate).

An important class of heuristics is based on knowledge-base complexity. Dialog Manager rules manage hierarchies of experts, cases, elements, and traits. One rule recommends that a rating grid be split into two or more grids when it is large and a cluster relationship between elements or traits exists. Another rule suggests that one expert's rating grid should be subordinated to that of another expert. Other rules attempt to simplify complex implicational relationships. Figure 10 illustrates examples of these heuristics.

Another useful class of heuristics illustrated in Fig. 11 stems from potential problems in the knowledge base: a high similarity between two traits or elements, high average similarity, ambiguities, too many or too few implications, etc. Heuristics from this category are also applied when there are missing grid ratings or trait weightings, or if inheritance relationships have not been specified. This behavior is similar to that of the "Watcher" in the KRITON system (Diederich, Ruhmann & May, in press) which monitors the intermediate knowledge representation for missing components and recommends using an elicitation method to complete the knowledge base.

Examples of dialog manager heuristics based on problems in the knowledge base

If   fill-in-rating-grid-complete and
      number-of-ambiguities > 0
then recommendation =
      (ANALYSE IMPLICATIONS AMBIGUITIES)
because
      "there   are   inconsistent   or   ambiguous   implications   in   the
      knowledge base"

if   fill-in-rating-grid-complete and
      number-of-elements < 6 and
      number-of-traits > 3 and
      element-similarity > 0.90
then recommendation =
      (ANALYSE SIMILARITIES ELEMENTS)
because
      "there is a high degree of similarity between two
      elements in the knowledge base. Analyse similarities to
      distinguish them."

if   number-of-elements < 6 and
      number-of-traits > 3 and
      fill-in-rating-grid-complete and
         average-element-similarity > 0.70
then recommendation =
      (ANALYSE SIMILARITIES ELEMENTS)
because
      "the average similarity between elements in the
      knowledge base is > 70%. Analyse similarities to
      distinguish the elements".

FIG. 11. Examples of Dialog-Manager heuristics based on knowledge-base problems.

ROLE OF LEARNING IN THE DIALOG MANAGER

The Dialog Manager is equipped with a learning mechanism. The data structures used to record interaction between the Dialog Manager and the Aquinas user (the recent events list, the permanent history) provide a wealth of information about how Aquinas is used to construct knowledge bases. Whenever the user enters a command sequence in *off* mode or confirms or overrules a Dialog Manager suggestion in *assist* mode, the learning mechanism records the action and scans the data structures for similar patterns in the past history. Detected patterns of user preferences are stored in the user profile, or may be used to create new heuristics applicable to the individual user or a more general class of users.

The Dialog Manager learning capability is illustrated in Figs 12 and 13. Our database management system expert is expanding the DBMS rating grid by adding elements, using the Dialog Manager's *assist* mode. The expert follows the suggestions to add an element and display the hierarchy map, but overrides the Dialog Manager's recommendation to fill in ratings and chooses to add a new trait instead. Later in the session, the expert repeats this same pattern. The Dialog

```
--[DM] Expand grid by adding new solutions
AQ**EDIT ADD ELEMENTS (CR)
Please enter a list of solution elements.
AQ**ADABAS
AQ**(CR)
---[DM] Now display map to show changes.
AQ**SHOW MAP (CR)
--[DM] Do you want to add elements, add traits, fill in ratings, or make
   hierarchies?
I recommend you FILL.IN RATINGS since you have added a new solution.
AQ**EDIT FILL.IN RATINGS
AQ**EDIT ADD TRAITS (CR)     (expert overrules)
                  •
                  •
                  •
---[DM] Expand grid by adding new solutions
AQ**EDIT ADD ELEMENTS (CR)
Please enter a list of solution elements.
AQ**ORACLE
AQ**(CR)
-[DM] Now display map to show changes.
AQ**SHOW MAP (CR)
--[DM] Do you want to add elements, add traits, fill in ratings, or make
   hierarchies?
I recommend you FILL.IN RATINGS since you have added a new solution.
AQ**EDIT FILL.IN RATINGS
AQ**EDIT ADD TRAITS (CR)     (expert overrules)

--[DM]I notice that you repeatedly follow a pattern of EDIT ADD
   ELEMENTS, SHOW MAP, and EDIT ADD TRAITS. Will you follow this
   sequence most of the time?
AQ**YES
---[DM]Adding new heuristic for expert ATN.
   Please explain why you do this.
AQ**I PREFER TO ADD ONE ELEMENT AND ONE TRAIT AT A TIME .

(Explanation is saved for analysis by Dialog Manager developers to
extract non-idiosyncratic heuristics)
```

Fig. 12. An example of *learning* in the Dialog Manager based on an idiosyncratic user pattern.

Manager's learning mechanism observes the repetition in command sequences, noting that in each case, the expert has overruled EDIT FILL IN RATINGS with EDIT ADD TRAITS. The Dialog Manager points out this pattern, and the expert confirms a preference for this command sequence. A new heuristic is created for this individual expert, ATN, to suggest EDIT ADD TRAITS after adding an element and displaying the hierarchy map. This is an example of the Dialog Manager's learning of idosyncratic heuristics based on individual preference patterns.

The Dialog Manager can also learn heuristics that apply to a more general class of users. Figure 13 illustrates the learning of a non-idiosyncratic pattern based upon observations of behavior of a group of users. In this case, the Dialog Manager notes that John, a member of the class Aquinas system developers, follows a pattern of adding an element, displaying the rating grid, and displaying implications, but overrules the Dialog Manager's suggestion to display the rules. As in the previous example, the Dialog Manager adds a heuristic for the individual user, but it also is aware that other Aquinas system developers, Jeff, Dave, and Cathy, also follow this

```
.. ADDING AN ELEMENT --
                •
                •
                •
--DISPLAYING RATING GRID--
-[DM]Now display rating grid to show changes.
AQ**SHOW UPDATE GRID (CR)
--DISPLAYING IMPLICATIONS--
-[DM]Now display implications to show changes.
AQ**SHOW UPDATE IMPLICATIONS (CR)
--DISPLAYING RULES--
-[DM]Now display rules to show changes.
AQ**SHOW UPDATE RULES
AQ**ANALYZE TEST CONSULTATION (CR)   (expert overrules)

Dialog Manager detects pattern occurring earlier.

---[DM] I notice that you repeatedly follow a pattern of  SHOW UPDATE
 GRID,  SHOW UPDATE IMPLICATIONS, but not SHOW UPDATE RULES. You
 TEST CONSULTATION instead. Will you follow this sequence most of the
 time?
AQ**YES

---[DM] Adding a new heuristic for expert JOHN.
 Please enter a short description of why you do this.
AQ**TO REDUCE SCREEN OUTPUT.
(Explanation is saved for analysis by Dialog Manager developers to extract
non-idiosyncratic heuristics)

---[DM] I notice that other members of class Aquinas-developers
 (JEFF,DAVE,CATHY) follow this pattern. Does this heuristic apply to all
 Aquinas-developers?
AQ**YES
---[DM] Adding new heuristic for Aquinas-developers.
```

FIG. 13. An example of learning in the Dialog Manager in which a non-idiosyncratic pattern is observed to apply to a class of users and new heuristic is added.

pattern. The user confirms that this is a non-idiosyncratic heuristic that applies to the entire user class of Aquinas system developers.

In both examples of learning (and in any case in which the expert overrules the Dialog Manager), the Dialog Manager seeks an explanation of *why* the particular pattern was entered. This textual explanation is stored for later analysis by the developers of the Dialog Manager as a further source of non-idosyncratic heuristics. In addition, if the Dialog Manager suspects a reason why it was overruled in *assist* mode, it will display its hypotheses and ask the user to confirm or deny them. For example:

"Did you overrule my recommendation to ANALYZE SIMILARITIES TRAITS because this did not result in improved performance when you did this earlier?"

This proposed explanation is stored for later analysis, along with the user's response.

We recognize the weakness in this purely statistical and pattern-recognition-based approach, but we feel that it offers promise as a basis for further work. Our intent is for the Dialog Manager to be able to "learn" broader concepts such as how experts organize knowledge hierarchically and how and when the expert should move to a more general or more specific level of abstraction.

Issues and future work

The implementation of the Dialog Manager and the experience of experts and knowledge engineers who have used Aquinas and the Dialog Manager to develop prototype expert systems have raised a number of issues. We are only beginning to understand how expertise can effectively be transferred: the techniques currently used by experts or knowledge engineers using an automated system such as Aquinas, their underlying heuristics, and whether there are more effective strategies for knowledge acquisition.

We expect to learn more about heuristics for effective transfer of expertise as more experts and knowledge engineers have the opportunity to use Aquinas with the Dialog Manager. We will observe and interview Aquinas users of varying backgrounds and experience in the development of expert systems. We will also examine the information recorded by the Dialog Manager when it adapts existing heuristics to derive new ones.

In addition, we are planning an experiment in which experts will use Aquinas without the Dialog Manager for entry of new knowledge bases, and then repeat the knowledge-base entry exercise with the Dialog Manager automatically directing or assisting the process. Transcripts for knowledge acquisition both with an without the Dialog Manager can then be compared and discrepancies discussed with the expert to identify where Dialog Manager heuristics could be improved.

LEARNING CAPABILITY

The learning capability of the Dialog Manager is an area where we are focusing attention. We recognize that the current approach, relying on statistical analysis of the command history and user profile files, is an oversimplified view, but we feel that it is a promising first step. Our objective is that the Dialog Manager improve its performance through adaptive learning.

MANAGING COMPLEXITY IN AQUINAS

As the scope of Aquinas is expanded, using the tool will become increasingly demanding. The recent implementation of Aquinas (Boose & Bradshaw, in press) allows hierarchically structured cases, experts, solution elements, and traits. This gives rise to a new set of questions to be considered in formulating hueristics for this complex environment. For example, when should the rating grid be split into two or more grids, and what is the best way to structure the knowledge? The novice user of Aquinas may find the multiple windows, rating grids, and implication graphs confusing. The need for guidance, explanation and tutoring becomes more critical as the knowledge acquisition environment becomes more complex.

ACQUIRING UNDERLYING CONCEPTS

One of the greatest challenges for Aquinas is acquiring underlying concepts in the problem domain. The ROGET system (Bennett, 1983) is a knowledge-acquisition tool that aids in conceptualization of knowledge bases. ROGET is aware of the organization of existing knowledge bases in the medical domain and attempts to structure a new knowledge base using categories common to related expert systems (for example, determined causes, laboratory tests, observed signs). Like ROGET, the Aquinas Dialog Manager carries on a dialog with the expert about the relationships between objects in the problem domain (traits, elements, etc). Both ROGET and Aquinas are concerned with acquiring an expert's conceptual structure. However, ROGET's success may be due in part to the fact that it deals with the medical domain, in which categories of advice and evidence are applicable to a whole family of expert systems. Aquinas is not restricted to a specific domain, however broad, and must handle a wider variety of classes of problems.

SELECTING KNOWLEDGE-ACQUISITION STRATEGIES FOR APPLICATION TASKS
We also anticipate that requirements for guidance from the Dialog Manager will increase as the ability is added to acquire knowledge for problem domains that do not fit the structured selection paradigm. We plan to extend Aquinas to handle knowledge acquisition for constructive problem solving, such as in the SALT system (Marcus & McDermott, 1987), and to represent domain models of qualitative causal relations in acquiring diagnostic knowledge, as in the MORE system (Kahn, Nowlan & McDermott, 1985) and its successor MOLE (Eshelman, Ehret, McDermott & Tan, in press). Aquinas may also be integrated with other knowledge-acquisition tools, for example, KNACK, a report-driven knowledge acquisition tool. (Klinker, Bentolila, Genetet, Grimes, and McDermott, in press).

GIVING PRIORITY TO ALTERNATIVE STRATEGIES
Another issue to be resolved is how the Dialog Manager should give priority to alternative strategies when more than one is justified. It must balance the severity of the problems requiring correction against the expected benefits of a modification. In our earlier example (Fig. 6), the Dialog Manager chose to correct the element similarity because it was the only current problem in the knowledge base. However, if there had also been an ambiguous implication, the Dialog Manager would have applied the first heuristic illustrated in Fig. 11 to correct the ambiguous relationship because of the severity of the condition (conflicting rules would be generated, giving inaccurate test results). Various schemes for evaluating the relative seriousness of problems and predicted success of alternatives will be attempted. A future issue is resolution of conflicts between problems of similar severity. How do we determine the command sequences leading to the highest payoff?

THE ROLE OF TEMPORAL REASONING
Also at issue is the role of temporal reasoning in heuristics for knowledge acquisition. Future work will explore the effects of absolute vs relative differences in time and the concept of "recency" in performing operations in a time-related sequence of commands. For example, if the knowledge has just been tested, and two new traits are added, the user may wish to test the knowledge again even if it was done recently.

USER PREFERENCES AND PAST EXPERIENCE
An open question is when the Dialog Manager should consider user preferences and past successes to select or rule out a strategy. As an example, the Dialog Manager

may suggest that the user volunteer data to expand the rating grid (additional solution elements, trait pairs, or even cases). This is appropriate if no data have been volunteered earlier or if many intervening operations have occurred since the grid was expanded. But the Dialog Manager must also consider user preferences and past performance. For example, when the user consistently answers "no" to prompts such as "Can you think of a trait which discriminates between IDMS and TOTAL?", the Dialog Manager should not repeat this request.

USER MODELS

A final research objective is to incorporate user models in the Aquinas system. Recent attention has been given to user modeling for tailoring system responses, explanation facilities, and tutoring for the user (Sleeman, Appelt, Konolige, Rich, Sridharan & Swartout, 1985). The Dialog Manager already maintains user profiles, and its learning facility can make inferences based on user performance. We will extend this ability to define and model the knowledge, intentions, goals, roles, activities, and communications protocols of Aquinas users, including the domain expert, knowledge engineer, and Aquinas system developer.

User models will be critical if the Dialog Manager is to be used as tutorial system to teach knowledge engineers and experts how to effectively transfer domain expertise. Woolf and McDonald specify four components in an effective tutoring system: the subject area (knowledge acquisition), the student model (the novice Aquinas user), teaching strategies, and communication strategies (Woolf & McDonald, 1984; Clancey, 1985). We anticipate that new heuristics for teaching and communication must be developed for the Dialog Manager to become an effective tutoring system. Additional consideration will be given to the interrelationship between the level of user expertise, complexity of the heuristics, the importance of the concept, and the level of detail in explanations (Wallis & Shortliffe, 1985) to customize the Dialog Manager's explanations for its use as a tutorial system.

The authors wish to thank Roger Beeman, Miroslav Benda, Jeff Bradshaw, Jackson Brown, Art Nagai, Dave Shema, Lisle Tinglof-Boose, and Bruce Wilson for their contributions and support. Aquinas and the Dialog Manager were developed at the Boeing Advanced Technology Center of Boeing Computer Services in Seattle, Washington.

References

BENNETT, J. S. (1983). ROGET: A knowledge-based consultant for acquiring the conceptual structure of an expert system: *Report No. HPP-83-24,* Computer Sciences Department, Stanford University.

BOSSE, J. H. (1985). A knowledge acquisition program for expert systems based on personal construct psychology. *International Journal of Man–Machine Studies,* **23,** 495–525.

BOOSE, J. H. (1986). *Expertise Transfer for Expert System Design.* New York: Elsevier.

BOOSE, J. H. & BRADSHAW, J. M. (1987). Expertise transfer and complex problems: Using AQUINAS as a knowledge acquisition workbench for expert systems. *International Journal of Man–Machine Studies,* in press.

CLANCEY, W. J. (1985). Use of MYCIN's rules for tutoring. In BUCHANAN, B. & SHORTLIFFE, E. Eds, *Rule-Based Expert Systems: the MYCIN Experiments of the Stanford Heuristic Programming Project.* Reading, Massachusetts: Addison–Wesley.

DIEDERICH, J., RUHMANN, I. & MAY, M. (1987). KRITON: a knowledge acquisition tool for expert systems. *International Journal of Man–Machine Studies,* in press.

ESHELMAN, L., EHRET, D., MCDERMOTT, J. & TAN, M. (1987). MOLE: a tenacious knowledge-acquisition tool. *International Journal of Man–Machine Studies,* in press.

GAINES, B. R. & SHAW, M. L. G. (1981). New directions in the analysis and interactive elicitation of personal construct systems. In SHAW, M. L. G. Ed., *Recent Advances in Personal Construct Technology.* New York: Academic Press.

KAHN, G. S. BREAUX, E. H., JOSEPH, R. L. & DEKLERK, P. (1987). An intelligent mixed-initiative workbench for knowledge acquisition. *International Journal of Man–Machine Studies,* in press.

KAHN, G., NOWLAN, S. & MCDERMOTT, J. (1985). MORE: an intelligent knowledge acquisition tool. *Proceedings of the Ninth Joint Conference on Artificial Intelligence,* Los Angeles, California.

KELLY, G. A., (1955). *The Psychology of Personal Constructs.* New York: Norton.

KITTO, C. M. & BOOSE, J. H. (1986). Heuristics for expertise transfer: the automatic management of complex knowledge acquisition dialogs. *Proceedings of the IEEE Expert Systems in Government Symposium.* Washington D.C: IEEE Computer Society Press.

KLINKER, G., BENTOLILA, J., GENETET, S., GRIMES, M. & MCDERMOTT, J. (1987). Report-driven knowledge acquisition. *International Journal of Man–Machine Studies,* in press.

MARCUS, S. & MCDERMOTT, J. (1987). SALT: a knowledge acquisition tool for propose-and-revise systems. *Carnegie–Mellon University Department of Computer Science Technical Report.*

SHAW, M. L. G. & GAINES, B. R. (1987). Techniques for knowledge acquisition and transfer. *International Journal of Man–Machine Studies,* in press.

SLEEMAN, D., APPELT, D., KONOLIGE, K. RICH, E., SRIDHARAN, N. S. & SWARTOUT, B. (1985). User modelling panel. *Proceedings of the Ninth International Joint conference on Artificial Intelligence,* Los Angeles, California.

WALLIS, J. W. & SHORTLIFFE, E. H. (1985). Customized explanations using causal knowledge. In BUCHANAN, B. & SHORTLIFFE, E. Eds, *Rule-Based Expert Systems: the MYCIN Experiments of the Stanford Heuristic Programming Project.* Reading, Massachusetts: Addison–Wesley.

WOOLF, B. & MCDONALD, D. D. (1984). Building a computer tutor: design issues. *IEEE Computer,* **17,** 61–73.

KNACK—Report-driven knowledge acquisition

Georg Klinker, Joel Bentolila, Serge Genetet, Michael Grimes and John McDermott

Department of Computer Science, Carnegie–Mellon University, Pittsburgh, Pennsylvania 15213, U.S.A.

This paper describes a knowledge-acquisition tool that builds expert systems for evaluating designs of electro-mechanical systems. The tool elicits from experts (1) knowledge in the form of a skeletal report, (2) knowledge about a large collection of report fragments, only some of which will be relevant to any specific report, and (3) knowledge of how to customize the report fragments for a particular application. The tool derives its power from exploiting its understanding of two problem-solving methods and of the different roles that knowledge plays in those two methods.†

1. Introduction

A key issue in developing any expert system is how to update its large and growing knowledge base. A commonly proposed solution is the construction and use of a knowledge acquisition tool, e.g. TEIRESIAS (Davis & Lenat, 1982), ETS (Boose, 1984), MORE (Kahn, Nowlan & McDermott, 1985), SALT (Marcus, McDermott & Wang, 1985), SEAR (van de Brug, Bachant & McDermott 1986), MOLE (Eshelman & McDermott, 1986). Such a tool typically interacts with domain experts, organizes the knowledge it acquires, and generates an expert system. A knowledge-acquisition tool also can be used to test and maintain the program it generates. The critical feature of such a tool is that a domain expert can use it to update a knowledge base without having to know about the underlying AI technology.

A large knowledge base can be kept maintainable by organizing it according to the different roles that knowledge plays (Chandrasekaran, 1983), (Clancey, 1983), (Neches, Swartout & Moore, 1984). Knowledge roles, the organizational units of the knowledge base, are made explicit by defining a problem-solving method. Some work has been done to analyse existing knowledge-acquisition tools with respect to the problem-solving method each assumes and the roles that knowledge plays (McDermott, 1986). We share the hope that a better understanding of different problem-solving methods will lead to better knowledge-acquisition tools in the near term and to expert systems with broader scope farther down the line.

KNACK is a knowledge-acquisition tool that assists an expert in creating expert systems that evaluate the designs of electro-mechanical systems. Each of the expert systems produced by KNACK is called a WRINGER. A WRINGER gathers information about a system's design, points out possible design flaws and makes suggestions to correct and improve the design.

KNACK guides a domain expert through the knowledge-acquisition session. It

† This research was sponsored by the Defense Nuclear Agency (DNA) and the Harry Diamond Laboratories (HDL) under contract DNA001-85-C-0027. The views and conclusions contained in this document are those of the authors and should not be interpreted as representing the official policies, either expressed or implied, of DNA or HDL.

195

asks the expert to create or modify a skeletal report and report fragments which describe the design of some specific class of electro-mechanical systems. KNACK also elicits knowledge of how to customize the report fragments for a particular application. That information is then transformed into a knowledge representation appropriate to evaluate a system design. KNACK helps the user by minimizing the amount of information the expert must provide to define a piece of knowledge and by using heuristics to infer new knowledge from previously acquired knowledge.

Section 2 gives an overview of the design evaluation task for a specific class of electro-mechanical systems. Section 3 describes the capabilities of the WRINGERs generated by KNACK for evaluating the design of such systems. Section 4 is meant to explicate the problem-solving methods and knowledge roles employed by the generated expert systems. Section 5 discusses KNACK.

2. The design evaluation task

The WRINGERs that we have developed so far do design evaluation within the nuclear hardening domain. Nuclear hardening implies the use of specific engineering design practices to increase the resistance of an electro-mechanical system to the environmental effects generated by a nuclear weapon. Our domain expertise is supplied by individuals who are technical design reviewers for nuclear effects on electro-mechanical systems. The following is a summary of the problems such experts encounter in their work.

Information about the design is usually provided by several different designers. This causes problems when different designers use conflicting terminology or have inconsistent or incomplete views of the overall system design. The evaluator integrates the information coming from different sources in order to understand the overall system design.

The evaluator tries to gather just enough information from the designer to do the evaluation. The designer takes into account an immense number of details about the system and about the environment within which it will function. Since the evaluation is focused along the nuclear hardening dimension, not every detail that was considered by the designer is relevant for the evaluator. An experienced evaluator knows which information to gather and how to elicit that information.

When one of our domain experts evaluates the design of an electro-mechanical system, he is really helping to design it. He evaluates the design for consistency, completeness, and possible design flaws. Although the designer can develop a system that meets all other requirements, he often does not know enough about nuclear hardening to design a hardened system. Therefore, the evaluation must be constructive. The experienced evaluator suggests improvements to the submitted design which would make it more acceptable.

The designer and the evaluator ordinarily go through several cycles of design presentation and design evaluation. Once the design has been evaluated, it is returned to the designer together with criticism and suggestions on how to correct possible design flaws. The designer then comes back to the evaluator with a revised design proposal. This is an iterative process which leads to an acceptable design proposal.

The evaluator also takes into account highly interdependent information. Restricting a system in some way may influence other design decisions. It may constrain future design choices or require revising previous design decisions.

We have organized these problems into two major tasks for an expert system that functions as a competent evaluator of electro-mechanical system designs: (1) how to gather just the requisite information from the designer to build a useful design description; and (2) how to evaluate the design for consistency, completeness and possible flaws in a constructive manner.

3. The WRINGERs

We decided to build our expert system (the first WRINGER) in two consecutive steps, corresponding to the problems involved. First, we built a system that gathered information. The output from a session with this system was a report describing the design of some particular electro-mechanical system. Because these reports contained all of the information necessary to evaluate the design, they were useful in themselves.† Second, we extended our initial expert system so that it evaluated the gathered information. An advantage of this stepwise approach was that our domain experts could critique the generated report and, in the process, show us how they evaluate a system design.

Each WRINGER is a member of a family of expert systems in a common domain area. The WRINGERs we have generated so far gather information about electro-mechanical systems, and evaluate this information with respect to nuclear hardening. They also produce, in report form, a description of the system design and a preliminary evaluation with suggestions on how to improve the design.

3.1. GATHERING INFORMATION

Usually, a team of designers will work together on the design of a system. It is thus likely that several different designers will interact with a WRINGER to give an adequate description of a system design. Different people might use conflicting terminology. A WRINGER discovers whether two designers use different words to describe the same fact by using its knowledge about synonyms. If a designer's answer to a question contains a synonym for a known expression, the WRINGER replaces it with that known expression.

To take into account the different sources of information available to an evaluator, a WRINGER has several ways to gather information: it can elicit the information from the user by: (1) asking a question; (2) interpreting a graphical design description, e.g. a drawing of a system's components; (3) asking the designer to fill in the slots of a table or diagram; or (4) asking the user to choose from the items in a menu. A WRINGER can fill in gaps based on information already available to it by: (5) directly applying specific domain knowledge; (6) computing numeric values; or (7) referring to a database. Some information-gathering

---

† Most design projects require a finished report containing information about general design objectives, tradeoff decisions, analysis and test results, and detailed parts specifications. Those reports are usually valuable even before they are finished. While it is being written, a good report indicates the benefit of continuing a project; it helps to organize the diverse activities within the scope of a large task and to identify potential problem areas within sub-tasks. A good design report contains all the data that an evaluator needs to determine the adequacy of a proposed design.

strategies will be more suitable than others for gathering a particular piece of information. Using an appropriate strategy makes it easier for the designer to interact with a WRINGER. For example, to give a spatial description of the system it is often more convenient to draw the system than to answer questions. Often more than one way exists to gather a piece of information. When this is the case, a WRINGER decides how to gather it.

An evaluator might have to try several ways to gather a piece of information before he is satisfied with the result. A strategy used to gather information might not be successful or the information received might be insufficient or incomplete. If a way to gather information was unsuccessful, a WRINGER tries another strategy. For example, a WRINGER uses a database when it has to determine the break-down voltage of a diode. If the database contains no entry for that diode, a WRINGER asks the designer. On the other hand, if the information received by using some strategy was insufficient or incomplete, a WRINGER will try another way to gather that information. For example, it is possible to infer that one of the subsystems of a system with an internal power supply will be a motor generator. This information might not be sufficient. It is likely that the motor generator is not the only subsystem. Therefore a WRINGER will ask for the remaining subsystems. A WRINGER might consult a database in order to determine the break-down voltage and the damage constant of a diode. If the database contains data on the break-down voltage but no entry for the damage constant, the latter has to be determined. It can be computed if the requisite information is available or else the WRINGER can ask for it.

It is often the case that only a fraction of a WRINGER's knowledge is applicable to the evaluation of any particular electro-mechanical system. A WRINGER selects the necessary information about the design of the system in a data-driven manner; the decision to gather a particular piece of information is based on previously gathered information. Generally more than one piece of information can be gathered at any time. The order in which the pieces of information are gathered may be important: an inference might make a question unnecessary, the designer might feel more natural providing information in a certain order, or information gathered in a certain order might reduce the amount of information needed. Accordingly, a WRINGER uses the following heuristics to select which piece of information to gather next:

Prefer to infer a piece of information whenever possible;

Prefer to gather a piece of information that allows the designer to feel comfortable with the order of giving this information;

Prefer to gather the piece of information which is most likely to reduce the subsequent number of necessary pieces of information, that is, select the piece of information to gather next which prunes the space of necessary pieces of information.

The purpose of the first heuristic is simply to avoid asking the designer unnecessary questions.

The goal of the second heuristic is that the information will seem convenient to the designer to provide next. This is accomplished by following the skeletal report, thereby eliciting information for a selected report part only, and by providing a WRINGER with a set of preference rules enabling it to decide which piece of information to gather next, for example, request the names of subsystems before asking about connections between them.

The third heuristic reduces the burden placed on the designer in gathering a piece of information. WRINGERs prefer to elicit a piece of information which is likely to enable inferences. For example, the type and the diameter of a cable might both be important to know. If a WRINGER has to decide whether to ask a question to determine the type or to ask another question to determine the diameter of the cable, it will prefer to ask the former question because it knows that it can infer the diameter once the type is known. Another way for a WRINGER to reduce the effort to gather a piece of information is to try to establish the requisite information enabling inferences with minimal effort. For example, a worst-case value for the damage constant of a semiconductor device can be inferred if the class (transistor, diode, etc.) and family (high-power, low-power, etc.) of the device are known. On the other hand, the damage constant can be computed precisely if class, break-down voltage, capacity of the junction, material (silicon, gallium arsenide, etc.) and geometry (planar, non-planar) are known. In order to determine the damage constant of a semiconductor device, a WRINGER will try to determine the worst-case value first. Therefore it will try to establish information about class and family. If the worst-case value confirms the system design (does not lead to a design flaw during evaluation), further information needed to compute the damage constant does not have to be gathered, even though the computation would have led to a more precise result.

3.2. EVALUATING DESIGNS

Before the design of a system is evaluated for design flaws, the information provided by the designer will be checked to ensure that it is correct, consistent and complete. A WRINGER immediately checks newly gathered information for validity. This includes finding out whether input provided by the designer is obviously wrong or merely implausible. In the first case, an answer might be outside of a predefined numeric range or it might not be a member of a predefined complete set of possible answers. In the second case an answer might be flagged as questionable because it is not a member of a predefined incomplete set of possible answers.

A WRINGER checks the gathered information for contradictions. For example, it makes sure that a cable carrying power is not connected to a cable carrying a signal. It also tries to determine whether it has all the information needed to evaluate the system. For example, it checks whether a power source is specified for the system and whether a defined antenna is connected to the rest of the system.

In the case of the WRINGERs we have built so far, the evaluation of electro-mechanical systems focuses on nuclear hardening. They ensure that a system will function in some predefined nuclear environment. A WRINGER's approach to this evaluation is to determine and use worst-case values for its analysis. An assumption is made that worst-case values are rough estimates of the precise values and that it takes less effort to determine worst-case values (in terms of pieces of information to gather) than to find out the precise values. If the worst-case analysis indicates a design flaw, a WRINGER gathers the additional information that allows it to replace the worst-case values with more precise values. If the evaluation still does not result in a hard system, a WRINGER points out possible flaws in the design of the system. It then suggests improvements. For example, if the energy coupled into an interface circuit through a power line exceeds an upper limit, the semiconductor devices of the interface circuit will be damaged. A WRINGER will suggest using a terminal protection device to limit that energy to an acceptable level.

As a result of the evaluation a designer might want to change his description of the system design or the system design itself. On the other hand it might be necessary to gather additional information. A WRINGER gives the designer an opportunity to review and correct the gathered information about the system being designed. It checks whether all the information necessary to evaluate the system is available. If some vital piece of information is missing, a WRINGER tries to elicit this information from the designer. If the designer cannot or does not want to provide the required information, a WRINGER assumes a worst-case value. For example, a WRINGER needs to know the transfer impedance of the solid shield for a cable in order to evaluate the protection provided by this shield. If the designer cannot provide this information, a WRINGER asks for the outer and inner radii and the resistivity of the solid shield in order to compute the transfer impedance. If this information is not available, a WRINGER assumes a worst-case value.

Finally, the description of the system design and the evaluation results are usually documented in some form. A WRINGER presents the gathered information and the results of the evaluation in the form of a report. It uses the skeletal report to determine the structure and the report fragments to determine the content of a report about an actual electro-mechanical system. The report fragments also guide a WRINGER in integrating the gathered information into a report. In some cases the designer will not agree with the results of the evaluation. For this reason a WRINGER allows the designer to add comments to a report.

4. The WRINGERs' problem solving methods

This section describes the knowledge a WRINGER uses to perform the tasks reported in section 3. It gives an overview of the problem-solving methods the WRINGERs use, along with the identified knowledge roles, and describes the knowledge bases of two implemented WRINGERs.

A problem-solving method is knowledge that establishes and controls the sequences of actions required to perform some task. This control knowledge dynamically defines the order in which subtasks have to be solved in order to perform the overall task. It also defines the kind of domain-specific knowledge that is applicable within each step. Thus, the problem-solving method helps to identify and classify the domain knowledge. It makes the different roles knowledge plays in the design evaluation task explicit and suggests ways to organize the knowledge base according to the knowledge roles. The granularity of the problem-solving method is determined by the demand that the knowledge represented by a knowledge role can be applied without further control knowledge, e.g. the order in which that knowledge will be brought to bear does not matter.

Information gathering and evaluation are treated as separate problems. A

WRINGER uses a different problem-solving method for each of them. Initially, it gathers the information necessary for the evaluation and then evaluates the information. If, as a result of the evaluation, additional information is required, the WRINGER then invokes the method for information gathering again. After that, another evaluation is performed. This iterative process ends when the designer is satisfied with the design.

4.1. A METHOD FOR INFORMATION GATHERING

The problem-solving method and the knowledge roles that WRINGERs use to solve the information gathering problem can be summarized as follows:

(1) Choose an appropriate part (chapter, section or subsection) of the report that is to be constructed (Report Structure). Identify all the pieces of information which are required for this part of the report (Information Identification).

(2) Determine the pieces of information which are appropriate to be elicited now from the set of all identified pieces of information. If no appropriate pieces of information remain to be gathered, continue with step 6.

(3) Select one piece of information to be elicited from among those appropriate to be gathered (Information Selection).

(4) Determine a strategy to gather the selected piece of information and apply that strategy (Information Gathering). If the strategy fails, try another one. If no strategy succeeds, continue with step 2; otherwise check the provided piece(s) of information for synonyms (Synonym) and errors.

(5) Make all appropriate inferences based on the gathered piece(s) of information (Information Gathering). Continue with step 2.

(6) If there are more report parts to be constructed, continue with step 1; otherwise, information gathering is tentatively assumed to be complete.

One role for knowledge is in regard to Report Structure; this includes knowledge about which chapters, sections and subsections are part of the report and knowledge about their order. Information Identification knowledge is used to identify pieces of information which are relevant to each part of the report; determining an initial set of pieces of information to be gathered. The Information Selection role represents knowledge about how to select a piece of information to be gathered from the set of all identified pieces of information. It organizes knowledge of how to prefer to gather one piece of information over others. The Information Gathering role describes the different ways to gather a piece of information (ask a question, interpret a graphical design description, fill in the slots of a table or diagram, choose among the items in a menu, apply specific domain knowledge to inferences, compute numeric values from formulas, refer to a database). Relying on previously elicited information and other pre-defined knowledge, it defines the circumstances in which these techniques can be applied. It also includes instructions about what to expect as a response and what to do with the elicited information. The role Synonym is a way to represent knowledge about making a user's answer consistent with the common way of expressing that answer.

4.2. A METHOD FOR EVALUATION

The problem-solving method and the knowledge roles the WRINGERs use to solve the evaluation problem can be summarized as follows:

(1) Check the gathered information for consistency (Consistency Evaluation) and completeness (Completeness Evaluation).
(2) Evaluate the design description for possible design flaws by using a worst-case analysis (Design Evaluation). If no indications of flaws are found, go to step 6.
(3) Evaluate the parts of the design description which showed indications of flaws again, this time using a precise analysis (Design Evaluation). If no indications of flaws are found, go to step 6.
(4) Make constructive suggestions which pieces of information need to be modified or completed (Design Fix). Gather any missing information.†
    Generate worst-case values for any required pieces of information still missing (Design Default). When there is nothing to be modified or to be completed, go to step 6.
(5) Continue with step 1.
(6) Integrate the gathered information into the associated report phrases (Report Phase), assemble the report phrases, include any evaluation messages, and write the report to an output device (Report Structure).

Consistency Evaluation knowledge and Completeness Evaluation knowledge include, respectively, how to uncover contradictory information and how to detect when information provided by the designer is incomplete. Design Evaluation knowledge identifies problem cues that are associated with possible flaws in the design of an electro-mechanical system. The Design Fix role includes knowledge about how the design could be improved. Design Default knowledge is about worst-case values for the necessary pieces of information the designer could not provide. A WRINGER uses Report Phrase knowledge to incorporate the gathered information into the report. Report Structure knowledge is applied to appropriately place the report phrases within the report.

4.3. TWO SAMPLE WRINGERs

In Autumn 1986 KNACK was used to develop two WRINGERs. The first, a PROGRAM PLAN writer, presents a definition of the activities necessary to design, produce, and maintain an electro-mechanical system capable of withstanding nuclear environments and completing its mission. The program plan is the primary top-level report covering all phases of the design project. It describes the comprehensive plan for management, assessment, hardening, implementation, and testing that a contractor will conduct for an electro-mechanical system. It identifies the specific methods to be used for analysis, design, testing and evaluation, explains the design philosophy, rationale behind various decisions, and assumptions underlying the design. It also projects a schedule of activity and completion for each segment of the program plan. Given several well-chosen sample reports, it took 1 person-week to

---

† The method described in section 4.1 for information gathering is used.

create the PROGRAM PLAN writer with KNACK. The domain dependent knowledge base contains 834 OPS5 rules: three rules describe the skeletal report (Report Structure knowledge), 386 rules define the report fragments (Report Phrase knowledge), 351 rules represent different ways to gather information in order to customize the report fragments for a particular application (Information Gathering knowledge), 19 rules define synonyms (Synonym knowledge), 46 rules identify the information relevant for each part of the report (Information Identification knowledge), and 29 rules describe which piece of information to gather next (Information Selection knowledge). The average condition part of one of the PROGRAM PLAN WRINGER's rules has 3·4 elements. Each element is a pattern that can be instantiated by an object. On the average the pattern will mention 2·0 of the attributes which define an object. The average action part has 7·2 elements. Each element creates either a new object or modifies an existing object.

The second expert system, a DESIGN PARAMETERS REPORT writer, presents and evaluates a detailed description of an electro-mechanical system. It documents the system description, analysis, design features, and assumptions required to assure the nuclear hardness and survivability of the system with respect to one nuclear environment: electromagnetic pulse (EMP). To evaluate the system, the WRINGER gathers detailed information about the electro-mechanical system design ranging from the level of major components to the level of individual semiconductors. After the gathered information is checked for completeness and consistency, a worst-case analysis is carried out for each interface circuit in the system, determining whether the EMP environment will induce currents about the operating voltage of the interface circuits. This analysis indicates either that the system is sufficiently refractory of the EMP environment or may not be. In the latter case a more detailed screen analysis, and if necessary an even more precise resistive analysis, is conducted to identify inadequacies in the system's response to the EMP environment. When such an inadequacy is pinpointed, the WRINGER suggests possible fixes, all of which are pre-checked for adequate strengthening properties in the interface circuits. The basis for the expert system was a single sample report and a series of interactions with our EMP expert. It took 3 person-weeks to create it with KNACK. The domain-dependent knowledge base contains 1444 OPS5 rules: three rules represent Report Structure knowledge, 620 rules Report Phrase knowledge, 610 rules Information Gathering knowledge, 32 rules Synonym knowledge, 47 rules Information Identification knowledge, and 29 rules Information Selection knowledge. One hundred and thirty-five rules evaluate the gathered information (Consistency Evaluation, Completeness Evaluation, Design Evaluation, Design Fix, and Design Default knowledge). The average condition part of one of the DESIGN PARAMETERS REPORT WRINGER's rules has 3·8 elements. On the average each element will mention 2·3 of the attributes which define an object. The average action part has 3·0 elements. Each element creates either a new object or modifies an existing object.

5. KNACK

KNACK is a knowledge acquisition tool capable of building WRINGERs, i.e. expert systems that can evaluate electro-mechanical system designs. Its task is to elicit the domain-dependent knowledge from the expert. The remaining part of the paper describes how KNACK aids an expert in creating a WRINGER: (1) it elicits knowledge from the expert about a skeletal report, report fragments, and how to customize the report fragments; (2) it uses heuristics to infer additional knowledge.

KNACK uses object–attribute–value tuples and relations as basic elements to represent knowledge. Each object may have multiple attributes. Dependencies between objects are represented by relations. These basic elements, object-attribute-value tuples and relations, are used to build the condition parts and the action parts of OPS5 rules. An OPS5 rule represents a piece of knowledge. The pieces of knowledge are organized into knowledge roles. A knowledge role is described by a corresponding knowledge role template.

5.1. ELICITING KNOWLEDGE FROM THE EXPERT

KNACK's knowledge-acquisition approach is based on the assumption that an expert can adequately present his knowledge about electro-mechanical design evaluation in the form of a skeletal report and report fragments. It is also assumed that the expert knows how to customize the report fragments for a particular application. The skeletal report and report fragments describe all the information that reports in a given domain might contain. An actual report will be the skeleton fleshed out with some subset of customized report fragments. In detail, the skeletal report defines the outline of an actual report and the order of report fragments within an actual report. A report fragment describes a small, possible piece of an actual report, the conditions under which the piece will be included in the actual report, the fixed text of a report part and the variable information of a report part. The knowledge of how to customize the report fragments for a particular application defines strategies for how to gather the variable information.

KNACK assumes that the expert knows what information is needed, how to evaluate this information and how a designer should present this information (i.e. the expert must have a clear idea of what constitutes an acceptable report about the design of electro-mechanical systems). We think this is a valid presupposition for a variety of evaluation tasks. In general, someone whose job it is to evaluate the work of others must have comprehensive and precise knowledge about that work.

KNACK provides support to the expert in defining that knowledge. The expert uses keywords to indicate chapter, section and subsection headings. From this KNACK determines the skeletal report. The expert then types the text for a report fragment. There are basically two kinds of text that can be included in a WRINGER report. One kind is "boiler plate" text and it is simply a sentence or paragraph which will appear exactly the way it was formulated by the domain expert, whenever the conditions for including it are satisfied. The other kind of text contains blanks which are filled in with information that is specific to whichever electro-mechanical system is the subject of the WRINGER report. The blanks are given variable names and it is the values for these variables that are collected by a WRINGER during its information gathering. Figure 1 illustrates how a report fragment is defined. The example contains the blanks "$\langle V1 \rangle$" and "$\langle V2 \rangle$" for variable information. In an actual report these variables would be instantiated; for example: "The power line interface-circuit is protected by a terminal protection device."

The expert then defines object/attribute pairs to represent the variable information.

```
REPORT DEFINITION:
chapter: 4 section: 13 subsection: 0 phrase: 1
[
   The <V1> interface-circuit is protected by a <V2>.
]
```

FIG. 1. Sample input for the report phrase knowledge. In this and following figures, the expert's input appears in bold italics; the implementation details (for rules) and the prompts (of KNACK) appear in lowercase and uppercase; the knowledge inferred by KNACK appears in small capitals. Default responses, enclosed by brackets, are used when the user types only a carriage return.

In the example in Fig. 2 "interface-circuit name" and "protection-device name" are used to define the variables "⟨V1⟩" and "⟨V2⟩" of Fig. 1. KNACK assumes that objects appearing in the same report sentence are related and routinely creates relations between them, asking the expert to name the relation. If the expert does not give a name for it, the relation is not created. "Protects" is the relation name used in the example.

KNACK guides the expert through the knowledge-acquisition process by exploiting a WRINGER's problem-solving methods. A WRINGER's problem solving methods represent the knowledge needed to control the task. They are defined so that the domain knowledge, organized in knowledge roles, does not include control knowledge. KNACK takes advantage of this separation of control knowledge and domain knowledge. It presupposes that a WRINGER's problem-solving methods are those described in section 4, thus freeing the expert from having to define the control knowledge.

KNACK also exploits a WRINGER's knowledge roles, which are described by templates. The knowledge role templates define implementation details for a piece of knowledge, they define what the expert has to provide for a piece of knowledge, and they define the optional parts of a piece of knowledge. The implementation details ensure that the domain knowledge can be accessed by the control knowledge. Because these details are already defined by a knowledge role template the expert does not have to be concerned with them. The following example of how to define the knowledge for the knowledge role Information Gathering points out how KNACK determines what the expert has to provide to define knowledge. Suppose the expert wants to define a question which a WRINGER will ask the designer. KNACK knows from the knowledge role template for Information Gathering that the expert must provide text for the question and that the expert has an option of providing possible and default answers. Therefore it prompts the expert for that input. The sample input shown in Fig. 3 demonstrates how the expert defines a

```
VARIABLE DEFINITION:
variable.......... [ V1 ]:
represents.......:
     object........ [ INTERFACE-CIRCUIT ]:
     attribute..... [ NAME ]:

variable.......... [ V2 ]:
represents.......:
     object........ [ INTERFACE-CIRCUIT ]: protection-device
     attribute..... [ UNKNOWN ]: name

name of the relation PROTECTION-DEVICE -> INTERFACE-CIRCUIT.. [ PART-OF ]: protects
```

FIG. 2. Sample input to define variables.

```
QUESTION DEFINITION:
variable......... [ PROTECTION-DEVICE.NAME ]:
represents.......:
    object.......: PROTECTION-DEVICE
    attribute....: NAME
is determined by.:
    [question, graphics, table, menu, inference, formula, database, quit] [ QUESTION]:


text............: Which protection device protects the interface-circuit
possible answers.. [ UNKNOWN ]:
default answers..: [ UNKNOWN ]:
```

FIG. 3. Sample input for the question knowledge.

question intended to gather information for one of the slots in the report fragment shown in Figs 1 and 2.

5.2. INFERRING ADDITIONAL KNOWLEDGE USING HEURISTICS

KNACK uses heuristics to infer additional knowledge. The heuristics can be specific to infer additional knowledge for a particular knowledge role or they can be applicable to more than one knowledge role. We now use the example of Fig. 3 to describe some of these heuristics. Figure 4 shows the question rule† for the input sample of Fig. 3 after KNACK extended it by using heuristics.

KNACK uses heuristics to insert conditions and relations between the objects of conditions into the question rule. These conditions and relations define the circumstances in which asking that question is appropriate:

> IF KNACK discovers known objects within the text of the question and if a way is known to gather information about these objects, KNACK adds a condition for each object to the question rule. The question text of the example contains the object "interface-circuit." This is a known object and a question strategy was defined to gather information about this object. Thus KNACK added the condition about the existence of an "interface-circuit" to the rule.

> KNACK adds a template element relation for each previously defined relation between objects in different conditions. In the example, KNACK added the relation "part-of" between the objects "interface-circuit" and "subsystem".

KNACK uses heuristics to make the text of a question more specific. It is easier to answer a specific question because it is more clear what the question is about. Also, it is easier to evaluate specific information than it is to evaluate some general statements:

> If a known object is used in the question text and if a way is known to gather information about this object and this object is related to another object by a "part-of" relation, KNACK includes this relation into the question text and it adds the corresponding condition to the rule. In the example, KNACK encountered the object "interface-circuit". This is a known object and a question strategy

---

† A question rule consists of two OPS5 rules: one rule to enable the asking of the question and another rule to handle multiple answers. In the case of multiple answers the second rule fires again for each answer and creates the appropriate basic elements for each of the answers.

```
If          a SUBSYSTEM WITH SOME NAME IS KNOWN
       and  a INTERFACE-CIRCUIT WITH SOME NAME IS KNOWN
       and  THE INTERFACE-CIRCUIT IS PART-OF THAT SUBSYSTEM
Then ask  "Which protection device protects the interface-circuit <INTERFACE-CIRCUIT.NAME>
             OF THE SUBSYSTEM <SUBSYSTEM.NAME>"
       and create the slot PROTECTION-DEVICE.NAME for the answer
       and create the relation PROTECTS between the object PROTECTION-DEVICE
                                    and the object INTERFACE-CIRCUIT
```

```
(p question-65
    (questioning-in-progress)
    (SUBSYSTEM   ^id <id-1>   ^NAME {<SUBSYSTEM.NAME> <> NIL})
    (INTERFACE-CIRCUIT   ^id <id-2>   ^NAME {<INTERFACE-CIRCUIT.NAME> <> NIL})
    (relation   ^name PART-OF  ^from-object INTERFACE-CIRCUIT   ^from-id <id-2>
                 ^to-object SUBSYSTEM   ^to-id <id-1>)
  -(question   ^number q65   ^id-list <id-1> <id-2>)
-->
    (bind <question-id> (gint))
    (make question-text   ^id <question-id>
          ^text Which protection device protects the interface-circuit <INTERFACE-CIRCUIT.NAME>
                OF THE SUBSYSTEM <SUBSYSTEM.NAME>))
    (make question   ^number q65   ^id-list <id-1> <id-2>)
    (make argument-list   q65 <question-id> <id-1> <id-2>)
    (make build-obj/att   q65 <question-id> <id-1> <id-2>)
)

(p question-obj/att-65
    {(build-obj/att   q65 <question-id> <id-1> <id-2>) <cb>}
--->
    (remove <cb>)
    (bind <o-id-1> (gint))
    (make object   ^id <o-id-1>   ^pointer <question-id>   ^name PROTECTION-DEVICE)
    (make attribute   ^pointer <o-id-1>   ^name NAME   ^value nil)
    (bind <n-id-1> (gint))
    (make object   ^id <n-id-1>   ^pointer <question-id>   ^name relation)
    (make attribute   ^pointer <n-id-1>   ^name name    ^value PROTECTS)
    (make attribute   ^pointer <n-id-1>   ^name from-object   ^value PROTECTION-DEVICE)
    (make attribute   ^pointer <n-id-1>   ^name from-id   ^value <o-id-1>)
    (make attribute   ^pointer <n-id-1>   ^name to-object   ^value INTERFACE-CIRCUIT)
    (make attribute   ^pointer <n-id-1>   ^name to-id   ^value <id-2>)
)
```

FIG. 4. Sample question rule extended by heuristics.

was defined to gather information about this object. It is further known that "interface-circuit" is a "part-of" a "subsystem". Therefore KNACK extended the question text with "of the subsystem" and added the corresponding condition about the existence of a "subsystem" to the rule.

If a known object is used in the question text and if a way is known to gather information about this object and if this object has a "name" attribute or a "type" attribute, KNACK will include a variable in the question text which will insert the name or type of the known object. The above example now contains the objects: "interface-circuit" and "subsystem". They are known objects and question strategies were defined to gather information about them. Also, a "name" attribute exists for both objects. Thus KNACK made the question text more specific by adding the variables "interface-circuit name" and "subsystem name".

KNACK uses heuristics to extend its knowledge about known objects, their attributes, and the relations between objects. It defines new objects, adds new attributes to objects, and creates the necessary relations between objects:

If the expert uses an object that KNACK does not know, KNACK asks whether it is a synonym for an existing object. If the expert indicates that it is not a synonym for an existing object, KNACK defines the new object.

If the expert describes a known object with an attribute that KNACK does not know, KNACK asks whether it is a synonym for an existing attribute of the known object. If the expert indicates that it is not a synonym, KNACK defines the new attribute for the known object.

If the expert mentions known objects in the text of a question and if a way is known to gather information about these objects and if the object of the answer is a different object, KNACK creates relations between the known objects of the question text and the object for the answer. KNACK also inserts these relations into the representation of the question. The expert has to define a name for each of these relations. The example in Fig. 4 shows that KNACK extended the question rule with an action to create the relation "protects" between the object for the answer "protection-device" and the known object "interface-circuit" which appears in the question text.

6. Conclusion

In this paper we described KNACK, a knowledge-acquisition tool for building expert systems that evaluate the design of electro-mechanical systems. KNACK's knowledge-acquisition approach is based on the assumption that an expert can adequately present his knowledge in the form of a skeletal report and report fragments. The skeletal report provides a framework around which report fragments relevant to the design of a specific electro-mechanical system can be organized. KNACK also elicits knowledge about how to customize the selected report fragments for a particular application. The skeletal report, the report fragments and the knowledge of how to customize the report fragments provide KNACK with all it has to know to present the design of an electromechanical system and to evaluate it. In order to acquire the knowledge necessary to solve the information gathering and the evaluation tasks, KNACK exploits a WRINGER's problem-solving methods and knowledge roles to guide the expert through the knowledge-acquisition process. KNACK determines what an expert has to provide to define the knowledge. Finally, KNACK uses heuristics to infer additional knowledge. For example, heuristics are used to define the circumstances in which it is appropriate to ask a question, to make the text of a question more specific, and to extend knowledge about objects, attributes and relations between objects.

We would be remiss if we did not mention our co-workers in this project. William Rodi (S-Cubed) made significant contributions. Casey Boyd (CMU) reviewed an earlier draft of this paper. Thomas Flory and Roland Polimadei of Harry Diamond Laboratories (HDL) and Rodney Perala of Electro Magnetic Applications (EMA) served as our domain experts. We would also like to thank Andrej Bevec (HDL), John Northrop (S-Cubed), William Proffer (S-Cubed), and Alex Stewart (HDL) for their support.

References

BOOSE, J. (1984). Personal construct theory and the transfer of human expertise. *Proceedings of the National Conference on Artificial Intelligence.* Austin, Texas, pp. 27–33.

VAN DE BRUG, A., BACHANT, J. & MCDERMOTT, J. (1986). The taming of R1. *IEEE Expert,* **1.**

CHANDRASEKARAN, B. (1983). Towards a taxonomy of problem solving types. *Al Magazine,* **4,** 9–17.

CLANCEY, W. (1983). The advantages of abstract control knowledge in expert system design. *Proceedings of the 3th National Conference on Artificial Intelligence,* Washington, D.C. pp. 74–78.

DAVIS, R. & LENAT, D. (1982). *Knowledge-Based Systems in Artificial Intelligence.* New York; McGraw-Hill.

ESHELMAN, L. & MCDERMOTT, J. (1986). MOLE: a knowledge acquisition tool that uses its head. *Proceedings of the 5th National Conference on Artificial Intelligence,* Philadelphia, PA, pp. 950–955

KAHN, G., NOWLAN, S. & MCDERMOTT, J. (1985). MORE: an intelligent knowledge acquisition tool. *Proceedings of Ninth International Conference on Artifical Intelligence,* Los Angeles, California, pp. 581–584.

MARCUS, D., MCDERMOTT, J. & WANG, T. (1985). Knowledge acquisition for constructive systems. *Proceedings of Ninth International Conference on Artificial Intelligence,* Los Angeles, California, pp. 637–639.

NECHES, R., SWARTOUT, W. & MOORE, J. (1984). Enhanced maintenance and explanation of expert systems through explicit models of their development. *Proceedings of IEEE Workshop on Principles of Knowledge-based Systems,* Denver, Colorado, pp. 173–178.

Taking backtracking with a grain of SALT

SANDRA MARCUS†

Department of Computer Science, Carnegie–Mellon University, Pittsburgh, Pennsylvania 15213, U.S.A.

SALT is a knowledge-acquisition tool for generating expert systems that can use a propose-and-revise problem-solving strategy. The SALT-assumed method incrementally constructs an initial design by proposing values for design parameters, identifying constraints on design parameters as the design develops and revising design decisions in response to detection of constraint violations in the proposal. This problem-solving strategy provides the basis for SALT's knowledge representation. SALT guides its interrogation of the domain expert using its identification of weaknesses in the knowledge base.

Introduction

A very successful approach to automating knowledge acquisition has been to focus a tool on expert systems that use the same problem-solving method (Davis & Lenat, 1982; Boose, 1984; Marcus, McDermott & Wang, 1985; Kahn, Nowlan & McDermott, 1984; van de Burg, Bachant & McDermott, 1986). Such tools gain their advantage from the way in which they represent the knowledge they acquire; that is, the representation can identify knowledge by the role it plays in finding a solution (Clancey, 1985; McDermott, 1986). Knowing how knowledge will be applied provides a strong lever for eliciting knowledge from a domain expert and analyzing the adequacy of the knowledge base. This paper will describe how SALT (Marcus *et al.*, 1985; Marcus & McDermott, 1986) uses its understanding of a constructive problem-solving strategy to guide knowledge acquisition.

SALT assumes that any expert system it creates will use a propose-and-revise strategy. The system will start incrementally constructing a design by proposing values for design parameters, one parameter at a time. As it extends the design, the system will also identify constraints on design parameters. Whenever it detects a constraint violation, the system will use domain expertise to consider past decisions that could be revised, choose the most preferred revision that remedies the violation, remove anything potentially inconsistent with that change, and continue extending the design from that point. For an unaided domain expert to describe how to perform a task using backtracking involves making explicit a great deal of control knowledge, which experts are usually fairly vague about. It is particularly difficult for the expert to keep in mind how steps to construct a design or plan should be ordered, which decisions affect compliance with constraints on the design, and how local refinements that remedy individual constraint violations interact with each other to affect overall progress toward a design that meets *all* constraints. The problem-solving strategy SALT assumes defines a knowledge representation SALT

---

† Dr Marcus is now a principal researcher with Boeing Computer Services, Advanced Technology Center, P.O. Box 24346, M/S 7L-64, Seattle, WA 98124.

211

KNOWLEDGE-BASED SYSTEMS Vol. 2
ISBN 0-12-115920-5

can exploit to assist users with these difficulties. SALT's knowledge base analyses can indicate when backtracking is needed, identify potential points to backtract to, and indicate potential problems in converging on a solution that may require additional domain knowledge.

Is backtracking needed?

Experts in design and planning are fairly good at describing individual considerations for constructing a solution for their domain. They can extemporaneously list many of the constraints the solution must satisfy. They can consult manuals of formulas and tables for producing individual output values. But they are less clear on how the individual steps fit together, how to organize them into a system. SALT aids users by allowing them to enter knowledge piecemeal starting at any point. Salt keeps track of how the pieces are fitting together and warns the user of places where pieces might be missing or creating inconsistencies.

SALT users typically start by specifying procedures for producing particular desired output values. They can start by specifying a procedure for any value. Users can describe a set of procedures from input to output if they wish to do so. Alternatively, users may start by giving a procedure for determining an output value that takes into consideration all information necessary to make a decision. SALT can then march the user backward to acquire procedures for the information necessary at that step, and so on. If each step includes all relevant considerations, the resulting expert system will be a least commitment system in the sense that, like MOLGEN (Stefik, 1981a, b), it will not make a decision until all necessary information is available. If steps cannot be ordered so as to make all information available before a decision is required, SALT will guide the expert in combining plausible reasoning to propose an initial guess with knowledge-based backtracking to revise guesses. Examples based on VT (Marcus, Stout & McDermott, 1986), an expert system for designing elevators, can illustrate how SALT exploits its knowledge of propose-and-revise problem-solving to guide the expert. These examples will follow a user whose strategy is to start with a procedure for specifying one of the desired output values of the expert system.

VT takes as input the customer's functional specifications, such as elevator speed and carrying capacity, and key architectural information about the elevator shaft, such as wall-to-wall dimensions and locations of sills and rail supports. VT's task is to select all pieces of equipment and produce a configuration and layout of parts that meet both those specifications and safety, installation and maintenance requirements.

At the start of a SALT interview, the user is shown the menu below for indicating the type of knowledge to be entered or viewed. Three basic kinds (or roles) of knowledge make up a propose-and-revise system: (1) procedures for proposing values for the pieces of the design the system will output, (2) identification of constraints on individual pieces of the design, and (3) suggestions for ways of revising the design if the constraints are not met.

In the interaction below, the user is electing to enter a procedure for determining the value of MACHINE-MODEL. SALT's messages are in sans serif type, user replies in sans serif italic. A word in brackets at the end of a SALT request for information is a default response which the user can issue by typing carriage return. (These conventions apply to all sample SALT dialogs in this paper).

1.   PROCEDURE   Enter a procedure for a value

2.   CONSTRAINT   Enter constraints on a value

3.   FIX   Enter remedies for a constraint violation

4.   EXIT   Exit

Enter your command [EXIT]: *1*

What is the name of the value for which you will specify a procedure?: *MACHINE-MODEL*

SALT next presents the user with a set of prompts. These are requests for information needed to specify a procedure for the SALT-assumed problem-solving strategy. The completed PROCEDURE schema for MACHINE-MODEL is as follows:

1	Name:	MACHINE-MODEL
2	Constraint type:	ACTUAL
3	Precondition:	NONE
4	Procedure:	DATABASE-LOOKUP
5	Table name:	MACHINE
6	Column with needed value:	MODEL
7	Parameter test:	MAX-LOAD > = SUSPENDED-LOAD
8	Parameter test:	DONE
9	Ordering column:	HEIGHT
10	Optimal:	SMALLEST

The user's choice of DATABASE-LOOKUP as the procedure type for determining MACHINE-MODEL indicates that the SALT-generated expert system will consult its database of equipment specifications to select an appropriate machine.† For a DATABASE-LOOKUP procedure, the user is presented with a set of subprompts asking for details for locating the value to be retrieved. In the schema above, the name of the table and column from which the value is retrieved are SALT-generated defaults. Parameter tests are tests to be performed on table entries (rows) to decide which are appropriate candidates for retrieval. In this case, the entry must have a listing under the column MAX-LOAD that is greater than or equal to the SUSPENDED-LOAD. Finally, if more than one entry under MODEL meets this

---

†SALT can also be used to collect and generate a database that is organized into tables of constants. The user will be reminded to enter constants for any table referenced in a procedure.

test, ORDERING-COLUMN and OPTIMAL values are used to determine which entry should be retrieved. Here the user indicates that the entry with the SMALLEST HEIGHT is the most deisrable.

This procedure in isolation is incomplete. SALT notices this and makes the query below if the user tries to exit from the interview at this point:

> I have no PROCEDURE for arriving at a value for SUSPENDED-LOAD which was mentioned
>
> as a contributor for MACHINE-MODEL . Do you wish to specify one now? [SAVE]:

The following three procedures are supplied by the user in response to SALT prompts:‡

1	Name:	SUSPENDED-LOAD
2	Constraint type:	ACTUAL
3	Precondition:	NONE
4	Procedure:	CALCULATION
5	Formula:	CAR-WEIGHT + CABLE-WEIGHT

Enter your command [EXIT]:

1	Name:	CABLE-WEIGHT
2	Constraint type:	ACTUAL
3	Precondition:	NONE
4	Procedure:	CALCULATION
5	Formula:	HOIST-CABLE-UNIT-WEIGHT * HOIST-CABLE-QUANTITY

Enter your command [EXIT]:

1	Name:	HOIST-CABLE-QUANTITY
2	Constraint type:	ACTUAL
3	Precondition:	NONE
4	Procedure:	CALCULATION
5	Formula:	SUSPENDED-LOAD / HOIST-CABLE-STRENGTH

Enter your command [EXIT]:

‡ This is a simplification of an example that occurred as SALT acquired the VT knowledge base. The original analysis involved a chain of 13 steps.

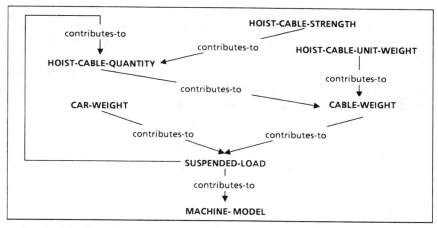

FIG. 1. SALT's representation of the user's input of procedures to propose a design.

Once the user enters these procedures, SALT stores that knowledge within a dependency network shown in Fig. 1. SALT will attempt to build an expert system that applies procedures for constructing a design in a least commitment order. Each procedure is eligible for use only after all the values needed for that procedure have been generated. Using the representation illustrated in Fig. 1, it is easy for SALT to detect the impossibility of applying three of the steps in a forward chain. SALT's aid in this situation is guidance in how to use propose-and-revise instead. First the user is warned that the situation exists:

In the procedures I have been given, there is a loop. The list below shows the values on

the loop; each value uses the one below it and the last uses the first:

    1   CABLE-WEIGHT

    2   HOIST-CABLE-QUANTITY

    3   SUSPENDED-LOAD

In order to use any procedure, I need some way of getting a first estimate for one of the

names on the list. Which one do you wish to estimate? [SUSPENDED-LOAD]: *2*

The user is asked to break the loop by providing an estimate for one of the values on the loop. The user indicates that an estimate will be provided for HOIST-CABLE-QUANTITY by typing its number, 2.

The format used for eliciting an estimate is the same as that used for any step to extend a design:

    1   Name: HOIST-CABLE-QUANTITY

    2   Precondition: NONE

    3   Procedure: CALCULATION

    4   Formula:

    Enter your command [EXIT]: *4   3*

Prompts on the left represent requests for information. Values on the right in the example are defaults. The user indicates that in extending any design, the system should initially use three hoist cables. (The user's "4" specifies the line of the prompt and "3" is the value the user wants to enter in the knowledge base for that prompt). SALT users are coached to use the most preferred value as an estimate. In this case, the smallest number of hoist cables that can be used on any job is most preferred. The completed procedure is shown below:

1	Name:	HOIST-CABLE-QUANTITY
2	Precondition:	NONE
3	Procedure:	CALCULATION
4	Formula:	3

Enter your command [EXIT]: < cr >

Once the user has settled on this procedure and exited from the procedure screen, SALT indicates that this will be a potential point for initiating backtracking, since the original procedure will be used to derive a constraint placed on this estimate. In this case, the user accepts the default, MINIMUM:

The procedure you originally gave for HOIST-CABLE-QUANTITY will be used as a check

of the estimate. How does the value arrived at by that procedure limit the estimate?

[MINIMUM]: < cr >

SALT's representation of the revised knowledge base that results from this interaction is shown in Fig. 2. The system is now set up to start with three hoist

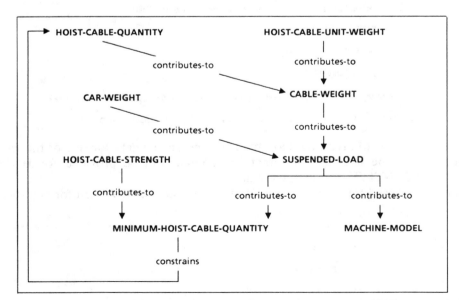

FIG. 2. The modified knowledge base after input of a new procedure for HOIST-CABLE-QUANTITY and identification of the constraint, MINIMUM-HOIST-CABLE-QUANTITY.

cables; use this value to compute CABLE-WEIGHT, then SUSPENDED-LOAD; and finally, compute MINIMUM-HOIST-CABLE-QUANTITY. If the computed minimum is greater than three, the system will register a constraint violation. SALT has essentially taken knowledge that the user originally defined as filling the role of extending a design and assigned it as part of the system's constraint knowledge. Because SALT now has knowledge of a new constraint, it must have a way of remedying a violation of that constraint, and it reminds the user:

> I have no knowledge of fixes for MINIMUM-HOIST-CABLE-QUANTITY. Would you like to
>
> specify one now [SAVE]? *YES*

The next section describes aid SALT can provide in suggesting potential fixes.

To what point should the system backtrack?

In many cases, it can be difficult to decide what parts of the proposed design to revise in order to remedy a constraint violation. In principle, any value that contributes to the constraint or its constrained value might serve as a potential "fix" value. This is the rationale behind dependency-directed backtracking, applied in expert systems such as EL (Stallman & Sussman, 1977; Sussman & Steele, 1980). But revisions may differ in cost and in likelihood of success. SALT assumes a method of *knowledge-based* backtracking; i.e. the generated system will use domain expertise to decide what values to change to remedy a constraint violation.† A user who wishes to suggest revisions in response to a constraint violation should at least consider any contributor that could have an impact. If the dependency network is very dense, the user may have difficulty recalling all contributors. SALT helps by reading out the relevant part of the network on request. The example below is for the knowledge base described so far, after the user elects to supply a fix for the MINIMUM-HOIST-CABLE-QUANTITY constraint.

> There are no fixes for MINIMUM-HOIST-CABLE-QUANTITY in the knowledge base.
>
> Would you like to see possible fix values? [YES]: < cr >
>
> There are no contributors to HOIST-CABLE-QUANTITY.
>
> Would you like to see the contributors to MINIMUM-HOIST-CABLE-QUANTITY? [YES]:
>
> < cr >
>
> Contributors to MINIMUM-HOIST-CABLE-QUANTITY:
>
> 1   HOIST-CABLE-STRENGTH
>
> 2   SUSPENDED-LOAD
>
> 3   CABLE-WEIGHT
>
> 4   HOIST-CABLE-QUANTITY
>
> 5   HOIST-CABLE-UNIT-WEIGHT
>
> 6   CAR-WEIGHT
>
> Give the number of the one you want to work on (0 for new) [0]: *4*

† AIR-CYL (Brown, 1985) and PRIDE (Mittal & Araya, 1986) also use domain-specific advice for recommending revisions but differ from SALT-generated systems in other architectural features.

Because HOIST-CABLE-QUANTITY was assigned a constant value of 3, there are no contributors to it. The indentation in the display of contributors to MINIMUM-HOIST-CABLE-QUANTITY indicates the remoteness of their contribution. The leftmost contributors, SUSPENDED-LOAD and HOIST-CABLE-STRENGTH, are used directly to calculate the constraint. CABLE-WEIGHT and CAR-WEIGHT, indented under SUSPENDED-LOAD, directly contribute to SUSPENDED-LOAD and thus to MINIMUM-HOIST-CABLE-QUANTITY. In principle, a change in any contributor to MINIMUM-HOIST-CABLE-QUANTITY, however remote, could change its value and, depending on the direction of change, remedy the constraint violation. Domain expertise is needed to determine what change to try because the domain expert knows which changes are most disruptive or expensive in the real-world, and also which are most likely to succeed.

In this example, the user suggests changing HOIST-CABLE-QUANTITY, a contributor to MINIMUM-HOIST-CABLE-QUANTITY. The proposed fix is shown below:

1	Violated constraint:	MINIMUM-HOIST-CABLE-QUANTITY
2	Value to change:	HOIST-CABLE-QUANTITY
3	Change type:	INCREASE
4	Step type:	SAME
5	Rating of undesirability:	4
6	Reason for undesirabiity:	Changes minor equipment selection

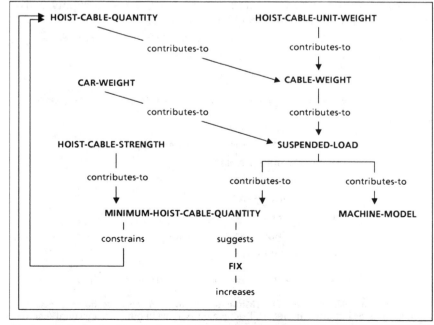

FIG. 3. The knowledge base with a fix for violation of MINIMUM-HOIST-CABLE-QUANTITY added.

SALT's representation of the knowledge base now looks as shown in Fig. 3. One final piece of SALT advice is a prompt for a ceiling on the increase of HOIST-CABLE-QUANTITY:

> I have no knowledge of a procedure for MAXIMUM-HOIST-CABLE-QUANTITY which
>
> could bound the increase of HOIST-CABLE-QUANTITY called for by a fix for MINIMUM-
>
> HOIST-CABLE-QUANTITY. Would you like to specify one now? [SAVE].

The knowledge base now calls for the generated system to start with the smallest possible number of hoist cables and use that estimate to make other equipment selection and sizing decisions. The system will then use the results of those decisions to calculate the smallest number of hoist cables required under those conditions. If the minimum is three or fewer, the current configuration is acceptable. If it is greater, HOIST-CABLE-QUANTITY will be increased by the same amount that it fell below the minimum (INCREASE SAME). The process will then be repeated using the new estimate for HOIST-CABLE-QUANTITY. If the calculated minimum ever exceeds the specified maximum, the system will stop increasing HOIST-CABLE-QUANTITY and reach a dead end. It will then declare that no solution is possible for this over-constrained job.

In this example, the search carried on by the mechanism that implements fixes is extremely simple. Since there is only one potential remedy for MINIMUM-HOIST-CABLE-QUANTITY, the generated system need not decide which potential fix to apply. When there is more than one possible fix, the system must choose among them in a way that ensures that the system will converge on a solution if one exists. SALT provides a map of the knowledge base to help sophisticated users assess the adequacy of any knowledge base collected by SALT. This map and its use are described in the next section.

Will the search converge?

A piece of knowledge supplied by the user to fix a violated constraint carries with it three crucial bits of information: a value that might be changed, the way it should be changed, and the desirability of the change. The first two pieces of information give the system potential remedies for constraint violation. The third influences the order in which the system attempts to apply those remedies.

Domain knowledge determines the relative desirability of potential constraint remedies. For VT, ordering largely reflects safety considerations, customer satisfaction and dollar cost to the company responsible for supplying, installing, and maintaining the equipment. Potential fixes are ordered according to their most severe negative effect on the configuration. For VT, potential fixes are investigated in that order, starting with the most preferred. However, this method excludes any use of information that might reflect the likelihood of convergence on a solution that satisfies *all* constraints. Evaluation of the likelihood of convergence requires examining the effect of fixes for the constraint violation on other potential constraint violations.

The kind of domain-specific information SALT collects to direct backtracking is relatively easy to elicit, since the expert can focus on one constraint violation at a time and give preference ratings that reflect local considerations alone. However, a search that relies solely on this local information and ignores potential interactions among fixes for different constraint violations may run into trouble. SALT helps manage knowledge-based backtracking by mapping out interactions among fixes for different constraint violations. The user can then examine cases of interacting fixes for their potential to cause trouble for convergence on a solution. Noninteracting fixes and certain configurations of interacting fixes can be dealt with using local information only. This treatment, the "standard treatment" for SALT-generated systems, ignores potential interactions among fixes for different constraints. Some configurations of interacting fixes might lead to failure under the standard treatment and are treated as special cases that take into account more global information.

The assumed standard treatment and its trouble spots

In the standard treatment, choice of where to backtrack to is conditioned on individual constraint violations. Only potential fixes identified by the domain expert as relevant to the current violation are considered, and these are selected in order of the expert's preference. All possible combinations of constraint-specific remedies will be tried until a remedy is found for the violation. If the system reaches a dead end—i.e. none of these combinations remedy the local constraint violation—the system will announce that there is no possible solution. If fixes for one constraint violation do not affect other constraint violations, this strategy guarantees that the first solution found will be the most preferred and that the system will correctly report failure if no successful fix is found for an individual constraint.

However, it is possible that remedies selected for one constraint violation may aggravate constraint violations that occur further downstream. This may result in failure to find a solution when one does exist in cases in which a fix that appears optimal based on local information would not be preferred if more were known about the search space.†

For example, the lowest cost successful fix for a particular constraint violation may aggravate a downstream constraint violation so much that the system reaches a dead end when exploring fixes for the downstream violation. If more expensive fixes for the first constraint do not have the same negative effect downstream, then a solution may be possible. If the standard treatment were used, the undesired behaviour of the system in this case would be a premature announcement of failure.

Another potential problem is that unproductive looping may occur between fixes for two constraint violations if their preferred fixes counteract each other. This will occur, for example, if fixing one constraint violation increases a certain value, which leads to violation of another constraint whose fix calls for decreasing the same value, and so on. Repeated violations of the same constraint are not necessarily pernicious, but such a case of antagonistic constraints might result in an infinite loop under the standard treatment.

Currently SALT displays a representation of the interactions among fixes in a knowledge base. This can be used to analyse a knowledge base for potential trouble

---

† A related but less serious problem is that a remedy not chosen may have an ameliorating effect on a downstream constraint violation. In such a case, the system might miss a solution in which the total cost of fixing the two violations might be less if a more costly fix were chosen for the first.

in a local, constraint-specific search. Special-case treatments for problem spots can then be hand-coded. This process will eventually be automated in SALT.

SALT's map of fix interactions

In order to identify trouble spots, we need to know whether and how a proposed change to a fix value will affect the relationship of constraints and their constrained values anywhere else in the network. To map these interactions, SALT uses a worst-case analysis. The dependency network that represents contribution in procedures for proposing design extensions and specifying constraints can be augmented in many cases by a notation for direction of correlation between values at adjacent nodes. For many algebraic formulas, SALT can assess whether an increase in a contributor will produce an increase in the result or the reverse. For example, if $z = x - y$, increasing x will increase z, while increasing y will decrease z. Procedures involving calls to the database cannot be similarly assessed because, by design, what is stored in the database could vary on a very short-term basis. Thus, anything involving a database call is marked unknown and considered to have a potentially aggravating effect on downstream constraint checks. Most fixes have an associated direction—increase or decrease of the fix value. Using the correlations, this direction of change can be propagated through the network to any constraints or constrained values. Since constraints involve relational tests between values, knowing the propagated effect on the constraint or constrained value will tell us whether the change to some upstream fix value will make the constraint more or less likely to be violated. For example, if a constraint is a maximum, a change that decreases the value of the constraint or increases the value it constrains makes it more likely that the constraint will be violated. Again, fixes without a clear direction—e.g. those involving calls to the database or substitutions of symbolic values—are assumed to have a potentially negative effect on downstream constraint checks.

SALT lists chains of interacting fixes. Each chain originates from a constraint whose tendency to be violated is not affected by fixes for any other constraint and whose own fixes make other constraints more likely to be violated. If fixes for any of the constraints in this second tier make other constraints more likely to be violated, these are added to the chain and so on. Loops are flagged when a constraint recurs in the chain. SALT users can then examine the chains and loops in a knowledge base to see whether they represent trouble spots for the standard treatment.

DIAGNOSIS AND TREATMENT OF TROUBLE SPOTS
The map displayed by SALT for the HOIST-CABLE-QUANTITY example is shown below. The starting point of the chain is the first constraint, shown between asterisks. There is no possibility that a fix for any other constraint violation will make it more likely that this first constraint will be violated. Constraints are shown without parentheses. All potential fixes for a given constraint are listed below the constraints that they might remedy and indented to the right. They are enclosed in parenthese along with the direction of change and a number representing the cost of the fix; higher numbers indicate higher cost. Below each fix value is a list of constraints that may be more likely to be violated because of that fix. "LOOP" indicates the occurrence in the chain of a constraint that has already appeared.

```
  *
MINIMUM-HOIST-CABLE-QUANTITY-----------------------------------------------------------------⌐
  *                                                                                           |
                                                                                              |
      (HOIST-CABLE-QUANTITY, Up, 4)                                                           |
                                                                                              |
                MINIMUM-HOIST-CABLE-QUANTITY------------*** LOOP ***-----------⌐
```

This figure displays a loop, but it is not an infinite loop because the system will stop increasing HOIST-CABLE-QUANTITY when the maximum hoist cable quantity is reached. When this happens a dead end will be declared. If increasing HOIST-CABLE-QUANTITY is the only possible fix, as the knowledge base shows, such a dead end would not be premature because the dead end would be unavoidable.

A knowledge base configuration symptomatic of a premature dead end might look like this:†

```
           *
    MAXIMUM-CAR-JAMB-RETURN
           *

        (PLATFORM-WIDTH, Down, 10)

        (DOOR-OPENING, Substitute, 8)

        (OPENING-WIDTH, Up, 6)

              MINIMUM-DOOR-OPERATOR-SPACE

            (DOOR-MODEL, Up, 4)
```

This map indicates that the less costly change to OPENING-WIDTH, although preferred for local considerations, may cause a violation of MINIMUM-DOOR-OPERATOR-SPACE. The more expensive fixes to PLATFORM-WIDTH and DOOR-OPENING have no negative downstream effects. If selecting OPENING-WIDTH as the fix to implement causes a dead end, this may constitute a premature announcement of failure. Selecting a change to PLATFORM-WIDTH, DOOR-OPENING, or some combination of the three potential changes may remedy the violation to MAXIMUM-CAR-JAMB-RETURN without making it impossible to fix MINIMUM-DOOR-OPERATOR-SPACE.

Currently, a system developer must hand-code a solution by customizing treatment for the potential site of the dead end. The control shell of the generated expert system must be modified so that whenever a dead end is found for a violation of MINIMUM-DOOR-OPERATOR-SPACE, the system will go back and try more expensive fixes at the relevant prior constraint violation, MAXIMUM-CAR-JAMB-RETURN. The SALT map helps the user locate this relevant prior constraint violation.

Below is an example of a potential infinite loop. Two of the fixes for MAXIMUM-TRACTION-RATIO can result in a violation of MAXIMUM-MACHINE-GROOVE-PRESSURE and in turn, two fixes for MAXIMUM-MACHINE-GROOVE-PRESSURE can loop back to cause a violation of MAXIMUM-TRACTION-RATIO. The details of this map reveal that these two

---

† This example is completely fictional, since no such trouble spots exist in the current VT knowledge base (Marcus, Stout & McDermott, 1986).

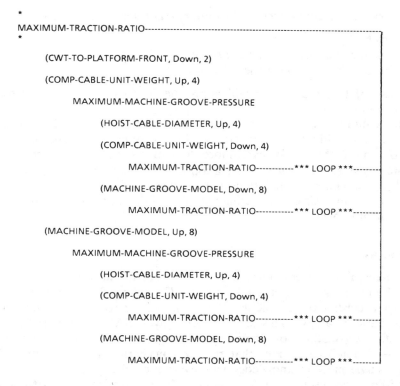

```
*
MAXIMUM-TRACTION-RATIO----------------------------------------------------------

*

        (CWT-TO-PLATFORM-FRONT, Down, 2)

        (COMP-CABLE-UNIT-WEIGHT, Up, 4)

                MAXIMUM-MACHINE-GROOVE-PRESSURE

                    (HOIST-CABLE-DIAMETER, Up, 4)

                    (COMP-CABLE-UNIT-WEIGHT, Down, 4)

                        MAXIMUM-TRACTION-RATIO-----------*** LOOP ***--------

                    (MACHINE-GROOVE-MODEL, Down, 8)

                        MAXIMUM-TRACTION-RATIO-----------*** LOOP ***--------

        (MACHINE-GROOVE-MODEL, Up, 8)

                MAXIMUM-MACHINE-GROOVE-PRESSURE

                    (HOIST-CABLE-DIAMETER, Up, 4)

                    (COMP-CABLE-UNIT-WEIGHT, Down, 4)

                        MAXIMUM-TRACTION-RATIO-----------*** LOOP ***--------

                    (MACHINE-GROOVE-MODEL, Down, 8)

                        MAXIMUM-TRACTION-RATIO-----------*** LOOP ***--------
```

potential fixes for each constraint—the changes to COMP-CABLE-UNIT-WEIGHT and MACHINE-GROOVE-MODEL—directly counteract each other. A closer look at SALT's knowledge representation, not in evidence here, indicates that decreasing the CWT-TO-PLATFORM distance to fix MAXIMUM-TRACTION-RATIO does not affect MACHINE-GROOVE-PRESSURE or its maximum. Increasing the diameter of the hoist cables to fix MAXIMUM-MACHINE-GROOVE-PRESSURE may actually ameliorate a problem with MAXIMUM-TRACTION-RATIO, although the effect is not substantial enough to warrant its inclusion as a fix for that constraint.

As long as only one of the two constraints is violated, the standard search for a solution based on isolated constraint violations is satisfactory. But if both constraints are violated, the system may thrash. The control shell was modified to treat this latter situation as a special case and investigate fixes for the two constraints in tandem. To do this, one extra piece of information not currently acquired by SALT was needed. If both constraints cannot be remedied at the same time, a VT domain expert would relax MAXIMUM-MACHINE-GROOVE-PRESSURE before violating MAXIMUM-TRACTION-RATIO. Under such a circumstance, the generated system will try to minimize the violation of MAXIMUM-MACHINE-GROOVE-PRESSURE.

Whenever a violation of one of these constraints is detected, the system will check to see if the other has been violated. If it has, the system will reset the values of all potential fix values to their last value before the first violation of either constraint. It will then try out potential fixes in this order, according to whether the fix:

(1) helps both;
(2) helps one and doesn't hurt the other;
(3) helps one but does hurt the other.

In the case of (3), the system will apply the fix to remedy the constraint most important to fix.

These examples show that special case treatment can require knowledge elicited from the user in addition to that required for the standard, locally based search. A better solution might call for even more domain expertise. For example, a domain expert may wish to consider a fix for a job in which two antagonistic constraints are violated that should never be attempted if either one alone is violated. SALT could make use of its analysis of interacting fixes to identify a potential need for additional search control knowledge.

Conclusion

SALT makes a strong commitment to the nature of the problem-solving strategy that will be used for any task it will acquire. This allows SALT to represent domain knowledge according to the role it will play in finding a solution for any task that can use this basic strategy. This commitment gives SALT considerable power in guiding its interrogation of domain experts in the area where they most need guidance—in making decisions that require consideration of the potential interactions of a single piece of knowledge with everything else in the knowledge base.

In guiding the user, SALT is constantly monitoring the adequacy of the knowledge base and sometimes uses its identification of weakness in the knowledge base to suggest changes in how the knowledge should be brought to bear. When SALT makes such suggestions, it is essentially deciding on variations in problem-solving strategy. As demonstrated, SALT starts with the assumption that procedures it is given for constructing the initial design will fit together in a least-commitment system. If this assumption is met by the user's input, SALT will generate a least-commitment system. Whenever SALT detects that the knowledge base does not meet this assumption, it recommends use of propose-and-revise. In doing so, it redefines a procedure that was intended to extend the design as a procedure that identifies a constraint. In deciding to use propose-and-revise, SALT assumes a very simple strategy for revising a proposal in reaction to a constraint violation—a strategy that uses only local, single-constraint-specific considerations. This assumption will produce an inadequate problem solver under certain conditions of interacting fixes. Future versions of SALT will identify such inadequacies and recommend a variation in strategy that takes into account just the kind of global information that would remedy the inadequacy observed.

SALT has been successfully used to build and maintain VT, an expert elevator designer. Yet another kind of variation in problem-solving strategy was needed when SALT was used in developing an expert system for production scheduling of elevators (Marcus, Stout, Caplain & McDermott, in press). VT and Scheduler differ in when they do constraint checking. VT checks constraints as soon as possible; the Scheduler delays checking until after a complete schedule has been generated for an order. The desirability of immediate vs delayed constraint checking lies in the nature of the interaction among constraints and their fixes.

SALT currently understands only a few variations on a problem-solving strategy. The ideal knowledge-acquisition tool would be a true knowledge-engineering expert that understands a large range of AI techniques. A research strategy that makes progress toward the goal of developing such a tool is the one followed so far for SALT: (1) focus the knowledge acquisition tool on the problem-solving strategy that will be used by the system it creates for one domain; (2) try the tool on another domain for which the problem-solving strategy looks promising; (3) when the problem-solving strategy breaks down, identify characteristics of the domain that made it break. This task will be tractable if the knowledge-acquisition tool makes explicit what the problem-solving strategy is and how knowledge is used by the strategy (McDermott, 1986); (4) automate the analysis of the knowledge base to diagnose the breakdown and treat it.

In addition to the author, Emile Servan-Schreiber contributed significantly to the coding of the SALT analyses described in this paper. Many of the ideas contained here were presented in a discussion group attended by Larry Eshelman, Gary Kahn, John McDermott, Tom Mitchell, and Allen Newell, and I am very grateful for their feedback. I would also like to thank Jeff Stout for his work on the problem-solving strategy and control shell assumed by SALT.

References

BOOSE, J. (1984). Personal construct theory and the transfer of human expertise. *Proceedings of the National Conference on Artificial Intelligence,* Austin, Texas.

BROWN, D. (1985). Failure handling in a design expert system. *Computer-aided design,* **17,** 436–441.

CLANCEY, W. (1985). Heuristic classification. *Artificial Intelligence,* **27,** 289–350.

DAVIS, R. & LENAT, D. (1982). *Knowledge-based Systems in Artificial Intelligence.* McGraw–Hill.

KAHN, G., NOWLAN, S. & McDERMOTT, J. (1984). A foundation for knowledge acquisition. *Proceedings of IEEE Workshop on Principles of Knowledge-Based Systems,* Denver, Colorado.

MARCUS, S., McDERMOTT, J. & WANG, T. (1985). Knowledge acquisition for constructive systems. *Proceedings of the International Joint Conference on Artificial Intelligence* (IJCAI), pp. 637–639.

MARCUS, S., STOUT, J. & McDERMOTT, J. (1986). VT: an expert elevator designer that uses knowledge-based backtracking. Carnegie–Mellon University Department of Computer Science technical report.

MARCUS, S., STOUT, J., CAPLAIN, G. & McDERMOTT, J. (1987). Toward automating recognition of differing problem-solving demands. Carnegie–Mellon University Department of Computer Science technical report. In press.

MARCUS, S. & McDERMOTT, J. (1986). SALT: A knowledge acquisition tool for propose-and revise systems. Carnegie–Mellon University Department of Computer Science technical report.

McDERMOTT, J. (1986). Making expert systems explicit. *Proceedings of the IFIP Congress,* Dublin, Ireland.

MITTAL, S. & ARAYA, A. (1986). A knowledge-based framework for design. *Proceedings of the National Conference on Artificial Intelligence,* Philadelphia, PA.

STALLMAN, R. M. & SUSSMAN, G. J. (1977). Forward reasoning and dependency-directed backtracking in a system for computer-aided circuit analysis. *Artificial Intelligence,* **9,** 135–196.

STEFIK, M. (1981a). Planning with constraints (MOLGEN: Part 1). *Artificial Intelligence,* **16,** 111–140.

STEFIK, M. (1981a). Planning and meta-planning (MOLGEN: Part 2). *Artificial Intelligence,* **16,** 141–170.

SUSSMAN, G. J. & STEELE, G. L., Jr (1980). Constraints—a language for expressing almost-hierarchical descriptions. *Artificial Intelligence,* **14,** 1–39.

VAN DE BRUG, A., BACHANT, J. & McDERMOTT, J. (1986). The taming of R1. *IEEE-Expert,* **1,** 33–38.

INFORM: an architecture for expert-directed knowledge acquisition

ERIC A. MOORE

Applicon/Schlumberger, 4251 Plymouth Road, Ann Arbor, MI 48105, U.S.A.

ALICE M. AGOGINO

Department of Mechanical Engineering, University of California, Berkeley, 5136 Etcheverry Hall, Berkeley, CA 94720, U.S.A.

This paper presents an architecture for INFORM, a domain-independent, expert-directed knowledge acquisition aid for developing knowledge-based systems. The INFORM architecture is based on information requirements and modeling approaches derived from both decision analysis and knowledge engineering. It emphasizes accommodating cycles of creative and analytic modeling activity and the assessment and representation of aggregates of information to holistically represent domain expertise. The architecture is best suited to heuristic classification problem-solving (Clancey, 1985), in particular domains with diagnosis or decision-making under uncertainty. Influence diagrams are used as the knowledge structure and computational representation. We present here a set of information and performance requirements for expert-directed knowledge acquisition, and describe a synthesis of approaches for supporting the knowledge engineering activity. We discuss potential applications of INFORM as a knowledge engineering aid, specifically as an aid for developing insight about the encoding domain on the part of its user.

1. Introduction

Hindrances to widespread application of expert systems include what are typically significant allocations of resources, of critical personnel (the expert) and of knowledge engineering effort and equipment. The knowledge engineer's efforts to replicate the knowledge underlying expert performance through encoding techniques that maintain the form of that knowledge are known as *knowledge acquisition*; the design of tools and techniques to manage and support the process, as well as the active guidance of the process, is known as *knowledge engineering*. Knowledge acquisition is by far the hardest and most time-consuming part of the expert-systems building problem.

"Knowledge-acquisition bottleneck" understates the significance of the effort required to assess from a domain expert the information necessary to achieve expert performance. The resources required to build an expert system seem to have funneled the application of knowledge-based technology to only high payoff projects, involving only experts with highly valued skills. Here, the more specialized the expertise, and the more significant the application, the harder it is for someone outside of the expert's domain—the knowledge engineer—to build a system to replicate it. "Knowledge-acquisition Klein Bottle" might be more appropiate.

What can one do? We could relax the performance requirement, and settle for a knowledge-based system without expert performance, or reduce the scope of the

227

target problem-solving domain, and settle for less functionality. Neither is likely to result in the most effective use of development resources. We could find persons with familiarity or proficiency with both knowledge-engineering tools and representation and the encoding domain (Fox, Lowenfeld & Kleinosky 1983), but even these persons are a scarce organizational resource. We could find less skilled persons in the domain that are likely to be more articulate about their problem solving (Dreyfus & Dreyfus 1980), but there is no assurance that these people will share their conceptual structure of the domain with that of the expert. Perhaps we could eliminate the expert knowledge engineer, and look for a way to let the expert encode directly.

The thought of having experts encode their expertise is compelling. Without an intermediary between the expert and the system, there is less noise introduced to the encoded knowledge, there is no time spent for the knowledge engineer to learn the language and concepts of the domain, and the resultant system has the expert's—and not an intermediary's—view of the domain (Friedland, 1981). For this, one risks losing process efficiency, for the expert must understand the knowledge representation and learn how to use the tool, one risks a potential loss of transparency, if the expert must recast his or her thinking in the tool's terms, and one risks failing to address objectively and fundamentally the expert's reasoning in the domain.

Like many established engineering organizations, the U. C. Berkeley Mechanical Engineering Department has many potential applications for knowledge-based technology, rich areas of domain expertise, and many senior and articulate experts, but it lacks readily available organizational knowledge engineering expertise, as well as tools demonstrably appropriate for the potential applications.

There is a very strong motivation to develop not just a toolkit, but a procedural aid, that will allow, for example, Master's level engineering students to successfully and efficiently employ knowledge engineering techniques and technology for practical problem-solving. Ongoing research has produced IDES, the Influence Diagram-Based Expert System, for doing probabilistic inference and planning using influence diagrams (Agogino, 1985, Agogino & Rege 1986] and (Rege, 1986a). This paper presents an architecture for INFORM, (INFluence diagram FORMer), an expert-directed knowledge-acquisition aid and interface for building knowledge-based systems in IDES.

2. Prior work on knowledge acquisition

We draw a distinction between *techniques, tools* and *aids.* A technique is a set of procedures, heuristics, or guidelines for performing Knowledge Acquisition (KA) or Knowledge Engineering (KE). A tool provides software support for application of the techniques, but no guidance on its own; knowledge engineers use tools. An aid is a tool that provides process guidance on its own. A domain expert undertaking any phase of a knowledge engineering project requires an aid.

KE tools, techniques, and aids in the literature address different areas of the knowledge engineering process: *encoding context,* the phase of determining how the characteristics of the domain, the expert, the user, and the application will affect or constrain KA procedure; *knowledge structuring,* the process resulting in an initial description of the knowledge base in the computational representation; and *knowledge refinement,* the process of model focusing and validation. Our research focus here is to provide tools that support KA in the context of developing techniques and aids for KE. Early work in KE was concentrated on developing tools and representations. The concept of the "knowledge level" (Newell, 1982), seeking to formally describe domain knowledge and problem solving at a level independent of implementation, has influenced the development of ontological representations of different problem solving domains, (Clancey, 1985; Alexander, Freiling, Staley, Rehfuss & Messick 1986), and languages specialized to problem-solving types (Bylander and Mittal, 1986). Recent emphasis has been on methodologies for structured KA (Freiling, Alexander, Messick, Rehfuss & Shulman 1985; Kline & Dolins, 1986 deGreef & Breuker, 1985), on assuring that the KA process meet the communication requirements of the application's organization (Grover, 1983), and on aids for rule refinement, (Kahn, Nowlan & McDermott 1985; Eshelman & McDermott 1986; Ginsberg, Weiss & Politakis 1985; Langlotz, Shortliffe & Fagan, 1986].

The organizational and structured knowledge-acquisition approaches are information-driven in the sense that they are a formalism, a set of activities, which produce documents and assure that information requirements and checks are met. These approaches emphasize building a paper knowledge base, or building a conceptual or knowledge-level structure of the domain, before committing programming resources; here, experts can describe their domain structure in some accessible representation freed from the implementation representation and with minimized reformulation by the KE. The KE is later involved, however, in rule encoding and refinement.

De Greef and Breuker (1985) see two basic approaches to knowledge engineering: the skills/programming-based rapid prototype and test approach (Hayes-Roth & Waterman, 1983; Brownston, Farrell, Kant & Martin, 1985) and the structured knowledge-engineering approach, which guides and supports an initial knowledge-acquisition phase while implementation is deferred. The INFORM architecture actually falls between the two; we employ model refinement techniques from decision analysis and knowledge engineering in an environment that is predominantly structured knowledge acquisition.

Successful KA aids for domain dependent systems in both KE and Decision Analysis (DA) exist; their design typically provides a domain-based encoding language and set of problem solving primitives, domain specific graphics, or some superset of domain concepts from which a temporal encoding problem will be identified (Holtzman, 1985; Musen; Fagan, Combs & Shortliffe, in press; Merkhofer, Robinson & Korsan 1979). "Domain-independent" implies that, for a given problem-solving approach, the user must create concepts, rather than select them, or that many meta-models of domain concepts are included in the tool model. Two aids for knowledge structuring, ETS (Boose 1984, 1985) and ROGET (Bennett, 1983) elicit the expert's structure of domain concepts though sequences of comparisons among sets of proposed objects. Both are intended for use by domain experts and result in "executable" rule bases. ROGET aids the user in choosing the appropriate inference technique and ontological representation, given information about the user's experience and the problem-solving type (as subsets of the classification problem-solving model). INFORM is intended to be domain independent across the range of heuristic classification problem-solving, but is potentially adaptable to specific domains.

3. Expert-directed knowledge acquisition

The notion behind "expert systems" is the desire to replicate an expert's problem-solving performance in a domain. While rule- and frame-based expert systems are proving to be effective computational representations of knowledge and expertise, they are not complete cognitive models (perhaps not even cognitive) of that knowledge or expertise. So the process of capturing knowledge, of transferring the expert's cognitive structures, representations, and methods to computational domain structures, knowledge representations, and procedures, will almost certainly entail its reformulation. If, for the expert, the act of articulating this knowledge to an audience is novel, then the expert is also reformulating his or her knowledge. Knowledge engineering is thus both a descriptive and creative modeling activity.

We view knowledge engineering as a model design and software engineering activity. A proportionally small amount of KE time is actually spent programming (Freiling *et al.*, 1985, Grover, 1983); much of the skills (and effort) of knowledge engineering are modeling skills—analysis and reduction, information management, and process decision-making—as well as the traditional emphasis on performance replication through incremental refinement. An expert-directed KA interface must support all of these activities to in turn successfully support a model's elicitation and eventual refinement.

The key assumptions behind any approach to self-encoding are that:

It is plausible that the expert can efficiently learn and use the encoding interface: that the expert understands how to use the tool, understands the problem, and is motivated enough to use the tool conscientiously;
The expert can think abstractly about the domain and problem-solving within it, i.e. identifying variables and influences;
A structured, analytic approach to thinking about one's domain knowledge and problem solving can achieve a refinable model;
The inevitable loss of transparency in encoded information is acceptable if the expert can somehow assure the performance of the model or if the expert is capable of thinking in the terms of the transformed model.

4. Decision analysis, influence diagrams, and knowledge-based systems

Decision analysis (DA) brings a body of experience to structured KA that meshes well with other approaches from within the AI community.

4.1. DECISION ANALYSIS

The *decision analysis cycle* (Matheson, 1977) is an iterative and interactive proscription for assuring that essential steps in the decision process or decision-making problem have been taken. It separates the process into deterministic structuring, probabilistic assessment, and informational phases. Assessment and modeling procedures direct the formation of choices, information, and preferences into the decision set.

Both practitioners of DA and KE face the problem of attention focusing, not in making analyses complicated enough to be comprehensive, but rather keeping them simple enough to be affordable and useful (Howard, 1980). DA structuring aids have taken a largely "top–down" approach to modeling a domain, and the KE aids a "bottom–up" approach to describing the relations in a domain based upon examples of problem-solving performance.

4.2. INFLUENCE DIAGRAMS

Influence diagrams (Miller, Merkhofer, Howard, Matheson & Rice 1976; Rege & Agogino, 1986b) are an intuitively attractive conceptual and operational representation for domain expertise. We use influence diagrams as a knowledge structure: a way of organizing knowledge that is operational, but that makes no cognitive claim. Influence diagrams have developed into a decision analysis tool that graphically represents the structure of the decision problem but maintains the computational utility of the decision tree (Shachter, 1985). They are a three-layered knowledge representation, consisting of information at three hierarchical levels: *relational, functional,* and *numerical.* This hierarchy accommodates well the way people tend to model from simple to complex, and from conceptual to numeric.

At the relational level, influence diagrams are directed acyclic graphs that represent the interdependence of uncertain events in a complex system. Nodes represent sets of possible events, or a range of properties for some object. The presence of an arc indicates the possibility that the outcomes of one node are somehow influenced by the outcomes of the other. At the relational level, they superficially resemble semantic nets and frames. A major distinction is that Bayes' theorem allows topological solution, or "re-orienting" of influence diagrams. Pearl's work with Bayesian networks (Pearl, 1985) uses inheritance in a frame-based system to propagate uncertainties in a structure that closely resembles influence diagrams, though without decision nodes.

The functional level is a specification of the type of relationship between nodes, or "how" a particular event or object influences another. The functional level is traditionally probabilistic, with quantitative relations compressed into the stochastic ones, but influence diagrams can readily accommodate fuzzy, logical, and other functional relations (Rege & Agogino 1986c). The numerical level is a quantitative measure of the "extent" of the relationship.

Figure 1 describes a diagnostician's model for a simple centrifugal pump. At the relational level, we can say that the pump's "discharge" is influenced by the "foot-valve state" and "stainer state". The likelihood that discharge is high, low, or nil, is influenced by the likelihood that the foot valve is open or closed and the likelihood that the strainer is clear, partially clogged, or clogged. At the relational level, we can specify that the arc from foot valve to discharge is "logical"; if the foot valve is closed, the discharge is nil. Or we could specify a probabilistic relation, and give a distribution on the probability of discharge being high, low, or nil, given some joint distribution of strainer and foot valve states. The diagnostic inference problem

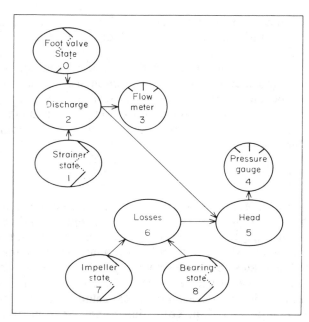

FIG. 1. Sample influence diagram.

is formulated as, for example: "given some flow meter reading X, and some pressure gauge reading Y, what is the probability that the strainer is clogged?"

4.3. BRINGING DECISION ANALYSIS TO KNOWLEDGE-BASED SYSTEMS

INFORM, because it is based on influence diagrams, is seen as best fitting applications under heuristic classification problem-solving (Clancey, 1985). The formal influence diagram representation is quite concise; there are nodes (a set of possible states for an event), states spanning the range of possible outcomes or values for the event, and probabilities on the occurrence of those states conditioned on other events. An arc in an influence diagram represents a heuristic link between a class of concepts in the domain. Data abstraction is subjective, rather than symbolic; the information lies in the uncertainty assessment or from further structuring, rather than in endorsements or in classification hierarchies.

Applying DA to knowledge-based systems means that we focus on designing problem-solving models that effectively replicate expert performance, rather than concentrating on implementing descriptions of that performance. It is important to separate replication of performance from duplication of procedure—at best, duplication is unlikely to result in performance improvement. Rather than implement actions emulating expert's problem solving actions, we want to use the expert's judgement to construct the model and to evaluate the model's performance.

Langlotz *et al.* (1986) point out one of the side benefits of doing first- and second-order sensitivity analysis on heuristics: the KE has to think more broadly about the concept, not just what its value is, but what it could be, and how likely those other values might be. Decision analysis is normally employed for significant non-routine decision-making where there is uncertainty about the state of the factors influencing the decision, the outcomes of the decision, or the extent to which the factors may influence the outcome. Knowledge-based systems are normally restricted to important but routine problem-solving, perhaps with the most frequency to heuristic classification style problems. In situations where it is uneconomical or impossible to replicate the expert problem-solving processes, the DA approach may be a viable way to approximate expert performance without explicitly relying on the processes behind it.

Barr argues for knowledge-based systems that provide insights, and not merely answers (Barr, 1985). He sees the largest measure of the utility of expert systems in the fact that their construction forces critical re-evaluation of one's own expertise. The same has been said of the utility of Decision Analysis (Howard, 1980). Non-transparency (reformulation, rather than replication of a true expert's problem-solving skills), represents a potential corruption of those skills, but can improve domain skills in non-experts, persons who would not ordinarily get the benefit of the KE's critical attention. Non-experts and experts alike may gain improvements through articulating, structuring, and recording for examination relationships and strategies in the problem-solving domain.

For knowledge acquisition and knowledge engineering, AI research and Knowledge-Based Systems practice offer:

information manipulation and management tools;
operational models of problem solving types;
passive and intelligent interface design concepts;
models of users and user problems;
prototyping/system development techniques;
tools and techniques for model refinement;
techniques for heuristic control;

and Decision Analysis offers:

Normative models for decision-making;
Robust techniques for modeling structure;
Practical encoding techniques for uncertainty;
Experience in organizational integration and acceptance.

We see particular appeal in bringing the top–down modeling and Bayesian uncertainty approaches of Decision Analysis and the influence diagram together with the software engineering tools and performance refinement techniques of Knowledge-Based Systems.

5. The information requirements for expert-directed knowledge acquisition

The design of an interface must be based upon the needs and abilities of the set of users for the set of tasks composing the application. However, the interface must also assure that it gets to the application the information it needs to run. In this sense, INFORM is a port for putting information into a program—subject to requirements for content, quality, and ease of expression.

There is no escaping the need to engineer information in order to represent knowledge. At issue, here, of course, is how best to give the expert some responsibility for knowledge engineering. INFORM is responsible not only for meeting the information needs of the computational knowledge representation, the influence diagram, but for meeting the information needs of a knowledge engineering process: context definition, model structuring, model refinement, and process decision-making.

In the context of assessment, an influence diagram is a framework for experimenting with a model's behaviour. The encoded diagram must represent information and must communicate an understanding. Much of this deeper information is descriptive, representing controlling assumptions, constraints on those assumptions and endorsement for or against them, intentions, histories, and alternatives. To communicate this understanding, we must represent information of different types: graph information, text, numerical, deterministic, logical, and uncertain.

There are three basic types of information INFORM must represent:

Model: the knowledge base;
Procedural: information revolving around the state, history, and direction of the
               KE process;
Insightful: information adjunct to analytic and creative thinking about and
               explanation of the model.

In this section, we discuss these information types in terms of their form and assessment.

5.1. MODEL INFORMATION

The information in the knowledge base is divided into *Computational, Structural* and *Uncertain* conceptual information types.

Computational model information. These are the representational requirements of the formal influence diagram. Nodes, states, probabilities, outcomes, and arcs map from a heterogeneous collection of C data structures to formatted matrices and probability distributions for topological transformation and numeric calculation within IDES.

Structural model information. An influence diagram represents a set of concepts and a way of associating related concepts. The underlying information may merely be descriptive to be useful. Augmented with context and assumption tags, and with their graphical representation, influence diagrams are an appealing way to structure the knowledge in a domain.

Uncertainty model information. Despite the naturalness of the influence diagram representation, both temporal and domain-acquisition problems are difficult for an expert or some other user to solve without experience or training and in some cases, without assistance. While Bayesian probability is a particular strength of the influence diagram, encoding for decision-making and diagnosis problems presents difficulty. Probability encoding is tedious. People's numeric estimates of uncertainty invariably do not accurately represent their underlying judgement without some structured revision and debiasing (Raiffa, 1970; Kahneman, Slovic & Tversky 1982). The process of encoding uncertain information may affect the values assessed and so is critical to the utility of that information (Spetzler & Holstein, 1977).

The many alternative uncertainty calculi are in part responses to these problems. The failure, however, of any one representation to win widespread acceptance as the "best" underscores the need for richer representations.

Bonissone & Tong (1985a) present further guidelines for assessment; these dovetail with what we already know from decision analysis to be important in terms of structuring the uncertain variable. Their discussion is valuable because it presents the uncertainty encoding activity explicitly as an information problem. So then, for each piece of evidence, one should determine the:

measure of certainty/uncertainty;
source of the evidence;
credibility of the source;
environmental conditions under which the source gathered information;
sensitivity of the goal to evidence;
cost of facility to gather information;
likelihood of succeeding in gathering information;
cost of this information gathering task;
default plan to accomplish this task.

The encoding of expert's uncertainty estimates is as least as important as the internal representation of that uncertainty in a knowledge base. One essential perspective on uncertainty representation which sometimes gets lost is that the representation must be intuitively agreeable to the expert—both the expert and the uncertainty representation must speak the same language. As Bonisonne (1985b) points out, it will ultimately take a mix of verbal and numeric representations to cover adequately the Babel of uncertainty representations used by different experts in different domains.

Influence diagrams are founded on Bayesian probability. Cheeseman (1985) argues that Bayesian probability, if properly used, can be worked around virtually all objections to it; in his view, the faults of Bayesian probability are based primarily on the misperceptions of its critics. On the other hand, a number is a rather sterile representation of a quantity that, cognitively, appears to be in large part verbal (Zimmer, 1985). A strictly Bayesian numeric estimate is very convenient, and axiomatically correct, but is often misleading without a complete view of the priors implicit in the assessment. Further, a single number overestimates the crispness of the state of knowledge about that uncertainty. A verbal assessment incorporates more factors than a numeric one, but computation, without loss of information, requires that the user's fuzzy functions be known as a context-specific mapping of verbal to possibilistic (Zimmer, 1985) or probabilistic numeric distributions. Evidential reasoning emphasizes articulating priors acting on an estimate and the decision-making power of simply ranking outcomes [much like the Analytic Hierarchy Process in decision-making (Saaty, 1980)]. All of these approaches, under some conditions, make a strong case for themselves. With influence diagrams, we are committed to representations that can ultimately be mapped to Bayesian probability.

Certainly a judgement on the strength or weakness of one representation or another should consider encodability of that representation. In assessing an uncertainty estimate, considering all the approaches, one would want to:

rank comparable outcomes in order of likelihood;
assess a verbal (qualitative) estimate;
assess numeric Bayesian values;
elicit underlying evidence for an assessment;
estimate the range of uncertainty;
elicit direct conditions on the validity of the assessment.

However, decision analytic information assessment calls for no less than all of this information. What we find is that, even though the computational representation may be considerably sparer, the conceptual representation must include an aggregate of information about the uncertain quantity. We contend that a well-designed encoding and representation environment can make the encoding of Bayesian probabilities for expert systems less forbidding and more accurate. Such an environment would support a composite conceptual representation of uncertainty (including linguistic, numeric, underlying and conditioning priors), a mapping from verbal to numeric, and from numeric to verbal, and a numeric Bayesian calculus.

For INFORM, the approach we will take is straightforward:

(1) first assess reference linguistic distributions in a broad context;
(2) use these linguistic assessments as a "first pass";
(3) for refinement, with more sensitive variables, or for variables misleadingly represented by the linguistic assessment, qualify the linguistic assessment for the specific context or employ traditional numeric encoding techniques.

5.2. PROCEDURAL INFORMATION

Supporting the KA process, for a self-encoding expert, or for some combination of KE and expert, requires information management tools (for representing the model and process state and history as basis for making choices about what to do next, and it requires guidelines and tools for making procedural decisions.

Many KA tools provide programming support, support interpreted incremental refinement, provide rule prompters, or a rule compiler based on a rule language. The DA framework is an approach that would complement all of these approaches. One view (Reboh, 1981) favors a system that requires the collaboration of the KE, but with techniques and tools for support of critical phases requiring little KE training. Such a system would in effect redistribute portions of the KE's expertise between the support tools and a domain expert or less skilled KE. This view is at the heart of the INFORM approach.

5.3. INFORMATION FOR INSIGHT

We regard "insight" as the creation and revision of a mental picture of the domain and processes within it, and the recognition and evaluation of possibilities and tradeoffs inside it. The modeling interface should provide the information and techniques for developing and maintaining insight about the model. Insight is supported by the ability to conveying timely information from the model to the user;

if it is not easy for the user to organize and convey appropriate information to the model, insight is impeded. The base issue is achieving a fit between user and interface. INFORM attempts to provide a familiar medium and acceptable stimulus for modeling effectively.

Essay writing is a metaphor for the "progressive formalization" (Holtzman, 1985) of a decision analytic model. A contention of the INFORM approach is that expository writing could accomplish (in effect) what the motivation and structuring phases are intended to accomplish in the probability encoding process (Spetzler & Holstein, 1977); give the user the opportunity to address critically the assumptions, intentions, and methods behind the model.

The "standard form" for writing an essay is a well-known and widely taught framework for expository thinking and discourse. As an encoding approach, it goes a step beyond simply writing rules into some subset of a natural or domain language. It puts relations into paragraphs and sections in support of a problem statement or thesis—the user thinks about components of the model in a structured sense, in the context of other model components, the modeling context, and the modeling goal.

In reviewing a knowledge base encoded through INFORM, the DA, expert, user, or KE is in a sense reading a story; from the contents of the KB, the reader is supposed to be able to piece together a problem-solving "narrative". Applications to be used with persons other than the encoding expert require explanations that are dependent on the line of reasoning, the model description, and the background of the users relative to that of the expert. A very critical element for KA is visualizing an audience for the application. Viewed this way, we can say that the "rules of journalism" apply here too. In this sense, the reader must know—and the interface must somehow assess *Who, What, When, Where, Why & How* for its concept and relation.

6. INFORM

These three performance goals capture the essence of what INFORM is intended to achieve as a KA aid:

(1) *sufficiency,* getting the encoded information right in terms of the influence diagram representation;

(2) *correctness,* avoiding and correcting conscious and unconscious misrepresentations of expert judgement; and

(3) *providing insight,* at minimum representing the correct information in a comprehendable form, at best completely capturing an expert's underlying model of the objects, relationships, and inferences in his domain.

6.1. ARCHITECTURE

There are four conceptual levels to the INFORM architecture. They build from satisfying information requirements to giving more sophisticated tools and advice for insight and finally to a system which could effectively tutor its user through the KE process.

The first level is to fill the diagram to sufficiency, through satisfying structural and computational constraints. The second is to employ the kinds of feedback that decision analysts and knowledge engineers employ: diagram drawing on demand, graphic feedback of distributions, ordinal, deterministic and stochastic sensitivity analysis, comfortable interaction language, and opportunity for and access to extensive explanation about the modeling process and the encoded model. The third is the "heuristic" approach, where the system provides hints and suggestions for encoding to the user based upon normative models of the encoding process and sticky points in the domain. Finally, with "expert aid", the system provides aid (hints, requests for explanation, reformulation) based upon encoding session information, normative models of the encoding process, and descriptive models of the problem domain and user's encoding style.

The INFORM user, in an encoding session, goes through a problem and session structuring module, and then a succession of editing and analysis phases. At any time, the user may get help about the syntax, options, or intent of the current phase, or comment about some aspect of the model or the modeling process, or review some graphic or textual aspect of the model. Figure 2 shows the main modules and editor sequence.

6.2. KNOWLEDGE STRUCTURING

There are two key ideas to INFORM's structuring and refinement approach:

(1) start modeling at the most general level of precision or specificity;
(2) increase specificity only for the best improvements in model performance.

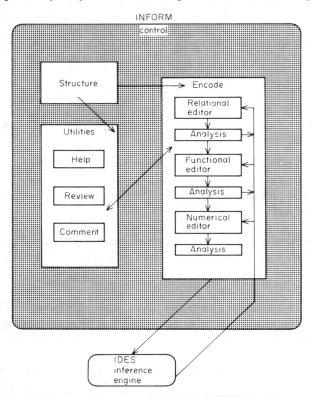

FIG. 2. Process paths and modules in the INFORM architecture.

The user is free to edit the model, and accept or reject advice on what task to choose next, but is guided through model analysis and refinement.

In the relational editor, the user specifies combinations of node name, node label, node description and arcs. On exiting the editor, this information is parsed and "incomplete information" is identified; the user is prompted to provide, for example, a description for a node identified only by a label.

The nodes operated on in the relational editor determine the nodes to be operated on in subsequent phases, in the functional and numerical editors. The analysis phases are directed by ordered lists: perform sensitivity analysis with the nodes the user is least confident about, expand the nodes that the outcome is most sensitive to, assess in a different way those uncertainty estimates the user is least (or most confident) about. The order of nodes operated on is determined by user ranking, or by some function of the rank of the node within the influence diagram.

Below are some of the activities in the INFORM architecture:

INFORM encoding activities

Set Context	System application? Encoding goal? Identify user group? Calibrate linguistic uncertainty? How much time is this encoding problem worth?
Model at Relational Level	
– Describe the Model:	Edit and compile nodes and arcs.
– Assure Completeness:	For each: name, label, description, givens, explanation.
– Look for Insight:	Potential modifications? Encoding plan?
– Offer Analysis:	Check for cycles, bushyness, sort objects by importance?
– Offer Advice:	"Might do this next"
Revise Model?	Does information about the state of "Node X" tell you something about the state of "Node Y"?
Model at Functional Level	
– Describe	Edit and compile functional form, states. Choose decision rule, or choose quantitative form or uncertainty representation?
– Assure Completeness:	Name, label, description, explanation, plan.
– Offer Analysis:	Estimate modeling effort?
– Offer Advice:	"Consider reducing the number of states in these nodes . . . "
Revise Model?	
Model at Numeric Level	
– Assure Completeness:	Assess aggregate uncertainty information.
– Offer Analysis:	Sensitivity, performance analyses.
– Offer Advice:	"Focus next on these most sensitive nodes . . . "
Revise Model?	

6.3. KNOWLEDGE REFINEMENT IN INFORM

"Refinement", in the DA context, is directed towards attention focusing, typically through ranking, and deterministic and stochastic sensitivity analysis, and towards balancing the modeling effort in terms of both structural granularity and value of additional modeling effort. Refinement in rule-based expert systems building is a process of rule addition and modification leading ultimately to performance replication. Performance improvement in a knowledge-based system generally comes with increases in specificity; because of the large assessment effort behind properly encoding probabilities, a good decision model will expand and contract through each refinement cycle. With influence diagrams, there is tradeoff between the granularity of the represented uncertainty and that of the model structure. Formally, influence diagrams rely on implicitly incorporating conditioning factors within the uncertainty assessment and in the concept's definition to result in a polished but condensed model. Rule-based expert systems representations, on the other hand, force this contextual information to be explicitly expressed as rules. Part of the refinement process in INFORM is the successive elaboration of what the model represents.

The success of our approach to encoding uncertainty during refinement is contingent on at least three things: that, given no new information, some consistency of uncertainty verbal to numerical mappings is maintained over time and domain; the success of linguistic revision given new contextual information; and the extent to which information from simulation and tests is incorporated into revised estimates.

6.4. INFORM IN THE FUTURE

The superstructure for INFORM has been implemented in C, and presently a single-display text and graph editor assesses relational information and automatically generates complex influence diagrams. We have written a linguistic calibration program; work is continuing at UC Berkeley with experiments to sample uncertainty vocabularies of graduate and undergraduate engineering students. Work is continuing with the re-implementation and development of the INFORM architecture at Schlumberger/Applicon with the Strobe/Impulse object programming and knowledge-base editing tools (Smith, Dinitz & Barth 1986; Smith, 1983).

The principal advantage of influence diagrams over decision trees is the explicit graphic representation of the interdependencies (or lack of) between events. Influence diagrams are fundamentally graphic entities; once a diagram has been created, the interface too should be organized graphically. Because we want to simultaneously represent different types of information about the model and the modeling process, a single view is inadequate. The interface under development will have static windows—for model graphics, model text, prompt window, editor/comments and "pop-up" windows—for agendas, menus, advisors, and uncertainty encoding and display. Given the need for a graphic representation, the interface should allow the diagrams to be created graphically (to be drawn on the screen), in addition to generating the graph from the user's entries of nodes and arcs.

INFORM is intended to be domain-independent; a specialization of the architecture could add to the interface the kind of checking rules that allow for domain and user dependent meta-knowledge about encoding. RACHEL (Holtzman, 1985) is one such system, a domain-dependent intelligent decision support aid for infertile couples.

Effective modeling approaches rely in part on the underlying domain and in part on the modeler's cognitive style. INFORM is a system intended to replace at least in part the expertise of the KE in directing and in giving advice to the encoder about the KE process, and in representing the encoded information. Implementation of the architecture may ultimately support active modeling and guidance of a particular expert's encoding effort. Prerequisites for such tutor include measurable or deducible standards of knowledge engineering performance and methodology for individual actors, and that these measures are conditionable on a fairly small set of inferable or directly assessable measures.

6.5. EVALUATION

We would like to test INFORM for absolute performance, as an interface and as a modeling tool, and for relative performance, against an encoding expert. The true test is application, taking an encoding problem from scratch with an acknowledged expert, and trying to build a working system in a nonlaboratory environment. The typical test of comparing system performance against that of an encoding expert is inappropriate at this point but ought to be an eventuality. At the interface level, we have used and continue to use "good design" checklists (Heckel, 1984), but that is no real assurance of a good interface without testing and experience. At this stage, while we are still developing an "integrated" system, user comments and ad hoc evaluation have been especially useful. More formal approaches to interface evaluation will be the next step.

There are further questions arising from the premises that we have based the INFORM architecture on. Are there correlations between level of skill and self-encoding ability? We would like to use INFORM in a group with measurably disparate levels of problem solving skill in a common domain. Does structured explanation support model articulation, or is this approach too much of a burden on the imagination and patience of the "typical" expert? Does having control over simulation and performance evaluation put the expert in a position where he or she is describing concepts and relations that exist near the problem-solving level, or will the expert still construct unrefinable models? These questions represent both sides of bets that we are making in this research.

A testing issue that is separable from the evaluation of the entire interface is the effectiveness and accuracy of our linguistic uncertainty encoding approach. Testing areas of interest include looking at differences in the language of uncertainty between estimates about uncertain events from inside and outside the encoding domain, consistency of judgements between subdomains, and the efficacy of different approaches to representing the encoding problem and conducting refinements.

6.6. POTENTIAL APPLICATIONS OF INFORM

When can we use a stand-alone aid such as INFORM for constructing a knowledge-based system or decision support system? We divide the spectrum of application problems down into significant and not-significant problems. Significant problems are "high stakes" problems, involving lives, or allocations of resources significant in the eyes of the sponsoring organization. For significant problems, in a novel domain, one would expect to be able to use a KA aid as a preprocessor (as in ETS) for initiating the model, but would certainly expect decision-analyst or knowledge-engineer involvement in model refinement and validation. Significant problems in a stable and well-understood context are liable to see the involvement of DA and KE, but it may not be always necessary. In both cases, the KA aid must accommodate well the involvement of DA and KE.

For problems whose solution is strongly driven by model structure, or where solution precision is not critical, INFORM is plausibly stand-alone. Other potential roles for INFORM in KE are as a "pre-processor", structuring the domain for explanation as a component of an intensive KA process; as a KA aid for supporting a novice knowledge engineer; as a personal KA tool for novel problems or where the modeling goal is oriented towards developing insight; as a domain-independent aid for non-significant problems; and as a domain-dependent aid for significant problems.

7. Conclusion

We feel knowledge-acquisition aids must support information assessment and presentation and must provide support for undergoing a sound modeling process. Fundamentally, the INFORM architecture is an aid for building models; it draws its knowledge structure and modeling approach from Decision Analysis, and its approach to handling information and heuristics about encoding from Knowledge Engineering. It is well suited for classification problem solving, especially under uncertainty. The support INFORM will provide for experts encoding is as a top down design aid, focusing on descriptions of the domain concepts and structure, rather than on examples of problem solving in the domain. Structure is edited, rather than induced. Such direct involvement of the expert in constructing an operational model of the domain we feel will aid *knowledge engineering for insight,* aiding the development of expert behavior not only on the part of the system, but on the part of the encoder as well.

This work was performed at the University of California, Berkeley, and was funded in part through grants from the National Science Foundation PYI Program, University of California's Project Micro, General Electric and IBM.

References

AGOGINO, A. M. (1985). Use of probabilistic influence in diagnostic expert systems. *Proceedings of the 1985 ASME International Computers in Mechanical Engineering,* Boston, MA, Vol. 2, pp. 305–310 (4–8 August 1985).

AGOGINO, A. M. & REGE, A. (1986). IDES: influence diagram based expert system. *Mathematical Modelling in Science and Technology Proceedings of the Fifth International Conference on Mathematical Modelling, 29–31 July 1985,* University of California, Berkeley.

ALEXANDER, J. H., FREILING, M. J., STALEY, J. L., REHFUSS, S. & MESSICK, S. L. (1986). Knowledge level engineering: ontological analysis. *Proceedings American Association for Artificial Intelligence 1986,* pp. 963–968.

BARR, A. (1985). Systems That Don't Understand. *Cognitiva: Artificial Intelligence and Neuroscience,* Paris, June 1985.

BENNETT, J. S. (1983). *ROGET: A knowledge-based consultant for acquiring the conceptual structure of an expert system,* Stanford HPP-83-24, October 1983.

BONISSONE, P. P. & TONG, R. M. (1985). Editorial: reasoning with uncertainty in expert systems. *International Journal of Man–Machine Studies,* 22, 241–250.

BONISSONE, P. P. (1985b). *Summarizing Uncertain Information With Aggregation Operators (draft),* General Electric Corporate Research and Development, New York, 11 March 1985.

BOOSE, J. H. (1984). Personal construct theory and the transfer of human expertise. *Proceedings American Association for Artificial Intelligence 1984*, pp. 27–33.

BOOSE, J. H. (1985). A knowledge acquisition program for expert systems based upon personal construct psychology. *International Journal of Man–Machine Studies*, **23**, 495–429.

BROWNSTON, L., FARRELL, R., KANT, E. & MARTIN, N. (1985). *Programming Expert Systems in OPS5*, Addison–Wesley Publishing Company.

BYLANDER, T. & MITTAL, S. (1986). CSRL: a language for classificatory problem solving and uncertainty handling. *The AI Magazine* August, 66–77.

CHEESEMAN, P. (1985). In Defense of probability. *Proceedings International Joint Conference on Artificial Intelligence 1985*.

CLANCEY, W. J. (1985). Heuristic classification. *Artificial Intelligence*, **27**, 289–350.

DREYFUS, S. E. & DREYFUS, H. L. (1980). A five stage model of the mental activities involved in directed skill acquisition. *ORC 80-2*, U. C. Berkeley Industrial Engineering and Operations Research Department, February 1980.

ESHELMAN, L. & MCDERMOTT, J. (1986). MOLE: a knowledge acquisition tool that uses its head. *Proceedings American Association for Artificial Intelligence 1986*, pp. 950–955.

FOX, M. S., LOWENFELD, S. & KLEINOSKY, P. (1983). Techniques for sensor-based diagnosis. *Proceedings International Joint Conference on Artificial Intelligence 1983*, pp. 158–163.

FREILING, M., ALEXANDER, J., MESSICK, S., REHFUSS, S. & SHULMAN, S. (1985). Starting a knowledge engineering project: a step by step approach. *The AI Magazine*, **Fall**, 150–163.

FRIEDLAND, P. (1981). Acquisition of procedural knowledge from domain experts. *Proceedings International Joint Conference on Artificial Intelligence 1981*, pp. 856–861.

GINSBERG, A., WEISS, S. & POLITAKIS, P. (1985). SEEK2: a generalized approach to automatic knowledge base refinement. *Proceedings International Joint Conference on Artificial Intelligence 1985*, pp. 367–375.

DEGREEF, P. & BREUKER, J. (1985). A case study in structured knowledge acquisition. *Proceedings International Joint Conference on Artificial Intelligence 1985*, pp. 390–392.

GROVER, M. D. (1983). A pragmatic knowledge acquisition methodology. *Proceedings International Joint Conference on Artificial Intelligence 1983*, pp. 436–438.

HAYES-ROTH, F. & WATERMAN, D. A. (1983). An overview of expert systems, Ch. 1. HAYES-ROTH, F., WATERMAN, D. A. & LENAT, D. R. *Building Expert Systems*. Addison–Wesley Publishing Company.

HECKEL, P. (1984). *The Elements of Friendly Software Design*. Warner Books.

HOLTZMAN, S. (1985). *Intelligent Decision Systems*, Ph.D. thesis, Stanford Engineering-Economic Systems, reprinted by Strategic Decisions Group, March 1985.

HOWARD, R. A. (1980). An assessment of decision analysis. *Operations Research*, **28**, 4–27.

KAHN, G., NOWLAN, S. & MCDERMOTT, J. (1985). *MORE: an intelligent knowledge acquisition tool. Proceedings International Joint Conference on Artificial Intelligence* 1985, pp. 582–584.

KAHNEMAN, D., SLOVIC, P. & TVERSKY, A. (1982). *Judgement Under Uncertainty: Heuristics and Biases*. Cambridge University Press.

KLINE, P. J. & DOLINS, S. B. (1986). Problem features that influence the design of expert systems. *Proceedings American Association for Artificial Intelligence 1986*, pp. 956–962.

LANGLOTZ, C. P., SHORTLIFFE, E. H. & FAGAN, L. M. (1986). Using decision theory to justify heuristics. *Proceedings American Association for Artificial Intelligence 1986*, pp. 215–219.

MATHESON, J. E. & HOWARD, R. H. (1977). Introduction to decision analysis. In *Readings in Decision Analysis*, Strategic Decisions Group.

MERKHOFER, M. W., ROBINSON, B. & KORSAN, R. J. (1979). A computer aided decision structuring process. *Technical Report 7320*, SRI International, Menlo Park, CA, June 1979.

MILLER, A. C., MERKHOFER, M. W., HOWARD, R. H., MATHESON, J. E. & RICE, T. (1976). *Development of Automated Aids for Decision Analysis*. SRI International, Menlo Park, CA, 1976.

MUSEN, M. A., FAGAN, L. M., COMBS, D. M., & E. H. SHORTLIFFE (1987). Using a domain model to drive an interactive knowledge editing tool. *International Journal of Man–Machine Studies*. In press.
NEWELL, A. (1982). The knowledge level. *Artificial Intelligence,* **18,** 87–127.
PEARL, J. (1985). Fusion, propagation, and structuring in Bayesian networks. *Workshop on Probability and Uncertainty in Artificial Intelligence,* UCLA, 14–16 August 1985, RCA and AAAI.
RAIFFA, H. (1970). *Decision Analysis: Introductory Lectures on Choices under Uncertainty.* Addison–Wesley Publishing Company.
REBOH, R. (1981). *Knowledge Engineering Techniques and Tools for Expert Systems. Linkoping Studies in Science and Technology No. 71,* Software Systems Research Center, Linkoping University, *S-581 83,* Linkoping, Sweden.
REGE, A. & AGOGINO, A. M. (1986a). Sensor integrated expert system for manufacturing and process diagnostics. *Proceedings of the Symposium on Knowledge-Based Systems,* ASME Winter Annual Meeting, Anaheim, CA, 7–12 December 1986.
REGE, A. & AGOGINO, A.(1986b). Representing and solving the probabilistic inference problem in expert systems. *Proceedings of the ICS-86, International Computer Symposium,* 15–19 December 1986, Tainan, Taiwan.
REGE, A. & AGOGINO, A. (1986c). Fuzzy influence diagrams. *UC Berkeley Expert Systems Lab Working Paper 06-86-01.*
SAATY, T. L. (1980). *The Analytic Hierarchy Process.* New York: McGraw–Hill.
SHACHTER, R. D. (1985). Intelligent probabilistic inference. *Workshop on Probability and Uncertainty in Artificial Intelligence,* UCLA, 14–16 August 1985, RCA and AAAI.
SMITH, R. G. (1983). Strobe: support for structured object knowledge representation. *Proceedings International Joint Conference on Artificial Intelligence 1983,* pp. 855–858.
SMITH, R. G., DINITZ, R. & BARTH, P. (1986). Impulse-86: a substrate for object-oriented interface design. *Proceedings of the ACM Conference on Object Oriented Programming Systems, Languages, and Applications.*
SPETZLER, C. S., HOLSTEIN, C.-A. & VON STAEL, S. (1977). Probability encoding in decision analysis. *Readings in Decision Analysis,* Decision Analysis Group, SRI International, Menlo Park, CA.
ZIMMER, A. C. (1985). The estimation of subjective probabilities via categorical judgements of uncertainty. *Workshop on Probability and Uncertainty in Artificial Intelligence,* UCLA, 1985, 14–16 August, RCA and AAAI.

Acquiring domain models

KATHARINA MORIK†

Technical University Berlin, Institute for Applied Computer Science, Computer-based Informations Systems, Project KIT-Lerner, Sekr. FR 5-8, Franklinstr. 28/29, D-1000 Berlin 10, West Germany

Whereas a Learning Apprentice System stresses the generation and refinement of shallow rules of a performance program, presupposing a domain theory, BLIP‡ is mainly concerned with the construction of a domain theory as the first phase of the knowledge-acquisition process. In this paper the BLIP approach to machine learning is described. The system design is presented and the already implemented knowledge sources are shown with their formalisms and functions for the learning process.

1. Introduction

Following from the growing interest in the application of expert systems, machine learning is now viewed as a means for building up and refining the knowledge base of an expert system for a particular domain and for a particular consultation class. This puts new requirements on machine learning and has led to a discontent with the former inductive-learning paradigm which can be characterized by a two-step procedure consisting of a training phase and a performance phase. In the training phase, a teacher has to present several examples, each classified as positive or negative, forming a complete set with regard to the concept to be learned. This set must be free of contradictions. The ordering of examples perhaps is important. In the worst case, all the system does is to abstract away features, thus acquiring a general concept. As far as the knowledge acquisition for an expert system is concerned, this procedure is, of course, unsatisfactory. Instead, real-world observations should be exploited as examples (Rajamoney, DeJong & Fattings, 1985). These can be a user's problem-solving activities (e.g. Brazdil, 1978; Mitchell, Mahadevan & Steinberg, 1985; Smith, Mitchell, Winston & Buchanan, 1985), visual data of objects (e.g. Phelps & Musgrove, 1986), or facts, as is the case with BLIP. No training mode should be necessary and no trainee should be in demand.

The new paradigms of machine learning, namely explanation-based learning, analytic learning, verification-based learning, deductive learning have overcome the limitations of the learning-from-example paradigm. However, there is still another constraint on these learning approaches: a complete domain theory is presupposed. Furthermore, in the case of deductive and verification-based learning, the domain theory must be such that the correctness of each rule can be shown with certainty. Thus the problem is to build up a consistent domain theory. The standard criticism

† The KIT-LERNER project is partially supported by the German Ministry for Research and Technology (BMFT) under contract ITW8501B1. Industrial partners are Nixdorf Computer AG and Stollmann GMbH.

‡ BLIP stands for 'Berlin Learning by Induction Program'.

245

of inductive learning techniques is that finding the right descriptive terms for the description language is the real learning task. This argument also applies to the new learning paradigms in a modified way: building up the domain model is the real problem. The first phase of knowledge acquisition is the hardest problem of the entire learning process (van Someren, 1986). This problem has been largely ignored in existing machine learning approaches. BLIP is an attempt to cope with this problem.

Of course, learning cannot start without any knowledge. One way out of the dilemma is to start knowledge acquisition with just two types of knowledge:

a "sloppy" domain model entered by the user;
general structures that reflect structures of human thought, rather than structures of the world (Anderson, 1975).

In knowledge-representation systems for domain modeling (e.g. KL-ONE and its derivates) a so-called knowledge engineer has to structure the domain, and define the relevant objects, their properties and relations between them. A learning program, however, should not require the user to do all this. An initial sloppy model of the domain should suffice, a well-organized model should be the result of the learning process. The learning process itself should be guided by domain-independent, general knowledge that reflects the human ability to adopt to new situations. This general knowledge can be incorporated into the system and, thus, need not be entered by the knowledge engineer.

In this paper, the system BLIP is described whose task is to aid in the construction of a domain model. The learning process is guided by meta-knowledge which can be viewed as the representation of cognitive structures that ease the knowledge acquisition process.

2. BLIP's approach to machine learning

BLIP is the learning part of an overall system called LERNER.† The performance element of the overall system is the expert system shell TWAICE.‡ BLIP requires the user to specify a sloppy domain model by:

defining predicates and the sorts of their possible arguments;
entering facts about the domain expressed with those predicates.

BLIP then discovers properties of those predicates and establishes relations between them thus structuring the domain. An example of the user's entries and the program's output is presented below. Finally, the domain model is transformed into the TWAICE-format rules (for the overall LERNER architecture see Emde & Morik, 1986). The rule part of the expert system that represents knowledge about a particular domain is then filled. Beyond the range of BLIP is the acquisition of problem solving knowledge which elsewhere has been called "domain principle" knowledge (Swartout, 1983) and which is acquired by systems like SEEK.2

---

† BLIP is implemented in MPROLOG and is fully operational under VM370 on an IBM4381. The learning algorithms are based on the METAXA.2 system (Emde, 1984).

‡ TWAICE is a registered trademark of Nixdorf Computer AG. It is in the framework of EMYCIN.

(Ginsberg & Weiss, 1985), LEAP (Mitchell *et al.* 1985) or others (cf. Steels & van de Velde, 1985).

To learn without bearing a particular consultation system in mind has several advantages. First, the learned domain model may be used more than once to construct several expert systems. Suppose BLIP has acquired a domain model of the "side-effects-of-drugs world". This knowledge may be used to build an expert system which assists a user in choosing a drug with a small number of side effects for a known complaint. But the knowledge may also be used to build an expert system for an agency which has to assess the risks of new drugs. The domain model that is necessary to solve these problems is by and large the same, but the problems differ in the domain principle knowledge that is necessary.

The same domain model may also be used to build an expert system which differs from a previously built system only in the number of questions that will be asked, e.g. because more information is available from the users. In such cases where even the domain principle knowledge is the same, the difference lies in the consultation knowledge (cf. Clancey, 1979). The term "consultation knowledge" is applied to knowledge about the goal of the consultation with an expert system (e.g. "Determine a fault in a computer system"), the knowledge about the data that have to be asked from the user, the knowledge about default assumptions that should be used if the user is not able to answer a question, and other dialog handling routines. The implications of choosing another consultation class are so important that expert systems are built from scratch even if expert systems similar with respect to domain principles and domain model already exist.

Second, as different kinds of knowledge are acquired and represented separately it is possible to explain the expert system behavior to the user with methods described by Swartout (Swartout, 1983).

Before we explain the learning process, let us have a look at the knowledge sources. First we will describe the constructions for sloppy modeling, then the meta-knowledge sources.

2.1. BLIP'S KNOWLEDGE SOURCES

Knowledge representation in BLIP is not homogeneous. Although the representation formalisms are all in the spirit of predicate logics (of higher order if meta-knowledge is involved), each knowledge source has its own format. This lack of uniformity can lead to redundant representations. However, the functionality of the knowledge sources and their efficient use was of particular importance to us.

Facts are represented declaratively as predicates with arguments, a representation that is natural to the user. We assume a sorted logic. The argument sort masks are stored in the lexicon of predicates (LEXICON). The superconcept relation can be defined for two argument sorts but need not be. Excerpts of the knowledge sources can be seen in Fig. 1.

Analogous to the sort restrictions for the arguments of a predicate there is a kind of sort restriction for the arguments of a meta-predicate, too. That is, the predicates are sorted in a tree structure and each layer of the tree is named. this tree-structure is stored in the knowledge source LAYERLEX. For an example, see a simplified diagram of the LAYERLEX for out pharmacy domain (Fig. 2).

These two knowledge sources are domain-dependent. The argument types of

RULE-SCHEMATA:
reductive (p1, s2, s):
  p1(x1, y1) => s2(x1).

opposite−1 (op1, op2, s):
  op1(x1) => not (op2(x1)).

opposite−2 (p1, r1, s):
  p1(x1, y1) => not (r1(x1, y1)).

STRUCTURE:
(**reductive** (p1, s2, s))
  lexikon (p1, sort1, sort2) &
  lexikon (s2, sort1)
  layerlex (p1, m1, n1) &
  layerlex (m1, mmn, 12) &
  layerlex (s2, x, 12)).

CHARACTERISTIC
  SITUATION:
cspos (**reductive** (p1, s2, s),
       p1(x1, y), s2(x1)).

csneg (**reductive** (p1, s2, s),
       p1(x1, y1), not (s2(x1))).

cspos (**opposite**−1(op1, op2, s),
       op1(x1) & not op2(x1).

csneg (**opposite**−1(op1, op2, s),
       op1(x1) & op2(x1)).

FACTS:
mono-substance (aspirin).

multi-substance (novalgin).

opposite−1 (mono-substance,
  multi-substance, all).

opposite−2 (opposite−1,
  inclusive−1, all).

LEXICON:
lexicon (**strengthen 2**,
  substance, symptom).

lexicon (**subsort**,
  pain, symptom).

LAYERLEX:
layerlex (**strengthen 2**,
  disadvantage, n0).

layerlex (**is-good-for**,
  recommendation, n2).

RULES:

mono-substance(x1) => not
  multi-substance(x1).

opposite−1(op1, op2, s) => not
  inclusive−1(op1, op2, s).

FIG. 1. Knowledge sources of BLIP.

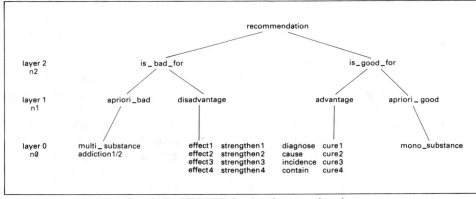

FIG. 2. LAYERLEX for the pharmacy domain.

predicates for a certain domain model are to be entered into LEXICON. The predicate layers can be declared in order to explicitly describe the effect of a certain consultation class on a domain model, here, the recommendation class as applied to the pharmacy domain. This is done filling the LAYERLEX.

For building up a sloppy model of side-effects of drugs, the knowledge engineer defines, for instance, the following predicates:

- CURE_1 ($\langle$drug$\rangle$, $\langle$illness$\rangle$)
- CURE_2 ($\langle$substance$\rangle$, $\langle$symptom$\rangle$)
- CURE_3 ($\langle$drug$\rangle$, $\langle$symptom$\rangle$)
- CURE_4 ($\langle$substance$\rangle$, $\langle$illness$\rangle$)
- CONTAIN ($\langle$drug$\rangle$, $\langle$substance$\rangle$)
- STRENGTHEN_1 ($\langle$drug$\rangle$, $\langle$illness$\rangle$)
- STRENGTHEN_2 ($\langle$substance$\rangle$, $\langle$symptom$\rangle$)
- STRENGTHEN_3 ($\langle$drug$\rangle$, symptom$\rangle$)
- MONO-SUBSTANCE ($\langle$drug$\rangle$)
- MULTI-SUBSTANCE ($\langle$drug$\rangle$)
- ADVANTAGE ($\langle$patient$\rangle$, $\langle$drug$\rangle$)
- IS_GOOD_FOR ($\langle$patient$\rangle$, $\langle$drug$\rangle$)
- DISADVANTAGE ($\langle$patient$\rangle$, $\langle$drug$\rangle$)

Further predicates can be defined by demand. The user is not forced to give the semantics of these predicates by explaining their relations. The relations which s/he might have in mind are to be made explicit by the machine. For example the following rules have been learned by BLIP:

> If a drug contains a substance, then its negative effects which are expressed by EFFECT, STRENGTHEN, DISADVANTAGE, and ADDICTION are to be inherited by the drug;
> If a drug is of advantage and not of disadvantage for a patient, then it is good for the patient;
> If a drug is a multi-substance, then it is not a mono-substance.

These rules have to be represented explicitly in a domain model. For a user, however, they are so "natural" that s/he might not want to write them down. In the BLIP framework, just after entering the predicate definitions the user can express facts. For example:

- CONTAIN (aetz, paracetamol)
- CONTAIN (aetz, ass)
- CONTAIN (aspirin, ass)
- STRENGTHEN_2 (ass, stomach-ache)
- STRENGTHEN_2 (paracetamol, kidney-trouble)
- STRENGTHEN_3 (aetz, kidney-trouble)
- STRENGTHEN_3 (aspirin, stomach-ache)

The user enters these facts just taking them from a text book on drugs. S/he needs not take care of the order of the facts or even of a clear definition of the predicates. BLIP then comes up with rules like those mentioned above. In BLIP's notation, a part of the first rule is written as follows:

CONTAIN (x, y) & STRENGTHEN_2 $(y, z) \Rightarrow$ STRENGTHEN_3 (x, z)

This rule corresponds to a meta-fact. In the next paragraph BLIP's meta-knowledge is explained.

2.2. META-KNOWLEDGE IN BLIP

Meta-knowledge plays the central role in our approach to knowledge acquisition. Meta-knowledge is used for:

 checking consistency;
 inducing rules from facts (the learning process);
 deducing rules from other rules.

Meta-predicates express relations between and attributes of predicates. Meta-meta-predicates express relations between meta-predicates. A distinction of types between meta-predicates and meta-meta-predicates is not made. A meta-predicate can be used at every meta-level. It is used to represent the relation between concepts of the level directly below.
   Example:

> fact1: MONO-SUBSTANCE (aspirin);
> fact2: MULTI-SUBSTANCE (novalgin);
> fact3: OPPOSITE_1 (mono-substance, multi-substance);
> fact4: OPPOSITE_2 (opposite_1, inclusive_1).

Fact3 is at the meta-level with respect to fact1 and fact2, it is at the object-level with respect to fact4. A meta-predicate, e.g. OPPOSITE, can be used at every meta-level; it can be a meta-predicate, a meta-meta-predicate, a meta-meta-meta-predicate, and so on.
   Meta-knowledge in BLIP does not refer to a rule format or a knowledge-representation formalism as does the meta-knowledge of AM, EURISKO, TEIRESIAS (Davis & Lenat, 1982). Nor does it refer to control knowledge or run-time behavior as described in (Hayes-Roth, Waterman & Lenat, 1983). Meta-knowledge in BLIP refers to predicate constants, describing properties or relations of certain properties or relations.
   A meta-predicate expresses a structural relation that is given by a RULE-SCHEMA. For example, the rule-schema for OPPOSITE_1 is:†

$$P(x) \Rightarrow \text{not } Q(x),$$
$$Q(x) \Rightarrow \text{not } P(x),$$

and for OPPOSITE_2:

$$P(x, y) \Rightarrow \text{not } Q(x, y);$$
$$Q(x, y) \Rightarrow \text{not } P(x, y).$$

---

† In another notation:

$$\forall P, Q, x: \text{OPPOSITE\_1}(P(x), Q(x)) \Leftrightarrow (P(x) \Rightarrow \text{not } Q(x))$$

The rule-schema for INCLUSIVE_1 is:

$$P(x) \Rightarrow Q(x).$$

The rule-schema for EQUIVALENT is:

$$P(x) \Rightarrow Q(x);$$
$$Q(x) \Rightarrow P(x).$$

It is easily seen that P or Q can be meta-predicates and that relations between meat-predicates can be expressed by meta-meta-predicates using the very same rule-schemata.

The restrictions on the applicability of meta-predicates to predicates are given by the knowledge source STRUCTURE. A meta-predicate can be applied to predicates if the argument structures of the predicates fulfill certain restrictions and the predicates are of the appropriate types. For example, the meta-predicate OPPOSITE can only be applied to two predicates of the same layer which have the same argument restrictions, because direct opposition of relations presupposes that the relations are comparable. Another function is to exclude antinomies: The distinction of types is obeyed, i.e. predicates of the first type are separated from those of higher types by the structural descriptions.

If a meta-predicate holds for a particular predicate this is represented in two ways. BLIP employs as well a procedural (inferential) representation as a declarative representation of the same information. This is, as Weyhrauch (Weyhrauch, 1980) puts it, a consequence of the procedural–declarative debate in AI. For example, the meta-fact:

W_TRANSITIVE (contain, cure_2, cure_3),

expresses in a declarative way the same information as the rule:

$$\text{CONTAIN}(x, y) \ \& \ \text{CURE\_2}(y, z) \Rightarrow \text{CURE\_3}(x, z).$$

On the one hand, a meta-fact is stored in the fact part of the inference engine. On the other hand, a rule is generated automatically for the meta-fact and stored in the rule part of the inference engine. The two representations have different functions. With the help of the rule new facts are inferred and thus the factual knowledge of the system is enhanced. For example, given:

CONTAIN (novopirin, ass), CURE_2 (ass, head-ache),

the new fact:

CURE_3 (novopirin, head-ache),

can be entered into the knowledge base. With the help of the declarative representation other meta-facts are inferred in the following way: when there is a meta-meta-fact whose corresponding representation as a rule has, e.g. W_TRANSITIVE as a premise and some other meta-predicates in its conclusion, these meta-predicates will be considered true with the argument bindings of the meta-fact concerning w_transitivity without testing. Also, negated meta-predicates as the conclusion of a meta-meta-fact are useful because the corresponding meta-facts then need not be tested.

For example:

  (i)   meta-meta-fact: OPPOSITE_2 (opposite_1, inclusive_1)
  (ii) meta-fact: OPPOSITE_1 (mono-substance, multi-substance)
 (iii) meta-fact: INCLUSIVE_1 (mono-substance, multi-substance)

Meta-fact (iii) need not be tested if (ii) is known because of the rule which corresponds to meta-fact (i):

  (i)   meta-rule: OPPOSITE_1$(p, q) \Rightarrow$ not INCLUSIVE_1(p, q)

In our example, p is MONO-SUBSTANCE and q is MULTI-SUBSTANCE. Only the declarative representation of rules enables us to deduce rules from other rules.

For entering a fact or a rule into the inference engine knowledge about representation format of the inference engine is used (FORMAT).

In order to verify whether or not a meta-predicate holds for certain predicates the criteria for the validity of a meta-fact are represented in such a way that can be used as pattern for a search process in the factual knowledge of the inference engine. These patterns are called "characteristic situations" (Emde, Habel & Rollinger, 1983). For each meta-predicate patterns for positive and negative situations are stored. The CHARACTERISTIC SITUATIONS are generated out of the rule-schemata automatically.

The main information about meta-predicates is captured by the rule-schemata and the structural descriptions. The characteristic situations could be generated at run-time as part of the testing process as well as the format knowledge could be part of the entering process of the inference engine. However,—as is well known—it is of advantage that most of the knowledge is extracted from processes, because it is then transparent (particularly in machine learning where the expert user requires control over the system's processing) and easy to change.†

There is a third knowledge source which could be realized as part of a process: the PRIORITIES of meta-predicates. there is an efficient ordering of meta-predicates to be tested for a predicate. It may be viewed as the knowledge of how to construct an "experiment" in order to prove a hypothesis. This knowledge may be coded in the hypothesis testing or—as we do—is concentrated into a knowledge source. The efficient ordering of hypotheses depends on the meta-meta-facts. The ordering itself is represented in a network-like knowledge source, which can be used for choosing the hypotheses which are to be tested next.

2.3. THE LEARNING PROCESS

The main components of the learning process are:

> the generation of hypotheses;
> the rating of hypotheses; and
> the testing of hypotheses.

The architecture of BLIP is shown in Fig. 3. The components interact via an agenda. The hypotheses are generated syntactically by taking advantage of the structural

---

† The interface for the meta-knowledge acquisition and the transducer for the automatic generation of redundant knowledge representations has been implemented by Sabine Thieme.

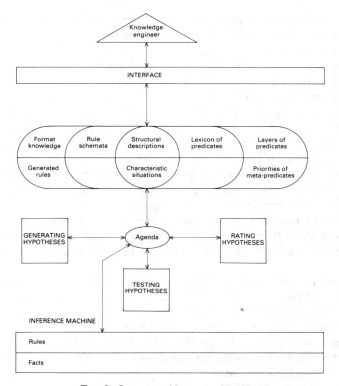

FIG. 3. System architecture of BLIP.

descriptions. For each predicate all possible meta-facts which take that predicate as an argument are constructed.

The rating component attaches a value between 0 and 1000 to each such hypothesis. There are several criteria for rating:

efficiency
the hypothesis is easy to test, or the hypothesis would exclude a lot of other hypotheses (this is the priority knowledge);
activeness
former tests of the particular hypothesis could not be accomplished with a clear result;
effectiveness
the number of stored facts which correspond to the predicate(s) for which a meta-predicate is to be tested.

Meta-facts which require no testing are immediately generated and entered into the inference engine. They always have the highest rating.

A hypothesis is tested by searching in the fact part of the inference engine for facts matching the characteristic situations of this hypothesis. The number of positive and negative examples are counted. If there are only positive examples and no negative one, and the number of positive examples exceeds a threshold, then the hypothesis is verified, the corresponding meta-fact is entered into the factual part, and the corresponding rule is generated and entered in the rule part of the inference engine. If sufficiently many negative situations found, but no positive ones, then the hypothesis is clearly falsified. If neither the number of positive nor the number of negative examples exceeds the threshold, nothing is entered into the inference engine, but the activeness of the hypothesis increases.

The difficult case is, of course, if facts support a hypothesis, but there is at least one exception. We prepared SUPPORT SETs for this case. Each meta-fact has as one argument the support set for which the meta-fact is valid. The default assumption is that the support set is ALL (see Fig. 1). But if exceptions occur, these are described and excluded from the support set. The description is given by a condition which is introduced as a supplementary premise in the corresponding rule. The condition can be very simple, e.g. the rule is not valid for a certain concept. If more is known about the exceptions the condition can become more complicated, e.g. the rule is not valid for all concepts with a certain attribute or for all concepts with a certain relation to other concepts. The exceptions are analysed searching for statements which are true for all of them. In this way new concepts can be introduced.

Meta-knowledge also assists in the manual acquisition of knowledge. Instead of typing in facts and rules for each object of the domain, meta-facts may be entered into the system. From these meta-facts rules are generated and from these facts are deduced. Checking sets of rules for consistency is a problem which is dealt with in, e.g. (Suwa, Scott & Shortliffe, 1982), (Keller & Nagel, 1981). Our approach of using declaratively represented consistency conditions saves theorem proving and allows for repairing inconsistencies easily. Consistency of meta-facts is checked with the help of meta-meta-facts. Consistency of facts is checked with the help of meta-facts.

3. Further research

The processes described above will be implemented on a SYMBOLICS 3670 in PROLOG. The main research topics will be:

improving and reorganizing the predicates and their typed arguments
developing the approach of the support sets further, so that the knowledge base can automatically be structured according to relevant subdomains
handling exceptions, noisy data, and evidence for the inappropriateness of the model built so far

If a meta-predicate cannot apply to a predicate only because of the order of the arguments, the order should be rearranged. Similarly, predicates with n arguments can be split into r predicates with m arguments ($m < n$). Of course, conflicts may occur. Criteria are then needed in order to decide which rearrangement is the most efficient.

If support sets or the exception sets become more complicated they can be used to structure the domain model. the model may be divided into sub-domains, in which certain relations hold. These sub-domains may be interrelated. If it were possible to construct a taxonomy of sub-domains, this could reflect the overall structure of the particular domain and could be used as overview knowledge. An approach in that direction has been made by Emde et al. (1983). Considering the taxonomy as the optimal "Gestalt" of a theory provides a guide as to how the sub-domains should be organized. It allows for improving even a consistent domain model (DeKleer & Brown, 1981).

Handling noisy data is another (although interrelated) topic. There are some problems with this. First, classifying facts requires a theory. But this theory is not fully known before the system has accomplished its task and no new facts are to be expected. There is no teacher who classifies the facts for the system as a "deus ex machina". Therefore, the system has to use the rules generated so far, which may be an incomplete or even false theory.

Second, improving a theory means not only to increase the amount of rules, but also to modify it. This may include the deletion of rules and those facts which have been deduced with the help of these rules (belief revision), or even the refutation of the theory and building up an alternative, more appropriate theory. Another modification of a theory is to introduce "invisible facts" by the help of which most of the rules and inferred facts can be kept but the counter-examples are also covered.

Third, building up a body of interrelated inference rules would become impossible, if each new incoming fact had the chance to change the former generated rules. The system were too busy to revise, its behavior would become oscillating.

It will be one of our prior tasks to operationalize criteria for the decision whether a fact should be rejected, a rule should be deleted with the dependent facts, or the theory should be refuted. Some ideas of how to deal with evidence for the inappropriateness of a model are presented in Emde (1986).

References

ANDERSON, B. F. (1975). *Cognitive Psychology*. Academic Press.

BRAZDIL, P. (1978). Experimental learning model. *Proceedings of AISB/GI*, Hamburg, p. 46.

CLANCEY, W. J. (1979). Tutoring rules for guiding a case method dialogue. *International Journal of Man–Machine Studies* **11**, 25–49.

DAVIS, R. & LENAT, D. B. (1982). *Knowledge-based Systems in Artificial Intelligence*. McGraw–Hill.

DEKLEER, J. & BROWN, J. S. (1981). *Mental Models of Physical Mechanisms and Their Acquisition*. In ANDERSON, J. R. Ed., *Cognitive Skills and Their Acquisition*. Lawrence Erlbaum, pp. 285–309.

EMDE, W., HABEL, CH. & ROLLINGER, C.-R. (1983). The discovery of the equator (or concept driven learning. *Proceedings of IJCAI-83*, Karlsruhe, 1983.

EMDE, W. (1984). Inkrementelles Lernen mit heuristisch generierten Modellen. *KIT-Report 22*, Technische Universität Berlin, 1984.

EMDE, W. (1986). Great flood in the blocks world (or non-cumulative learning). *Proceedings of the European Workshop Session on Learning*, Paris-Orsay, 1986.

EMDE, W. & MORIK, K. (1986). The BLIP System. *KIT-Report 32*, Technische Universität Berlin, 1986.

GINSBERG, A. & WEISS, SH. (1985). Seek2: a generalized approach to automatic knowledge base refinement. *Proceedings of IJCAI-85*, 1985, pp. 367–374.

HAYES-ROTH, F., WATERMAN, D. A. & LENAT, D. (1983). *Building Expert Systems*. Addison Wesley.

KELLER, R. M. & NAGEL, D. (1981). Some experiments in abstraction of relational characteristics. *Technical Report DCS-TM-15*, Rutgers University, May 1981.

MITCHELL, T. M., MAHADEVAN, S. & STEINBERG, L. I. (1985). LEAP: a learning apprentice for VLSI design. *Proceedings of IJCAI-85*, 1985.

PHELPS, B. & MUSGROVE, P. (1986). Representation and clustering in conceptual learning. *Proceedings of the European Workshop Session on Learning,* Paris-Orsay, 1986.

RAJAMONEY, S., DEJONG, G. & FALTINGS, B. (1985). Towards a model of conceptual knowledge acquisition through directed experimentation. *Proceedings of IJCAI-85,* 1985, pp. 688–690.

SMITH, R. G., MITCHELL, R. M., WINSTON, H. A. & BUCHANAN, B. G. (1985). Representation and use of explicit justification for knowledge refinement. *Proceedings of IJCAI-85,* 1985, pp. 673–680.

STEELS, L. & VAN DE VELDE, W. (1985). Learning in second generation expert systems. In KOWALIK, J. S. Ed., *Knowledge-based Problem Solving.* New Jersey: Prentice–Hall Inc.

SUWA, M., SCOTT, A. C. & SHORTLIFFE, E. H. (1982). An approach to verifying completeness and consistency in a rule-based expert-system. *Report No. STAN-CS-82-922,* Stanford, California: Stanford University.

SWARTOUT, W. R. (1983). XPLAIN: a system for creating and explaining expert consulting programs. *Artificial Intelligence* **21,** 285–325.

VAN SOMEREN, M. W. (1986). Constructive induction rules: reducing the description space for rule learning. *Proceedings of the European Workshop Session on Learning,* Paris-Orsay, 1986.

WEYHRAUCH, R. W. (1980). Prolegomena to a theory of mechanized formal reasoning *Artificial Intelligence* **13,** 133.

Use of a domain model to drive an interactive knowledge-editing tool

MARK A. MUSEN, LAWRENCE M. FAGAN, DAVID M. COMBS AND EDWARD H. SHORTLIFFE

Medical Computer Science Group, Knowledge Systems Laboratory, Departments of Medicine and Computer Science, Stanford University School of Medicine, Stanford, California 94305–5479, U.S.A.

The manner in which a knowledge-acquisition tool displays the contents of a knowledge base affects the way users interact with the system. Previous tools have incorporated semantics that allow knowledge to be edited in terms of either the structural representation of the knowledge or the problem-solving method in which that knowledge is ultimately used. A more effective paradigm may be to use the semantics of the application domain itself to govern access to an expert system's knowledge base. This approach has been explored in a program called OPAL, which allows medical specialists working alone to enter and review cancer treatment plans for use by an expert system called ONCOCIN. Knowledge-acquisition tools based on strong domain models should be useful in application areas whose structure is well understood and for which there is a need for repetitive knowledge entry.

1. Introduction

Knowledge acquisition for expert systems can be a laborious process because of difficulties in communication between the knowledge engineers who build the systems and the domain experts whose knowledge is to be represented in the computer. Knowledge engineers typically lack the background needed to pose optimal questions about a particular application area. At the same time, domain experts may find it hard to introspect on their problem-solving strategy and often have little appreciation for how knowledge engineers formalize expertise as a knowledge base. While the use of protocol analysis and structured interviewing techniques (de Greef & Breuker, 1985) has begun to define an established methodology for knowledge engineering, many cycles of potentially unnecessary programming, system evaluation, and reprogramming still occur simply because of miscommunication (Buchanan *et al.*, 1983). It has long been recognized that the development of new expert systems might be greatly expedited if experts could somehow enter their knowledge directly into computers without relying on knowledge engineers as intermediaries (Davis, 1976).

Although domain experts should not be expected to become programmers or to learn knowledge representation techniques, it is still desirable to reduce their dependence on knowledge engineers during construction of expert systems. One approach is to provide the experts with some type of *knowledge editor* to aid in updating and reviewing the contents of the knowledge base. To varying degrees, such computer-based tools attempt to hide the technicalities of encoding knowledge

257

KNOWLEDGE-BASED SYSTEMS Vol. 2
ISBN 0-12-115920-5

from the user, permitting information to be entered in more familiar terms. The more the user can be insulated from the implementation details of representing knowledge, the easier it is to view the knowledge intuitively and abstractly. Knowledge editing programs consequently attempt to transform an expert's knowledge from some higher level, external representation entered into the editor to the internal format required by the target expert system.

Every computer program is written with particular semantic assumptions about the data on which it operates. These assumptions, which are reflected in the way users interact with the program, form a *conceptual model* of the data (Brodie, Mylopoulos & Schmidt 1984). For example, simple text editors generally employ a conceptual model in which the data represent characters in a document; such editors accept commands whose semantics relate to modifying characters or lines of text. Spreadsheet programs, on the other hand, conceptualize their data as rows and columns of interdependent numbers. However, a knowledge editor such as Davis' (1976) program TEIRESIAS must assume a different sort of model. The data on which TEIRESIAS operates represent rules in the knowledge base of an expert system. Interaction with TEIRESIAS involves identifying erroneous or missing rules and making necessary corrections. Although all of the rules in the knowledge base collectively define a problem-solving strategy, TEIRESIAS does not address the knowledge from that perspective; the system is designed to focus on the individual rules in a single chain of reasoning.

OPAL, the knowledge editor for a cancer-therapy management system known as ONCOCIN (Shortliffe, Scott, Bischoff, van Melle & Jacobs, 1981), is based on a more abstract kind of conceptual model—that of the structure of the domain itself. We refer to this structural characterization of the application area as a *domain model*. In OPAL, a domain model for cancer therapy gives the program the ability to solicit and display knowledge of cancer treatment plans using graphical "forms" and other visual representations that correspond to the way expert physicians seem to think about oncology treatments (Musen, Combs, Walton, Shortliffe & Fagan, 1986*a*). An example of an OPAL "form" is shown in Fig. 1. Knowledge specified graphically using OPAL is first stored internally in an intermediate representation and then automatically converted to a format used by ONCOCIN to provide clinical consultations. OPAL's use of a detailed model of the domain minimizes dependence on knowledge engineers by allowing entry of new treatment plans directly by physicians.

Constructing an expert system requires identification and conceptualization of a task—a problem to be solved in some application domain. To perform the task requires application of a method—a problem-solving strategy appropriate for the task. Whereas many tools for knowledge acquisition have been built concentrating on problem-solving methods which might be applied to new tasks, our orientation has been to focus first on the task domain. This paper examines the use of a domain model as the foundation for an interactive knowledge-acquisition tool with which expertise can be entered independent of the representation required by the target expert system. We show that a domain model which includes strong assumptions about the application area can greatly facilitate the knowledge engineering process. Because we base our discussion on our experience with OPAL, it is first necessary to describe ONCOCIN and its area of application.

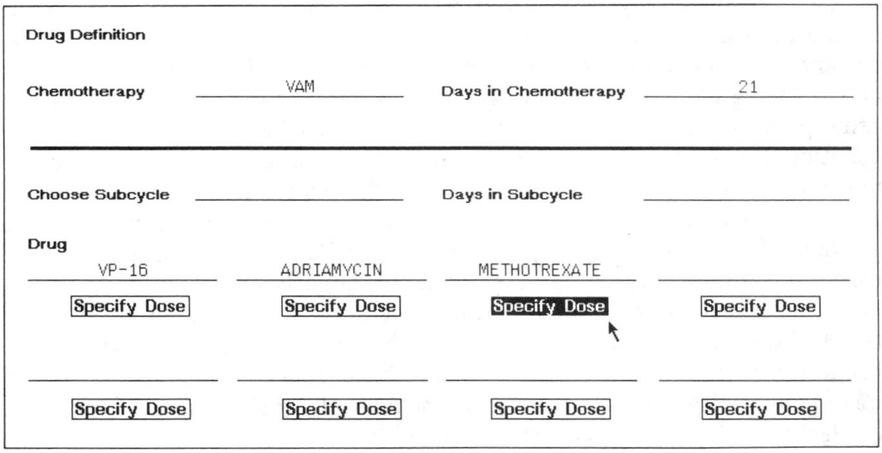

FIG. 1. Sample OPAL "Form". This table, which has been reproduced directly from the computer screen, displays information concerning the drug combination "VAM", consisting of VP-16, Adriamycin, and methotrexate. For each specified drug, OPAL creates a separate object in the intermediate representation of the ONCOCIN knowledge base. These drug objects are linked to the object for VAM chemotherapy, thus defining their "context".

2. The performance element: ONCOCIN

Therapy for most cancers is constantly being refined on the basis of medical experiments. In academic medical centers, patients are often enrolled in clinical trials that study the efficacy of alternative treatment plans for given types of cancer. The written descriptions of these complex treatments, called *protocols,* contain detailed specifications for how patients with particular tumors should be managed by their physicians. Protocols dictate combinations of drugs (called *chemotherapies*) that are given in a specific order over time. Required laboratory tests and radiation treatments (if any) are also specified. The complexity of oncology protocols can make it difficult for physicians to remember precisely what treatments may be required whenever standard therapy must be modified either because of continued growth of a patient's tumor or because of the presence of serious side-effects. The written protocol descriptions may also contain areas of vagueness or ambiguity that may be difficult for practitioners to resolve (Musen, Rohn, Fagan & Shortliffe, 1986*b*). As a result, the need for precision in carrying out these clinical experiments and the difficulties inherent in administering intricate treatment make cancer therapy an excellent domain for the application of expert systems technology.

ONCOCIN uses a knowledge base of cancer protocols to make therapy recommendations. Physicians enter required data into the system each time a patient is seen in the clinic. ONCOCIN then uses its knowledge of the protocol in which the patient is enrolled to suggest appropriate treatment given the clinical information supplied. If physicians should disagree with the program's suggested therapy, they are free to modify ONCOCIN's recommendation.

ONCOCIN's task may be viewed as a problem in skeletal plan refinement (Friedland & Iwasaki, 1985). The program identifies the appropriate protocol for a patient and constructs a treatment plan by selecting and instantiating plan elements at successively greater levels of detail. For example, ONCOCIN might determine that the plan for a particular patient visit should be initiation of a new drug combination (chemotherapy). The general plan to begin a chemotherapy is then refined into separate plans for giving each of the component drugs. Next, the dose and route of administration (e.g. intravenous or oral) for each drug must be determined. The problem-solving method in ONCOCIN is consequently one of successive instantiation of component skeletal plans. Because the component plans tend not to interact, there is, in general, no need for backtracking.

The ONCOCIN knowledge base is encoded heterogeneously using three basic representations. First, a hierarchy of *frames* encoded using an object-oriented language (Lane, 1986) defines the various structural entities for each protocol in the knowledge base (Fig. 2). Each treatment plan has a unique *protocol* object that identifies other objects representing the constituent radiation treatments and chemotherapies. The *chemotherapy* objects in turn specify objects that describe the component drugs.

Production rules, the second form of knowledge representation in ONCOCIN, are linked to each object in the planning hierarchy. The rules are invoked during skeletal plan refinement to conclude the values of special variables called *parameters,* establishing such concepts as the health of the patient, interpretations for various laboratory tests, and required adjustments of drug dosages (Shortliffe *et al.,* 1981). Associating rules with specific objects representing the components of the planning task explicitly defines the context within which each rule is applicable, enhancing the efficiency of the consultation system. For example, the rules linked to

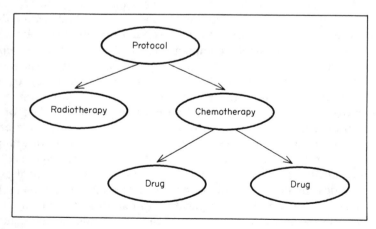

FIG. 2. Hierarchy of Objects in ONCOCIN. Both the ONCOCIN knowledge base and the intermediate knowledge representation used by OPAL maintain a hierarchy of objects that reflects the components of each protocol's treatment plan. A protocol is comprised of specific radiation treatments and chemotherapies. The chemotherapies are made up of various drugs. In the knowledge base used by ONCOCIN, production rules are linked to each object. The consultation is conducted by traversing the object hierarchy and invoking appropriate rules.

an object representing a particular chemotherapy conclude the values of parameters related just to that combination of drugs.

The third form of knowledge representation encodes the sequences of chemotherapies and radiotherapies to administer to the patient over time. This procedure-oriented knowledge is represented in finite state tables—lists of potential states in the treatment plan and the conditional transitions that define how one state may be followed by others. Each stage of therapy is represented by a state in the table that marks the particular situation. A finite state table and the name of an ONCOCIN parameter whose value keeps track of the table's patient-specific state is stored in a special object called a *generator* (Musen, Fagan & Shortliffe, 1986c).

Defining knowledge of a new protocol for ONCOCIN therefore requires: (1) creating an object hierarchy describing the component elements; (2) linking appropriate production rules (and the parameters they conclude) to the various objects; and (3) specifying the temporal sequence of chemotherapies and radiation treatments in terms of a finite-state table. Each of these representational issues is handled transparently by OPAL and subsequently will be discussed in more detail. Because OPAL uses a detailed model of the domain of cancer therapy as its conceptual model for the knowledge in ONCOCIN, users can think about protocol knowledge independently of how that knowledge is ultimately encoded in the expert system.

3. Knowledge-level analysis

Analysis of a domain at the "knowledge level", regardless of whatever notations might be used to *encode* such knowledge, has been suggested as an important first step in the development of expert systems (Newell, 1982). Once the intended actions, goals, and vocabulary of the application are understood, a system of symbols can then be used to represent the knowledge. The particular choice of symbols is in some ways arbitrary.

This view of knowledge as a set of specific goals and behaviors needed to achieve those goals bears directly on the domain model in OPAL. OPAL's model, derived from a "knowledge-level analysis" of therapy planning in oncology, is applied as a template for instantiating the concepts present in particular cancer protocols. Knowledge of the goals and behaviors that can be anticipated from protocol to protocol guides all of the program's interactions with its users. Thus, the domain model in OPAL represents a type of knowledge-level description of the application area in machine-usable form.

It should be emphasized that in practice there is little consensus on how one should go about describing tasks at the knowledge level. Newell (1982) and Nilsson (1981) advocate the use of predicate logic. Clancey (1985) is less emphatic about the particular notations one should choose, and instead stresses modeling the application task in terms of an abstract problem-solving method. For example, Clancey's model for the method of *heuristic classification* provides a precise set of terms and relations by which knowledge can be characterized. He argues that knowledge-level analysis for classification tasks can accordingly be viewed as a matter of identifying: (1) the particular elements in the application area from which the solution is selected; (2) data that bear on the selection process; (3) the kinds of abstraction hierarchies in the domain; and (4) heuristics that can link one abstraction hierarchy to another. By defining a heuristic classification task in terms of this model, complete specification of a reasoning system's behavior can be achieved, independent of any particular implementation. However, few problem-solving methods are as well formalized as the method of heuristic classification. Many applications will consequently have to await development of more complete models for their problem-solving behavior before this form of method-oriented, knowledge-level analysis can be applied.

Viewing knowledge-level analysis from a different perspective, one knowledge engineering group has de-emphasized models of problem solving and focussed more on the intrinsic structure of domain tasks. Using a methodology called *ontological analysis,* Alexander, Freiling, Shulman, Staley, Rehfuss & Messick (1986) choose to describe systems at the knowledge level in terms of the entities, relations, and transformations between entities that occur while performing a given task. Ontological analysis involves describing the structure of domain knowledge within three broad categories: (1) *the static ontology,* consisting of the physical objects, attributes, and relationships in the domain; (2) *the dynamic ontology,* defining the states that may occur as a result of problem solving and possible transformations from one state to another; and (3) the epistemic ontology, the knowledge that bears on the state transformations within the dynamic ontology. Although ontological analysis assumes that a task can be viewed at some level as a search problem, the structures generated by the technique are derived by asking the knowledge engineer to focus primarily on the application domain, not the method of search. As a result, an inference strategy for the reasoning system does not accrue explicitly from the analysis. Alexander *et al.* believe the technique's greatest strength lies in its ability to conceptualize knowledge engineering problems at meaningful levels of abstraction.

Like ontological analysis, knowledge-level modeling in OPAL has concentrated on the task (therapy planning for cancer patients), rather than on the problem-solving method (skeletal plan refinement). Analogous notions of static, dynamic and epistemic knowledge components are present in OPAL. However, OPAL is designed to convert a user's task description into a representation that can actually be interpreted by an expert system. An ontological analysis alone would be insufficient for this purpose because the technique is unable to specify how the actions in the dynamic ontology might be performed. OPAL's model of the domain therefore includes additional specifications to permit the mapping of a task description onto ONCOCIN's particular inference mechanism. Unlike an ontological analysis, the OPAL model makes assumptions about the methods by which task-level actions take place.

4. The domain model in OPAL

Although at the knowledge level there is a single, unified model for cancer therapy, OPAL *encodes* the domain model using two different, isomorphic representations (Fig. 3). First, OPAL stores entered protocol knowledge in an intermediate representation that can later be translated into a knowledge base for ONCOCIN. The specification of the object-based format for this intermediate representation is

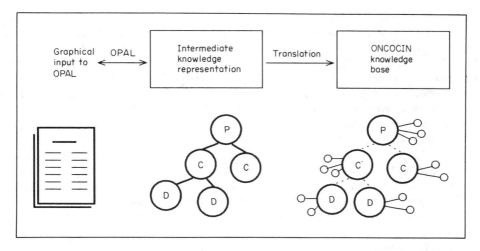

FIG. 3. Transfer of knowledge from OPAL to ONCOCIN. Knowledge specified graphically using OPAL is transferred to an *intermediate knowledge representation*. The intermediate representation is a hierarchy of frames encoded in an object-oriented language, with specific objects for the protocol ("P"), chemotherapy ("C"), drug ("D"), and radiotherapy constituents of a cancer-treatment plan. Once a treatment plan has been entered using OPAL, the program translates the intermediate representation into the format used by ONCOCIN, merging the knowledge with that of existing protocols in the ONCOCIN knowledge base. Like the intermediate representation, the knowledge base is organized as a hierarchy of objects. The translation process generates executable production rules, stored in association with the objects whose properties they conclude.

one embodiment of the domain model. The second incarnation of the same model is reflected in OPAL's graphical user interface.

The two parallel representations of the domain model are necessary for logistical reasons. Because OPAL displays knowledge for the user in terms of two-dimensional, bit-mapped images, protocol descriptions within the OPAL interface must be stored as graphical structures that cannot be transformed directly into knowledge bases for ONCOCIN in a convenient fashion. At the same time, transmuting ONCOCIN production rules, which are "symbol-level" entities (Newell, 1982), back into their knowledge-level assertions for presentation to the user is also computationally cumbersome. Thus, the intermediate knowledge representation serves as a useful buffer between the OPAL interface and the target expert system.†

We now consider OPAL's domain model in terms of its knowledge-level components and physical implementations. Although we have not attempted to apply formal ontological analysis in any rigorous fashion, we can describe the domain model in OPAL with respect to the ontologies proposed by Alexander *et al.* (1986) as a consequence of our similar, task-oriented approaches.

---

† One could, of course, use the intermediate representation *directly* as the knowledge base for a consultation program. Such an approach would require a highly specialized, *task-specific* inference mechanism (as in Gale, in press), rather than the more general skeletal planning method now used in ONCOCIN.

4.1. ENTITIES AND RELATIONSHIPS

The first component of the domain model consists of an identification of the entities in the application area and the relationships among them (the *static ontology*). In the ONCOCIN domain, the "entities" are the therapeutic elements that make up the planning problem (Fig. 2). The "relationships" are defined in part by the composition hierarchy that specifies how each plan (e.g. treatment according to a particular protocol) may be defined in terms of more specific plans (e.g. administration of various chemotherapies). The model also defines attributes of individual entities (e.g. that drugs have *dosages* and *routes of administration*).

At the implementation level, the intermediate knowledge representation for a cancer treatment plan is based on a hierarchy of objects describing the necessary *protocol, chemotherapy, radiotherapy* and *drug* entities, with appropriate links to establish the compositional relationships. OPAL creates new objects in this hierarchy and stores and retrieves the values of slots that define attributes of each instance.

The same entity-relationship model is implicit in the OPAL user interface. For example, the OPAL form in Fig. 1 allows the user to specify the names of the individual drugs that make up a particular chemotherapy. The program presumes that chemotherapies and drugs are entities in the domain and that they are related compositionally. When a user interacts with OPAL, the names of the drugs are entered into the blanks of the graphical form by selecting appropriate choices from a predefined menu. (If a required drug does not appear in the list, the drug name can be typed in from the keyboard).

Whenever a blank requesting a drug name is filled in, knowledge stored in the definition of the graphical form causes OPAL to create a new drug object in the intermediate representation and link it to the object for the related chemotherapy. Additional forms in OPAL contain blanks that can define values for the slots in the generated objects. For instance, selecting the box labeled *specify dose* beneath one of the drug names in Fig. 1 causes another form to be displayed in which certain properties of the designated drug can be entered (Fig. 4). By noting the pathway used to access the form in Fig. 4 (i.e. which box in Fig. 1 was selected), OPAL can store the knowledge specified via the second form in the appropriate drug object. Thus, the user's path through the various forms in the system determines the particular entities to which entered knowledge is related at each step. Furthermore, whenever knowledge is specified graphically using the OPAL forms (one embodiment of the domain model), it is simultaneously translated internally to the intermediate representation, whose structure denotes the same model in a different conformation.

4.2. DOMAIN ACTIONS

Much of ONCOCIN's skeletal planning task is predefined by the hierarchical relationships among entities in the domain (Fig. 2). Initiating a plan to begin a new chemotherapy, for example, tacitly requires invoking plans to administer the component drugs. Because the planning hierarchy is built into OPAL's model of the domain, such actions do not have to be specified explicitly when new protocol knowledge is entered. These refinement operations are assumed constant from protocol to protocol.

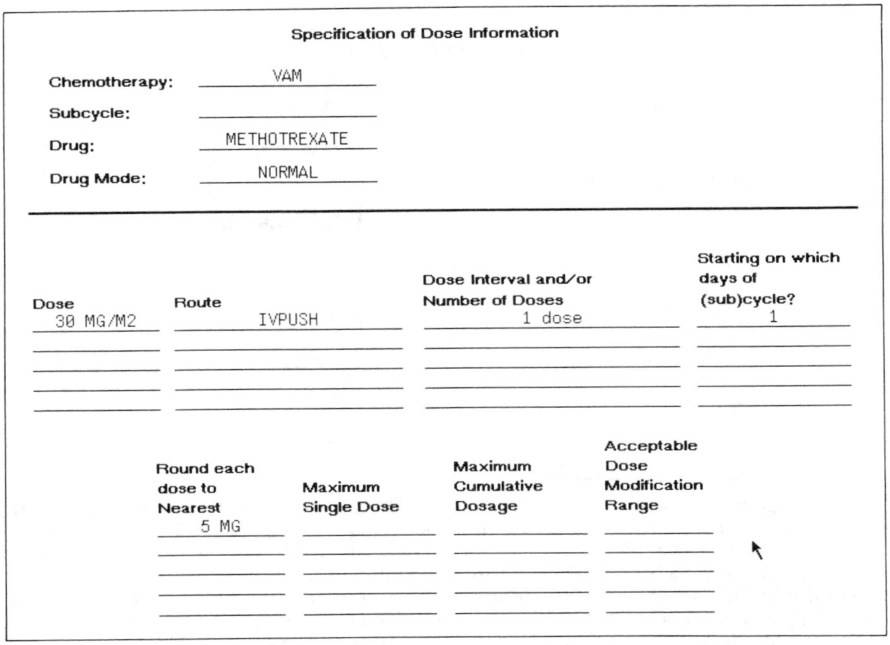

FIG. 4. Attributes of the "Drug" entity. This form was invoked from the one shown in Fig. 1 by selecting the region labeled *Specify Dose* beneath the blank for the drug methotrexate. The blanks in this figure allow physicians to enter knowledge about the administration of a drug in the context of a particular chemotherapy, in this case a drug combination called "VAM".

On the other hand, there are several ways in which the simple instantiation of the skeletal plans defined by the domain entities may be modified. Fortunately, the list of these possible actions is small. At the knowledge level, we must deal with such behaviors as altering the customary dose of a drug, substituting one drug for another, or aborting or delaying chemotherapy. Alexander *et al.* (1986) would classify these concepts as part of the *dynamic ontology* of the domain.

OPAL's semantic assumptions about the knowledge in ONCOCIN form a conceptual model that is derived directly from the domain model. Accordingly, the knowledge-level actions that form the dynamic ontology can be selected directly from menus when physicians enter descriptions of new protocols (Fig. 5). The subsequent translation of the intermediate knowledge representation into the knowledge base used by ONCOCIN requires conversion of the knowledge-level specifications from OPAL into expressions that operate on internal ONCOCIN parameters. For example, when a physician uses OPAL to specify that chemotherapy should be delayed in a particular clinical context, the corresponding "DELAY" entry in the intermediate knowledge representation causes a number of ONCOCIN production rules to be created in generating the final knowledge base. The right-hand sides of these rules evaluate LISP expressions to conclude values for arcane ONCOCIN parameters such as VISIT.TYPE, VISIT.NEXT.DAYS, and DRUGS.TO.GIVE. The user of OPAL, however, needs only to be concerned with actions at the knowledge level.

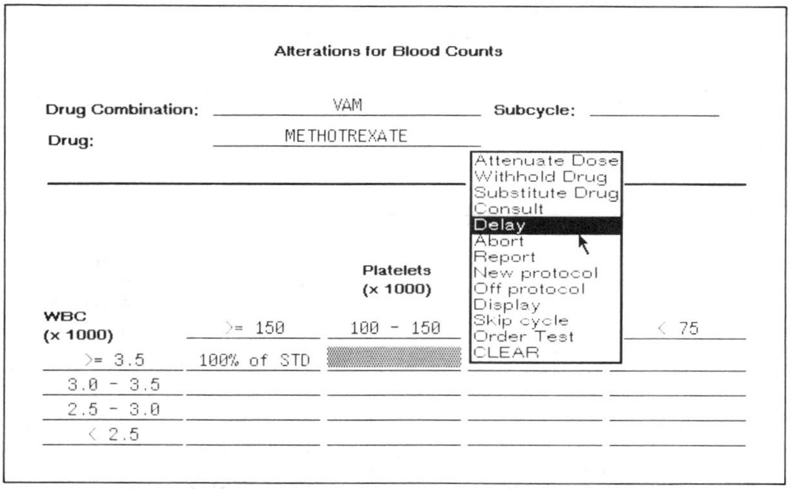

FIG. 5. Knowledge-level actions in OPAL. Operations that modify the plan of the protocol are specified in OPAL by selecting knowledge-level actions from menus, such as the one toward the right hand side of the figure. These knowledge-level actions are translated into expressions involving ONCOCIN parameters when the knowledge base is generated from the intermediate representation. The OPAL "form" shown here displays actions to take with the drug methotrexate in a chemotherapy called "VAM". The user is specifying that when a patient's white-blood-cell count (WBC) is greater than or equal to 3500 and the platelet count is between 100 000 and 150 000, treatment should be delayed.

4.3. DOMAIN PREDICATES

Just as there is a limited set of actions at the knowledge level, there are limited classes of *conditions* that can cause modification of the basic treatment plan. The results of laboratory tests, certain patient symptoms, and manifestations of treatment-induced toxicity are the principal factors that can dictate particular actions in OPAL's domain.

Much of the knowledge needed to specify ONCOCIN's planning task consists of a mapping of specific conditions onto corresponding domain actions. This is part of the *epistemic ontology* of Alexander *et al.* (1986). OPAL simplifies entry of this portion of the knowledge by using a different graphical form for each class of conditions. For example, in Fig. 6, OPAL displays a predefined list of all the relevant laboratory tests known to the system. When one of the laboratory tests is selected by the user, "rules" predicated on the results of the test can be entered. In Fig. 6, the expert has indicated that when a patient's serum creatine is greater than 1·5, the drug methotrexate should be withheld from "VAM" chemotherapy. The values entered by the physician using OPAL correspond to a high level production rule: **If** creatinine is greater than 1·5 **then** omit the drug. The rule is applicable only within a specific context—in this case, when giving a particular drug (methotrexate) in a particular chemotherapy ("VAM") in a particular protocol. As in the specification of the static attributes of domain entities (Figs 1, 4), the context of the knowledge is determined from the manner in which the user invoked the form.

OPAL must translate predicates that are based on knowledge-level concepts such as laboratory tests into expressions that evaluate parameters internal to the

```
                            Alterations for Lab Tests
TEST:
  Hematology              ————————Chemistries————————      Miscellaneous
  CBC and PLTs        Alkaline Phosphatase                  DLCO
  CBC and PLT w/dif.  Bilirubin                             ECG
  Granulocytes        BUN                                   Pulm. Function
  Hematocrit          Creatinine Clearance
  Hemoglobin          Serum Creatinine
  Platelets           SGOT
  PT                  SGPT

          Selected Test:       Serum Creatinine.


Test Alterations for Chemotherapy: _____VAM_____   Subcycle: _____

Value              Action                Value              Action
_____   _____      _____   _____
_____   _____      _____   _____
_____   _____      _____   _____


Test Alterations for Drug: ____METHOTREXATE____  (You must select a chemotherapy first)

Value              Action                Value              Action
____> 1.5_____   ___Withhold_____     _____   _____
_____   _____      _____   _____
_____   _____      _____   _____
```

FIG. 6. Knowledge-level rules in OPAL. The blanks in this form allow the expert to specify how the results of laboratory tests should cause modification of the protocol. The knowledge entered is ultimately converted to production rules that can be invoked by the ONCOCIN inference engine. In this example, the user has specified that when the patient's serum creatinine is greater than 1·5, the drug methotrexate should be withheld from "VAM" chemotherapy.

ONCOCIN knowledge base. The resultant expressions form the left-hand sides of production rules used by ONCOCIN.

4.4. PROCEDURAL KNOWLEDGE

Another part of the epistemic ontology is the recognition that elements of the treatment plan are not static, but rather vary over time according to predefined specifications. For example, some protocols call for one or more chemotherapies to be administered a fixed number of times during the course of treatment; other protocols give sequences of drugs until the tumor is controlled or severe side-effects occur. The potential complexity of these treatment algorithms has required us to equip OPAL with a comprehensive visual programming language that can be used to describe the general procedure associated with each protocol (Musen et al., 1986c).

A graphical environment permits the user to create special icons that represent the various procedural elements of oncology treatment plans (Fig. 7). By positioning these icons appropriately on the computer display and drawing connections between them, physicians can create diagrams that mimic the flowcharts typically found in

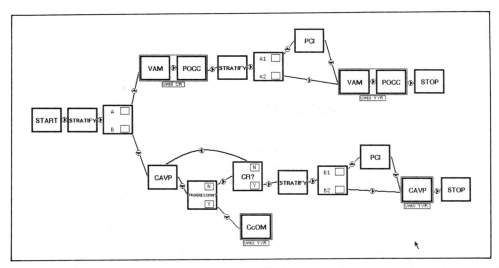

FIG. 7. Procedural knowledge in OPAL. This is a modified version of the sequence of steps in a protocol for lung cancer entered into OPAL. Patients are randomly assigned to either Arm *A,* which tests the chemotherapies "VAM" and "POCC", or Arm *B,* which tests the chemotherapy "CAVP". Patients who respond to either treatment arm may be randomly assigned to receive "PCI" radiation treatments. The visual flowchart in OPAL is coverted to a finite state table (*generator*) for use by ONCOCIN.

printed protocol descriptions. Concepts associated with traditional programming languages such as sequential control, conditionality, iteration, exception handling, and concurrency can all be specified using a graphical syntax.

OPAL converts the visual program created in this environment into one or more finite state tables (*generators*) that are stored as part of the intermediate knowledge representation. The same generators are ultimately incorporated in the ONCOCIN knowledge base, where they serve as a declarative representation for procedural protocol specifications.

5. Discussion

Now that tools for knowledge engineers to build expert systems are readily available commercially, increasing attention is being placed on the problems of creating and maintaining large knowledge bases. In the case of the prototype version of ONCOCIN, developed before work began on OPAL, difficulties in knowledge acquisition were particularly apparent; encoding the systems's protocols for lymph node cancer required two years of effort and some 800 h of an oncology expert's time. The addition of three protocols for breast cancer chemotherapy took several more months, most of which involved the usual cycles of programming by knowledge engineers and system testing by domain experts.

A principal goal of our current work is to solve the practical problem of expediting knowledge acquisition for ONCOCIN by reducing dependence on knowledge engineers as intermediaries. In OPAL, we have attempted to ease the interchange between experts and the computer by providing a visual model of oncology knowledge that is familiar to physicians. The model incorporates sufficient assumptions about the domain that clinicians can describe new protocols by means of a simple "fill in the blanks" approach. As a result, some three dozen oncology protocols have been entered using OPAL during the past year; complete specification of new protocols can generally be performed in a matter of a few days.†

Other workers have emphasized the usefulness of visual representations in facilitating knowledge entry by experts. ETS (Boose, 1985), for example, allows construction of knowledge bases for certain classification tasks. Once a prototype knowledge base has been specified by means of a textual dialog, ETS displays a directed graph that allows the user to visualize how classifying particular entities in the application area may entail additional classifications. A program called ESSA (Hannan & Politakis, 1985), on the other hand, allows users themselves to define classification hierarchies graphically. The actual knowledge, however, must be specified as production rules in the EXPERT language, thus requiring that the user be familiar with a particular expert-system "shell". Neither ETS nor ESSA uses graphics for specification or display of knowledge-level concepts.

Knowledge entry tools such as INKA (Phillips, Messick, Freiling & Alexander, 1985) come closer to using visual representations in the manner adopted by OPAL. INKA permits experts to employ a structured subset of natural language to define PROLOG rules for diagnosis of faults in electronic circuits. The program displays a schematic diagram of the circuit under discussion, specified in advance by a knowledge engineer. Experts simply point to components in the diagram when composing new rules, causing descriptions of the indicated circuit elements to be incorporated within the entered text. INKA relies on this graphical display of domain objects to acquire part of the knowledge from experts. The program also incorporates concepts such as "transistor" and "voltage" into its structured rule language. INKA thus adopts a strong domain model that facilitates knowledge entry. However, the domain model in INKA is *not* reflected in the program's conceptual model of the knowledge base. The conceptual model is one in which the knowledge is viewed as a collection of isolated "rules"; there is no framework that can help the domain expert recognize what knowledge is *expected* by the system. As a result, INKA itself cannot inform the expert if any rules are missing or whether a new rule interacts with previously entered statements.

Because the conceptual model in OPAL directly reflects the domain model, physicians learn immediately that defining protocol knowledge for ONCOCIN is simply a matter of filling out all the OPAL "forms". Once a particular fact has been entered into OPAL, the appropriate blanks remain filled in unless the knowledge is later retracted by the expert; previously entered knowledge can therefore be perused easily at any time. Because entering new knowledge into a blank always overwrites prior specifications, certain classes of contradictions in the knowledge base can be avoided. At the same time, portions of the knowledge can be recognized as missing if particular blanks are not filled in.

In general, previous knowledge editors have been based on either of two types of conceptual models. The first and most common approach has been to provide a

---

† Knowledge entered using OPAL is validated by observing ONCOCIN's performance on test cases before the knowledge is incorporated into the version of ONCOCIN used by physicians in the clinic. Validation and refinement of new protocols may require several additional days of effort.

model of *the knowledge representation itself*. Typical expert-system building shells such as EMYCIN and more specialized tools such as INKA have adopted this type of conceptual model. TEIRESIAS (Davis, 1976), for example, allowed its users to examine and modify faulty knowledge in the MYCIN system. TEIRESIAS was a landmark program in that it demonstrated that inferring a domain model from an existing knowledge base could be used to assure the syntactic and semantic integrity of new knowledge entered by an expert. However, the conceptual model of the MYCIN knowledge base presented by TEIRESIS to its users—that of a collection of rules—was the same model adopted by the consultation program. Although the system took great pains to attempt translation between natural language and LISP code, if experts could not convey their thoughts in terms of MYCIN-style rules, it was impossible to interact with TEIRESIAS.

The second, more abstract approach has been to conceptualize knowledge in terms of a *problem-solving method*. ROGET (Bennett, 1985), for example, acquires knowledge for EMYCIN-based systems using a model akin to heuristic classification (Clancey, 1985). By asking the user what hypotheses are to be considered and what kinds of evidence can support or refute those hypotheses, the EMYCIN rule-base for a new expert system can be produced from what is essentially a knowledge-level analysis of the domain. In a similar fashion, ETS (Boose, 1985) can generate prototype knowledge bases using a weaker model of classification based on "personal construct theory", a system used by psychologists for evaluating how people categorize elements in their environment. Because ETS and ROGET are derived from such general strategic models, the systems are most useful in eliciting the basic framework for a knowledge base; neither is intended to generate production-version expert systems.

A system called SALT (Marcus, McDermott & Wang, 1985) models a different problem-solving method, one for *constructing solutions*. The program has actually been used by engineering experts to specify knowledge for configuring elevators in new buildings. SALT requires a structured language for entry of specific concepts such as methods for determining values, constraints on values, and corrections for constraint violations. The system then generates rules in OPS5. Like ROGET, SALT assumes that the user will be able to conceptualize the solution to the problem in terms of the model provided by the system. Although it may be easier for non-programmers to think in terms of *strategies* rather than individual *rules*, the approach requires users to describe their applications in terms of models of problem solving that may seem artificial or unnatural.

The conceptual model used in OPAL, based on the domain model itself, is perhaps the most categorical way in which the contents of a knowledge base can be viewed. Unlike previous knowledge-acquisition tools, OPAL's model is simply one of what knowledge should be expected. As a result, the user is not given the flexibility found in other systems to specify new concepts. Novel instantiations of existing concepts can be entered (e.g. a previously unknown drug can be defined), but the general classes of concepts in OPAL are predetermined. The domain model, however, tends to be sufficient because of the highly structured, stylized nature of oncology treatment plans.

In choosing a conceptual model for a knowledge-acquisition tool, program designers implicitly determine who will be responsible for the knowledge-level analysis required for knowledge engineering. For instance, when the conceptual model is based on symbol-level representations (as in TEIRESIAS), knowledge-level analysis is left entirely to the *user*; the knowledge-acquisition program makes no assumptions about any of the goals or behaviors associated with particular tasks. On the other hand, when the conceptual model reflects the problem-solving method (as in ROGET), *the knowledge acquisition program itself* assists the user directly in performing knowledge-level analysis. By instantiating a desired task in terms of a predefined model of problem solving, such programs guide their users in analysing the application domain at the knowledge level in the manner advocated by Clancey (1985). However, if the conceptual model is derived from a domain model (as in OPAL), knowledge-level analysis must be completed *a priori* by the *system designers*. In this case, the knowledge-level description originates from the ontology of the task (Alexander *et al.*, 1986) and must be pre-programmed into the knowledge-acquisition tool. Current work in our laboratory concerns the development of techniques to define and edit such knowledge-level descriptions.

The limitations in OPAL are thus the limitations of the domain model. OPAL could obviate the need for knowledge engineers entirely if the domain model were sufficiently complete. Yet regardless of the thoroughness with which one can understand the application area at the knowledge level, it is impossible to anticipate all of the constructs one might encounter in oncology protocols. Even if one had the necessary prescience, designing acceptable graphical forms to capture the knowledge for such an all-inclusive model would be unwieldy. Knowledge acquisition is nevertheless expedited when physicians can use OPAL for the bulk of the knowledge entry, recognizing that specialized knowledge editing by computer scientists may often be necessary later. Previous workers have stressed the great advantages of having preliminary knowledge specification performed by domain experts working alone (Boose, 1985; Phillips *et al.*, 1985). Our goal in OPAL is to maximize the knowledge that experts can enter independently by providing a conceptual model that matches the way oncologists seem to think about the application area. The model then serves as the basis for a visual language that makes it easy for experts to express ideas relevant to their domain.

OPAL's strategy of adopting a domain model to guide the acquisition of new protocols for ONCOCIN presumes a knowledge-level understanding of cancer-treatment plans. The approach is practical in our setting primarily because encoding oncology protocols is a repetitive task that can be greatly accelerated when physicians enter the knowledge themselves. Developing expert systems in other application areas, such as process control, data analysis (Gale, in press), and fault diagnosis for electronic instruments (Phillips *et al.*, 1985), similarly requires the reiterative specification of knowledge bases that are in many ways homologous. Tools that allow experts to define new knowledge-base congeners in terms of explicit, knowledge-level models should greatly facilitate creation of expert systems in these domains.

This work has been supported by grants LM-04420, LM-07033, RR-01631, and LM-04316 from the National Institutes of Health. Computer facilities were provided by the SUMEX-AIM resource under NIH grant RR-00785 and through gifts from Xerox Corporation and

Corning Medical. Dr Musen and Dr Shortliffe have also received support from the Henry J. Kaiser Family Foundation. Joan Walton implemented the first prototype version of OPAL. We thank oncologists Joel Bernstein, Robert Carlson, Charlotte Jacobs, and Richard Lenon for their evaluations of the developing system. We are grateful to Michael Kahn, Samson Tu, and Cliff Wulfman for valuable discussions.

References

ALEXANDER, J. H., FREILING, M. J., SHULMAN, S. J., STALEY, J. L., REHFUSS, S. & MESSICK, S. L. (1986). Knowledge level engineering: ontological analysis. *Proceedings AAAI-86,* American Association for Artificial Intelligence, Philadelphia, Pennsylvania, pp. 963–968 (August).

BENNETT, J. S. (1985). ROGET: a knowledge-based system for acquiring the conceptual structure of a diagnostic expert system. *Journal of Automated Reasoning,* **1,** 49–74.

BOOSE, J. H. (1985). A knowledge acquisition program for expert systems based on personal construct psychology. *International Journal of Man–Machine Studies,* **23,** 495–525.

BRODIE, M. L., MYLOPOULOS, J. & SCHMIDT, J. W. (Eds) (1984). *On Conceptual Modeling.* New York: Springer–Verlag.

BUCHANAN, B. G., BARSTOW, D., BECHTAL, R., BENNETT, J., CLANCEY, W., KULIKOWSKI, C., MITCHELL, T. and WATTERMAN, D. A. (1983). Constructing an expert system. In HAYES-ROTH, F., WATERMAN, D. A. & LENAT, D. B. (Eds) (1983). *Building Expert Systems,* Ch. 5, pp. 127–167. Reading, Massachusetts: Addison–Wesley.

CLANCEY, W. J. (1985). Heuristic classification. *Artificial Intelligence,* **27,** 289–350.

DAVIS, R. (1976). Applications of meta-level knowledge to the construction, maintenance, and use of large knowledge bases. *Ph.D. Thesis,* Stanford University. Rep. No. STAN-CS-76-564.

DE GREEF, P. & BREUKER, J. (1985). A case study in structured knowledge acquisition. In *Proceedings of the Ninth International Joint Conference on Artificial Intelligence,* Los Angeles, California, pp. 390–392 (August).

FRIEDLAND, P. E. & IWASAKI, Y. (1985). The concept and implementation of skeletal plans. *Journal of Automated Reasoning,* **1,** 161–208.

GALE, W. A. (1987). Knowledge-based knowledge acquisition for a statistical consulting system. *International Journal of Man–Machine Studies.* In press.

HANNAN, J. J. & POLITAKIS, P. ESSA: an approach to acquiring decision rules for diagnostic expert systems. In *The Second Conference on Artificial Intelligence Applications,* IEEE Computer Society Press, Miami, Florida, pp. 520–525 (December).

LANE, C. D. (1986). Ozone Reference Manual. *Technical Report KSL-86-40,* Knowledge Systems Laboratory, Stanford University.

MARCUS, S., McDERMOTT, J. & WANG, T. (1985). Knowledge acquisition for constructive systems. In *Proceedings of the Ninth International Joint Conference on Artificial Intelligence,* Los Angeles, California, pp. 637–639 (August).

MUSEN, M. A., COMBS, D. M., WALTON, J. D., SHORTLIFFE, E. H. & FAGAN, L. M. (1986a). OPAL: toward the computer-aided design of oncology advice systems. In *Proceedings of the Tenth Annual Symposium on Computer Applications in Medical Care,* Washington, D.C., pp. 43–52 (October)

MUSEN, M. A., ROHN, J. A., FAGAN, L. M. & SHORTLIFFE, E. H. (1986b). Knowledge engineering for a clinical trial advice system: uncovering errors in protocol specification. In *Proceedings of AAMSI Congress 86,* American Association for Medical Systems and Informatics, Anaheim, California, pp. 24–27 (May).

MUSEN, M. A., FAGAN, L. M. & SHORTLIFFE, E. H. (1986c). Graphical specification of procedural knowledge for an expert system. In *Proceedings of the 1986 IEEE Computer Society Workshop on Visual Languages,* Dallas, Texas, pp. 167–178 (June).

NEWELL, A. (1982). The knowledge level. *Artificial Intelligence,* **18,** 87–127.

NILSSON, N. J. (1981). The interplay between theoretical and experimental methods in artificial intelligence. *Cognition and Brain Theory,* **4,** 69–74.

PHILLIPS, B., MESSICK, S. L., FREILING, M. J. & ALEXANDER, J. H. (1985). INKA: the INGLISH knowledge acquisition interface for electronic instrument troubleshooting systems. In *The Second Conference on Artificial Intelligence Applications,* Miami, Florida, pp. 676–681 (December).
SHORTLIFFE, E. H., SCOTT, A. C., BISCHOFF, M. B., VAN MELLE, W. & JACOBS, C. D. (1981). ONCOCIN: An expert system for oncology protocol management. In *Proceedings of the Seventh International Joint Conference on Artificial Intelligence,* Vancouver, British Columbia, pp. 876–881 (August).

Multiple-problem subspaces in the knowledge-design process

Alain Rappaport†

Neuron Data, 444 High St, Palo Alto, CA 94301, U.S.A.

Designing a knowledge base is viewed as a problem-solving task in which the skilled individual's knowledge and behavior must be mapped into the system, preserving the compiled knowledge acquired by experience. The expert's problem space is complex, but its breakdown into three major subspaces allows one to formalize this approach. Selective interfaces and high-level primitives as well as a flexible knowledge representation not only elicit knowledge and the learning of the design task by the expert. High-level programming, stressing the importance of the psychological as well as the physical descriptions, should allow the expert to bypass the current bottleneck of having to decompile the knowledge into a low-level language and then reconstruct the control structures to recover the expertise. Hence, knowledge design becomes a function available to domain experts themselves.

The following reflections aim at the construction of a comprehensive theory of knowledge acquisition and transfer, in the context of a direct relation between the domain expert and the machine. This work is linked to the development and use of the NEXPERT™ hybrid knowledge-based system.

Knowledge design

A problem is an event which requires the immediate allocation of resources because it cannot be dealt with in an automated fashion and/or it is new or too different. Thus, the dependence between the notions of problem and that of observer of that problem makes this observer's behavior a critical element of the description of problems in general.

The apparent lack of formalism of human knowledge is not merely due to its variety of expressions or to the complexity of the thought processes, but also to the fact that much of the powerful human knowledge is compiled knowledge, resulting from more or less long experiential learning. This is reflected at the behavioral level, by the rapid allocation of the correct resources and a high efficiency in the problem-solving activity through effective management of the focus of attention.

The task of formalizing knowledge from a domain and the associated mental processes in the form of a knowledge-base application is itself a problem-solving task. The progressive assembly of chunks of knowledge reflects a task of search through a particular problem-space: the expert's domain knowledge. We call this task of incrementally discovering and refining elements of knowledge from one's expertise "knowledge design". It can be studied from a "problem-space" perspective (Newell, 1980).

† Also The Robotics Institute, Carnegie–Mellon University, Pittsburgh, PA 15213.

KNOWLEDGE-BASED SYSTEMS Vol. 2
ISBN 0-12-115920-5

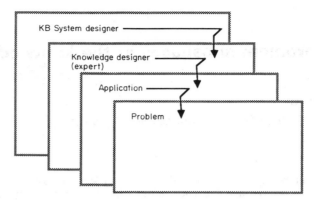

FIG. 1. Recursive problem-solving tasks in the design and use of knowledge-based systems. The knowledge environment designer has to solve the problem of building the system. To do so, information on how knowledge designers solve the problem of building a knowledge base is useful. In turn, the application solves the problem. The knowledge designer is the domain expert in this model.

Experiential learning results in compiled knowledge, which key characteristics is to embody control knowledge, indexing the memory and controlling the focus of attention. A fundamental consequence is that the problem-space is necessarily reduced compared of that of a novice. Real-world problems as perceived by experts are *simpler* than abstract problems such as puzzles solved by weak methods. In the design of the specifications for a knowledge base building tool, we can see that we have a recursive embedding of problem-solving tasks (Fig. 1):

The problem space of the task performed by the expert is simplified by the use of experiential knowledge;

The expert, when designing a knowledge base, is performing search through a problem-space which is its own knowledge.

Decompilation or not

The behavioral, or control level is critical in the nature of expert knowledge. It is naturally the case that two people could have the same book knowledge. However, the distinction between the expert and the novice will be in the speed of recognition and in the nature of the problem-solving techniques used when confronted to a problem. The expert has accumulated experience which results in rules of thumb, intuitions, inductive reasoning and knowledge about control.

The difference in behavior between the expert and the novice in real life can be best noticed for instance at the attentional level. The expert rapidly focuses on the most relevant knowledge and then organizes the agenda in a structured fashion. On the other hand, by that time the novice has not infered yet the important discrimination factors; s/he has not dynamically indexed the long-term memory and has not replaced enough search by knowledge.

These elements account for a key difference in performance. Is expert knowledge only an increase in performance of the search functions? Learning processes are certainly not only limited to skill acquisition. Rather, they consist in the incremental acquisition of compiled knowledge, or elements of knowledge which properties have somehow emerged from the assembly and/or transformation of past, more elementary or obsolete descriptions. It is the complex result of linear mechanisms (practice) and, most importantly, non-linear ones (analogy, discovery, examples. . .). A given element of knowledge, be it a rule or a structured object, embodies both objective textbook knowledge and subjective, proprietary heuristics for its manipulation relative to the others during problem-solving. We shall focus on the translation of human knowledge into a machine program with a maximum transfer efficiency.

How much of this human knowledge needs to be decompiled for its translation into a knowledge-based system? There is an obvious high cost in performing the decompilation, both at the elicitation and implementation levels. Retrospection in a process such as long-term learning by experience is difficult. Furthermore, artificial agents would have to relearn by experience in order to reach again the same level of competence and performance. Decompilation induces the risk of losing the control knowledge and having to use standard weak methods to solve problems and improve their performance over time. Although decompilation may be sometimes necessary and non-compiled knowledge must be expressed, it is important to develop languages allowing to map directly this compiled knowledge.

Thus, we need an appropriate mix of functions and representations allowing both the preservation of the compiled knowledge and the decompilation of other aspects of the expert's corpus of knowledge requiring the representation of lower level, algorithmic functions. The preservation issue requires the availability of high-level primitives in the system. If the expert (the designer) is aware of his/her compiled knowledge, knowledge systems must be able to directly capture those heuristics and not force the designer into a low-level representation of the task requiring a decompilation effort. This effort would moreover have to be followed by another aiming at reconstructing the efficient behavior using the system's functions.

In order to work towards a comprehensive theory for the design of such systems, we chose to approach the knowledge-acquisition issues from the problem-solving perspective. We need to explore how the problem space of the domain-expert knowledge can actually be searched so as to have their problem-solving technique formulated by the experts themselves.

Since we assume that the domain expert is performing a problem-solving task, we may consider what techniques are being applied from the computational point of view. First and foremost, problem-solving cannot be separated from learning. To progress in the knowledge-design task, the expert must learn how to use the formalization tool. Working with knowledge-design tools involves a critical learning period during which the expert acquires experience and actually modifies his/her problem-solving techniques accordingly.

In the very initial phase, the expert may not have any well-structured goal. Either he basic notions of problem-solving and representations are unknown to the expert and cannot yet be related to the overall goal of building an application, or no particular task or domain has been identified yet. The design task thus consists more in an exploration than in a structured, goal-driven task. This period is most critical to keep the expert's attention focused on the task in general, so s/he does not delegate it. The tool must be able to show its function and potential. Past this early phase, the task of the expert becomes to implement knowledge about particular problems in a given domain. The absence of previous reflections on knowledge and in particular of experience with the tool from which to draw upon will gear the expert into a behavior typical of domain-independent, weak methods such as means-ends analysis (creating subgoals and achieving them). As the expert becomes more experienced with the tool, s/he can draw upon experience to design new functions or primitives to reflect particular subtasks of their behavior, and example applications. From then on, higher level techniques such analogical reasoning become relevant. There must be an environment for the design of knowledge bases which favors this type of evolution in the problem-solving techniques used in order to gain in performance. Knowledge design is primarily dependent upon a learning task, in a reactive environment, and, as for autonomous learning devices (Rappaport, 1985), one will observe a progression along a gradient of problem-solving methodologies. Prior to any other considerations in knowledge acquisition, we believe that such knowledge-acquisition issues must be taken into account at the time of the tools' specifications design (Fig. 1). The resulting interactive tool will then be able to elicit the expression of both compiled and less compiled knowledge.

Decomposition of the problem space

The designer's problem space is made of all the knowledge available to the expert. Although the problem space is simplified by the presence of experiential knowledge, search through this space is a complex task to formulate. In order to progress, we have chosen to decompose this problem space in subspaces corresponding to particular functions of the knowledge-design task. The following decomposition into three subspaces allows us to formalize some important specification design issues. The problem space is divided into three subspaces: (i) the application space covers all the factual knowledge of the expert and its representation; (ii) the methodological space addresses the representation of control knowledge; and (iii) the processing space concerns the execution functions, or the reactiveness of the system. This division is clearly for analysis purposes only and the three subspaces are naturally strongly overlapping in the actual task.

THE APPLICATION SPACE

The application space corresponds to the corpus of domain specific chunks of knowledge used by the expert. From the specifications point of view, it addresses more specifically the representational components of the design task and the nature of the man–machine interface to elicit knowledge.

Representation

From the point of view of the tool's design, unless one voluntarily limits the type of problems to be addressed, the system must support various, though interrelated, knowledge representations. The lowest level of representation should be of a high enough symbolic level, such as *objects* with a local and global organization, describing the percepts (instances) or concepts (generalizations) as sets of properties and relations. Such static representations must coexist with more dynamic ones from various types of constructions to rules, which by definition give a sense of cognitive progression and problem-solving to the developer. The representation environment can be seen as a multi-dimensional space of structures related one to the others. For instance, rules address objects, perform pattern-matching on their multi-level organization, modify their characteristics and their values.

Whether a unification of the mental and physical models is possible or even desirable is difficult to assess and is case-dependent. The observer-dependent components of the knowledge base can be rules as well as objects. Previous studies (Larkin, 1983) have shown the shift in the nature of the representation from novices to experts. What we would like to stress is the need to be able to represent the psychological representation of problems in the expert's mind.

In modelling processes for example, the description of the device can often be more or less abstracted and reduced to the main events which may occur and their impact on the system. This description can be very dependent upon the expertise and experience of the domain expert. More classic simulations aim at linking an intelligent system to or using the language to program a very precise description of the system's functioning. The result is a greatly increased difficulty in both the debugging and the maintenance of the system. The implementation of the expert's model of the key events and functions can be as powerful and provide a more dynamic, maintainable model.

Another example of adaptability of the representation is the composition of models in terms of instances and classes or generalizations. These notions are useful to direct the transfer process from the expert to the system. However, one must be able to reflect, in the organization of those structures not only material, physical relations but also *psychological* manipulations. Down-inheritance allows one to describe the hierarchical physical nature of things. Whilst such descriptions may be correct, their *perception* by the human mind makes the reality look often more like a heterarchical world. Operations such as generalizations or dynamic classification are constantly performed in problem-solving. When one sees the front side panel of a car one can surely infer the color of that car's door before seeing the entire object. The system must thus allow rapid transformations from prototypical objects to generalizations and vice versa, as experts do. The dynamics of the structural representation is a graph of uni- or bi-directional relations.

Although one can argue that many representation techniques are used in human reasoning, the sole representation in terms of rules needs to be somewhat transformed. Because expert reasoning is different from solving abstract puzzles for the most parts, rules must contain a high level of control information. This allows them to be used in a *symmetric* fashion. This symmetry avoids having to defined the rule artificially as a forward or backward structure. The compiled nature of the knowledge makes it much more suitable for an event-driven, opportunistic general control as opposed to a specific, often unadapted algorithm. We shall come back to these points in the section on the methodological space.

Interactive editing environment
Manipulating such primitives requires the building of specific editors and interfaces. Because of the variety of domains, tasks and even approaches to similar tasks, we need to insure a basic flexibility in the editing mechanisms, so that the designer can

mention objects, classes or properties in a rule before creating the latter if s/he has a better sense of the dynamics than of the overall, more static representation. Indeed, the high-level implementation—not exclusive of the rest, is best allowed when not forcing any particular framework of development such as static knowledge first, followed by dynamic operations on the knowledge space. Rather, an approach allowing a permanent shift between the different aspects of the domain (mainly the static and dynamic components) should best capture the natural equilibrium between those concepts in the actual task.

Hence, being able to extract as much information about the structures from the rules at compilation is critical, for the rule compiler then automatically assures part of the work at the descriptive level as well. The rules involving previously created objects should be able to bring about new important information about the more precise nature of objects and their properties. We call this concept of editing objects and classes from their description in rules *cross-compilation* of knowledge structures. Furthermore, in order to allow a continuous, incremental and interactive development, incremental compilation of all structures is necessary. This will also allow the dynamic creation of objects and the incrmental modifications of their relationships.

Selective interface

Whatever the application domain, it is necessary to capture the chunks of knowledge involved in the task to be modelled. These chunks can be rules, schema, frames or any other representation. In any case, there is, for the domain-expert, the task of finding or discovering what those chunks are and entering them into the system. Thus, the primary work takes place at what we call the *microscopic level*. Even though the designer certainly has in real life a global vision of his/her task, this perception may be lost when it becomes necessary to work at the microscopic level.

It is thus important that the tool allows one to take a global view at the space of knowledge elements, objects or rules, that is to say automatically reconstructs the structural links between them, thereby generating a global image of the corpus of knowledge (as a whole or of part it). To provide such functions, one must take advantage of the selectivity of visual perception (Arnheim, 1969) and its powerful global/local relation. It maintains the correct focusing of the attention on more or less complex arrangements of chunks of knowledge. Such visual thinking provides a powerful incentive to create new chunks and structure the knowledge.

Provided that the visual tool is part of an interactive environment, the visualization greatly enhances the tasks of unification, organization and integration of knowledge. It also allows the reformulation of parts of or entire problems. This elicitation factor is even more important when one knows that mental representations of a problem are by essence more fluid, changing more often than the physical ones.

NEXPERT allows one to represent the macroscopic structure of the knowledge chunks via the *Network* functionality. In general, the meshed structure of knowledge does not only result from the fact that certain concepts share attributes in their definition, but also from the way they are processed by the rules. Thus, there are *functional* links between the elements of a knowledge base, as follows in the figures showing examples of the Network of rules (Figs 2–4).

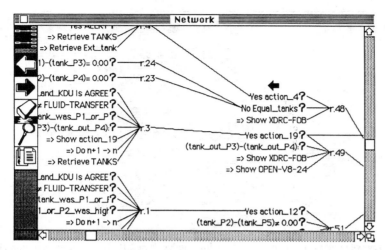

FIG. 2. Deductive navigation in a knowledge-base (rule plane) using the NEXPERT network.

The possibility of *navigating* through a knowledge base by simulating/viewing inference functions (deductive/backward and evocative/forward), and the structural organization of objects is crucial in the understanding of the knowledge-processing task by domain experts and the progression in their knowledge space. The evocative navigation simulates some of the forward processing notions, such as the organization of the agenda. Furthermore, in both ways, the declarative conflict resolution method in NEXPERT can also be visualized, as well as the object representation.

The cognitive continuum between the user and the knowledge thus results from two important elements: (i) the representation must attract the user's attention with the highest gain; and (ii) the actions resulting from this observation must be rapidly integrated.

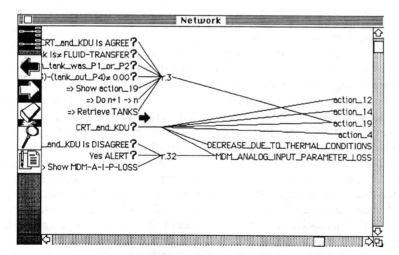

FIG. 3. Evocative navigation. Clicking on the CRT_and_KDU datum with the forward icon displays the goals or subgoals in which this attribute is involved.

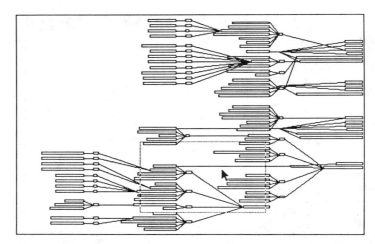

FIG. 4. Overview of a navigation in parts of a knowledge base. It was noticed that domain experts recognize the visual patterns of rules belonging to their knowledge base, facilitating the use of this zooming mechanism.

At the same time as the interface can correctly keep the designer's attention on the incremental editing of knowledge, lower-level interface optimizations must prevent the perturbation of this effort by distractions due to a bad display organization and/or non-optimized click distances (number of clicks separating functions).

THE METHODOLOGICAL SPACE

The methodological space addresses the system's ability to model the behavior of the expert, or the mental model in terms of available inference functionalities. It thus addresses the functional or control component of the overall problem space.

Human reasoning vs theorem-proving

There are fundamental issues to tackle as well concerning the logical mechanisms available to the developer. The philosophical attempts to establish a relation between formal logic and identity has been overcome by a large body of work, and new approaches to logic tend to formalize a more psychological approach to logic (McDermott & Doyle, 1980; Doyle, 1982; Harman, 1985). Flexibility in the representation of facts and logical dependencies is thus necessary. In theorem-proving situations, the facts cannot be contradicted because of their universal validity, whilst in human reasoning, new data come and contradict previous inferences at all times. Inferences at the mental level reflect the application equivalence relations based on the permanent matching to the environment. On the contrary, formal logic approaches do not clearly distinguish facts from theorems and are search-driven instead of being event/concept-driven. The logic underlying design tools must be somewhat more adapted to the non-monotonic nature of human reasoning. More formal approaches can be applied to local subproblem spaces to which they are relevant.

The main characteristic we emphasize is the need for the knowledge designer to be able to concentrate on the implementation (mapping) of his/her thought process rather than on having to focus permanently on the consistency of the underlying representation language, as in prolog-like systems. The result is an acyclic graph of rules representing the directions of the focus of attention.

Agenda levels

As mentioned above, a major way of distinguishing an expert's behavior from that of a novice is to study the focus of attention, which reflects a compiled set of heuristics to perform an optimized search in the problem space.

In NEXPERT for instance, the *context* function allows sets of related rules to be linked together by what are called *weak* links. Such links represent shifts in the focus of attention, products of highly compiled knowledge. They allow the easy sequencing of a job, the representation of intuitive, inductive knowledge (which does not need to be decompiled). The first result from a computational and knowledge design point of view is an important economy in the number of rules used to represent the problem.

Different levels of granularity in the focus of attention can be distinguished, from the prompting order directed by knowledge of a cost-efficiency measure to the selection of overall goals on experience-defined criteria. These agendas are easily implemented using declarative mechanisms at different levels of the representation. This corresponds to a controllable, dynamically updated, declarative agenda, opposed to the lack of accessible control structures of lower level languages which operate while generating of large quantities of eventually useless information. Sets of rules can be as small as one desires.

In order to insure all levels of implementation, the system must integrate various methodologies for such mappings as well as more classic issues, from agendas to production-system-like mechanisms. Figure 5 shows an architecture where different *granularity levels* for the focus of attention are used in the same knowledge based in the NEXPERT system. It shows a sample architecture of a knowledge base, with its different levels of knowledge processing.

Each ellipse encircles a *knowledge island,* an independent set of rules, sharing no attributes with one another. Within each island, progression occurs in an integrated forward (fwd) and backward (bwd) fashion. The islands are linked by a forward indexing mechanisms, the *context,* indicating future focus of attention. New directions of search can also be selectively induced as a result of right-hand side (RHS) actions. The flow of control from one island to another or the effects of any RHS actions can be controlled from the rules themselves. For instance, the consequences of RHS actions may or may not be investigated. The overall result is the possibility to organize the search according to psychological evidence. The fluctuations of the focus of attention are not necessarily trivial and declarative access to this mechanism should enable the implementation of many variations.

The concepts of contexts and knowledge islands represent the type of short cuts necessary to embody intuitive reasoning without having to go back to a description of the physiology of the problem or of the causal mechanisms (deep knowledge). Contexts act as declarative heuristics limiting the search space. However, within each island, the problem-solving task can be quite similar to more classic systems.

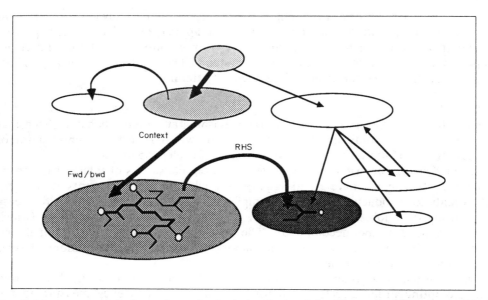

FIG. 5. Management of the focus of attention by declarative heuristics. The top-level flow of control from the original task is concerved by the system. Horizontal (e.g. scheduling) as well as hierarchical refinement) or mixed representations can thus be implemented.

Still, inside each island the focus of attention can be controlled as well, simply at a lower granularity scale.

Control primitives

The control of the flow of information must be accessible by the use of "control primitives": local and global priorities, context links, revisions, conflict detection, generalizations... At the same time, more classic approaches, closer to the algorithmic calculations and searches, such as Prolog or OPS5 can be used to perform *subroutine* work in adequate, relevant problem subspaces. Thus, these primitives represent the high-level programming while languages that lack control structure should be used to perform subtasks (recognition, filtering, tree searching etc...) of a more algrorithmic nature, as treated by some production systems.

To summarize this notion, we can represent problem-solving tools or languages along an axis which indicates the degree of control available for any language (Fig. 6). At one end of this spectrum lie languages which have very little control. The use of such languages, because it requires to program even the most natural functions in human problem-solving, does not allow direct access by the domain expert. The knowledge-acquisition efforts are thus directed towards the building of task-specific molds. At the other extreme are found systems based on languages with built-in control strategies which severely limit the possibilities of the system. This lack of flexibility greatly affects the interest of interfaces or knowledge-acquisition tools on top of such inference systems. Our research is focussed on sets of primitives allowing the design of the task, as well as the discovery of arrangements of such primitives to provide more powerful and new functionalities.

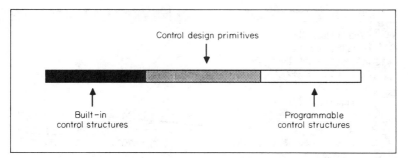

FIG. 6. The spectrum of knowledge nase languages along the "control axis". At one end are the control-free languages such as LISP or OPS5. Since they require programming the cognitive functions, they force the decompilation of knowledge. At the other end, built-in control languages, such as EMYCIN, are greatly limiting in their representation capacities of reasoning except for a very narrow set of problems. Prolog is a language which belongs to both extermities of this scale. Research on control primitives focusses on designing functionalities which reflect a natural equilibrium between built-in and lack of control, thereby defining higher-level AI languages.

THE PROCESSING SPACE

The processing space is the problem-space in the design task concerned with the execution of the program. It precisely addresses the relation between form and function, and makes a bridge between the two subspaces described above. The execution environment for the designer must allow a selective reduction of the overall search space, setting its boundaries by allowing to interactively discover inconsistencies, irrelevances, redundancies as well as potential unifications and refinements. The co-existence of a performance system in a knowledge-base building tool is thus a fundamental asset.

Insuring the cognitive continuum between the user and the system requires that the relevant design tools remain available during the verification phase, in which the user tests the current state of the knowledge base. The notion of example and trial execution is central to the development process, addressing the refinement and verification functions. Execution of the inference process based on the available knowledge at any time focuses the designer's attention on selecting the most relevant chunks of knowledge.

While the use of the Network in a non-interactive manner favors a rapid growth of the corpus of knowledge, the same visual information obtained during execution (Fig. 7) is of a different order: it sets boundaries to the designer, search space, and prevents the designer's inference process from drifting to unnecessary subspaces of knowledge.

Hence, it is necessary to integrate these functions into a coherent development environment. The execution phase brings new information which needs to be rapidly included in the system. Since such modifications stemming from testing the dynamics of the system's knowledge are of a particular nature, they should be tested as quickly as possible within the same execution environment. This functionality requires an incremental compiling mechanism (creating, modifying or deleting a rule) available during the execution. Coupled with dynamic visualization, this allows one to maintain the designer's focus all along the debugging of knowledge. These facilities constitute an interactive knowledge-design environment.

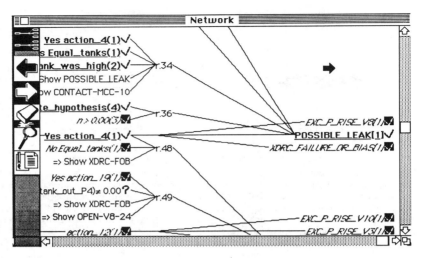

FIG. 7. This display of a Rule Network graph shows the state of part of the body of knowledge during a session. The icons and different fonts and styles indicate the various states of the conditions and goals. Rules can be edited during the session by calling the rule editor which then compiles modifications incrementally.

Yet another important issue addressed in the processing space is the tracking of inconsistencies. When knowledge based systems use formal logical statements, thereby confusing rules with theorems, inconsistencies exist only in the internal anatomy of the knowledge (theorem) base. The consistency checking becomes therefore mostly independent of the problem solved, and is pre-processed according to laws and constraints which may have little to do with the nature of the problem and its treatment by the expert. Because of the necessity to represent reasonings such as default reasoning or to live with inconsistencies which are actually dynamically solved by the data of the problem, the high transparency of the execution phase is a critical asset for the design environments. Inconsistencies are incrementally discovered, and different techniques can be implemented to deal with them.

Methodological progression

LEARNING BY SHIFTING PROBLEM-SOLVING STRATEGIES

Considering this breakdown of the problem space and the relevant elements described above, we can now come back to the actual search process taking place in the expert's mind. Initially, the expert is lacking knowledge on how to make a knowledge-base and must rely on an intensive exploration of the tool's capabilities. This will involve the use of the many different mechanisms but can only be useful if certain properties such as incremental compilation and fully interactive environments are available, with a minimal amount of low-level tasks (variable declaration for instance which can be handled automatically as in NEXPERT from reading the structures). In this first phase, the approach is weak, in the sense of weak methods for problem-solving, i.e. domain-independent (Laird & Newell, 1983). At this level, the interface issues as well as the format and editing mechanisms of the knowledge structures are critical to gain acceptance and keep the attention focused.

The tool is then supposed to elicitate not only the extraction of knowledge from the domain expert, with the incremental discovery of new knowledge chunks and refinements, but also to trigger shifts in the approaches to the construction of the knowledge-base, which will reflect a better understanding of the tool and its use to formalize a problem. We shall not dwell here upon the obvious practice effect on the use of the tool's text and graphic, menu-oriented interface. One important thing in this regard is of course the adaptiveness of the commands' access as practice is acquired and most skills are built. We are concerned here rather with the internal representation and approaches of the knowledge design task in the designer's mind.

The visual navigational tools have the major advantage of combining a macroscopic reconstruction and a complete description of the world of inferences and structures involved in the task. The visualization helps to develop models which are symbolic descriptions of rules or objects which perform certain functions in given contexts. This occurs with any individual learning a tool's use, but we are concerned here with the rapid facilitation of this process in order to make the reasoning functionality available to domain experts directly.

Thus, there is a clear progression from what are initially weak, domain-independent approaches to more structured, domain-dependent thinking involving in particular the notions of chunking and reasoning by analogy. The design process starts with an exploratory technique. It is followed by a more goal-oriented behavior. Chunking behavior (as in Rosenbloom & Newell, 1985) is facilitated by the interactive interface which favors the unification of elements of knowledge as part of the refinement process. While chunking may result in the generation of new structures, the interface also favors the exploding of too compact chunks, the reverse process. Further along, reasoning by analogy is elicited, in particular at the control level and architecture level. Design by analogy occurs: (i) at the elementary chunk level; (ii) at the local dependencies level (arrangement of a few elements to perform a function); (iii) the task level, being able to derive an overall plan from past experience with the tool; and (iv) at the architecture level, allowing to make abstract mapping between problems to direct the development.

Table 1 shows an example of an account of a knowledge-aquisition process by a domain expert in chemical engineering with no prior knowledge of artificial-intelligence techniques. A rapid analysis of the report in Table 1, paragraph by paragraph, allows us to distinguish the use of some interesting mechanisms:

(i) description of the nature of the task at the basis of the application;

(ii) exploration phase based on previous models and design of an overall architecture, from the focus of attention viewpoint;

(iii) work on a sub-problem using specific methodologies provided by the tool (reset, categories, meta-rules. Then notion of "cloning", or mapping the same structure to another part of the problem. This is the simplest level of analogical reasoning, where the problems (or subproblems) are very similar;

(iv) modifications are suggested at the cognitive level (cognitive debugging) concerning the temporal course of the task. The overall progression described before is reused (analogy) and the system is updated. The notion of "cloning" is

TABLE 1

Protocol obtained from a designer with NEXPERT™

Expert-system building steps with NEXPERT™

(1) General description of the problem

This expert system (ES) is a troubleshooting–dianostic program for quality defects on a production line. In the past, the operators were instructed by a line specialist. This system attempts to replace the line specialist for most of the routine problems, while recognizing the possibility of a difficult problem that might still require the line specialist.

The operator will identify a defect and then use the ES to correct the production line. He will be guided through several steps to correct the problem, anyone of these steps or actions might correct the problem, but there is no real certainty which of the actions will do it. Therefore it is important to check constantly to see if the action was carried out and if the problem was corrected.

(2) Identify knowledge islands

At first I implemented a set of rules from an old troubleshooting guide. I then realized that this problem was fairly nicely divided into five knowledge islands. I spent some time learning how to organize the overall problem. It took me a while to grasp how the rules could both be forward and backward chaining and then to understand the use of context to control "weak links".

(3) Develop meta-rule for ordering the rules

Concentrating on the first knowledge island, I worked out a system for setting the order in which the rules would be fired. At first I used categories, but I then decided that it would be better to use a meta-rule to control the rule order. Once I had debugged this structure I cloned the same structure for the other knowledge islands.

(4) Develop method for cycling each rule

After demonstrating the initial ES several people commented that in the real world the expert will verify if the action was in fact taken and if it worked, until a positive response is given, he will not procede. Therefore, I developed a method for cycling each question and checking to see if the problem was solved. I again debugged this procedure on the first knowledge island and then cloned the procedure for the other islands.

---

adopted as a problem-solving technique. The problem-solving strategy used previously is mapped to the current problem, in a derivational analogy-like process. A technique has been acquired for solving a particular problem and is reinstanciated as a whole after having been identified as relevant.

In reporting the structure of the knowledge base, the designer also describes the use of a technique applied recursively. In this instance the system can use the same control strategy at different scale levels of the architecture. The implementation is made possible by means of the reset operator and control over the propagation of new information.

Finally, it is of interest to note the learning process exposed by the expert. We can observe the shift in methodology and representation from what seems to be a type of exploratory approach to an experienced based approaches, somewhat as observed throughout cognitive development (Piaget, 1954; Carey, 1986). In this particular case, the overall architecture built here is currently being transposed to a similar task to be modelled.

The protocol described in Table 2 by a knowledge designer working on a complex task reflects both similarities with the previous example and another aspect of the knowledge design task. The initiation of the project with *textbook knowledge* is

TABLE 2

Protocol of an application development illustrating the major role of the domain expert in the design process

(1) Map sequential textbook steps into intermediate hypotheses (DE).
(2) Determine use of certainty factors [how, what for, thresholding, techniques (DS, fuzzy sets. . .)] (DE).
(3) Code and debug first set of rules (DE).
(4) Demonstrate to human experts (DE).
(5) Select the right approach for easy extension (DE + AI eng).
(6) Determine operator-prompting sequence.
(7) Generate Show and Apropos files (DE, long task).
(8) Code and debug a second set with a new architecture taking into account more assumptions, concepts and ideas (DE + AI eng).
(9) Categories to achieve prompting sequence (DE + AI eng).
(10) Determine appropriate strategies (DE + AI eng).
(11) Extend second set of rules (DE).
(12) Debug with intensive use of the Network, this task was extremely simple (DE + AI eng).
(13) Multiple-level Apropos, multiplication of the second set into many such sets to deal with other aspects of the problem and complete the knowledge base, and linking the sets (DE).
(14) Demonstrate to human expert (DE).

DE, domain expert; AI eng, AI engineer. The expert did all the coding. The AI engineer identified problems in the way the DE implemented the problem and was there to provide advise and debugging help. Furthermore, the AI engineer did not have to know much about the application.

rapidly followed by an implementation of the expert's knowledge. As in the previous example, textbook knowledge serves as a primer example on which the initial learning takes place. The interactivity of the tool is critical in this phase, for the domain expert to focus on the tool and obtain a sense of the problem-solving methodology.

This example also illustrates the replication method, allowed by the ability to test and understand the behavior of the system on small but representative sets of rules. Moreover, and this is the second aspect, the tool is in the hands of the domain expert and the AI knowledgeable person intervenes by "looking over the shoulder", providing (important) advise. This transfer of power to the expert is critical in the efficiency and quality of the overall process of modelling its thought process.

Eliciting problem-solving methodologies

We are thus concerned here with the optimization of the elicitation of such processes by means of automated tools. The examples above concerns specific tasks to be modelled. Other types of applications have been built where the same type of reasoning process takes place with the expert. The ability to provide quickly and concisely a report on the making of an application by an AI novice is illustrative, in our sense, of the "mapping" effect looked for. The extensive use of the Network also recalls the notion of "perception of analogies" put forward by Polya (1945) in problem-solving activities.

Such behaviors can only be elicited and maintained if the tool's mechanisms are close enough to the cognitive mapping concept and is thus based on very high level primitives, the rest of the knowledge involved being dealt with classical methods (by the same system though).

A critical factor has been to be able to initialize the learning process by the expert, by means of interface and representation tools. Then, we observe a progression in the problem methodologies used by the domain expert. Applications in complex domains have thus been developed in a very short amount of time. Much research and implementation remains to be done though in this direction, to find more adapted techniques. The shift in methodology is typical of a basic learning process, involving first weak methods and progressively showing capabilities in reasoning by analogy or discovering macro-operators for the design of a task. As those techniques are applied, the body of knowledge on how to construct a knowledge base increases and can be used for new, different domains, allowing the rapid identification of similarities between tasks and domains. The aim is to considerably reduce the overall learning curve.

INTEGRATED TOOLS

The technique described in this paper advocates the use of interactivity and the design of high-level primitives to allow the incremental elicitation of knowledge. Such an approach can however be associated to other forms of automated interviewing tools for knowledge acquisition. Studies based on Personal Construct Psychology for interactive interviewing (Boose, 1985; Gaines & Shaw, 1981) illustrates the progress of such techniques. Such structural analyses can yield rules to be used by an expert system. A forward-only or backward-only inference mechanism would be too "prejudiced" to allow a correct cognitive debugging. On the other hand, a more opportunistic system with symmetric rules will allow one to fully test the meaning of the resulting rules and, along with the visualization mechanism, will allow the progressive refinement (unification, selection etc...) of the initial knowledge (Shaw & Gaines, in press). Also relevant are automated techniques based on the analysis of reports from skilled individuals (Nisbett & Wilson, 1977; Ericsson & Simon, 1983) but protocol analysis itself is a lengthy process. Compiled knowledge should be directly elicited by the knowledge tool. This integration of techniques illustrates the importance of having a performance system associated with any tool.

Furthermore, learning techniques performing comparable tasks to those sought from experts during the knowledge-design task (Winston, 1980; Rosenbloom & Newell, 1985; Carbonell, 1985; Cheng & Carbonell, 1986) could be progressively included into the tool so as for the latter to analyse automatically the structure of the knowledge and adapt its reasoning methodologies. Learning mechanisms could also enhance the quality of the interactivity and communication between the tool and the domain expert.

Conclusion

While graphic interfaces were not emphasized in previous work (Card, Moran & Newell, 1983), they actually play a fundamental role in the design of intelligent systems. As in the case of automatic algorithm design (Kant, 1985), the problem-solving approach is a powerful heuristic for building knowledge systems with the preoccupation of knowledge-acquisition issues. New issues in the psychology of the human–computer interface arise from systems as the one described here, leaving plenty of perspectives for a hardening of the psychological approach (Newell & Card, 1985).

Based on a cognitive analysis of the task of formalizing knowledge, key issues in the design of knowledge-based systems can be identified which limit the need for the knowledge engineer and gears the technology towards the status of a functionality *per se,* directly available to the domain-experts. The resulting concept is that of high-level programming (Fig. 8) in knowledge-based systems. In general, progress is sought both on the impact of artificial systems on the reasoning of the human experts and on computational methodologies allowing an implementation of the expert's design of a task as opposed to an implementation of the expert itself. Basic research in cognitive processes and artificial-intelligence techniques, particularly in the context of problem-solving and learning in interactive environments, should allow to progress notably towards allowing experts to map their efficient knowledge derived from experience.

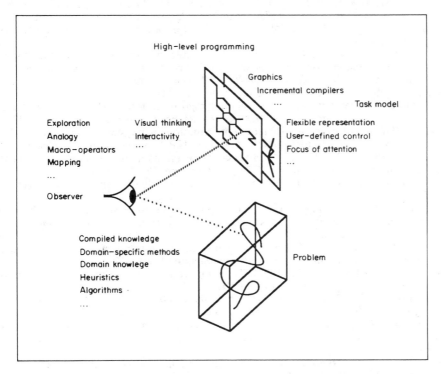

FIG. 8. The distance between the problem-solving activity and the model being implemented must be minimized. While low-level programming requires the decomposition of the problems into many, small elements of knowledge and then the reconstruction of the control structure, high-level programming attempts to preserve via elicitation and high-level operators a maximum of compiled knowledge.

The author thanks Albert Gouyet, Bruno Jouhier, Patrick Perez and Chris Shipley for most helpful comments on earlier drafts. Special thanks are also given to Jaime Carbonell and Brian Gaines for some insightful discussions. I naturally extend my thanks to the domain experts who provided an account of their experience with the tool. This research was made possible by the support of Neuron Data.

NEXPERT™ is a trademark of Neuron Data Inc. Figures 2, 3, 4 and 7 were obtained using NEXPERT™, with the permission of Neuron Data.

References

ARNHEIM, R. (1969). *Visual Thinking*. Berkeley: University of California Press.

BOOSE, J. H. (1985). A PCP-based method for building expert systems. *Boeing Computer Services Report BCS-G2010-24.*

CARBONELL, J. C. (1985). Derivational analogy: a theory of reconstructive problem solving and expertise acquisition. In *Machine Learning II*, pp. 371–392. Los Altos, CA: Morgan Kaufmann.

CARD, S. K., MORAN, T. P. & NEWELL, A. (1983). *The Psychology of Human Computer Interaction*. Hillsdale, NJ: Lawrence Erlbaum Associates.

CAREY, S. (1986). *Conceptual Changes in Childhood*. Cambridge MA: MIT Press.

CHENG, P. & CARBONELL, J. G. (1986). The FERMI system: inducing iterative macro-operators from experience. *Proceedings of the Fifth National Conference on Artificial Intelligence*, Los Altos, CA, **1**, pp. 490–495.

DOYLE, J. (1983). Some theories of reasoned assumptions. *Technical Report,* Carnegie–Mellon University, Department of Computer Science, CMU-CS-83-125, Pittsburgh, PA.

ESHELMAN, L. & McDERMOTT, J. (1986). MOLE: a knowledge acquisition tool that uses its head. *Proceedings of the Fifth National Conference on Artificial Intelligence*, Los Altos, CA, **1**, pp. 950–955.

GAINES, B. R. & SHAW, M. L. G. (1981). New directions in the analysis and interactive elicitation of personal construct systems. In SHAW, M. L. G. Ed., *Recent Advances in Personal Construct Technology,*. New York: Academic Press.

HARMAN, G. (1985). *Change in View*. Cambridge MA: MIT Press.

KANT, E. (1985). Understanding and automating algorithm design. *Proceedings of the Ninth International Joint Conference on Artificial Intelligence* Los Altos, CA, **2**, pp. 1243–1253.

LARKIN, J. (1983). The role of problem representation in physics. In GENTNER, D. AND STEVENS, A. L., Eds, *Mental Models*. Hillsdale, NJ: Lawrence Erlbaum Associates.

LAIRD, J. & NEWELL, A. (1983). A universal weak method. *Technical Report,* Carnegie–Mellon University, Department of Computer Science, Pittsburgh, PA.

McDERMOTT, D. & DOYLE, J. (1980). Non-monotonic logic. *Artificial Intelligence*, **13**, 41–72.

NEWELL, A. (1980). Reasoning, problem solving and decision processes: the problem space as a fundamental category. In NICKERSON, R. Ed., *Attention and Performance*. Hillsdale NJ: Lawrence Erlbaum.

NEWELL, A. & CARD, S. K. (1985). The prospects for psychological science in human–computer interaction. *Human Computer Interaction*, **1**, 209–242.

NISBETT, R. E. & WILSON, T. D. (1977). Telling more than we can know: verbal reports on mental processes. *Psychological Review* **84**, 231–259.

PIAGET, J. (1954). *The Construction of Reality in the Child*. New York: Basic Books.

POLYA, G. (1945). *How to Solve It*. Princeton NJ: Princeton University Press.

RAPPAPORT, A. (1985). Goal-free learning by analogy. In MITCHELL T., CARBONELL, J. G. & MICHALSKI, R. Eds, Machine Learning: a Guide to Current Research. Boston MA: Kluwer Academic.

ROSENBLOOM, P. S. & NEWELL, A. (1985). The chunking of goal hierarchies. In *Machine Learning II*. Los Altos, CA: Morgan Kaufmann.

SHAW, M. L. G. & GAINES, B. R. (1987). Interactive elicitation of knowledge from experts. *Future Computing Systems*. In press.

WINSTON, P. H. (1980). Learning and reasoning by analogy: the details. *Technical Report,* Massachusetts Institute of Technology, Artificial Intelligence Laboratory, AIM 520.

Creating the domain of discourse: ontology and inventory

STEPHEN REGOCZEI

Computer Studies, Trent University, Peterborough, Ontario, K9J 7B8, Canada

EDWIN P. O. PLANTINGA

Department of Computer Science, Redeemer College, Ancaster, Ontario, L9G 3N6, Canada

> Ontology recapitulates philology.
> (James Grier Miller as quoted by W. V. O. Quine)
>
> If you can't build a model of it, it isn't true.
> (Buckminster Fuller)
>
> The science of personal relations is not assisted by the fact that only a few psychologists are concerned to discover valid personal ways in which persons, and relations between persons, can be studied by persons.
> (R. D. Laing)

The paper describes the foundations of a methodology for natural language-based knowledge acquisition. It concentrates on a special type of context: the case in which an analyst interviews an informant who is a domain expert and the text of the discussion is carefully recorded. In this context the following paradox arises: the analyst is after knowledge, but all he gets are words. Matching concepts to the words—or, more precisely, constructing conceptual structures which model the mental models of the informant—is the task of the analyst. The conceptual structures are to be specified as sets of conceptual graphs.

To carry out this task, the clear specification of the domain of discourse in terms of an ontology and an inventory becomes necessary. The discourse is considered to include not only the text of the discussion between the analyst and the informant, but also the ever-changing mental models of both parties. The mental models are construed as modelling some object domain "out there", but the domain of discourse is created through discourse.

A step-by-step technique is given for specifying the domain of discourse with careful attention paid to version control. It is noted that different interviews about the "same" object domain may give rise to several different domains of discourse.

1. Introduction

Systems analysis, software requirements definition, conceptual database design and knowledge engineering for expert systems can all be viewed as activities which have essentially the same structure. The goal of all these processes is to acquire the world knowledge possessed by an informant who, depending on the situation, may be called an expert or a user. Through the mediation of at least one other person, generally called the analyst, programmer, or knowledge engineer, the process culminates in a "smartened-up machine".

293

The bottleneck in developing knowledge-based software is the knowledge acquisition (KA) phase. Given the importance of this problem, why is the literature in this area so small, especially when compared with the literature addressing the knowledge representation (KR) issues?† We suggest three reasons for this phenomenon.

The first reason is obvious. The problems associated with the representation of knowledge are easier to deal with than the problems of "acquiring" knowledge. Representational issues are also easier to write about and discuss since they ignore the informant–analyst relation. This is the first reason why the literature on knowledge representation is so much more extensive than the knowledge acquisition literature.

The second reason is slightly more complex. KA is a real dollar-and-cents issue in industry where software must be pushed through the door within budget and on time. In most industrial settings, the analyst needs those crucial bits of knowledge which the informant possesses. In order to construct a working and workable knowledge-based system, this knowledge must be acquired.

Contrast this with a typical situation in the academic world. An academic computer scientist, engaged in research, is not producing software for some user community. The academic already knows what he wants to knows so there is no need for a KA phase. In the academic world, the analyst and informant are one and the same. The key issue from this point of view is representation. The academic wonders how he should encode or represent the knowledge in his head in such a way that it is useable by a machine.

When academics publish in the domain of knowledge-based systems, they, in clear conscience, address those issues which they consider to be crucial. Although we agree with academics that there are important representational issues, we also side with those in industry who stress that the acquisition of knowledge is the crucial problem at present. However, people in industry do not publish their results for fear of losing their competitive advantage in the marketplace. This, we submit, is the second reason for the imbalance in the favour of representation in the knowledge engineering literature.

But there is a third reason. The view of the human mind, which is dominant in our culture, is simply too static to explain the difficulties analysts encounter in the KA process. Systems analysts frequently complain that "the user keeps changing his mind". We believe that this is to be expected, that the user "changing his mind" is the rule rather then the exception. Daniel McCracken and Michael Jackson have argued that

Systems requirements cannot ever be stated fully in advance, not even in principle, because the user doesn't *know* them in advance—not even in principle. To assert otherwise is to ignore the fact that the development process itself changes the user's perceptions of what is possible, increases his or her insights into the applications environment, and indeed often changes that environment itself. We suggest an analogy with the Heisenberg Uncertainty Principle: any system development activity inevitably changes the environment out of which the need for the system arose (McCracken & Jackson, 1982, p. 31).

† A good recent summary of KR is Ronald Brachman's and Hector Levesque's *Readings in Knowledge Representation*.

We take these comments by McCracken and Jackson very seriously. How can someone construct a system for a user if the user keeps changing his or her mind? We take this question as a challenge, and in response to this challenge we have developed our KA methodology.

The human mind is not well understood. When confronted with a poorly understood phenomenon, people invariably search for metaphors or analogies whereby they can think of the abstract entity in terms of a more concrete entity. We think that it is a distinct possibility that many of those currently involved in knowledge engineering view the human mind as an expert system. Using this metaphor, the KA problem becomes one of acquiring the production ruleset of the informant. Presumably this ruleset is fairly static. An analyst who works with the *expert system metaphor* becomes upset when the informant "changes his mind". We believe that it is time for a new metaphor: mind as an anthill in which the ants are constantly in motion. We develop this metaphor in Section 3 of the paper under the heading, "The mental models hypothesis".

To give a comprehensive account of KA, we have to depart from the standard descriptions of KA practices as published in the academic computer science literature. We believe that it is essential that the "architecture" of the informant and the acquirer be considered. While studying the "architecture" of these persons could be considered to be outside the bounds of computer science, it is very much in the domain of cognitive science and, therefore, not at all out of place in a paper dealing with issues of artificial intelligence and expert systems.

2. Overview of the methodology

This paper presents the foundations for a natural language-based knowledge acquisition methodology. Our methodology seeks to provide the best possible system description within the constraints imposed on the project, while taking the words of the informant very seriously.

The methodology relies on interviewing, diagramming, and conceptual analysis. An analyst interviews an informant and then diagrams the sentences produced in the interview in a graphic notation. When the analyst and informant have agreed that the text that forms the corpus for the domain of discourse is complete enough, the analyst performs conceptual analysis on the text (Sowa, 1984; Sloman, 1978). This leads to an ontology (a list of entity types) and an inventory (a list of instances of these entities).

The purpose of the ontology is to reduce the inherent fluidity of the KA process which McCracken and Jackson (1982) have described. The ontology list, the list of entities that "exist", defines the entity population of the domain of discourse. The document, in a sense, is a contract between the informant and the analyst that these are the only entities that will be talked about in the future and that these are the only entities the machine is expected to be able to recognize. Without such a contract, the expectations placed upon the machine are infinite. This phenomenon is well known to constructors of expert systems. For example after having constructed a well-functioning system in a limited problem domain such as medical diagnosis, users of the system may be shocked that the system cannot, for example, answer questions about baseball.

The ontology gives to both constructors and evaluators of expert systems a reasonable framework that defines what "exists". An ontology is, in fact, a definition of what constitutes the domain of discourse.

Trying to construct an expert system on the basis of collecting rules or propositions is only possible in clearly defined knowledge domains such as medicine. If the knowledge domain is not clearly defined and codified, so that it is possible to state clearly what is in, and what is not in, the domain, then project management, budgeting, time schedules, and evaluation criteria become uncontrollable. Not only do users change their minds, so do managers. As a matter of sound, practical project management practice, the ontology defines the problem domain in a field not previously codified.

3. The mental models hypothesis

In Fig. 1, we show the essential components of the person-to-person KA process based on the mental models hypothesis. The mental models hypothesis states that an individual understands the world by forming a mental model, that a cogniting† agent understands the world by forming a model of the world in his or her head.

Suppose you want to form a mental model of Alberta. You cannot look at Alberta because your eyes are not big enough to take in all of Alberta, so what you do is consult a map of Alberta. A map of Alberta is a physical model of Alberta. You fold the map up and put it away. Whatever fragmentary information remains in your head is your mental model of Alberta based on looking at the map. It is not your mental model of Alberta based on "reality"; you have not seen Alberta—you were looking at a map. But if you do want to to look at Alberta, you can get in a car and go for a ride. After the trip, your head will contain fragments of information about Alberta based on the trip; after the trip you will have a mental model of Alberta based on "reality".

How do different people's mental models get harmonized? Harmonization cannot be done directly—we cannot rub mental models together. What actually transpires is that the informant and the analyst are constantly revising their mental models (MMs) using the technology of natural language (Hagman, 1982). This is the complaint of the systems analyst: the ants keep moving. This revision of MMs takes place under the influence of input such as text. The stochastic process which connects text input with mental model revision is just as little understood as the "reminding" (Shank, 1982) process discussed in Section 8 of this paper.

MMs are rarely harmonized. But in order to construct knowledge-based software, the analyst and informant must come to an "understanding". In the interests of attaining "understanding", the knowledge must become accessible. Although the knowledge in people's heads is not publicly examinable, the KA process requires that the knowledge be represented in a fixed, publicly examinable form. We believe that the publicly examinable representation should be pictorial, or graphical, or diagrammatic. Words are a refuge which either analyst or informant might hide

---

† We will make use of the word "cogniting" which is a gerund formed from the verb "to cognit". We believe (tongue in cheek) that this is what the French philosopher René Descartes had in mind when he claimed *Cognito, ergo sum*. Through a typographical error, this has become *Cogito, ergo sum*. Agents who cognit are studied by cognitive science.

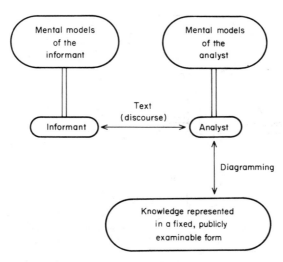

FIG. 1. A model of the person-to-person KA process.

behind to avoid making explicit the contents of the mental models. Our methodology requires that the analyst diagram his "interpretation" of what the informant said. If the informant does not "agree with the interpretation", the process is repeated until both analyst and informant converge on a set of diagrams. We expect the informant to keep "changing his mind"; we expect the ants to keep moving. We believe, however, that confronting the informant with the "meaning" of his own words (as interpreted by the analyst) will help him to "make up his mind". Is it not striking that before the recent invention of tape recorders, there did not even exist a fixed, publicly examinable way of recording what actually was said?

There are a number of candidates for representation languages. Our choice of John Sowa's conceptual graphs (Clancy, 1985; Fargues *et al.*, 1986; Sowa, 1984, 1986) as our fixed, publicly examinable form of knowledge representation was made on the basis of the following considerations:

1. Conceptual graphs stay close to the structure of natural language used by both informant and analyst.
2. Conceptual graphs are a clear notation in which to build models of MMs for public examination.

Other obvious choices are KL-ONE graphs (Brachman & Levesque, 1985) and the object-role information model of ENALIM (Evolving Natural Language Information Model) diagrams used in Control Data's Information Analysis methodology (Olle, Sol & Verrijn-Stuart, 1982).

4. Providing machines with mental models

One of the advantages of Sowa's conceptual graph notation is that the graphs (in their linear form) are directly machine representable. If the analyst can diagram the text which he receives from the informant, and if the informant can agree with the diagrammed representation, and if the diagram can be programmed into the machine, then we can provide the machine with a mental model. This process is

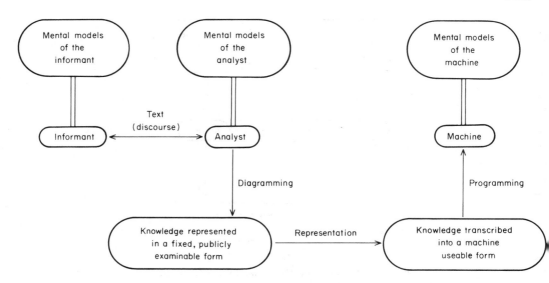

FIG. 2. A model of the knowledge acquisition process.

shown in Fig. 2 and we believe that this figure captures the essence of what any KA methodology must provide.

Sowa's notation is preferable over other notations for the following reasons:

1. The translation of a conceptual graph from its pictorial form to its linear form (the representation portion of Fig. 2) is a trivial operation.
2. The linear forms of the graph can be directly represented *without programming*.

Notice (from Fig. 2) that an automated version of this KA methodology would coalesce the role of the analyst and the machine.

The knowledge acquisition methodology which we present is based on the following hypotheses:

1. Cogniting agents, including computers, understand the world by forming MMs.
2. MMs have a structure.
3. The structures of MMs can be modelled with conceptual graphs.
4. The operations on MMs can be modelled using operations on conceptual graphs.

5. Knowledge acquisition and terminological confusion

There is a good deal of terminological confusion surrounding many KA kinds of activities. Let us consider the word "knowledge" which, in English, is used as a mass noun, indicating something of substance and bulk. "Acquiring" knowledge suggests that it is a concrete entity that could be "acquired". Reality does not support the metaphor.

Contrary to the way that English speakers use the word "knowledge", it is obvious that the concept is as intuitively elusive and as difficult to define precisely as the concepts of information and entropy. Yet the successful handling of entropy in thermodynamics and the precise and fertile definition of the Shannon–Weaver concept of information should give us hope that the concept of knowledge will also yield to a fruitful and operationally meaningful definition. Unfortunately, that time has not yet arrived.

As a substitute, and following suggestions made in the literature (Sowa, 1984; Johnson-Laird, 1983), for the purposes of this paper, we define knowledge as the semantic content of mental models. Tying knowledge to a mental model implies that there is no knowledge without a knower. This is our intent. Knowledge is possessed by a knower only in so far as the MMs "contain" this knowledge.

We assert that:

1. There is no knowledge without a knower.
2. There is no acquisition without an acquirer.
3. There is no acquisition without a source and, for us, the source is a cogniting agent.

Now let us consider systems analysis as a typical KA process. The role of analyst is played by the "systems analyst" and the role of informant is played by the "user". Let us consider the problems in this scenario:

1. The "user" may in fact have nothing to do with the use of the system under construction. The "user" may only act as a source of expertise in creating specifications for the future system. In what sense is this kind of a "user" a user?

2. The systems analyst thinks that he is analyzing a system, but this system does not exist, except perhaps in the mind of the analyst. In trying to analyze a non-existent system, certain distortions and inaccuracies are created as a side effect of the informant–analyst knowledge transfer.

3. The systems analyst would normally use the systems approach: he would interpret information received in terms of his view of the system which is usually an input–process–output model. At times, the crucial issue is the structure of the information which goes through the input and output processes and not so much the nature of the processes or the nature of the transformation which the information undergoes. While information flows are analyzed and carefully diagrammed on data flow diagrams, the structure of the information that flows is ignored. It is pushed over to database design.

Actually, a process of fact-finding does take place. Knowledge is being acquired by the analyst and this knowledge will be built into the computer system. If the systems analyst is analyzing anything, he is analyzing chaos. His job is create order out of chaos. Attempts to describe exactly what goes on during the process of systems analysis, conceptual database design, and requirements specification writing illustrate the confused state of the discourse about KA issues.

6. Providing machines with ontologies and inventories

How does a machine know what is "out there in the world"? Write a program in the Fortran programming language which accepts as input two integers, and returns, as output, their sum. Run the program and enter a real number and the letter k. What happens? The program aborts. Somewhere between the programmer and the user, somebody lied to the machine. The machine, when executing this program, "thinks" that there are only integer numbers "out there in the real world".

Does the computer, when executing this program have an ontology? Only implicitly. We define an *explicit ontology* to be a publicly examinable list of entity types. In a similar vein, we define an explicit inventory to be a publicly examinable list of instantiations of concept types listed in the explicit ontology.

Each cogniting agent has, as a minimum, an implicit ontology: man, animal, and machines all have implicit ontologies. Very few cogniting agents have explicit ontologies. The clearest example of an explicit ontology is a database schema which can be printed and is comprehensible to those who understand the data definition language. Databases also have explicit inventories in the form of population tables.

Fire insurance companies sometimes request that their policy holders complete an explicit ontology and an explicit inventory. Many accounting procedures (such as recording an inventory) can be viewed from the point of view of ontology and inventory. Philosophers are also interested in compiling ontologies although inventories are a foreign notion to them. Anthropologists, it could be argued, are also in the ontology and inventory business. They visit foreign cultures and, as part of their field work, attempt to compile an explicit ontology. We believe that KA for systems development is fundamentally an anthropological activity.

How does a machine know what is "out there in the world"? Let us compare a computer to an anthropologist. The anthropologist, who wants to find out, initiates an inquiry and so discovers what is "out there in the world". The machine has no way of finding out and must rely on humans to tell it which entities are "out there". The analyst or programmer ultimately decides which entities in the world will be known to the machine. If the analyst or programmer misses a few, the system might fail at some point. This makes a complete ontology list imperative. In fact, the entities defined by the analyst-programmer team constitute the domain of discourse.

What should be the basis for the ontology constructed for the machine? The obvious choice would be to use "things in the world", things like employees, managers, employee numbers, departments, and department budgets.

There is a problem with this approach.† Both informants and analysts speak of nonexistent entities—things like systems-to-be-built. The system will only exist (hopefully) at some point in the future. And in what sense is an employee number a "thing in the world"? If we base the ontology on "things in the world", we are restricting ourselves unnecessarily.

A second possibility is to use the names of entities as the basis for an ontology. This approach leads to three problems. First, names are also entities. Thus this approach requires distinguishing between lexical and non-lexical entities as is done in ENALIM diagrams with a distinction between LOTs (lexical object types) and NOLOTs (non-lexical object types) (Olle, Sol & Verrijn-Stuart, 1982). Second, the same name, as we all know, can refer to different entities. An ontology based on names is bound to lead to confusion. Third, many entities in the "real world" lack a name although they are part of the implicit ontology of an informant. Let us

---

† The relationship between "data" and "reality" is discussed very thoroughly in William Kent's *Data and Reality*.

TABLE 1

1	system	subsystem	component
2	set	subset	element
3	domain of discourse	subdomain	entity
4	mental model	model fragment	concept
5	conceptual graph	subgraph	concept-node

consider an example from systems analysis. In a manufacturing environment, some partially assembled structure must be moved from one department to another. The analyst wishes to describe this inter-departmental transfer and asks the informant for the name of the sub-assembly. The informant can provide no name: the sub-assembly is an unnamed object.

Restricting the ontology to "real world" entities will not work. Nor will a name-based ontology work. We believe that the only basis for constructing an ontology is concepts. Concepts are components of MMs and can be connected to entities which are unnamed. Concepts can be named allowing the informant and analyst to discuss entities such as "system" for which no "real world" referent exist. While there are those who wish to keep their ontologies pure of "non-existing entities", we believe that a KA methodology should be more descriptive than normative.

To clarify our terminology, and to allow the reader a glimpse of our mental models, we offer Table 1.

Items in a given column of Table 1 are in the same taxonomic relationship to items in the other columns. Lines 1 and 2 give the hierarchical taxonomy of systems theory and set theory, respectively. The ontology of the computer is restricted to line 5. The inventory of the computer consists of instantiated concept-nodes.

7. Knowledge acquisition through text

If there is no knowledge without a knower, then knowledge is not to be found "in" a text. All the same, discourse, whether oral or written, does deservedly occupy a special, privileged place in KA.

How does a person go from words to knowledge? Words "create" knowledge by causing a cogniting agent to form new MMs or alter existing MMs. During discourse, the MMs of both informant and analyst are harmonized; the MMs are "brought together" using language as a technology of harmonization.†

From our point of view, KA reduces to Natural Language Understanding (NLU). We seek knowledge; we are given words. KA reduces to NLU: generating meaning for words. To generate a meaning for a word means to map a word into a concept where the concept can be represented as a conceptual graph.

Sowa has provided a mechanism for connecting words and concepts. That mechanism is a conceptual lexicon which Sowa (1984), in an example, organizes as a look-up table. For example, the lexeme "occupy" maps into the concepts [OCCUPY-ACT], [OCCUPY-STATE], and [OCCUPY-ATTENTION]. These three

---

† We owe this key insight to R. Hagman (1984, pp. 104–107).

concepts are illustrated by the following sentences:

- The enemy occupied the island with marines.
- Debbie occupied the office for the afternoon.
- Baird occupied the baby with computer games.

Some would say that the word "occupy" is being used in different senses. The "sense"of a word is a fairly crucial issue which will require further elaboration.

The sense of a word is defined in the *Concise Oxford English Dictionary* as: "meaning, way in which word etc. is to be understood". For the purpose of this paper, we define the "sense" of a lexeme "lex", where "lex" could be—and in fact typically would be—a phrasal lexeme, as the ordered pair

$$\text{("lex", [LEX } n])$$

where [LEX n] is the nth concept associated with the lexeme "lex". The sense predicate

$$\text{S("lex", [LEX } n])$$

asserts that ("lex", [LEX n]) is a sense of the lexeme "lex".

It is doubtful that lexemes and concepts are associated in human memory as a simple look-up table. The process of "reminding" in the human mind is not very well understood.† Likewise, very little is known about the process that associates a lexeme with a concept.‡ However, from the point of view of KA, only the resulting concept [LEX n] is of significance and not the process that forms the pair

$$\text{("lex", [LEX } n])$$

in the mind of the informant or analyst.

Having acquired the concept [CONC], the analyst can describe [CONC] to the informant using both natural language and the formalism of conceptual graphs. Feedback from the informant further modifies the MM of the analyst. On the basis of the feedback, the analyst may create a new concept [CONC1]. This process can continue until both the analyst and the informant are satisfied or until the allotted time for the KA phase of the project has expired.

It should be noted that there are more sense relations than are defined in a dictionary. These "extra" senses are particular to individuals and hence idiosyncratic. Dealing with these complexities can be accomplished through a formalization of the meaning triangle (Regoczei, 1987).

8. An interviewing procedure for knowledge acquisition

While the interviewing process associated with a knowledge acquisition process may be quite extensive, in this paper we will restrict our attention to the particular task of compiling an ontology and inventory list for a particular domain of discourse. Statements by the informant would be about entities. A complete ontology list

---

† All this talk of reminding reminds us of Roger Schank's book *Dynamic Memory*.

‡ There is a body of psycholinguistic literature on this subject but there seem to be little agreement in the literature on how the lexeme-concept association process works.

contains all the concept types and a complete inventory list contains all the instances that statements of the informant might refer to. We note that these statements are of no concern to us during the interview, except in so far as they give clues about the "existing" population of entities in the domain of discourse. Descriptive information is of use only in so far as it describes the conceptual components of the mental models of informant and analyst.

With these restrictions, the step-by-step procedure of interviewing is as follows:

Step 1. Establish a text. The text should be in a permanent, publicly reference-able form. In practice, this would mean a written document, a voice tape, or a videotape.

Step 2. Select the contentives. Select all contentive lexemes, paying special attention to all the phrasal lexemes and subfragments of noun phrases.

Step 3. Produce a lexeme-to-concept mapping. The mapping is done either through a conceptual lexicon, if one exists, or through free association by the informant or analyst. This step associates senses with the lexemes. It gives sense to the words.

Step 4. Diagram the concepts. Concepts that are semantic primitives are dia-grammed as a single concept node containing the concept itself. For non-primitive concepts, the conceptual graph is as elaborate as necessary.

Step 5. Test the concepts. Elicit further comments from the informant on the appropriateness of the graphs. This step may produce more text which is to be cycled to Step 1 to produce a new version of the text.

Step 6. Model mental models. Model, using conceptual graphs, the relevant mental models of the informant to test the adequacy of the coverage. The main techniques are conceptual analysis and further dialogue with the informant. This step may produce only diagrams, in which case the interviewing procedure is complete, or more text, in which case cycle back to Step 1.

Clearly, the process may not terminate within a preset time limit. Cutoff criteria may have to be established for termination conditions.

The final product of this algorithm consists of two lists:

1. The Ontology List: a list of concepts, each defined by a conceptual graph. A conceptual graph consisting of a single concept node is a semantic primitive relative to this ontology.
2. The Inventory List: a list of instantiations of concept types relative to the particular domain of discourse.

It is assumed that there probably is an object domain "behind" the domain of discourse. The mental models of the informant are assumed to represent this object domain. As a matter of practical fact, the mental models of the informant define the domain of discourse, if it is assumed that knowledge about the domain is only accessible through the informant. The analyst's task is to establish a set of mental models in his own mind which are coherent with the set of mental models of the informant. The analyst makes a publicly examinable record of his own mental models by drawing diagrams. If the diagrams do not adequately model the mental models of the informant, then a process of adjustment will have to take place. If we look upon language as a form of technology, then the process can be described as follows: the analyst and the informant are asked to synchronize mental models using the technology of language (Hagman, 1982), assisted by a diagramming technique such as conceptual graphs.

9. Knowledge acquisition—an example

To illustrate our methodology we will run through a typical knowledge acquisition problem. In our example, the analyst is trying to find his way to a party and the informant provides directions. Admittedly, the matter is not one that requires a high degree of sophisticated expertise, but we have all been confronted by cases where the directions were so ineptly phrased that careful conceptual analysis was required to create order out of chaos.

To make the example more interesting, and to illustrate how two different ontologies and two different domains of discourse can be established for what, at an abstract level, are the "same" instructions, we shall give two versions of the text:

1. An object-oriented version.
2. A procedure-oriented version.

Both sets of instructions are about the "same" object domain, yet they create two different domains of discourse. **The domain of discourse is defined by the discourse.** Giving the full analysis of the two texts would be too lengthy for this paper. Some selected examples will illustrate the techniques.

The following texts are two sets of instructions given by two informants to an analyst on how to get to a party:

1. Text 1—Object-oriented:
   "We live at 251 Elm St.. Elm is a north–south street. The nearest major intersection is George and Hunter. We are in the southwest quadrant."
2. Text 2—Procedure-oriented:
   "Where are you now? OK. Drive down George until you get to Hunter. Turn right. Turn left after the fourth block. That's Elm. Now go down six houses and we are on the right."

We believe that it will become apparent that the ontology and the domains of discourse are quite different for the two examples, in spite of the fact that they are talking about the "same" thing.

Let us step through the procedure described in the previous section. This is artificial because the two cogniting agents, the person who gave the instructions and the person who received the instructions, are not present. We have to invent their responses and we have to make some guesses about the mental models of both analyst and informant.

Let us take the object-oriented version first.

Step 1. Establish the text. This is done above.

Step 2. List the contentives.

Normally, this would be a very long list, but this text is relatively short. We produce this list in Table 2.

Step 3. Produce a lexeme-to-concept mapping.

Looking at this list of contentives for Text 1, the analyst may decide to try to compile the first version of the ontology list. The concepts associated with the

TABLE 2

we	live	251
Elm	St.	Elm St.
251 Elm St.	north	south
north–south	street	north–south street
nearest	major	intersection
major intersection	nearest major intersection	George
Hunter	southwest	quadrant
southwest quadrant		

lexemes may turn out to be semantic primitives with no further definition, or may be defined by conceptual graphs which are constructed out of primitives and other non-primitive concepts. We show the lexeme-to-concept association in Table 3.

Lexemes such as "intersection" and "quadrant" may be difficult to handle at this stage for the analyst. We shall illustrate some possible techniques for dealing with this later. We note that at this stage that the ontology and inventory lists for Text 1 may look as shown in Tables 4 and 5.

We note that conceptual graphs would be required to connect the concepts [COMPASS-DIRECTION] and [STREET-TYPE]. The analyst may also want to connect this object-oriented text to procedural information. In this case he may ask at some future point in the process: "Yes, I hear what you are saying, but how do I actually get to your house"? At this point more text will be generated.

To contrast, let us look at the first two steps for Text 2.

Step 1. Establish the text.
This is done above.

Step 2. List the contentives.
The contentives are shown in Table 6.

We note that Text 2 is not only procedure-oriented, but also more colloquial. Colloquial language is usually ill-formed and idiosyncratic, and also makes references to entities which require a great deal of background knowledge to understand. But the analyst can still try to associate concepts with lexemes, although the process may require further information from the informant.

TABLE 3

Contentive lexeme or phrase	Associated concept
we	[PARTY-HOST]
live	[RESIDENCE]
251 Elm St.	[ADDRESS]
251	[HOUSE-NO]
north	[COMPASS-DIRECTION]
street	[STREET]
north–south street	[STREET-TYPE]
nearest	[NEAR]
George	[STREET:George]
southwest	[COMPASS-DIRECTION]

TABLE 4

Text 1 ontology list: version 1

[PARTY-HOST]
[RESIDENCE]
[ADDRESS]
[HOUSE-NO]
[COMPASS-DIRECTION]
[STREET]
[STREET-TYPE]
[NEAR]

TABLE 5

Text 1 inventory list by concept type: version 1

[ADDRESS: 251 Elm St.]
[HOUSE-NO: 251]
[STREET-TYPE: north–south street]
[COMPASS-DIRECTION: north, south, southwest]
[STREET: Elm, Hunter, George]

TABLE 6

where	you	now
OK	drive	drive down
George	get	get to
Hunter	turn	turn right
turn left	block	fourth
fourth block	after the fourth block	Elm
go	go down	six
houses	six houses	we
right	left	on the right

Now let us return to the processing of Text 1.

Step 3. Produce a lexeme-to-concept mapping (cont.)

The analyst may now want to tackle some of the more difficult concepts. Let us say that the analyst starts with the lexeme "intersection". Relying on his own mental models, and using his own "reminding" processes, the analyst may come up with the following natural language phrasings to capture the various senses of the lexeme "intersection":

1. "a place where one can pass from one street to another"
   (captures the concept [INTERCHANGE])
2. "a place where two streets meet"
   (captures the concepts of [T-JUNCTION], as well as [FORK-IN-THE-ROAD])
3. "a place where two streets meet at right angles creating four quadrants"
   (capturing the concept of [CROSSROADS])

The analyst may not be satisfied with any of these natural language phrasings of the sense for "intersection" and may, if there is no conceptual lexicon available, consult dictionaries and other sources for further information.

Suppose the analyst decides that Sense 2 and Sense 3 are the best candidates. For the sake of version control, he may not add the statements of Sense 2 and Sense 3 to the text as yet.

Step 4. Diagram the concept using a conceptual graph.
The analyst decides initially that for [INTERSECTION2] the concept will be [JUNCTION] and that for [INTERSECTION3] the concept will be [CROSSROADS].

He draws conceptual graphs for [INTERSECTION1] and [INTERSECTION2] and shows them to the informant.

Step 5. Elicit comments from the informant.
The informant expresses his opinion that [CROSSROADS] is the concept that best matches his mental models, i.e. that [CROSSROADS] is what he "had in mind" when he was giving instructions. He volunteers the following extra prose:

Well, think of analytic geometry. The two axes intersect, dividing the plane into four quadrants. The four city blocks around an intersection, provided it is an intersection formed by two streets intersecting at right angles, are similar to the four quadrants. You remember how they are labelled: the first quadrant, the second quadrant, the third quadrant, and the fourth quadrant. Well, when you look at a compass rose, you see the same thing. Obviously, the southwest quadrant according to the compass rose is the third quadrant of analytic geometry.

This step provided more text, namely the natural language description for the sense predicate S ("intersection", [INTERSECTION3]) above, plus the extra information provided by the informant. This text should be added to the original version to produce Version 2 of the text. Now the analyst can enlarge the list of contentives above to produce Version 2 of the contentive list. Then, he may update the ontology list by adding the conceptual graph for [INTERSECTION3] to the list.

At the end of this iteration from Step 1 to Step 5 we have

- Text—version 2
- Contentives list—version 2
- Ontology list—version 2

Step 6. Model, using diagrams, the mental models of the informant.
Making an appropriate decision on the depth of the analysis, the analyst could proceed to elicit additional information about the mental models of the informant. Conceptual analysis is described by Sloman (1978) and Sowa (1984), as well as by Riesbeck (in Schank, 1975). The process may not coverge, unless decisions are taken by informant and analyst on what does, or does not, belong to the domain of discourse.

The final product is an ontology list which contains all the concepts that are semantic primitives, as well as the concepts that are defined by more complex conceptual graphs. The inventory list is assembled on the basis of the contentives list. Each item in the inventory is an instantiation of a concept type. Matching up items on the contentives list with concept types is based on information from the informant.

For example, the concept [STREET] may be accepted as a semantic primitive and the contentives "Elm", "George", and "Hunter", as instances of [STREET]. This could be recorded as a population table, or in the linear notation of conceptual graphs, as

[STREET: Elm, George, Hunter]

10. Conclusion

The necessity of relying on an outside expert as the source of the knowledge in the creation of knowledge-based systems forces us to state—more clearly than ever before—exactly what steps must be carried out during the KA process. Writing such a "procedures manual" for people engaged in person-to-person KA work is a prerequisite for creating the architecture and specifications for an automated knowledge acquisition methodology. We are still a long way from formulating a methodology which can be automated. We offer our methodology as a workable approach for performing natural language-based, person-to-person knowledge acquisition for knowledge-based systems development in a present-day environment.

References

BRACHMAN, R. & LEVESQUE, H. Eds (1985). *Readings in Knowledge Representation*, Los Altos, CA: Morgan Kaufmann.
CLANCEY, W. J. (1985). Review of J. F. Sowa's *Conceptual Structures. Artificial Intelligence*, **27**, 113–128.
FARGUES, J., LANDAU, M.-C., DUGOUND, A. & CATACH, L. (1986). Conceptual graphs for semantics and knowledge processing. *IBM Journal of Research and Development*, **30**(1), 70–79.
HAGMAN, R. S. (1982). *Language, Life, and Human Nature*. Current Inquiry into Language and Human Communication 41. Edmonton: Linguistic Research.
JOHNSON-LAIRD, P. (1983). *Mental Models*. Cambridge, MA: Harvard University Press.
KENT, W. (1978). *Data and Reality: Basic Assumptions in Data Processing Reconsidered*. New York: Elsevier Science Publishers.
LAING, R. D. (1961). *Self and Others*. Harmondsworth, England: Penguin Books.
McCRACKEN, D. D. & JACKSON, M. A. (1982). Life cycle concept considered harmful. *Software Engineering Notes*, **7**(2), 29–32.
OLLE, T. W., SOL, H. G. & VERRIJN-STUART; A. A. Eds. (1982). *Information Systems Design Methodologies: Proceedings of the IFIP WG 8.1 Working Conference, Noordwijkerhourt, The Netherlands, 10–14 May 1982*. Amsterdam: North Holland, 1983.
PLANTINGA, E. P. O. (1986). Who decides what metaphors mean? *Proceedings of the Conference on Computing and the Humanities—Today's Research, Tomorrow's Teaching* Toronto, pp. 194–204.
QUINE, W. V. O. (1960). *Word and Object*, Cambridge, MA: MIT Press.
REGOCZEI, S. Formalizing the meaning triangle. *Trent University Technical Report* (to appear).
REGOCZEI, S. Can computers—or, for that matter, people—understand natural language, and if not, why not?—the impact of the cognitive revolution (to appear).
SCHANK, R. C. Ed. (1975). *Conceptual Information Processing*, Amsterdam: North Holland.
SCHANK, R. C. (1982). *Dynamic Memory: A Theory of Reminding and Learning in Computers and People*. Cambridge: Cambridge University Press.
SLOMAN, A. (1978). *The Computer Revolution in Philosophy: Philosophy, Science, and Models of Mind*, Harvester Studies in Cognitive Science, Atlantic Highlands, NJ: Humanities Press.
SOWA, J. F. (1984). *Conceptual Structures: Information Processing in Mind and Machine*, Reading, MA: Addison-Wesley.
SOWA, J. F. & WAY, E. (1986). Implementing a semantic interpreter using conceptual graphs. *IBM Journal of Research and Development*, **30**(1), 57–69.

KITTEN: Knowledge initiation and transfer tools for experts and novices

Mildred L. G. Shaw and Brian R. Gaines

Department of Computer Science, University of Calgary, Calgary, Alberta, Canada T2N 1N4

This paper gives a state-of-the-art report on the use of techniques based on personal construct psychology to automate knowledge engineering for expert systems. It presents the concept of knowledge support systems as interactive knowledge engineering tools, states the design criteria for such systems, and outlines the structure and key components of the KITTEN implementation. KITTEN includes tools for interactive repertory grid elicitation and entailment analysis that have been widely used for rapid prototyping of industrial expert systems. It also includes tools for text analysis, behavioral analysis and schema analysis, that offer complementary and alternative approaches to knowledge acquisition. The KITTEN implementation integrates these tools around a common database with utilities designed to give multiple perspectives on the knowledge base.

Knowledge support systems for automating knowledge engineering

Problems of knowledge engineering have been recognized since the early days of expert systems. It was possible that knowledge engineering might develop as a profession on a par with systems analysis and programming, and that an initial shortage of skilled knowledge engineers would cause problems to be overcome eventually as the profession developed. However, this scenario now appears less and less likely. There is certainly a shortage of knowledge engineers and problems in developing applications, but doubts have been cast on the notion that human labor is the appropriate solution to the knowledge engineering problem:

* The decline in costs of both hardware and software support for expert systems has brought the technology into a mass-market situation far more rapidly than originally envisioned;
* This has led to a growth in demand for expert systems that is proceeding far more rapidly than the growth in supply of trained and experienced knowledge engineers;
* The declining costs of expert system technology are also making the expense of human labour in tailoring the technology for particular applications appear to be the dominating constraint and an excessive cost;
* A move towards a labor-intensive activity such as knowledge engineering is contrary to all trends in industry;
* In particular it is contrary to the trend towards automatic programming techniques in the computing industry;
* The role of the knowledge engineer as an intermediary between the expert and the technology is being questioned not only on cost grounds but also in relation to

309

its effectiveness—knowledge may be lost through the intermediary and the expert's lack of knowledge of the technology may be less of a detriment than the knowledge engineer's lack of domain knowledge.

The considerations of the previous section have heightened interest in the possibility of providing knowledge support systems (KSSs) to automate knowledge engineering as a process of direct interaction between domain experts and the computer. In 1980 we proposed that personal construct psychology (Kelly, 1955; Shaw, 1980) could provide foundations for expert systems, particularly in systems that combined interactivity with database access and expert advice to provide decision support, and gave examples of algorithms and programs that extracted entailment rules from repertory grid data (Gaines & Shaw, 1980). In 1983 we reported further enhancements of these techniques and a preliminary experiment to validate them empirically as a knowledge engineering technique for priming expert systems (Shaw & Gaines, 1983). This work led to industrial studies of the methodology applied to the development of expert systems: Boeing Computer Services (Boose, 1984, 1985, 1986) and Lockheed Software Technology Center (Wahl, 1986) have reported success in applications; and validation has been reported in a statistics domain (Gammack & Young, 1985).

This paper gives a state-of-the-art report on the use of techniques based on personal construct psychology to automate knowledge engineering for expert systems. It is based on four areas of advance since the previous paper:

- Improved techniques for the derivation of rules from repertory grid data which give: a natural knowledge representation for uncertain data combining fuzzy and probabilistic logics; and an information-theoretic measure of the significance of a derived rule (Gaines & Shaw, 1986a);
- Widespread applications experience in prototyping expert systems using the methodology (Boose, 1985; Gaines & Shaw, 1986b);
- Improved interactive techniques for on-line knowledge engineering from groups of domain experts interacting through a computer network (Shaw, 1986; Shaw & Chang, 1986);
- The KITTEN implementation, a knowledge engineering workbench that provides next generation KSS facilities including textual analysis, induction of models from behavior, multi-level and multi-expert repertory grid elicitation, and hierarchical construct laddering, to automate knowledge engineering for a wide range of problem domains.

Personal construct psychology

Kelly developed a systemic theory of human cognition based on the single primitive of a construct, or dichotomous distinction. For an individual, constructs are:

transparent templets which he creates and then attempts to fit over the realities of which the world is composed (Kelly 1955).

He proposes that all of human activity can be seen as a process of anticipating the future by construing the replication of events:

Constructs are used for predictions of things to come, and the world keeps rolling on and revealing these predictions to be either correct or misleading. This fact provides a basis for the revision of constructs and, eventually, of whole construct systems (Kelly 1955).

Hence his psychological model of man is strongly epistemological and concerned with the way in which man models his experience and uses this model to anticipate the future. The anticipation may be passive, as in prediction, or active, as in action.

Kelly developed his theory in the context of clinical psychology and hence was concerned to have techniques which used it to by-pass cognitive defenses and elicit the construct systems underlying behavior. This is precisely the problem of knowledge engineering noted above. His repertory grid (Shaw, 1980) is a way of representing personal constructs as a set of distinctions made about elements relevant to the problem domain. In clinical psychology this domain will often be personal relationships and the elements may be family members and friends. In the development of expert systems the elements will be key entities in the problem domain such as oil-well sites or business transactions.

Repertory grids have been widely used: in clinical psychology (Shepherd & Watson, 1982); to study processes of knowledge acquisition in education (Pope & Shaw, 1981); and to study decision making by individuals and groups in management (Shaw, 1980). PLANET (Shaw, 1982) is an integrated suite of programs that operationalizes Kelly's work and may be used for the interactive elicitation and analysis of repertory grids. These programs have been widely used internationally in clinical psychology, education and management studies (Shaw, 1981), and this paper describes their application to knowledge engineering for expert systems.

Kelly's personal construct psychology is important because it develops a complete psychology of both the normal and abnormal, which has strong systemic foundations. In the long term these foundations may be more important to knowledge engineering than the techniques currently based on them. However, this paper concentrates on the repertory grid as a technique for eliciting information from an expert.

Repertory grids

A repertory grid is a two-way classification of data in which events are interlaced with abstractions in such a way as to express part of a person's system of cross-references between his personal observations or experiences of the world (elements), and his personal constructs or classifications of that experience.

The elements are the things which are used to define the area of the topic, and can be concrete or abstract entities. For example, in the context of: inter-personal relations the elements might be people; attitudes to life the elements might be critical events; job change the elements might be careers; expertise about metal joining the elements might be types of rivet; expertise about medical diagnosis the elements might be symptoms. Before choosing the set of elements, the user must think carefully about the area of the topic and relate the elements to his purpose. The elements should be of the same type and level of complexity, and span the topic as fully as possible. It is usual to start with about six to twelve elements.

The universe of discourse is determined by the elements. The elements originally suggested by Kelly in his work as a psychotherapist were role titles such as: Self, Mother, Father, Best Friend, Threatening Person, Rejected Teacher. This has been carried over into industry with such role titles as: Myself, My Boss, My Boss's Boss, Subordinate, Person Likely to Get On, Person Not Likely to Get On, and so on. The subject in both cases is required to supply names of individuals well known to her/him to fit these and other roles as closely as possible. When choosing elements care must be taken to ensure that each one is well known and personally meaningful to the subject. Each element must be significant to the person in the context of the particular problem.

The constructs are the terms in which the elements are similar to or different from each other. Each construct therefore has two poles, each of which has a meaning with respect to its opposite. Any construct or dimension of thinking which is important to the subject is a valid construct. For example, to distinguish between people by saying that x and y are **blue-eyed** whereas b and c are **brown eyed** may be trivial, and not concerned with the important qualities of $x, y, b,$ and c. However, if you are an eye specialist concerned with prescribing tinted contact lenses, this may be a significant construct. Thoughts and feelings, objective and subjective descriptions, attitudes and rules-of-thumb all constitute valid constructs. The verbal description of the construct and the labelling of the poles need not be a publically agreed meaning in the outside world, but only a memory aid to the thinking process. The mapping of the elements onto the constructs produces the two-dimensional grid of relationships.

ELICITING CONSTRUCTS BY TRIADS

The most common method used for eliciting a construct is the minimal context form or triad method. The elements are presented in groups of three—this being the least number which will produce both a similarity and a difference. The subject is asked to say in what way two are alike and thereby different from the third. This is the emergent pole of the construct. The implicit pole may be elicited by the difference method (in what way does the singleton differ from the pair) or by the opposite method (what would be the opposite of the description of the pair).

As an example, thinking of the three Artificial Intelligence books *Handbook of AI, Winston's AI,* and *AI Applications for Business* in what way are two alike and thereby different from the other one? We might first of all say that *Handbook of AI,* and *AI Applications for Business* are alike since they are **multi-authored**, whereas

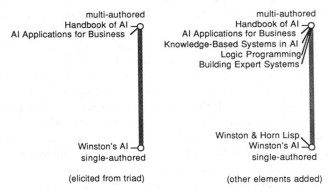

FIG. 1. Triadic elicitation of a construct about AI books.

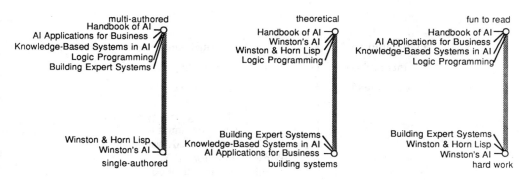

FIG. 2. Three constructs applied to AI books.

Winston's AI is **single-authored**. This is, then, the first construct with its two poles or opposite descriptions. Now all the elements in the set must be rated on this dimension as either 1 being **multi-authored**, or 2 being **single-authored** as shown in Fig. 1. This also shows the significance of the term personal in personal construct since it would not obviously be a publicly agreed description that *Winston and Horn's LISP* is single-authored whereas Davis and Lenat's book is multi-authored. In this case it reflects a single concerted effort as opposed to more than one topic.

Then the second and subsequent constructs are elicited in exactly the same way using different triads each time. Figure 2 shows the grid of Fig. 1 with a further two constructs elicited. The third construct shown here illustrates that constructs can be factual, imaginary, emotional, or whatever is important to the person generating the grid.

ELICITING CONSTRUCTS USING RATING SCALES

A scale allowing more distinctions than the pair 1 and 2 may be used as required. If a 1 to 5 scale is used then the above example might become the grid shown in Fig. 3. Thus, in this case, the third construct means that *Logic Programming* and *Knowledge-Based Systems in AI* are considered the most **fun to read** books, *Winston's AI* is both **fun to read** and **hard work**, and *Building Expert Systems* and *Winston & Horn LISP* are the most **hard work**.

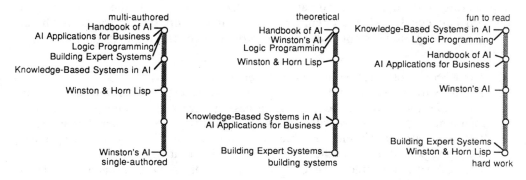

FIG. 3. Three multi-point scale constructs applied to AI books.

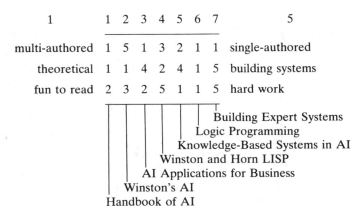

FIG. 4. Repertory grid data structure for three multi-point constructs applied to AI books.

Note how the use of a multi-point scale with an odd number of values allows for a central rating which does not force the user to choose either pole. It may be desirable to apply more discrimination to this central rating and allow the subject the choice of the two possibilities: neither, that the element belongs to neither pole; or both, that the element belongs to both poles (Landfield, 1976). It is also possible to extend these possibilities to allow separate ratings on each pole (Shaw & Gaines, 1980; Gaines & Shaw, 1981b).

The mapping of the elements onto the constructs produces the two-dimensional grid of relationships which can be represented as a numeric data structure as shown in Fig. 4. This structure may be viewed as a component of a database in entity-antribute form (Chen, 1980): a repertory grid has elements as entities, constructs as attributes and allocations of elements to poles of constructs as values.

Knowledge support system design considerations

We see knowledge engineering in very broad terms as: the acquisition, elicitation, structuring and encoding of knowledge for application in inferential, goal-directed, explanatory, decision and action support systems. We see knowledge support systems as having even broader scope, encompassing both aids to knowledge engineering and support of human knowledge processes—in the long term the division between knowledge engineering tools and expert system shells will break down, and integrated systems will be necessary. The general requirements for a KSS are:

1. The KSS tools should be domain independent;
2. The KSS tools should be directly applicable by experts without intermediaries;
3. The KSS tools should be able to access a diversity of knowledge sources including text, interviews with experts, and observations of expert behavior;
4. The KSS system should be able to encompass a diversity of perspectives including partial or contradictory input from different experts;
5. The KSS system should be able to encompass a diversity of forms of knowledge and relationships between knowledge;

6. The KSS system should be able to present knowledge from a diversity of sources with clarity as to its derivation, consequences and structural relations;
7. Users of the KSS should be able to apply the knowledge in a variety of familiar domains and freely experiment with its implications;
8. The KSS should make provision for validation studies;
9. As much of the operation of the KSS as possible should be founded on well-developed and explicit theories of knowledge acquisition, elicitation and representation;
10. As the overall KSS develops it should converge to an integrated system.

All of these requirements are subject to caveats—some domain dependency may be appropriate for efficiency in specific KSSs—some human intervention may be helpful or necessary when an expert is using a KSS—and so on. However, the broad design goals stated capture the key issues in KSS design currently.

The PLANET system for repertory grid elicitation and analysis (Shaw, 1980, 1982; Shaw & Gaines, 1986*b,c*) is a primitive KSS satisfying requirements 1 and 2 for domain independence and direct use. Its foundations in personal construct psychology, which itself has strong systemic and cognitive science foundations (Gaines & Shaw, 1981*a*; Shaw & Gaines 1986*a*), are attractive in terms of requirement 9. Boose (1985) in evaluating ETS has noted the limitations of basic repertory grid techniques in terms of requirement 5—that the methodology is better suited for analysis than for synthesis problems, for example, debugging, diagnosis, interpretation and classification rather than design and planning, and that it is difficult to apply to deep causal knowledge or strategic knowledge—and is attempting to overcome these use grid hierarchies in NeoETS (Bradshaw & Boose, 1986). The TEIRESIAS extension to MYCIN is an early form of KSS providing debugging support for an expert system using basic analogical reasoning (Davis & Lenat, 1982). The development of KSSs has become a major area of activity recently, for example, MORE (Kahn, Nowlan & McDermott, 1985), MDIS (Antonelli, 1983), DSPL (Brown, 1984), MOLE (Eshelman *et al.* 1987), SALT (Marcus, McDermott & Wang, 1985; Marcus & McDermott, 1987, Marcus, 1987), SEAR (van de Brug, Bachant & McDermott 1985), and TKAW (Khan *et al.*, 1987).

The following section describes our work on KITTEN, a knowledge support system that draws on many concepts and techniques for knowledge engineering to begin to encompass requirements 3 through 8, while attempting to satisfy 9 by relating them all through personal construct psychology, and 10 by building a workbench of tools around a common database.

KITTEN: a knowledge support system

Figure 5 shows the structure of KITTEN: Knowledge Initiation & Transfer Tools for Experts and Novices. KITTEN consists of a: knowledge base; various analytical tools for building and transforming the knowledge base; and a number of conversational tools for interacting with the knowledge base. The KITTEN implementation is written in Pascal and currently runs on a network of Apollo workstations.

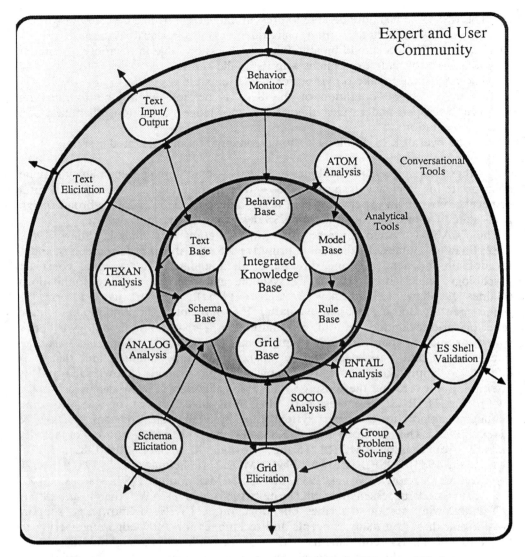

FIG. 5. KITTEN: Knowledge Initiation and Transfer Tools for Experts and Novices.

The KITTEN structure is best understood by following sequences of activity that lead to the generation of a rule base and its loading into an expert system shell.

A typical sequence is text input followed by text analysis through TEXAN which clusters associated words leading to a schema from which the expert can select related elements and initial constructs with which to commence grid elicitation. The resultant grids are analyzed by ENTAIL which induces the underlying knowledge structure as production rules that can be loaded directly into an expert system shell (Gaines & Shaw, 1986a).

An alternative route is to monitor the expert's behavior through a verbal protocol giving information used and decisions resulting and analyze this through ATOM which induces structure from behavior and again generates production rules (Gaines, 1977).

These two routes can be combined. KITTEN attempts to make each stage as explicit as possible, and, in particular, to make the rule base accessible as natural textual statements rather than technical production rules. The expert system shell being used in KITTEN currently is Nexpert (Roy, 1986) which gives a variety of textual and graphical presentations of the rule base enabling the expert to see the impact of different fragments of knowledge.

The group problem-solving component of KITTEN is particularly important because it goes beyond the stereotype of an **expert** and **users**, and allows the system to be used to support an interactive community in their acquisition and transfer of knowledge and mutual understanding. The SOCIO analysis allows members of a community to explore their agreement and understanding with other members, and to make overt the knowledge network involved (Shaw, 1980, 1981, 1986).

The KITTEN implementation is an initial prototype offering a workbench with minimal integration of the knowledge base, but each of tools has already proven effective, and their combination is proving very powerful in stimulating experts to think of the knowledge externalization process from a number of different perspectives. The following sections describe and illustrate some of the tools.

ELICITATION

The following screens show KITTEN eliciting data on staff appraisal using techniques that contrast with the prompt/response style of other systems (Shaw & Gaines, 1986b). When starting a new topic the working window must first be completed. A new user will have a topic with a specific purpose which should be entered in the appropriate box, and kept in mind as the interaction proceeds. In this example Bill is construing **managers** to see which of the ones he knows are **effective** and why. Figure 6 shows the screen after the user has entered his name, purpose, and the type of element that he will be using.

The next thing for Bill to do is to think of some managers and add these as elements. He does this by clicking on the **ELEMENTS** button, then typing in the names of the managers he would like to think about one on each line. Bill knows that about six is the best number to start with, and that less than three will make triadic elicitation impossible. If a typing error is made he can just go back and correct it by selecting that name and clicking on **Edit Name** as shown in Fig. 7.

As Bill is just starting his grid, he decides to elicit a construct from a triad, so he clicks **CONSTRUCTS** button, then on the **Do Triad** button. Bill sees the three elements in the triad, and decides that CY is the one which is different from CN and MT. This is shown in Fig. 8. Now Bill has to decide why he thinks CN and MT are alike and different from CY. He types in the description of the pair, **intelligent**, on one pole of the construct as shown in Fig. 9. Then Fig. 10 shows how he names the other end of the construct. That is, the way in which CY is different is that he is **dim**. This defines Bill's scale from **intelligent** to **dim**. He now has to rate all his other elements on this scale too. If he finds that his original triad CN, MT and CY need to be moved to accommodate the others he can do that. Figure 11 shows that he moves

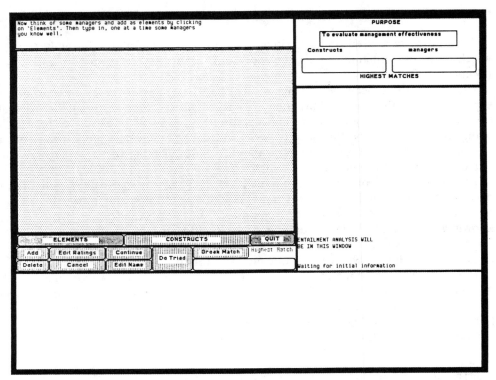

FIG. 6. KITTEN initial screen.

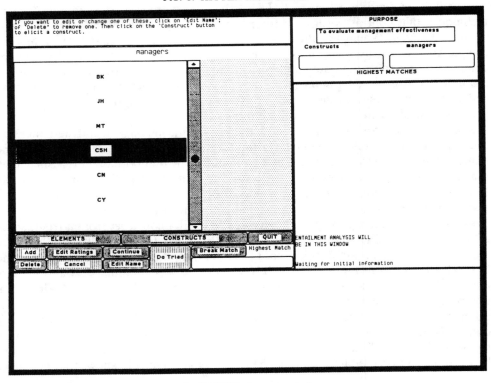

FIG. 7. KITTEN elements window.

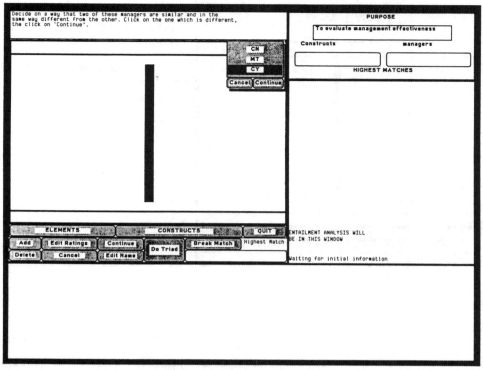

FIG. 8. KITTEN triad elicitation.

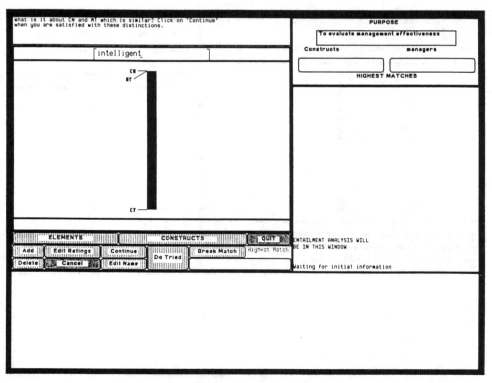

FIG. 9. KITTEN adding pole name for the similarity.

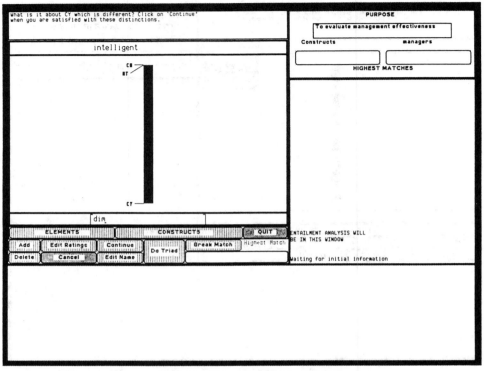

FIG. 10. KITTEN adding pole name for the difference.

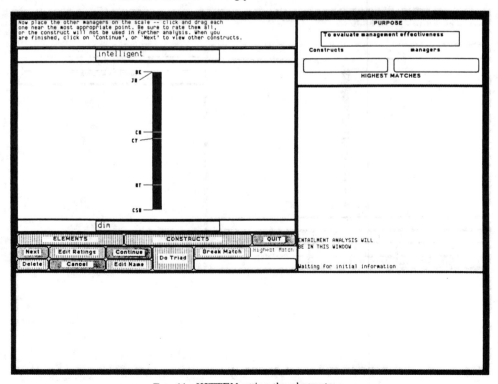

FIG. 11. KITTEN rating the elements.

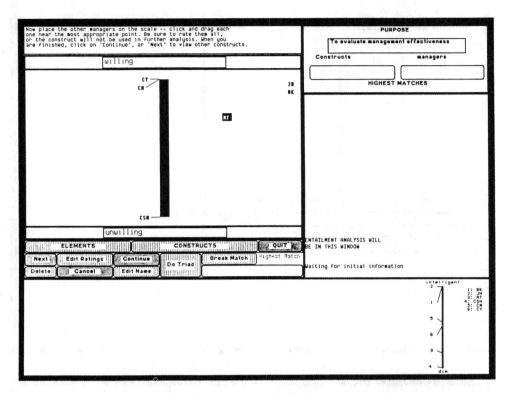

FIG. 12. KITTEN click and drag.

CY up to the middle of the scale, and puts CSH at the bottom. He also moves CN and MT as he re-thinks how the scale should be. Now BK and JH are at the top, CN and CY towards the centre, and MT toward the bottom. However, MT is not quite so dim as CSH.

Bill has now got his first construct. He continues adding several more constructs from triads before he decides to look at high matches. Figure 12 shows the first construct recorded in the bottom window, and the dragging of an element onto the construct bar for the second one. Figure 13 shows the completed construct.

After the next construct shown in Fig. 14, Bill notices that the top right window is showing a high match between two of the managers. He goes to the **ELEMENTS** window by clicking on that button, and chooses to split them by clicking on **Break Match**. This takes him to a new screen (Fig. 15) showing which elements are matched, and placing one at either end of the construct bar. He also notices the first entailment in the right-hand window: dim implies unwilling, but realises that it is formed on very little data and chooses to ignore it for now. The first thing he does after naming the poles, is to move one of the elements back close to the other, indicating that he cannot easily distinguish between them, as shown in Fig. 16. Figure 17 then shows the completed construct.

Bill then looks at the construct match by clicking on **Break Match** box when he is in the **CONSTRUCTS** window. This takes him to a new screen showing which

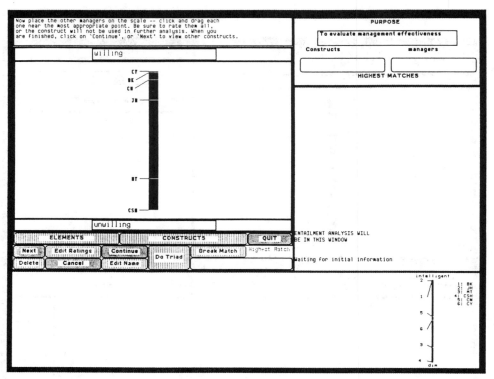

FIG. 13. KITTEN the second construct.

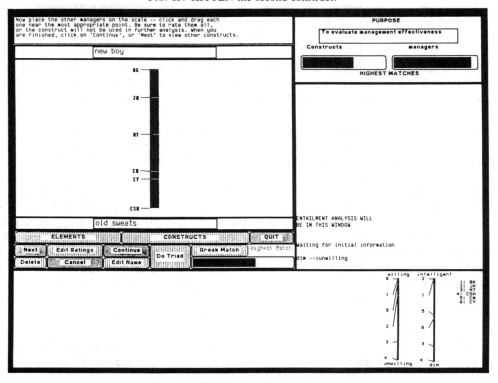

FIG. 14. KITTEN the third construct.

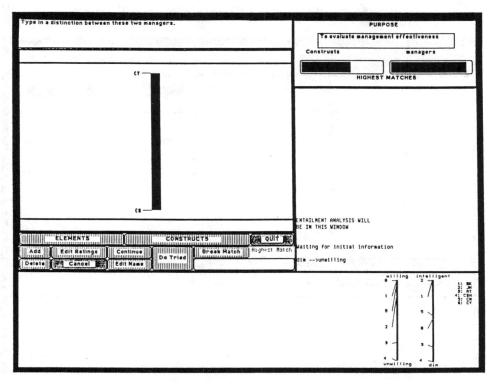

FIG. 15. KITTEN splitting matched elements.

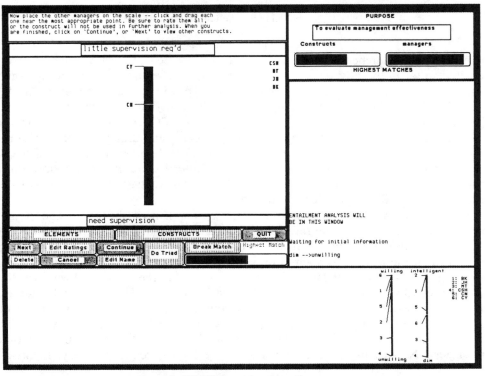

FIG. 16. KITTEN revising the ratings.

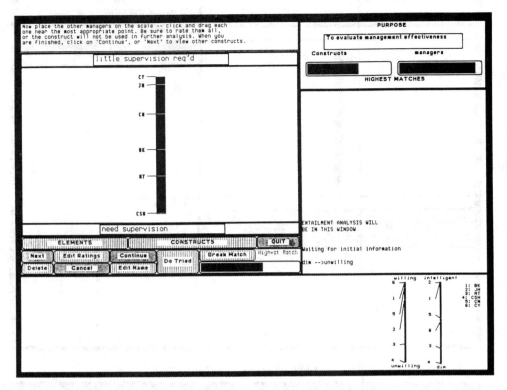

FIG. 17. KITTEN the fourth construct.

constructs are matched, shown in Fig. 18. This screen also shows the constructs elicited so far in the bottom window, and a new set of entailments in the right-hand window. Bill decides to add an element so he types in a new manager **NTM** (Fig. 19). Now he will have to rate **NTM** on each of his constructs in turn. He then has to go through each construct already elicited, adding NTM on to each scale in turn where Bill thinks he best fits. He does this by clicking and dragging that manager on the construct, then clicking on the **Next** button to get the next construct until he has done them all. Figure 20 shows one of these. Note that he may still choose not to rate NTM on opposite ends of the two matched constructs, but if he does not then the constructs will still be highly matched.

Figure 21 shows the constructs Bill has got so far. If he wishes to change the pole name of any one, or edit the ratings he could click on that and then on the **Edit Name** or **Edit Rating** button. It also shows that the new manager NTM has been added to all the constructs elicited previously, as shown in the bottom window. Bill sees that a new set of entailments has been produced in the right-hand window. Now Bill wishes to see how he has rated JH on each construct. He does this by going to the bottom window and clicking on the name JH. The number representing this manager is the highlighted on each construct, showing the relative positions which can be seen in Fig. 22. Figure 23 shows him looking at the positions of another manager CN. Any one of the elements can be highlighted in this way. Figures 24

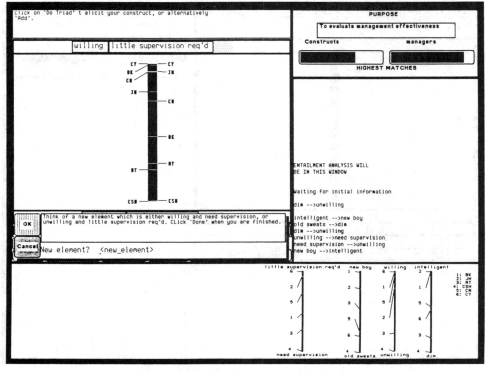

FIG. 18. KITTEN construct match.

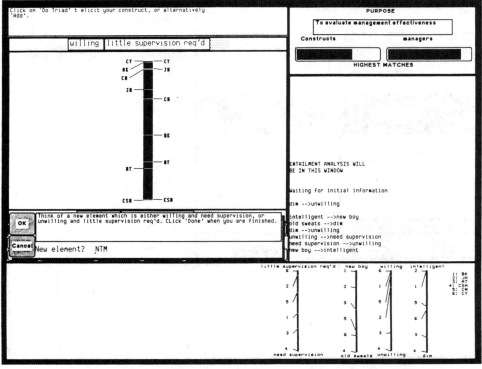

FIG. 19. KITTEN adding an element to break the construct match.

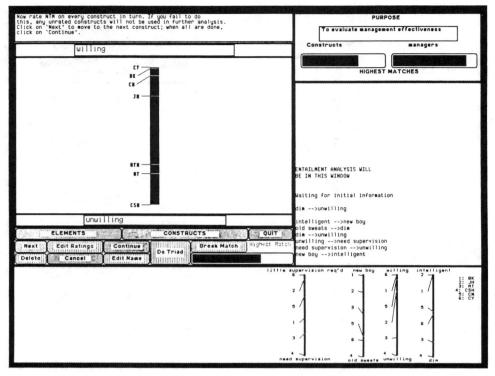

FIG. 20. KITTEN rating the new element.

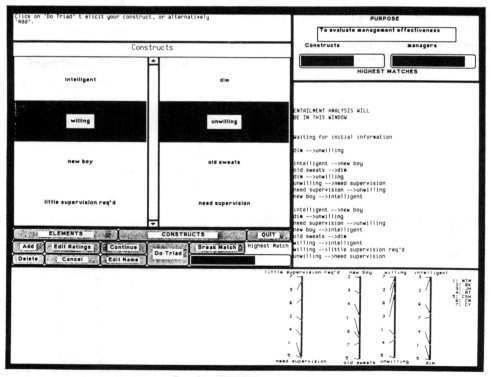

FIG. 21. KITTEN constructs.

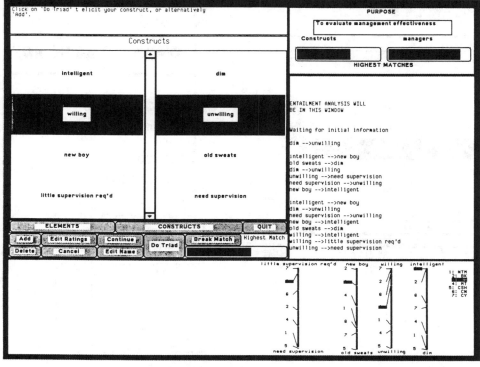

FIG. 22. KITTEN highlighting an element.

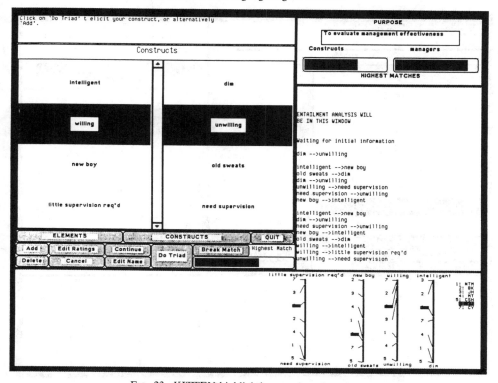

FIG. 23. KITTEN highlighting another element.

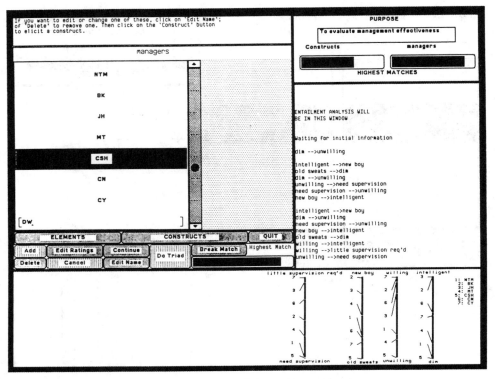

FIG. 24. KITTEN adding a new element.

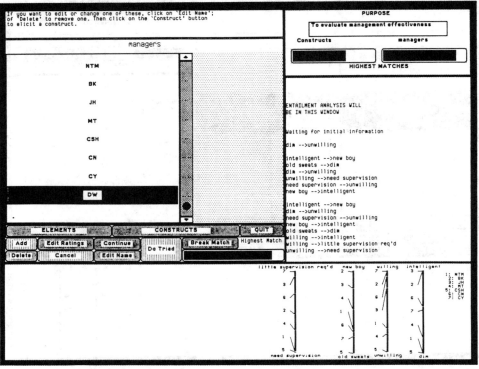

FIG. 25. KITTEN the list of elements.

and 25 show how Bill can add a new manager anytime he chooses by clicking first on the ELEMENTS button to bring up the screen in Fig. 24, and then just typing in the name of the new element. In Fig. 25 the manager is listed with all the others.

Bill continues to elicit his grid with the options available as described. At any time he can add or delete elements or constructs, use triads or just type in names and ratings. When he chooses to finish he can **QUIT** the elicitation by clicking on the button in any window. The grid will then be stored so that he can print it out or analyse it.

CLUSTER ANALYSIS

Repertory grids in themselves encode information about an expert's way of looking at the world. This information can be used in its own right for some purposes since it is an aid to remembering the basis for decisions and actions. It can also be analysed in a variety of ways to bring out possible underlying structures, or construct systems, in the expert's world view and its relationship to those of others. There are a number of forms of analysis that are widely used for different purposes and KITTEN offers all the commonly used techniques plus new developments in recent years. What form of analysis should be used in a particular case is partly a matter of personal preference and partly a matter of purpose. Comparisons have been made in the literature of different analyses with the same data (Shaw, 1981). In exploring the use of repertory grids for knowledge engineering in a specific domain it is worth repeating such comparisons with familiar data to determine what are the most applicable analyses and presentations.

The FOCUS algorithm is a distance-based hierarchical cluster analysis technique that sorts the constructs into a linear order such that constructs closest together in the space are also closest together in the order. It provides a hierarchical clustering of an expert's construct system that preserves the data elicited from him so that the sources of the analysis are evident and can be discussed.

Standard principal component analysis techniques give a non-hierarchical cluster analysis based on principal components that can be used to gauge the major dimensions along which an expert is making distinctions.

ENTAIL: ENTAILMENT ANALYSIS

PLANET and KITTEN access the expert's personal construct system by interactively eliciting a repertory grid of constructs classifying elements characterizing to part of the domain of expertise. Figure 26 shows the resultant grid elicited in a study of personnel selection.

The entailment analysis of a repertory grid treats each pole of a construct as a fuzzy predicate to which the elements have degrees of membership given by their ratings, and induces the logical implications between these predicates. The original ENTAIL program produced all entailments consistent with the grid and allowed the expert to prune any that seemed spurious before using them as inference rules in an expert system. ENTAIL II rank orders entailments in terms of the uncertainty reduction they induce in the distribution of the data, and hence tends to reject spurious entailments (Gaines & Shaw, 1986a).

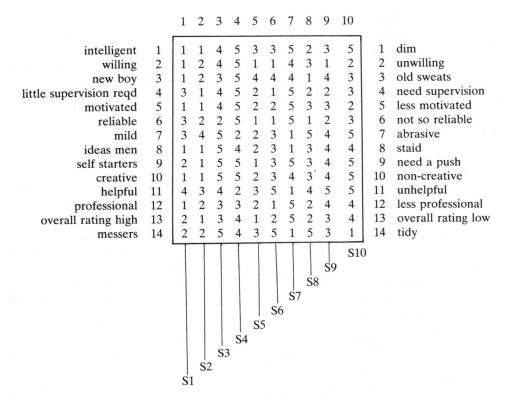

FIG. 26. Repertory grid elicited on staff appraisal.

Figure 27 is an ENTAIL II analysis of the grid of Fig. 26. The entailments are shown with three values in the range from 0 to 1: first, the truth value of the hypothesis; second, the probability of the hypothesis being true; and third, the information content (uncertainty reduction generated) of asserting the hypothesis. For example, $L1 \rightarrow L9$ has a truth value of 0·80, a probability of 1·00, and an information content of 0·29. The information content measures the significance of the hypothesis and is used to ensure that trivial entailments consistent with the data are pruned.

The data of Fig. 26 may be regarded as that of an expert on staff appraisal concerned with deriving his overall rating (construct 13) from behavioral assessments such as intelligent and creative. The ENTAIL analysis of Fig. 27 shows that L1, L4, L6, L9, L10 and L12 imply L13, that intelligent, creative, reliable and professional self-starters requiring little supervision receive a high overall rating, whereas R2, R4, R5, R6, R9 and R12 imply R13, that being unwilling, less motivated, not so reliable, less professional, needing supervision and needing a push leads to a low overall rating.

Figure 28 shows Nexpert in operation loaded with the entailments of Fig. 27. Interaction with Nexpert enables the expert to see the derived rules in action. He can determine their consequences with test data, analyze new hypothetical cases,

Entail	Truth	Prob.	Inf.	(Cutoff 0·17) Implication usually
L1→L9	0·80	1·00	0·29	intelligent→self starters
L9→L13	1·00	1·00	0·29	self starters→overall rating high
R9→R1	0·80	1·00	0·28	need a push→dim
L10→L8	1·00	1·00	0·28	creative→ideas men
L1→L10	0·80	1·00	0·26	intelligent→creative
R8→R10	1·00	1·00	0·26	staid→non-creative
L10→L9	0·80	1·00	0·26	creative→self starters
R13→R6	0·80	1·00	0·26	overall rating low→not so reliable
L9→L10	0·80	1·00	0·24	self starters→creative
R10→R1	0·80	1·00	0·24	non-creative→dim
L10→L1	0·80	1·00	0·23	creative→intelligent
R13→R9	1·00	1·00	0·23	overall rating low→need a push
R4→R13	0·80	1·00	0·22	need supervision→overall rating low
R5→R4	0·80	1·00	0·22	less motivated→need supervision
R5→R13	0·80	1·00	0·22	less motivated→overall rating low
R9→R10	0·80	1·00	0·22	need a push→non-creative
L1→L3	0·80	1·00	0·21	intelligent→new boy
L6→L13	0·80	1·00	0·21	reliable→overall rating high
R10→R9	0·80	1·00	0·20	non-creative→need a push
R1→R6	0·60	1·00	0·19	dim→not so reliable
R1→R10	0·80	1·00	0·19	dim→non-creative
R9→R4	0·60	1·00	0·19	need a push→need supervision
R9→R12	0·60	1·00	0·19	need a push→less professional
R9→R13	0·60	1·00	0·19	need a push→overall rating low
R12→R13	0·80	1·00	0·19	less professional→overall rating low
R13→R4	0·80	1·00	0·19	overall rating low→need supervision
R13→R12	0·80	1·00	0·19	overall raing low→less professional
L4→L5	0·80	1·00	0·18	little supervision reqd→motivated
L4→L9	0·60	1·00	0·18	little supervision reqd→self starters
R6→R4	0·80	1·00	0·18	not so reliable→need supervision
R6→R13	0·80	1·00	0·18	not so reliable→overall rating low
L12→L9	0·60	1·00	0·18	professional→self starters
L13→L4	0·80	1·00	0·18	overall rating high→little supervision reqd
L13→L5	0·80	1·00	0·18	overall rating high→motivated
L13→L9	0·60	1·00	0·18	overall rating high→self starters
L1→L8	0·80	1·00	0·17	intelligent→ideas men
R2→R4	0·80	1·00	0·17	unwilling→need supervision
R2→R5	0·80	1·00	0·17	unwilling→less motivated
R2→R13	0·80	1·00	0·17	unwilling→overall rating low
R3→R1	0·80	1·00	0·17	old sweats→dim
L4→L13	0·80	1·00	0·17	little supervision reqd→overall rating high
L12→L13	0·80	1·00	0·17	professional→overall rating high
L13→L12	0·80	1·00	0·17	overall rating high→professional

FIG. 27. ENTAIL analysis of repertory grid on staff appraisal.

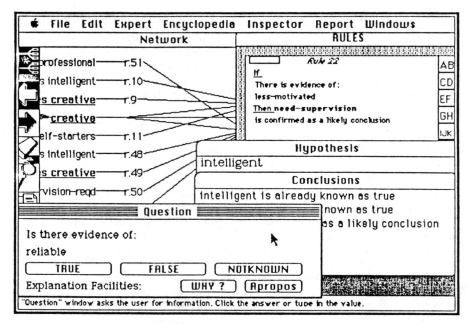

FIG. 28. Inference rules derived by ENTAIL in use in Nexpert expert system shell.

and see the inter-relations between rules presented graphically. The logging and explanation facilities of Nexpert enable him to track down spurious inferences that may arise with the rules derived by ENTAIL, or proper inferences that are missing. He can then edit the rules and test the revized system using Nexpert's facilities.

TEXAN: TEXT ANALYSIS

Repertory grid techniques depend on eliciting elements and constructs from experts that are representative of a domain and comprehensive in their classification. The interactive elicitation program PEGASUS in PLANET uses online analysis of the grid to feed back comments to the expert which stimulate the addition of elements and constructs to achieve comprehensiveness (Shaw, 1980). However, this structural feedback is only applicable when a grid has been partially completed and the initial selection of elements has had no computer-based support.

TEXAN is a text analysis program designed to pump-prime the grid elicitation process when a manual or text book is available that the expert regards as having reasonable coverage of the domain. It uses techniques that were originally designed to map subject matter concepts against student concepts in computer-managed instruction systems (Smith, 1976). The text is fully indexed by all non-noise words grouped by their stems, and a coupling matrix of word associations is calculated using a simple distance-in-text measure. The high-frequency associations in the text are clustered and presented to the expert as a prototypical schema for the subject area which he can edit for spurious words and associations, and then use to suggest knowledge islands and associated elements and constructs.

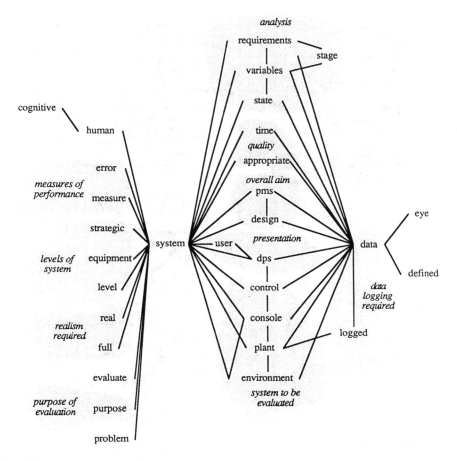

FIG. 29. TEXAN clustering of word associations from text with annotation showing knowledge islands.

Figure 29 shows a TEXAN clustering of an evaluation study of data logging, analysis and presentation methodologies for human performance evaluation in complex systems (Gaines & Moray, 1985). Figure 30 shows an independent mapping of the main knowledge islands for an expert system design based on the analyzed report (Gaines, 1986). The TEXAN analysis was done some time after the production of Fig. 30, and the shading of Fig. 29 shows the relationship of some of the groupings in the schema with the knowledge islands. There is not a one-to-one correspondence but this, and similar analyses, show that basic text analysis can focus attention on salient features of the domain and pump-prime the knowledge elicitation process.

In the long term more sophisticated text analysis techniques may be used to derive knowledge from text without human intervention. However, for many domains the knowledge is not yet that explicit and pump-priming of elicitation from experts will remain a significant requirement.

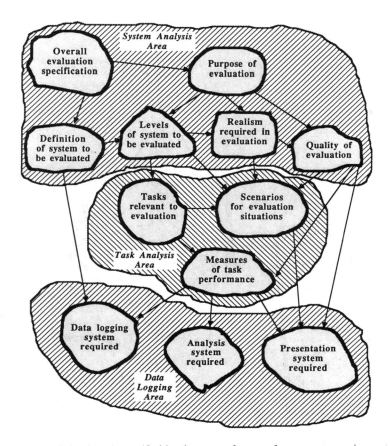

FIG. 30. Knowledge islands specified by the expert for a performance measuring system.

ANALOG: SCHEMA ANALYSIS

The groupings of Figs 29 and 30 when combined with the construct classifications of repertory grids as in Fig. 26 may be viewed as schema structuring a knowledge domain. ANALOG is a program that maps schema to schema based on their structure without regard to content. It is based on a theory of analogy that explicates analogies as pullbacks of faithful functors between categories (Gaines & Shaw, 1982) and generates maximal sub-graph isomorphisms between two classificatory data structures. It may be regarded as a generalization of the copy-edit process being used in the encoding of commonsense knowledge in CYC (Lenat, Prakash & Shepherd, 1986). ANALOG produces meaningful results on artificial examples and grids in related domains. It will also find meaningless analogies between unrelated domains which cannot be rejected by information-theoretic statistical procedures such as those used in ENTAIL and ATOM. It seems likely that effective application of ANALOG depends on the expert pump-priming the matching with known or hypothesized relations and the program extending these rather than attempting to generate them completely.

ATOM: BEHAVIOR ANALYSIS

Michalski and Chilausky (1980) have demonstrated that inductive modeling of an expert's behavior may produce effective rules when those elicited by interview techniques are clearly inadequate. ATOM is an algorithm for inducing the structure of a system from its behavior using a search over a model space ordered by complexity and goodness of fit. As in ENTAIL, models are evaluated in terms of the uncertainty reduction induced by the model in the distribution of the modeled behavior (Gaines, 1976; 1977; 1979). We have incorporated a version of ATOM in KITTEN that takes a set of sequences of arbitrary symbolic data and generates a set of production rules that will reconstruct it. These can be loaded into the expert system shell to give a simulator of the behavioral system. This has proved effective with inter-personal interaction data such as that analyzed by Mulhall (1977) and interactively elicited by Stevens (1985).

SOCIO: MUTUAL AGREEMENT AND UNDERSTANDING ANALYSIS

We have already emphasized the need for knowledge elicitation methodologies to cope with a group of experts as well as the individual. Much expertise only resides within the social context of cooperating individuals and requires elicitation across the group. The SOCIO analysis program supports group elicitation techniques in which the construct systems of a number of users are compared. Grids are elicited separately but then exchanged in two ways: a user can place elements on a colleague's constructs from his own point of view, and the analysis system then allows him to explore their agreement; or he can attempt to place them from his colleague's point of view and hence explore his understanding.

Conclusions: steps toward an integrated knowledge support system

This paper has presented the concept of knowledge support systems as interactive knowledge engineering tools, stated the design criteria for such systems, and outlined the structure and key components of KITTEN. KITTEN consists of a set of knowledge engineering tools, some of which already have track records of successful use in knowledge acquisition studies. In developing KITTEN we have preserved the integrity of each of these tools, enabling each to be utilized effectively in a stand-alone mode. However, we have also made the first steps towards an integrated knowledge support system by building the tools around a common database, providing access to the same data in each of its intermediate forms, and providing conversion utilities between different data forms.

The objective of integrating the tools has raised a number of new and significant questions. ENTAIL transforms a repertory grid to a set of production rules—is it possible, and useful, to convert production rules to a repertory grid? Technically the result is a possible world of grids that might have generated the rules, and the capability does prove useful, particularly given the other grid analysis tools available in KITTEN. Similar considerations apply to the transformations between other forms of knowledge representation. We see the next generation of knowledge support tools as being increasingly flexible in handling all aspects of knowledge acquisition, representation, processing and presentation. They will not be optimized with a particular knowledge representation, uncertainty calculation, inference mechanism, and so on, that are in some sense right. Rather they will provide a wide range of perspectives on the knowledge base, preserving source data and chains of derivative processes, so that users can freely explore the knowledge or follow a very specific path according to their choices and needs.

Financial assistance for this work has been made available by the National Sciences and Engineering Research Council of Canada. The KITTEN system is made available by the Centre for Person Computer Studies; the initial Apollo implementation is being carried out at the Knowledge Sciences Institute, University of Calgary. We are grateful to John Boose and Jeff Bradshaw of Boeing AI Center, for stimulating discussions relating to knowledge support systems.

References

ANTONELLI, D. (1983). The application of artificial intelligence to a maintenance and diagnostic information system (MDIS). *Proceedings of the Joint Services Workshop on Artificial Intelligence in Maintenance*, Boulder, CO.

BOOSE, J. H. (1984). Personal construct theory and the transfer of human expertise. *Proceedings AAAI-84*. California: American Association for Artificial Intelligence, pp. 27–33.

BOOSE, J. H. (1985). A knowledge acquisition program for expert systems based on personal construct psychology. *International Journal of Man–Machine Studies, 20*(1), 21–43 (January).

BOOSE, J. H. (1986). Rapid acquisition and combination of knowledge from multiple experts in the same domain. *Future Computing Systems, 1*(2), 191–216.

BRADSHAW, J. M. & BOOSE, J. H. (1986). NeoETS. *Proceedings of North American Personal Construct Network Second Biennial Conference*. University of Calgary: Department of Computer Science (June), pp. 27–41.

BROWN, D. E. (1984). Expert systems for design problem-solving using design refinement with plan selection and redesign. Unpublished Ph.D. dissertation, Ohio State University, CIS Department, Columbus, Ohio, August, 1984.

CHEN P. P. (ed.) (1980). *Entity-relationship Approach to Systems Analysis and Design*. North-Holland, New York.

DAVIS, R. & LENAT, D. B. (1982). *Knowledge-Based Systems in Artificial Intelligence*. New York: McGraw-Hill.

ESHELMAN, L, EHRET, D., McDERMOTT, J. & TAN, M. (1987) MOLE: A tenacious knowledge acquisition tool. In: special issue on the AAAI Knowledge Acquisition for Knowledge-Based Systems Workshop. *International Journal of Man–Machine Studies* *26*(1), 41–54.

ESHELMAN, L. & McDERMOTT, J. (1986). MOLE: a knowledge acquisition tool that uses its head. *Technical Report*. Carnegie-Mellon University: Department of Computer Science.

GAINES, B. R. (1976). Behaviour/structure transformations under uncertainty. *International Journal of Man–Machine Studies, 8*(3), 337–365.

GAINES, B. R. (1977). System identification, approximation and complexity. *International Journal of General Systems, 3*, 145–174.

GAINES, B. R. (1979). Sequential fuzzy system identification. *International Journal of Fuzzy Sets and Systems, 2*(1), 15–24.

GAINES, B. R. (1986). Development of performance measures for computer-based man–machine interfaces: Application to previous SHINMACS evaluation. *Technical Report DCIEM-PER-SUP: MAT 86.*

GAINES, B. R. & MORAY, N. (1985). Development of performance measures for computer-based man–machine interfaces. *Technical Report DCIEM-PER-FIN :JUL 85.*

GAINES, B. R. & SHAW, M. L. G. (1980). New directions in the analysis and interactive elicitation of personal construct systems. *International Journal of Man–Machine Studies, 13*(1) 81–116.

GAINES, B. R. & SHAW, M. L. G. (1981a). A programme for the development of a systems methodology of knowledge and action. In RECKMEYER, W. J., Ed. *General Systems Research and Design: Precursors and Futures*. Society for General Systems Research, pp. 255–264.

GAINES, B. R. & SHAW, M. L. G. (1981b). New directions in the analysis and interactive elicitation of personal construct systems. In SHAW, M. L. G., Ed. *Recent Advances in Personal Construct Technology*. Academic Press, London, pp. 147–182.

GAINES, B. R. & SHAW, M. L. G. (1982). Analysing analogy. TRAPPL, R., RICCIARDI, L. & PASK, G., Eds. *Progress in Cybernetics and Systems Reserach, Vol. IX*. Washington: Hemisphere, pp. 379–386.

GAINES, B. R. & SHAW, M. L. G. (1986a). Induction of inference rules for expert systems. *Fuzzy Sets and Systems*, **8**(3), 315–328.

GAINES, B. R. & SHAW, M. L. G. (1986b). Knowledge engineering for an FMS advisory system. In LENZ, J. E., Ed. *Proceedings of Second International Conference on Simulation in Manufacturing: AMS'86*. Bedford, UK: IFS Conferences, pp. 51–61.

GAMMACK, J. G. & YOUNG, R. M. (1985). Psychological techniques for eliciting expert knowledge. Bramer, M., Ed. *Research and Development in Expert Systems*. Cambridge University Press, pp. 105–116.

KAHN, G. S., BREAUX, E. H., JOSEPH, R. L., & DEKLERK, P. (1987). An intelligent mixed-initiative workbench for knowledge acquisition. In: special issue on the AAAI Knowledge Acquisition for Knowledge-Based Systems Workshop. *International Journal of Man–Machine Studies*, **27** (in press).

KAHN, G., NOWLAN, S. & MCDERMOTT, J. (1985). MORE: an intelligent knowledge acquisition tool. *Proceedings of the Ninth International Joint Conference on Artificial Intelligence*. California: Morgan Kaufmann, pp. 581–584.

LANDFIELD, A. (1976). A personal construct approach to suicidal behavior. In SLATER, P. Ed. *Dimensions of Intrapersonal Spaces* Vol. 1, John Wiley, London, pp. 93–107.

LENAT, D., PRAKASH, M. & SHEPHERD, M. (1986). CYC: Using common sense knowledge to overcome brittleness and knowledge acquisition bottlenecks. *AI Magazine* **6**(4), 65–85.

MARCUS, S. (1987). Taking backtracking with a grain of SALT. In: special issue on the AAAI Knowledge Acquisition for Knowledge-Based Systems Workshop. *International Journal of Man–Machine Studies*, **26**(3), 383–398.

MARCUS, S., and MCDERMOTT, J. (1987) SALT: a knowledge acquisition tool for propose-and-revise systems technical report, forthcoming, Carnegie–Mellon University Department of Computer Science.

MARCUS, S., MCDERMOTT, J. & WANG, T. (1985). Knowledge acquisition for constructive systems. *Proceedings of the Ninth International Joint Conference on Artificial Intelligence*. California: Morgan Kaufmann, pp. 637–639.

MICHALSKI, R. S. & CHILAUSKY, R. L. (1980). Knowledge acquisition by encoding expert rules versus computer induction from examples—a case study involving soyabean pathology. *International Journal of Man–Machine Studies*, **12**, 63–87.

MULHALL, D. J. (1977). The representation of personal relationships: an automated system. *International Journal of Man–Machine Studies*, **9**(3), 315–335.

POPE, M. L. & SHAW, M. L. G. (1981). Personal construct psychology in education and learning. In SHAW, M. L. G., Ed. *Recent Advances in Personal Construct Technology*. Academic Press, London, pp. 105–114.

ROY, J. (1986). Expert systems in Nexpert. *MacTutor*, **2**(2), 48–51.

SHAW, M. L. G. (1980). *On Becoming a Personal Scientist*. London: Academic Press.

SHAW, M. L. G. (1981). *Recent Advances in Personal Construct Technology*. London: Academic Press.

SHAW, M. L. G. (1982). PLANET: some experience in creating an integrated system for repertory grid applications on a microcomputer. *International Journal of Man–Machine Studies*, **17**(3), 345–360.

SHAW, M. L. G. (1986). PCS: a knowledge-based interactive system for group problem solving. *Proceedings of 1986 International Conference on Systems, Man and Cybernetics*. pp. 1353–1357.

SHAW, M. L. G. & CHANG, E. (1986). A participant construct system. *Proceedings of North American Personal Construct Network Second Biennial Conference.* University of Calgary: Department of Computer Science, pp. 131–140.

SHAW, M. L. G. & GAINES, B. R. (1980). Fuzzy semantics for personal construing. *Systems Science and Science.* Society for General Systems Research, Kentucky, pp. 59–68.

SHAW, M. L. G. & GAINES, B. R. (1983). A computer aid to knowledge engineering. *Proceedings of British Computer Society Conference on Expert Systems.* Cambridge, pp. 263–271.

SHAW, M. L. G. & GAINES, B. R. (1986a). A framework for knowledge-based systems unifying expert systems and simulation. LUKER, P. A. & ADELSBERGER, H. H., Eds. *Intelligent Simulation Environments.* La Jolla, California: Society for Computer Simulation, pp. 38–43.

SHAW, M. L. G. & GAINES, B. R. (1986b). Interactive elicitation of knowledge from experts. *Future Computing Systems,* 1(2), 151–190.

SHAW, M. L. G. & GAINES, B. R. (1986c). An interactive knowledge elicitation technique using personal construct technology. Kidd, A., Ed., *Knowledge Elicitation for Expert Systems: A Practical Handbook.* Plenum Press (to appear).

SHAW, M. L. G. & McKNIGHT, C. (1981). *Think Again.* Englewood Cliffs, NJ: Prentice-Hall.

SHEPHERD, E. & WATSON, J. P. (Eds.) (1982). *Personal Meanings,* John Wiley, London.

SMITH, R. A. (1976). Computer-based structural analysis in the development and administration of educational materials. *International Journal of Man–Machine Studies,* 8(4), 439–463.

STEVENS, R. F. (1985). An on-line version of the personal relations index psychological test. *International Journal of Man–Machine Studies,* 23(5), 563–585.

VAN DE BRUG, A. BACHANT, J. & McDERMOTT, J. (1985). Doing R1 with style. *Proceedings of the Second Conference on Artificial Intelligence Applications.* IEEE 85CH2215-2. Washington: IEEE Computer Society Press, pp. 244–249.

WAHL, D. (1986). An application of declarative modeling to aircraft fault isolation and diagnosis. LUKER, P. A. & ADELSBERGER, H. H., Eds. *Intelligent Simulation Environments.* La Jolla, California: Society for Computer Simulation, pp. 25–28.

Index